Land, Language, and Women

JULIE L. REED

Land, Language, and Women

ᏎᏫᎥ, ᏎᏍᎯᎦᎣᎯ, ᎠᏐ ᎠᏂᎨᏆ

A Cherokee and American Educational History

The University of North Carolina Press *Chapel Hill*

This book was published with the assistance of the Z. Smith Reynolds Fund of the University of North Carolina Press.

Set in Arno by Jamie McKee, MacKey Composition
Manufactured in the United States of America

Cover art: Lilith at Kituwah in North Carolina, June 2021. Photo courtesy of the author.

Library of Congress Cataloging-in-Publication Data
Names: Reed, Julie L., 1976– author
Title: Land, language, and women : a Cherokee and American educational history / Julie L. Reed.
Description: Chapel Hill : The University of North Carolina Press, 2026. | Includes bibliographical references and index.
Identifiers: LCCN 2025035321 | ISBN 9781469684895 cloth alk. paper | ISBN 9781469684901 pbk alk. paper | ISBN 9781469684918 epub | ISBN 9781469687353 pdf
Subjects: LCSH: Cherokee Indians—Education—History | Cherokee educators—History | Indian girls—Education—History | Indian women educators—History | Cherokee women—Social life and customs—History | Indians of North America—Education— Social aspects | BISAC: SOCIAL SCIENCE / Ethnic Studies / American / Native American Studies
Classification: LCC E99.C5 R358 2026
LC record available at https://lccn.loc.gov/2025035321

For product safety concerns under the European Union's General Product Safety Regulation (EU GPSR), please contact gpsr@mare-nostrum.co.uk or write to the University of North Carolina Press and Mare Nostrum Group B.V., Mauritskade 21D, 1091 GC Amsterdam, The Netherlands.

Dedicated to my mom
In memory of my dad

Contents

Illustrations

Acknowledgments

If this book represents an educational history that traces Cherokee pedagogical practices and people together over time, then acknowledgments should be understood as intellectually and personally cumulative as well. This book wouldn't exist without my first one, *Serving the Nation*. Therefore, those same people and institutions mentioned in the acknowledgments there contributed to this book, too, and deserve my continued thanks for fueling my scholarly life and interests. That said, there are people, groups, and institutions that have been integral to my more recent process and deserve credit for getting me to the finish line of this second book.

First the funding, which is increasingly limited and concentrated with those who often have the most resources to begin with. In many ways, institutionally, I fall into this category. Nonetheless, personally, I would not be able to do this work without financial support. If not for the Spencer Foundation, which awarded me a Small Research Grant in 2019 and a Spencer Communications Grant in 2022–23, and the individual mentorship of Emily Crone-Phillips and OiYan Poon, this book would not exist as it does.

I cannot express what a difference it makes when the people who work in grants and contracts and strategic development at your university care about securing funding for faculty in every discipline, especially the humanities. I want to personally thank Mark Williams, Rocco Zinobile, Penny Leach, Kathy Totino, and Heather Winfield, who may consider what they do as simply part of their jobs but by doing their jobs have made a huge difference in my scholarly life.

In 2019, I participated in the *William and Mary Quarterly*–Early Modern Studies Institute Workshop at the Huntington Library titled "Archaeology, History, and the Problem of 'Early America.'" There, I was able to test out my early experiments drawing from archaeology and centering a girl in chapter 1. Robin Beck, Emerson Baker, Juliana Barr, Denise Bossy, Robert Cook, Alejandra Dubcovsky, Carrie Heitman, Greg Waselkov, and Josh Piker all workshopped an early version of chapter 1. Rob Beck advised me to stay focused on Cherokee spaces and not veer too far into the larger Mississippian world to sharpen the archaeology, which ended up grounding each chapter in this book in place in a way it needed to be. Greg Waselkov, one of the dearest and most generous scholars I have come to know because of that workshop, read versions of chapters 1 and 2 to check my archaeological work, so to speak.

Nothing I say in these acknowledgments is enough. The people listed here wrote with me, mentored me, taught me the difference between sherds and shards, inspired me, guided me through institutional changes, witnessed my life changes, made room for my grief, reminded me to celebrate my wins, walked with me, ran with me, hiked with me, ironed out the details for annual Jamaica writing retreats, answered genealogical questions, opened their homes to me, nourished me, and listened to me cry, laugh, and talk through ideas—there are no amount of words on a page that can thank the people below for what they have contributed to this book or to my life.

Writing is hard. Formal writing groups at both the University of Tennessee and at Penn State have helped rein me in and keep the swelling down when writing bumped and bruised me. In my final year at the University of Tennessee, my interdisciplinary writing crew included Millie Gimmel, Jessie Grieser, Amy Mundorf, Melanie Beasley, and Caela O'Park. At Penn State, thanks to a program launched by Dr. Jenny Hamer, who deserves separate thanks for the support she has offered me since her arrival at Penn State, I joined a writing group with Niki vonLockette, Lori Francis, Kim Blockett, and Shirley Moody Turner several days a week throughout the pandemic. These women, these mothers, these academic dynamos, are keeping my writing, my self-care, and the academy honest.

Jan Simek's invitation to join him, Beau Carroll (Eastern Band of Cherokee Indians), Alan Cressler, and Stephen Alvarez in a cave changed my professional life, and this book is evidence of it. As my archaeology interests grew, so did the archaeologists in my circle. Kandy Hollenbach, Tim Baumann, Sarah Sherwood, Arthur Bogan, Benjamin Auerbach, and Ben Steere have pushed my thinking further. Brett Riggs has been a model of all that is right in archaeology since I was in graduate school, and that remains true.

I have been grateful to have supportive communities at Penn State. The people making up the Indigenous Peoples' Student Association and the Indigenous Faculty and Staff Alliance, including Tim Benally, Tracy Peterson, Nicole Peterson, Hollie Kulago, and Adriana Peterson, are a small but mighty bunch who help make the Indigenous people on the campus less invisible. Within the history department, a special thanks goes to Michael Kulikowski, Ellen Stroud, Jacob Lee, Cathleen Cahill, Rachel Shelden, Amy Greenberg, and Chris Heaney, though the entire faculty of the department inspire me with all they accomplish. The graduate students I work closest with at Penn State each assisted with pieces of this book, ranging from Jamie Henton's more complete transcriptions of some of the poems by girls at Dwight Mission to Ed Green's scanning the entire copy of *The Rollo Code of Morals* for me in the archives to Chris Thrasher's reminding me of key accounts by Benjamin Hawkins at exactly the moment I needed them. My sincere gratitude goes to all of them.

I feel lucky to be in conversation and collaboration with other Cherokee people who care about Cherokee history as much as I do: Travis Owens and Karen Shade of Cherokee Nation Cultural Tourism; Ross Mulcare at the Cherokee National Archives; and genealogists and community historians Twila Barnes, David Hampton, David Cornsilk, Jack Baker, Catherine Foreman Gray (whose love of Cherokee history matches my own), and Troy Wayne Poteete. OsiyoTV staff, past and present, including LeeAnn Dreadfulwater, Jen Loren, Rory Crittenden, Danielle Culp, and many other up-and-coming creative young people who work or have worked for OsiyoTV over the last few years, have provided conversations and opportunities for me to reconsider and clarify pieces of this project.

The Trail of Tears Association continues to be an organization filled with people with deep knowledge of Cherokee history. TOTA member Mike Wren has fielded questions from me at critical points along the way as well.

Emerging Indigenous scholars showing me the way include Alaina Roberts, Meredith McCoy, Jen Rose Smith, Ben Frey, Patricia Dawson, Constance Owl, and Frankie Bauer. *Wado.*

I would be remiss if I did not take a moment to acknowledge that I could not have written this book without the work of artists who see the world differently than I do, without people compelled by and who derive meaning from tasks and creative pursuits that do not drive me but whose work inspires me. Lisa Rutherford, Roy Boney Jr., Candace Byrd Boney, Joseph Erb, Sherry Quinton Berndt, Daniel Horsechief, Kelly Gonzalez, Dorothy Sullivan, Shawna Cain, Roger Cain, and Victorian Vasquez Mitchell let me see parts of the world I might not be able to see otherwise.

I owe first language speakers and second language learners and teachers Tom Belt, Bobbie Smith, Gil Jackson, Ed Fields, Lawrence Panther, Corey Still, Bo Taylor, Ben Frey, and Candessa Tehee thanks as they keep modeling for the rest of us what the future of our language looks like.

As a member of Digadatseli'i ᏗᎦᏓᏤᎵ, I have come to know or have an excuse to gather with Cherokee scholars I have known for many years. This group grounded me in a Cherokee academic community when I might otherwise be alone as a Cherokee scholar at my institution. To Candessa Tehee, Daniel Heath Justice, Melissa Lewis, Courtney Lewis, Ben Frey, Clint Carroll, Jaquetta Shade, Jeff Corntassel, Jeanette Haynes Writer, Sean Teuton, Chris

Teuton, Kirby Brown, Tiffanie Hardbarger—*wado*. My special thanks goes to Stacy Leeds for underwriting the call by language and culture keepers Benny Smith, Durbin Feeling, and Andy Girty to keep this group moving forward for us. I am so grateful Stacy was a Cherokee girl who grew into a Cherokee woman who is my friend.

Even though I said something similar in my first book's acknowledgments, I have to say it again. When Theda Perdue and Mike Green took me on as a graduate student at the University of North Carolina, little did I know I joined an extended academic family. I could not do this academic thing without Christina Snyder (and Zeke, Maybelle, and Ellie), Rose Stremlau (and Rio and Optimus), Brooke Bauer (and Charley), Liz Eilis (and Biscuit), and Malinda Lowery (and Lydia and Goliath). Being back at UNC in early 2023 reminded me what an incredible American Indian studies community I emerged from. I thank Miguel and Kathleen for asking the right kinds of questions and seeing beauty in my work as I headed down this final stretch.

My time at the University of Tennessee–Knoxville came to an end as this project was picking up, but my friendship with and the writing accountability provided by Kristen Block continues unabated. She deserves a byline on this book for the sheer number of hours she has spent listening to me talk through research conundrums, cry through unsaved pages lost, and work through the challenges of life, teaching successes, teaching disasters, writing fails, and writing wins. She has coached me through negative self-talk, set daily writing goals with me, been the only other member of my book club, and held me accountable to planning my academic week almost every Sunday for the last five years. Kristen is an incredible ally and an even more incredible friend; this book belongs to her, too.

To Nick, one phase of our life together ended, but you were and remain a part of this story, too.

To the anonymous readers who offered critical and generative feedback, thank you for helping me improve the manuscript. Our careers are not possible without the silent, unpaid behind-the-scenes labor you provide. To Jeani O'Brien and Kēhaulani Kauanui, thank you for pointing to places in the manuscript that could shine a little brighter.

To Mark Simpson-Vos, you encouraged me to remember I used to be writer, and you gave me the room to try to become one again—what a gift you have provided.

To Kellee, Stewart, Lynn, Valerie, Michele, who reach the pages of this book in various ways, thank you for being my teachers and my oldest friends.

To my family—the Reed, Dabb, Haas, Hardy, Mueller, Duffield, Quinton, and Smith strands—thank you for the pieces of support you have offered throughout my life and on my continuing educational journey.

To Lilith—you continue to be the multiauthored work I am most honored to have played a part in drafting. I remain thankful that I am your mother, but as you start this next phase of life, I am equally grateful to be your friend.

Note on the Cherokee Language

I am and will always be a Cherokee language learner. As a learner, I feel like I take two steps forward and three steps back, but it remains my responsibility to keep trying. I approached my use of the Cherokee language in this book much like a young child (or a full-grown adult) hearing and learning the language might. The words of family and animals often come first, as well as others repeated often because of their significance. Below is a list of words found in this book for those reasons. If I were further along in my studies, verbs would drive this list and provide an even more powerful set of Cherokee people's actions in the past.

Words listed singly are vocabulary words shared between Cherokee Nation and Eastern Band of Cherokee Indians speakers today. Words listed before the forward slash (/) are more common to Cherokee Nation speakers. Words after the forward slash are more common to Eastern Band speakers.[1] In the text itself, I am taking plurals out of their Cherokee context and, therefore, there is no perfect way to express them. Because of this, I leave them as singular words for the sake of English-language readers and hope Cherokee readers offer me some grace. A few words, like *anitsutsa*, which roughly translated as the "boy people," is more easily transferred to an English-language sentence. In a few instances, I have included those plurals.

- ageyutsa (girl); anigeyutsa (girls)
- ama (water)
- anyni (March)
- Asgeyvligei (Beloved Woman)
- ata (teenage girl)
- atsina (cedar)
- atsi nahsa'i (slave, one who is owned, one who is employed)
- atsutsa (boy); anitsutsa (boys)
- awina (teenage boy)
- awohali (white golden eagle, bald eagle)
- dasodaquali / tili (American chestnut)
- dehaluya (June)
- dewi (flying squirrel)

- dideyohvsgi (teacher)
- dinadanvtli / dinatlanvtsi (brother)
- diniyoli / diniyotli (children)
- dlaiga / tsayaga (blue jay)
- duwa (warbler)
- dvlasuga / tsusugv (native rhododendron)
- edutsi / agidutsi (uncle)
- eduda (grandfather)
- elisi / agilisi (grandmother); digvgilisi (grandmothers)
- eloqua (snail)
- equoni (river)
- etsi / agitsi (mother)
- gadugi (working together to elevate everyone)
- galoni (August)
- gu da ge wi (wild potato)
- gv na / kvna (wild turkey)
- kawogv (wood thrush)
- kayu se qua / wagigi (squash)
- nuna (sweet potato, potato)
- osi / asi (winter home, hot house)
- sa sa equa (white swan, goose)
- selu (maize, corn)
- sikwa (pig)
- squalequali (western whippoorwill)
- taline etsi / taline agitsi (second mother)
- tawodi (hawk)
- tsiguenalsa (red-bellied woodpecker)
- tsiyadvga (black-throated blue warbler)
- tsi yes sdi (Carolina parakeet)
- tsuwetsi (son)
- tuya (bean)
- ulv (sister)
- usdi / udage (baby, small)
- uyvtla ama / uyvtsa ama (cold water)
- waca / waga (cow)
- wa da lo ni (passenger pigeon)
- wagule (eastern whippoorwill)
- yona (bear)

Land, Language, and Women

Introduction

I am an educational success story in all the ways that educational institutions like to mark academic success. I credit my educational attainments to the foundation provided by my mother. For more than thirty years, she was an elementary school teacher. I have no recollection of the first time she read to me because that started even before I could form memories. My mom often read books to me and my older brother at his reading level. My reading comprehension benefited from this. I attended Department of Defense schools until I was eight. Then I attended public schools in Florida until I graduated from high school. Sunday school attendance supplemented my education throughout. I devoured *Highlights*, the kids' magazine with covers that asked, "What's Wrong?" with the cover art. I loved libraries. In my mom's downtime, especially when we returned to Florida, when she wasn't teaching or volunteering at our church, she remained inside reading. As I grew older, I read my mom's monthly *Reader's Digest* issues and the weekly Sunday paper supplement *Parade Magazine*. In many ways the path I followed was my mother's. I attended seminary after I received my undergraduate degree in literature. Then I became a public school teacher, just like my mother.

But it was in my attempt to make sense of the incongruity of my parents' lived experiences of school, education, and religion that initially drove my professional undertakings. My dad, whose Cherokee family shaped his childhood but who spent his formative years with his white mother's parents, struggled throughout his years in public schools. He felt ostracized by teachers. College wasn't the path for him. Instead, he enlisted in the military. He worked with his hands. He raced stock cars before I was born. As a parent, he rarely attended church except when he visited his mother. He worked hard physically. He spent a lot of time tinkering on cars, keeping up with our yard, and repairing things. He could spend hours outside in the Florida heat on projects in "his building," a makeshift garage constructed out of spare lumber. The first and only time I remember having a garden as a kid, my dad enlisted my brother and me to plant and care for it. Just a few months before he passed away in November 2022, my dad told me how glad he was that my mom had read to my brother and me when we were kids. He sometimes said that I "got all my smarts" from my mom.

The truth is that both of my parents shaped and formed my intellectual pursuits. My commitments to education and the satisfaction I derive from physical work—my professional life—is a love letter to them for the foundations they provided, even if I turned away from some aspects of their lives when they failed to provide the short- or long-term tools I needed to complete the love letter. The education I received wasn't simply in a school or the church (my mom's domains) and places historically associated with schooling, or in the hot garage or the yard (my dad's venues); it has been in all those spaces and more. I used those foundations to find my way to other educational spaces.

The origins of this book and my career as an ethnohistorian are rooted in family history. I started trying to make sense of people's relationships to institutions long before I became a historian. I continued that effort in my first book, *Serving the Nation*, and now in ᏚᎦᎠ, ᏚᎣᎯᏗᎣᎠᎵ, ᎧᏊ ᎠᎯᏈᏦ / *Land, Language, and Women: A Cherokee and American Educational History*. This book honors not only the Cherokee women who have served as educators, whether that labor was acknowledged, rewarded, or simply taken for granted for millennia, but also the intermarried, non-Cherokee women like my mother who were the first in their families to receive a college degree because they dreamed of becoming teachers, as well as their predecessors, immigrant women by force or consent, who served as teachers of their languages, histories, and cultures when they tended to the children who came to be theirs.

Rather than focus on the "feminization of teaching" as a change in history tied to women outnumbering men in the teaching profession and its relationship to economics, this book takes seriously that women as mothers, sisters, aunts, aunties, friends, caregivers, and unacknowledged supporters have provided a continuous foundation and necessary building blocks for all children's educational trajectories.[1] This teaching also represents the unpaid, domestic labor that women have performed for their families and communities since time immemorial. In a Cherokee context, an education required a deep knowledge of matrilineal and matrilocal practices, a system that foregrounded the significance of female kin for all learners and gender complementarity, not impenetrable walls between men's and women's roles in Cherokee society. Written records more times than not obscure, silence, or compartmentalize the activities of women, especially Black and Indigenous women, as irrelevant to educational history unless they are serving in an official capacity in institutions, receiving wages for their work, or engaging in educational activism or deviance.[2] The chronologies we choose to study can also contribute to the obscurity of women's holistic roles as educators even more.

This book assumes that Cherokee women universally provided primary education for all children during their formative years and that by and large they continue to do so. Kitchen gardens, community fields, and matrilocal households controlled and passed down through women served as the first and most prominent classrooms for children. Children remained close to their mothers, aunts, and grandmothers until they honed basic skills and identified other teachers who could help them obtain more specialized learning. Unlike boys, who eventually received more focused education from men, first from maternal uncles and, to a lesser degree, fathers, and later largely the reverse, girls primarily remained the ongoing students of women. The power of homes and primary caregivers remains a major and fundamental educational force in children's lives today.

Beyond their households, Cherokee women maintained political and economic voices at the local and sometimes a national level through the late eighteenth century. The curriculum was "matriarchal in psychological orientation, matrifocal in cultural meaning, and matrilineal in social power."[3] Through clans passed from women to their children or through ceremonial adoptions carried out by women, women universally determined who was Cherokee until the nineteenth century when the Cherokee government centralized and passed laws in the East usurping that power. The ecosystem of political, social, and economic power connected to and flowed from women's ability to wield substantial educational authority. Even after the American Revolution, which radically restructured many Cherokee communities, Cherokee women continued to act as educators to wider swaths of Cherokee society. When women claimed their authority as mothers and sisters at treaty negotiations or in petitions in the late eighteenth and early nineteenth centuries, they also invoked their authority as educational leaders.[4] They offered refresher courses to Cherokee people on their history, and they aimed to educate outsiders about political and social structures that existed within Cherokee communities. Even when the centralization of the Cherokee Nation in the early decades of the nineteenth century robbed women of their public political voice in national and international policy, the Cherokee Nation could not erase the voices of women in their homes and communities. In fact, certainly to persuade women of the legitimacy of the educational elements of the new governing structures, schooling opportunities were opened to provide one avenue for women to participate in the new system. And yet, even as elite Cherokee men, including John Ross and Major Ridge, appealed to federal officials and secured schooling for their daughters, Sequoyah with the aid of his wife Sallie and daughter Ayohka created and distributed a new technology with vast possibilities for other Cherokee educational futures.[5] The syllabary was available to Cherokee men and women, young and old, the reach of which extended far beyond the newer Euro-American educational institutions. Cherokee people readily adopted coeducation and embraced the availability of schooling for women and girls because it represented an intellectual continuity. The role of educator had been and continued to be a path available to and expected of Cherokee women.

Ethnographer Albert L. Wahrhaftig wrote of the Cherokee people that they changed to remain the same.[6] In many ways this book traces the changes in Cherokee educational history to highlight the continuities. ᏒᎥᎠ, ᏕᏉᏂᎠᏬᎠᎯ, ᎠᏙ ᎠᎲᏫᎶ / *Land, Language, and Women: A Cherokee and American Educational History* begins an exploration of what the primary educators in Cherokee society—linked to the larger Mississippian and Appalachian worlds (and later Trans-Mississippi West)—knew, how they learned what they did, and what value those skills provided for them and the next generation they passed them on to. I also consider why some skills and information may not have been passed along to future generations and why certain teachings and curricula faced interruptions only to be renewed in other moments in time. Even more so, I am interested in systems of education, which are multidirectional and intergenerational. The dynamics between learners and teachers can shift in real time, reversing the roles.

Methodologically, this book is first and foremost ethnohistory, but the interdisciplinary tools and sources I draw from have expanded since the publication of my first book. I have spent time in caves attempting to read spatially complex primary documents to make sense of how caves fit into a larger and older educational landscape. I have read hundreds of pages of reports written by archaeologists over the last few years. I consistently have two responses to archaeological reports. The first is guttural: The dehumanization in the reports is overpowering. I often take breaks, especially from grave site descriptions, because I need to sit with the humanity of the people's lives, likely some of my ancestors, people who have been whittled down to bones, body positions, measurements, an approximate age, and grave goods.

My second response is intellectual: Why don't archaeologists tell us more definitively what they think all these data mean? Archaeology in combination with Indigenous knowledge systems has aided me in answering basic questions I have about the everyday lives of ancestral Cherokees in the late Mississippian world. As Catawba ethnohistorian and potter Brooke Bauer notes in her 2023 prize-winning *Becoming Catawba: Catawba Indian Women and Nation Building, 1540–1840*, pottery sherds indicate the everyday presence of Indigenous women. I admire archaeologists whose work provides the *so what* of their field reports and who spend time adding complexity to research on the everyday lives of Indigenous peoples. I cite many of those archaeologists in the pages of this book.

Yet, the limitations in archaeological records—the lack of evidence of people's lived existences—led me to make a choice. In chapters 1 and 2, I created two composite girls to walk us through an educational landscape that is both knowable and unknowable simultaneously. It was a fortuitous discovery to realize that archaeologists Janet Spector and friend Kandi Hollenbach along with her coauthor Stephen Carmody provided a model for this very exercise. Janet Spector created a Dakota girl in her influential work *What This Awl Means: Feminist Archaeology at a Wahpeton Village.* Hollenbach and Carmody wrote, "By imagining the daily seasonal activities through the eyes of a young girl, we can give those individuals identities and begin to think about the social relationships among [Indigenous] peoples and the landscape."[7] Leanne Simpson, in her article "Land as Pedagogy," genders the main character in a traditional Michi Saagiig Nishnaabeg story as a girl and names her Kwezens, which means "little woman" or "girl."[8] Taking inspiration from them, I aim to extend their efforts further. I wanted the girls I created, rooted in what we know about the worlds where actual Cherokee girls resided and learned, to link us to the Cherokee girls and women who descended from them metaphorically. I see this book as creating a lineage—one that is simultaneously intellectual and social and familial.

I admit, as a historian, that the composite girls in the first two chapters may challenge the comfort of some readers, but to humanize the lives and realities of my ancestors, I couldn't simply rely on the data from sherds, shards, and skeletal remains. I needed flesh and blood. I needed the stories carried in people. The girls I created, Ageyutsa and Climber of Trees, are not rooted in fiction; instead, they emerge from an intellectually based creativity that pulls from relevant and vetted archaeology, oral narratives, the earliest ethnographies from the Native South, and the articulations of Cherokee master artists and teachers willing to share their processes with me or from published sources that exist with similar information. They also come from an awareness I gained by taking my daughter Lilith to sites I visited and allowing myself to think like a mother attuned to her child on the sides of bluffs covered with rock art created 800 years ago or in caves containing syllabary.[9] Combing through these sources, I have attempted to reconstruct pedagogical practices and curricula with long histories of use in Cherokee adult education and education aimed at children, and I often did so by paying attention to my own daughter's experiences of space and how what she learned in those places might have compared with what her ancestral cousins learned.

By choosing to write a book that spans a long chronology, I use what historian of education Adrea Lawrence refers to as "epic learning," an examination of knowledge acquisition and transmission that considers multiple generations and thus enables an examination of both Native and non-Native educational techniques and adaptations. This approach comports with Robert Warrior's point that a "generational view" enables us to see contemporary connections to centuries-long processes within Indigenous communities.[10] Additionally, as Lawrence writes, "Time within the framework of epic learning loses its directional privilege. In part, this is because the event grounds the epic learning in place and experience. But time also becomes backgrounded as a structural feature of epic learning because the scope of inquiry—the duration of epic learning—is significantly expanded to include multiple generations and thus multiple contexts for learning."[11] This approach also asks readers to abandon the language of prehistory, as Juliana Barr called upon us to do in her article "There's No Such Thing as 'Prehistory'" and was recently echoed in Robbie Ethridge's 2021 American Society for Ethnohistory presidential address titled "Ancient America: Connecting America's Deep Past to American History and Why It Matters."[12] In this spirit, I invoke the terms "ancestral Cherokees" to describe the people in the places where Cherokees claim their origins, regardless of when they arrived or how they emerged. I understand that the people who resided at Kituwah, a townsite continually occupied for the last 8,000 years, influenced those who came after them through their shared social and cultural patterns. As my mentor Theda Perdue has often reminded me, "It takes a long time to change culture."

Although I am examining education through the lives of girls, this book is not a true history of childhood for several reasons. Though all these girls had an individual experience with education, they existed within larger educational systems—constellations of teachers, spaces, and geographies—and were inextricably tied to the decision-making of those who came before them. Each girl's experience reflected and was the result of thousands of others. This relationality, a concept that Indigenous peoples and scholars are acutely aware of, exists at an individual point in time and across generations.[13] Second, as scholars of childhood point out, historians draw upon sources very often written about children by adults as opposed to being the voices of children.[14] I confront the same problem throughout the book, with a few exceptions. Chapter 4 draws upon the writings of girls attending Dwight Mission during the Long Removal Era, a mission that first opened in Arkansas Territory in 1821 and later moved to Indian Territory in 1829. Chapter 6 includes letters written by Nancy Joan and Doug, my aunt and father, to their mother when they were children. And chapter 7 relies heavily on the archive of my childhood that I began curating in 1979, when I was not even four years old. Although this book is not a history of childhood, per se, I hope it serves as some small inspiration for those on a path to writing histories or collecting archives of childhood.

I have increasingly turned to autoethnography for reasons that may already be apparent. Institutions, including universities, often demand the compartmentalization of our lives; this often falls hardest on women, mothers, BIPOC, 2SLGBQT+ individuals, and people with disabilities. Autoethnographers, for reasons more related to discussions of subjectivity and intellectual bias, contend that one's personal experiences and relationships to others can exist with "intellectual rigor."[15] I agree. I chose the classroom spaces I did because they were and continue to be spaces of learning for me and for other Cherokee and non-Cherokee people.

I am in the book in a number of obvious ways. I chose to write my introduction in the first person, and my narrative voice interrupts throughout the book to add asides. My courses in women's studies at the University of South Florida and pastoral care and counseling at Southern Methodist University used autoethnography as a pedagogical tool. Those courses inadvertently resulted in some of the primary documents I cite in this book.

However, my colleagues, co-thinkers, and mentors in Native American and Indigenous studies would ask, Rigor as defined by whom and for what ends? Native American and Indigenous studies and decolonizing studies often encourage and privilege statements of relationality—relationships to land, space, communities, and kin—so that we know who and where we are in relationship to each other. Indigenous education scholars, Indigenous historians of education, and Cherokee scholars have gifted the profession with and honored their communities by sharing a rich set of methodological tools grounded in our own communities' values; they inspire me to infuse my own family's story to better understand Cherokee educational history and to contribute to a body of work rooted in a Cherokee epistemology.[16] As Linda Tuhiwai Smith writes, "Indigenous peoples want to tell our own stories, write our own versions, in our own ways, for our own purposes. It is not simply about giving an oral account or a genealogical naming of the land and the events which raged over it, but a very powerful need to give testimony to and restore a spirit, to bring back into existence a world fragmented and dying. The sense of history conveyed by these approaches is not the same thing as the discipline of history, and so our accounts collide, crash into each other."[17] This book is a collision of writing Cherokee educational history and then "rewriting and re-righting" Cherokee educational history.

Beyond affirming "land as pedagogy," readers may ask how I chose the classroom spaces at the center of each chapter. The answer is multilayered. Pragmatically, all the locations have a documentary record associated with them. Moreso, as educators know, where we learn matters; simplistically, space can contribute to or inhibit certain kinds of learning. For Indigenous peoples and for Cherokee people, the land itself was and for some remains a literacy and a teacher. I'm not sure I fully understood this lesson until I was drafting this book and walked into spaces older than humans in places like Wills Valley, the classroom of chapter 3, an area occupied briefly by Cherokee people in the period between the American Revolution and forced removal but where old and new converged, geographically, socially, and educationally. This region could have been where this book began.

In another version of this project, before I entered caves at the invitation of a team of archaeologists in 2015 to examine what appeared to be Sequoyan syllabary on the walls and ceilings, I envisioned a starting point that privileged missionary-run schools and Sequoyah's syllabary. In so doing I would have elevated literacy in the form of written alphabetic languages above other kinds of Indigenous literacies, including sign languages, wampum, quipu, and older intellectual traditions. When I stood in the cave in Willstown—a space Mississippian peoples and their ancestors had ventured into long before their Cherokee grandchildren—I marveled at the use of such spaces in the nineteenth century to demonstrate the efficacy of the syllabary, a new technology of writing to convey very old ideas and teachings.[18] The educational commitments of those writers to convey their ideas reached back in time to even older social and cultural norms, even as it also reached forward in time to me. It was a place where changes and continuities exploded into view. It was so clear to me at that moment that Sequoyah didn't provide a starting point for Cherokee educational trajectories when he debuted the syllabary in 1821; he was, at best, a midpoint and another fork in an already forking road.

The limestone caves I entered were multidimensional, multisensory, and intergenerational spaces. Light and sound work differently there. Caves are otherworldly, forcing me to reckon with an embodied understanding of Cherokee conceptions of the world as a three-level underworld, middle world, and upper world. I was standing between those worlds. I needed to be in this classroom for an intellectual lesson to truly take root. I needed the land to teach me. It was more than simply applying what I had learned; it was the land itself. The caves contain stalactites and stalagmites that formed over thousands of years within some of the oldest mountains on the planet. In one of the caves, a unique species of snail has adapted itself to that single cave.[19] The first time I entered these caves, the awe, the skepticism, and the excitement all distilled into a set of questions that the team I was with has only partially been able to answer over the last eight years.

Why did my ancestors choose this place to use the language in the ways they did? What does it mean that a room in a cave has writing on the walls and ceiling? Should we be reading those collectively? Why did they choose to invert some of the writing so that it appears backward to humans below? What kind of engineering was necessary to write on the ceiling, a ceiling a twenty-first-century climber and caver has yet to figure out how to reach? What are the translation issues involved with the early syllabary script, as opposed to the syllabary adapted to the printing press just a few years after its invention? What does this say about the continuities of Southeastern Indigenous peoples entering caves for millennia? Should I have been there? What right did I have to be there, as opposed to all other Cherokee people? I will never possess the ability to fully read and understand what my forebears wrote in those caves, but the land taught me something: The land itself demands a longer chronology. This and other caves I entered (and the other places in the book) have been my classrooms, spaces where my Cherokee education has unfolded and continues to grow.

As I began delving into the primary documents related to Sequoyah to contextualize the caves and the areas surrounding them historically for our team *and* tried to grapple with a cave as a classroom space, I ran up against a second problem—revisionist history. In both of the earliest accounts related to Sequoyah's development of the syllabary, he mentions the role his wife and daughter played in helping him create it.[20] Some public memory exists as it relates his daughter Ayohka when she accompanied him to the Cherokee National Council and helped him demonstrate the efficacy of the syllabary.[21] But his wife's and daughter's phonological awareness—their ability to discern and hear the individual sounds that make up larger words (a term I know because this is a skill many people with dyslexia, my daughter and father included, and people with hearing impairments struggle with), a skill that enabled them to support his efforts and would have required a lot of their time—is less well known. Instead, his wife Sallie becomes a villain who destroyed his early drafts, and Ayohka becomes a dutiful student. Within a generation, the contributions of Sallie and Ayohka to his creative process disappear from future accounts.[22]

How we have remembered Sequoyah and his familial educational partners is not accidental. Non-Native writers obsessed over Sequoyah's possible non-Native father, with whom he never had any documented relationship, projecting their own anxieties over families and fathers onto Indigenous peoples. This obsession deserves no more oxygen. It denigrates Cherokee family systems and Indigenous genius by crediting his intellect to some non-Native source and ignores Cherokee women's educational contributions to their children's lives in the past and now. Through these retellings, Sequoyah emerged as a Cadmus, a lone genius, a self-taught man.[23] This is in keeping with "Big Men's History" more broadly, which privileges the actions of a few powerful men in shaping human history and ignores the actions of women and children in men's orbits as an inconsequential sidenote to men's greatness. But this version stands at odds with longer views of Cherokee educational history and with the records themselves. Rather than read Sequoyah as an individual genius, I ask us to read him as a son to Cherokee women, a nephew to Cherokee men facing down violent change, and a father to a Cherokee daughter in a time when Cherokee views on fatherhood were in flux. Did he seek solitude at various moments as he created the syllabary? Yes. Did he and the community acknowledge the role of his wife and child to his process at the time it debuted? Yes. Sequoyah and, I would argue, Ayohka democratized the syllabary's distribution, an ancient and abiding approach to Cherokee educational opportunities. Extracting him from Cherokee women and girls, from the place he was raised, and from the community he remained committed to, as most scholars have done, sets him outside of Cherokee educational history, not within it.

Finally, brief mentions of women in records designed and in service to men are not nothing; they are often everything. The records support Ayohka's central role and front-row seat in the process to create the syllabary. Making Ayohka a central character in Cherokee educational history restores Sequoyah's place within it, too.

This book is about rewriting, re-righting, and reenvisioning Cherokee educational history; centering Ayohka is a part of that. To help me accomplish this, I commissioned Roy Boney Jr. to create a unified set of illustrations so that we can see these girls individually and collectively. Roy, along with other Cherokee artists featured in the notes of this book and whose work is a different kind of Cherokee-centered primary source, helped me see and read sources more deeply. I asked Roy to let Ayohka grow up. Artists nearly always depict her as a six-year-old and in the shadow of Sequoyah. I am so grateful to Roy for helping me to see her as the young Cherokee woman she became. I hope you sit with the illustrations and discover something new about these young women each time, as I have.

Equally central to my decision to center girls is the lived reality of my educational and intellectual life. Existing in a world of institutions, academia included, so many of us—through bureaucratic mechanisms, new technologies to learn and integrate, endless committee work, large class sizes, loss of time to simply be—forget we are humans knitted to others. I began my PhD work with a nursing infant daughter in tow. She attended classes with me the first few weeks because my day care situation collapsed. When I took a boat with a team of archaeologists to see a bluff with 800-year-old rock art more than three stories high and stretching more than half a football field in length with a cave behind it eleven years later, that same daughter was with me. On that bluff, 100 years before we visited, a girl had written her name and the date. In that moment, on that bluff, as a mother, a Cherokee woman, and a scholar, I thought about all the ways girls entered a range of educational spaces again and again and again over long stretches of time. My daughter didn't write this book, but my choices, or lack of choice at times, to include her in my scholarly life altered the questions I have asked and the observations I have made about educational history. As Daniel Heath Justice, professor of critical Indigeneities, writes, "Without the teachings about the *who*, *how*, and *why* of us, something is profoundly, almost existentially amiss."[24]

Learning is not a one-way street. How, what, and where we learn and in relationship to whom all matter as well. Each chapter title in this book includes a primary classroom space and the name of a girl who lived and learned within that classroom. All the classrooms featured continue to exist, but the degree to which Cherokee people have uniformly acknowledged, controlled, had access to, or been educated in these spaces has waxed and waned over time. Also, these geographies represent classrooms and teachers. The girls featured in each chapter provide an entry point into a larger educational world. Their experiences are those of students and potentially teachers. Through more expansive definitions of classrooms and through the foregrounding of girls, the book seeks not only to make spaces of learning more visible but also to prompt a reconsideration of who was teaching and learning in those spaces.

Chapter 1, "Kituwah: Ageyutsa," examines our ancient Mother Town, a town with a sacred and elevated status that occupies a central role in Cherokee history. The girl's name literally translates to "girl." Many Cherokee people refer to themselves as AniKituwah, the people of Kituwah. Kituwah rests on the Tuckasegee River near present-day Bryson City, North Carolina, and has been continually occupied for more than 8,000 years. Indigenous informants and mapmakers consistently prioritized its presence on eighteenth-century maps; this speaks to its continued significance to Cherokee people even after its international diplomatic significance to outsiders waned in the years following European settlement. Kituwah is an ancient, abiding, and intellec-tually significant place for Cherokees, past, present, and future. It is one of our oldest classrooms, nestled within our original homelands, and a place that Cherokees residing in the East and West have attended over time. It is a classroom that Cherokee girls millennia ago and Cherokee girls today know about and study.

Chapter 2, "Overhill Towns: Climber of Trees," largely explores the educational systems at Chota and its sister town of Tanasi, located in present-day Monroe County, Tennessee. I chose the name Climber of Trees because it shows up in the archival records as a common Cherokee girl's name. Like Kituwah, Chota and Tanasi are also old and politically significant communities. Like Kituwah, mounds swelled from the surface until the Tennessee Valley Authority dam projects in the 1960s flooded large portions of the towns. Despite damming projects, the Little Tennessee River still flows past. In the early decades of the eighteenth century, numerous educational continuities extended across time and across Cherokee towns, even after contact with Europeans. Rather than focusing on Chota and Tanasi's rise and fall from international prominence in the mid- to late eighteenth century, the chapter focuses on the first decades of the eighteenth century and enables larger discussions of what were first slow and then more rapid changes wrought by settler colonial violence—changes that reconfigured the educational futures available to and sought by some Cherokee people.

Chapter 3, "Wills Valley: Ayohka," examines how Wills Valley existed briefly as a Cherokee region, in what is today northern Alabama, but connected Cherokee people to older and still familiar educational landscapes within the Native South. And yet, it also provided a space for missionaries, Sequoyah, Cherokee refugees, and political elites to debate and test out a variety of educational futures free from some of the familiar classroom tools of older spaces. It played a central role in the period immediately following the American Revolution, and its life as a Cherokee town effectively ended at the close of forced removal. But the educational possibilities it spawned informed the people who moved west before and after forced removal, including Sequoyah and his daughter Ayohka. Focusing on Wills Valley enables a richer discussion of the Long Removal Era, a period marked by multiple internal and external displacements leading up to massive forced removal from 1838 to 1839. Debates over educational futures offer a way to understand why Western Cherokees, also called Old Settlers, moved west earlier. The syllabary, completed in Wills Valley, offered an educational technology with vast possibilities, some of which dovetailed nicely with the aims of federal officials and Cherokee officials amenable to elements of the Civilization Policy, and some of which aimed to provide a tool for the transmission of much older forms of knowledge and enabled intellectual acts of resistance to the educational futures proposed by federal officials and embraced by some Cherokee people.

Chapter 4, "Skin Bayou District: Caroline Fields," focuses on the area first called the Lees Creek District under the Western Cherokees, then the Skin Bayou District after reunification, and then later renamed the Sequoyah District in 1851. It is where Ayohka and her father lived in the wake of their subsequent removals to Arkansas Territory (1820s) and then to Indian Territory after the 1828 treaty with the Western Cherokees. The Presbyterians also relocated Dwight Mission, first established in Arkansas Territory in 1821, to what became the Skin Bayou District (1841) in 1829. Dwight Mission continually operated as a school providing education to Cherokee youth from then until well into the twentieth century, though the student demographics ebbed and flowed over time. After removal, Dwight Mission became one school among many as the Cherokee Nation established its public schools throughout the Nation and its seminaries in Tahlequah. For a brief period after Cherokee removals, most of its students were elite Cherokee daughters of predominantly slaveholding Cherokee families. By examining the experiences of two girls named Caroline Fields—Caroline Eliza Fields and Caroline Matilda Fields—side by side with the educational paths of girls like Ayohka, we can see the range of educational possibilities that existed in the post-removal era. It demonstrates how Cherokee progressive educational policies, especially those related to women, impacted a variety of girls and women. Some Cherokee girls, just by being born, benefited economically from a system tied to newer racial ideologies and to the labor of enslaved Black people, including other children. Some families redefined education as schooling. By doing so, they worked to erase the teaching provided to girls by enslaved Black women and by teachers adhering to older curriculums. Other women continued to exercise their economic rights, not through acquisitive wealth but by holding fast to matrilineal and matrilocal structures and more egalitarian ways of being. Other women benefited from the employment offered through schools. Still others walked paths between, continuing to define education in far more expansive ways. The Skin Bayou District, where Ayohka grew to adulthood and had children and where the two girls named Caroline Fields attended Dwight Mission, laid the groundwork for Indian Territory educational futures.

Oklahoma provides the educational space for chapters 5, "Oklahoma Indian Schools: Rachel Johnson," and 6, "Oklahoma Public Schools: Nancy (Aincy) Joan." These two chapters are where I knew my family history entered this history, although by the end of writing this book I realized it began much earlier and that I am distantly related to Ayohka and a number of the girls who attended Dwight Mission. Rachel Johnson is my great-grandmother, Nancy Joan's (and my father's) grandmother. Nancy Joan is my dad's sister, my aunt. I chose the area and these women because, to quote Richard White, "most of us live with our family stories, but generally we don't think about them all the time. I think about them constantly."[25] The historian in me appreciated that although many Cherokee people stayed where they were, control over schooling did change. A range of educational pathways remained available to Cherokee students, albeit not evenly or equally, in the period following allotment, which broke up Cherokee communal landholdings (1898–1914) and led to Oklahoma statehood in 1907. Oklahoma housed boarding schools and mission schools formerly operated by the Native nations and the various denominations that had operated at the pleasure of those respective nations. It assumed control of many of the educational institutions, including the Cherokee Female Seminary and the various public school systems, which gave way to the Oklahoma public school system and formed the basis of some institutions of higher education. It also benefited from the human resources provided by the Five Tribes. Cherokee women assumed their place as public school teachers in the state of Oklahoma. Oklahoma continued to face the same struggle previously faced by Native nations and by rural districts across the country as they worked to make schools both physically accessible and of a similar quality and duration to more urban areas.

Chapter 7, "Global Education: Julie," traces the impact of major changes in the postwar period from the 1970s to the first decade of the twenty-first century. It charts the impact of imperialism, military service, *Brown v. Board of Education*, and globalization on my educational life. I am the product of European colonization, the United States' first efforts at imperialism against Native peoples, and its global reach against Indigenous peoples in places like the Philippines. Unlike the Cherokee girls you meet in this book, I have traveled the farthest and lived in the most places. My early educational history reflects the realities of many Cherokee children whose families moved away from the Cherokee Nation and have come to make up the Cherokee at-large communities today.[26] And yet, my life is unrepresentative compared with that of girls born and raised in the Cherokee Nation. For this reason, I introduce readers to two of my peer teachers, Catherine and Candessa, whose knowledge of towns, kinship, language, community, and Cherokee history is far deeper than mine and whose work as peer teachers has contributed to my Cherokee education. Their educational trajectories mirror mine in many ways and yet diverge in ways that enable a richer view of the educational futures created by the Cherokee women who came before us.

This book is not about changes over time; instead, it is about continuities amid change. When we expand our chronological frame, focus on the daily lives and activities of Cherokee women and girls, and consider a range of intellectual and educational spaces, we see that women were and have always been the central arbiters of Cherokee educational history and intellectual paths, not at the expense of boys and men but side by side with them. Cherokee women embraced educational futures rooted in distant pasts and paved new educational ground; some embraced the educational possibilities of the Civilization Policy and the racializing constraints it placed on wide swaths of Cherokee people; others paid this policy little heed; and still others remained enslaved by it. Many Cherokee women and girls continue to do the quiet behind-the-scenes work of language teaching and preservation in families, the sharing of family and community histories, and the transmitting of knowledge of place and space. Others do and have done the more civic work of teaching, public relations, and legal advocacy necessary to protect the Nation and its descendants from a loss of control over their families' and community's educational futures. ᏌᎤᏗᎢ, ᏌᏫᎮᏗᏓᎶᎯ, DᏙ DᎭᎮᎷᏍᎣ (land, language, and women) form the bedrock of Cherokee educational pasts, presents, and futures.

Ageyutsa of Kituwah. Artwork by Roy Boney Jr.

CHAPTER 1

Kituwah

Ageyutsa

By the time my daughter Lilith was twelve, she had been to Kituwah nearly a dozen times. She knows the name AniKituwah connects to "the People," although she is less clear on Kituwah's exact meaning.[1] She knows a mound is there and a river runs along the site. When she was younger, she was always eager to swim there, though she never has. She knows there is a farm at Kituwah and that it is close to Cherokee, North Carolina. She recognizes the site is important to Cherokee people, but she has never taken a class about Kituwah or visited for official reasons. She knows these details about Kituwah because as her mother I have shared them with her or because she has engaged in "landscape learning"; she paid attention to her environment.[2] My daughter, an enrolled Cherokee Nation citizen, has never lived in a Cherokee community, despite the fact that we lived in the Cherokee homelands in Knoxville for seven years. What she knows about Kituwah and how she knows it is not completely dissimilar to the ways a girl, Ageyutsa, who resided at Kituwah before the Spanish entradas and after it had already undergone major changes long before she was born, would have learned about the place she lived.[3] And yet, Ageyutsa's knowledge of that place would have been far deeper, richer, and more embodied and essential to her existence than my Cherokee daughter's understanding today. Rather than relying only on a biological mother or intermittent gatherings of family and community, Ageyutsa's learning opportunities were diverse and ever-present. Ageyutsa learned from a standard curriculum shared by everyone, but she also learned from a gendered curriculum and could excel in advanced teachings if she chose to (or was chosen to) and demonstrated a commitment to that learning. This chapter traces the educational life of Ageyutsa from the time she was an *usdi*, baby, until she was an *ata*, teenage girl. While the space she resided in largely remained the same, she changed and grew in relationship to it. As Cherokee Nation citizen and first language speaker Tom Belt often says of our connections to the homelands, she was "of Kituwah," not from it.[4]

Just as babies distinguish themselves from their mothers over time, Ageyutsa and other babies first began developing their relationships to the physical world around them at Kituwah swaddled on their mother's backs.[5] By her fifth moon, Ageyutsa regularly grasped the braid hanging down her mother's back and reached her hands for the women and children in her mother's orbit.[6] The first other-than-human relations Ageyutsa tracked may have been the wild turkeys skirting the woods, but she may have been more enamored by the flight of "millions [of passenger pigeons] in a flock . . . sometimes split[ting] off the limbs of stout Oaks" and by the chatter and colorful flashes of green, yellow, and red of Carolina parakeets moving across the sky.[7]

While mothers and aunties farmed, gossiped, discussed pottery making and feather cape construction, expressed frustration with local leaders or husbands, and framed ideas for women's councils, they also imparted to babies, toddlers, and young children linguistic, social, political, and economic knowledge. Those women's daily activities provided all *diniyoli*, children, with a standard curriculum. *Diniyoli* remained close to their mothers until they expressed an interest in more advanced learning. In doing so, they witnessed the range of skills and expertise that women possessed. They watched their mothers gather water when older *diniyoli* were not around to assist. They helped their mothers gather medicinal herbs for teas and medicines. They witnessed women working together across the community to grow corn, beans, and squash for the wider community and saw the women in their household maintain family kitchen gardens containing tobacco, smaller ears of corn that matured more quickly, and peas.[8] By assisting their mothers when they gathered nuts, they benefited from the range of breads prepared from them afterward and the knowledge of how to make them. When women dug up clay for pottery, it wasn't just girls who shaped and formed smalls wads of clay; boys did as well.[9] When they processed pottery temper to keep pottery from expanding while fired, *diniyoli* helped and learned. Although girls would be the primary creators of pottery for a variety of purposes, including preparing and mixing, cooking, serving, and storing foods, boys gained comfort with the clay they would use to make pipes.[10] Beyond the labor they modeled, Cherokee women introduced *diniyoli* to a range of disciplines.

When her mother returned from the community fields, Ageyutsa passed from her back to that of her *taline etsi*, second mother, what today might be called an aunt, and then to the lap of her *elisi*, grandmother. Who she was as a member of the Bird Clan, one of the seven clans that determined Cherokee belonging and identity, passed from her *elisi* to her *etsi*, mother, to her. She would always be AniKituwah and Bird Clan because of these women. Her mother's brother, her *edutsi*, uncle, was Bird Clan too. Although he hung around the council house when he was home from hunts, he brought her *etsi* deer and shared meals with them sometimes. And when he did, he took Ageyutsa on his lap and imitated her facial expressions, which made her smile.[11] This was her family.

By the time she was two winters, she understood these were the most important adults in her life. Beyond determining belonging, these women reinforced that belonging through the songs they sang, the stories they told, the medicines they grew, the skills they shared, and the relationships they explained when people or other-than-human beings passed through her world. They would teach her that Bird Clan people resided in every Cherokee town and that those kin had the same obligations and responsibilities to her that her household kin did and she to them. If she traveled to Coweeta or Watauga or Nikwasi, members of the Bird Clan would be there to welcome her, share food, and provide safety and care. Her children would eventually live among these same women and learn similar lessons. They were her past, present, and future.

Ageyutsa, like nearly all *diniyoli* throughout history, learned to speak and communicate by listening to the conversations around her, first the voices of her *etsi, taline etsi,* and *elisi*.[12] On the fourth or seventh day of her life, she received her first name. Ageyutsa didn't need to see her mother's lips to hear the sounds that would shape her world. As if to reinforce the skill of listening, because of how Cherokee sounds are formed in the mouth, it is extremely difficult to read the lips of a Cherokee speaker.[13] Most of the sounds are created in the mouth itself, not with the lips.[14] Listening and watching were essential educational skills.

Ageyutsa learned at Kituwah, but the built environment around her paralleled other town structures in other places and in later moments. Cherokee towns often contained paired summer and winter homes, also known as the *osi* (winter home), which dotted the landscape around plazas and town fields.[15] The *osi* provided refuge from the cold during the winter months and, like the summer house, required a hearth for cooking. Cherokee people in towns across the region replicated this paired structure.[16] This reinforced a larger and universalized curriculum of "social egalitarianism," which avoided placing power in the hands of a small group of people and valued the contributions and strengths of all of a community's members, men and women.[17] Specialized teachers, the hothouse people, "superintended the building of hothouses" to nearly exact specifications across time and space, providing another opportunity for some children to both learn from and aspire to become a teacher themselves.[18]

The realities of her living conditions did set her apart from her ancestors. She spent far more time inside than her ancestors had due to the colder and dryer conditions that prevailed and as a result created more challenging agricultural conditions across the region.[19] She also learned that Cherokee people still knew where these towns were; they could return when the towns were ready for them. She was growing up in a world that had taken steps toward rejecting the older hierarchies of the larger Mississippian world that spread from Cahokia eastward. Many communities had begun building council houses next to mound sites as opposed to on top of them; people built structures that created less social and physical distance between themselves and community leadership.[20] Governing took place on the ground among the entire community.

Ageyutsa's classroom from her birth reinforced the central place she and her siblings, who today might be referred to as cousins, and friends occupied in the Cherokee world. As she was swaddled to her mother's back, the world that first came into focus for Ageyutsa would have been the fields, possibly cleared using fire first, then broken at the start of planting by the community as a whole, and then cultivated by her grandmothers and mothers. Ancestral Cherokees cultivated fields of sunflowers, *kayu se qua* (squash), gourds, and, after AD 900, *selu* (maize). Tuya (bean) joined her sisters Selu (First Woman, Corn Mother) and Kayu se qua around 300 years later.[21]

This coming together of women, literally and figuratively, serves as one of the foundations of Cherokee history and explains the origin of staple crops absent from the region just a handful of centuries earlier. Selu, the Corn Mother, the First Woman—this was one of Ageyutsa's first and most embodied curriculums. From the place on her mother's back she rocked in motion, napped, and awakened to the planting, tending, and harvesting of those crops. Ageyutsa listened and absorbed the narratives, language, laughter, gossip, and concerns of the women who labored in those fields. In the fields, Ageyutsa learned about Selu's and Cherokee women's willingness to sustain the community even at great risk to themselves.

This may have been the context in which Ageyutsa first heard about Selu's centrality to Cherokee cosmology. When the *tsuwetsi*, Corn Mother Selu's sons, discovered her rubbing her abdomen to produce a bountiful supply of corn and beans (two of the three sisters), they thought she was a witch. They decided to kill her for her perceived transgression. Selu, as so many mothers do, knew what her boys were planning, but she also knew that without her ability to produce, life ceased to exist. With that knowledge, she provided a final lesson and gave explicit instructions:

> "Clear a large piece of ground in front of the house and drag my body seven times around the circle. Then drag me seven times over the ground inside the circle, and stay up all night and watch, and in the morning you

will have plenty of corn." The boys killed her with their clubs, and cut off her head and put it up on the roof of the house with her face turned to the west, and told her to look for her husband. Then they set to work to clear the ground in front of the house, but instead of clearing the whole piece they cleared only seven little spots. This is why corn now grows only in a few places instead of over the whole world. They dragged the body of Selu around the circle, and wherever her blood fell on the ground the corn sprang up. But instead of dragging her body seven times across the ground they dragged it over only twice, which is the reason the Indians still work their crop but twice. The two brothers sat up and watched their corn all night, and in the morning it was full grown and ripe.[22]

Embedded in this story of matricide and maternal sacrifice is a whole series of lessons about women's relationships to their children but also about men in general. Ageyutsa learned from her mother that mothers sacrifice for their children; that sacrifice might be life itself. For Ageyutsa, this story reinforced the central cosmological and agricultural role women played in the community. It also may have served as the reason that men and boys couldn't be trusted exclusively to tend to the agricultural landscape. Despite clear instructions, they might not follow through and thereby compromise the entire community's well-being. The story reminded all community members of what was lost if women's knowledge of and lessons related to the land weren't followed fully. Ageyutsa absorbed the lesson that producing corn and beans and having sisters, literally and figuratively, not only supported her but contributed to the entire community's and her specific family's well-being. Ageyutsa learned that her productive and reproductive knowledge was instrumental to the future of Cherokee society. She learned that political power emanated from this labor.

Intensive farming strengthened and changed women's bodies; it was also more physically taxing over time. Just as Ageyutsa's mother's labor increased her physical strength, women's agricultural pursuits served as a reminder to the entire community of the centrality of crops to their present well-being, their future possibilities, and their origins as a people.[23] Women planted the "three sisters" in hills using digging sticks and hoes. Likely with *diniyoli*, small children, assisting or in close proximity, they placed four to ten grains in each hill. Sometimes, the women planted squash and beans between the hills. In others, they planted squash and beans within the hills, which enabled the beans to climb the maize stalks. Women, with the assistance of *diniyoli*, thinned the plants, weeded, and hoed the soil around the crops to promote root development. As the season continued, they harvested and prepped the crops for storage. Women used mortars and pestles to pound corn into meal that could be used to prepare bread; they also stored some for the months ahead. In fall and winter, when Cherokee men left for hunting or raids, initially those men were sustained with the agriculture produced by women's labor, as were the elder men, women, and *diniyoli* who remained at home, sending up smoke for bountiful hunts.[24] Women's bodies underwent physical changes as the political and economic power attached to their more intensive farming took hold.

Six major seasonal ceremonies attuned to calendars dictated by solar and lunar cycles punctuated the everyday lessons provided and exemplified by women. Ceremonies tied to agriculture, and at the center was Selu—"a female . . . held in special honor, and identified with Indian Corn, or Maize. Most of the All Night Dances refer in some way to her, as did some of the Ceremonies in the Green Corn Festival. . . . A female called 'The Woman of the East' is also mentioned with much reverence."[25]

When Ageyutsa's mother first informed her kin she was pregnant with Ageyutsa, kin accompanied her to water every new moon to perform ceremonies that maintained the health and well-being of both mother and child. Women's experiences of pregnancy added another layer of meaning and knowing to the ceremonies they had attended but until then not as the bodily caretaker of a Cherokee *usdi*.[26] The Spring New Moon Festival acknowledged grass growth; the New Corn Feast recognized when new corn emerged; the Green Corn Ceremony celebrated when corn had become "perfect"; the Great New Moon Feast coincided with the first autumnal full moon, when the world was made anew and people were restored to one another to begin again; and finally the festival of Bounding Bush occurred.[27] Alongside these ceremonies marking the agricultural life cycle, Ageyutsa grew inside her mother's belly, just as the mounds in Cherokee communities swelled from the surface of the ground. Long before the Cherokee ceremonial leader recited the reasons for these rituals at the events themselves, Cherokee women provided the primer, preparing and modeling the significance of the ceremonies to their *diniyoli* and the larger community. Women's growing bellies provided a mnemonic device for children making sense of the world around them.

Across the region, men led most of the community ceremonies that reinforced the legal and spiritual educations of all community members; some still did so from a council house built atop a mound. But they could do so only because women provided the primary lessons in their homes, which shared the same proportions and shape of the council house, and in the community fields and kitchen gardens, which formed the building blocks of these public curricula. And because many of these ceremonies reinforced the central role that Selu and, by extension, women occupied in Cherokee society, they provided another important curriculum to Cherokee people.

Although she may not have remembered the first time she watched Asgeyvligei (Beloved Woman), an elder woman who had achieved an elevated status within the community, Ageyutsa's interest in feathers may have come from watching the Asgeyvligei gracefully swipe a *sa sa equa* (white swan) wing feather fan at a council meeting to drive home her lesson. She witnessed a parallel act by the local priest with an *awohali* (white golden eagle) feather.[28] She may have heard stories in all these educational spaces; sometimes, listening and learning also required seeing for mastery. The eagle, for example, because it could fly the highest and had the widest frame of vision, was known for its foresight and symbolized knowledge. Both public actions with feathers reinforced lessons and knowledge within the community. Mnemonic devices used by town leaders at ceremonies and council meetings reinforced the oral lessons and history of Cherokee people and may have reminded her of her responsibilities as a member of the Bird Clan.

Beyond the associations that feathers created for Ageyutsa in relationship to women's power, as she grew, feathers reinforced other lessons of history, culture, and kin. Whether she paid close attention or not, over time feathers acted as one of those mnemonic devices triggering a connection to lessons heard month after month, year after year. The eagle feathers waved by the priest came from a sacred flier. She learned that eagles could be killed only during the late fall or winter by those trained in the ceremonies of eagle killing. As a young child, she learned that feathers resided in their own spaces on the edge of dance grounds, where she witnessed the eagle dance.[29] The dance itself could be performed only after women, including her *etsi*, prepared the appropriate teas. She remembered watching an eagle feather touch the ground during a ceremony.

Everything stopped.

Rituals occurred.

Only then could the dances resume.[30]

Collectively, these events mutually reinforced key curricula shared by the community, but they may also have led Ageyutsa to take note of the significance of feathers and inspired her to learn more.

For Ageyutsa, Beloved Men and Women were some of her teachers, but Kituwah itself was a classroom and so much more. As Ageyutsa and her counterparts grew within that space at Kituwah and others like it across the region, Ageyutsa's natural environment served as her home, textbook, teacher, and classroom. In that classroom, Ageyutsa also was a student and a teacher to others. In addition to the learning she mastered on her own, her peers, older students, elders, the landscape, and the other-than-human beings with which she shared her world stepped in to act as teachers. The clear demarcations of what we most closely associate with schools today—students, teachers, textbooks, classrooms, public buildings, though currently undergoing rapid changes—fall away when we think about a Cherokee school environment a millennium ago. And yet, when we consider outdoor schools, debates centered on un-schooling, or arguments for vocational classes, or even look to alternative approaches to education that have competed with modern public educational systems like those offered by Montessori or Waldorf, we see reflections of the more expansive and holistic definitions of intellectual development and growth for the masses throughout human history but only recently rigidly defined as formal education confined to graded, age-determined classrooms based on differentiation.[31] By heeding dissatisfactions articulated about schooling today, we move closer to the Cherokee educational settings Ageyutsa encountered a millennium ago.

School calendars have always existed. Beyond the new moon ceremonies, women shifted their teaching materials seasonally. For the spring, summer, and portions of the fall, the outdoors nearly exclusively served as a classroom for Ageyutsa. Fields dominated by women absorbed Ageyutsa's time, in a space shared with an entire community. By the time she was five winters old, Ageyutsa entered the classroom that had operated at her periphery when she was an *usdi* tied to her mother's back.

Even if Ageyutsa never ventured beyond the thirty square miles of Kituwah, she lived and learned in one of the most biodiverse ecosystems in the world.[32] When she looked beyond the fields, a canopy of 60-to-100-foot-tall mature yellow poplar, white oak, and *dasodaquali* (American chestnut) trees protected her from harsh sun and rain.[33] These mythical "giants" surrounded her. Now nearly extinct, *dasodaquali* trees ranged from what is today Massachusetts to northern Georgia and resided on both sides of the Appalachian Mountains. They connected her to her Iroquoian linguistic kin to the north.[34] Even though she may have lived only within the bounds of Kituwah, her Muscogee (Creek) counterparts to the south performed ceremonies when the *dasodaquali* nuts emerged.[35] Ageyutsa's Iroquoian kin, separated by time and geography, played, explored, and learned under *dasodaquali* trees, too. Trees provided a common curriculum across vast distances, but local variations in educational content existed. Despite the omnipresence of *dasodaquali*, one key difference between a similar oral narrative of an other-than-human relative protecting a sacred plant shared by Iroquoian speakers is the protection of the chestnut for the Haudenosaunee and a tobacco plant for Cherokee people.[36]

Sense also played a key role in how Ageyutsa learned. During the late summer, a season associated with women due to the key agricultural labor they
carried out every morning and evening, a distinct odor from the long, spindly,
creamy white male flowers of the *dasodaquali* wafted throughout the woods.
Smelled once, it would be recognizable to her year after year. My daughter
and I memorized a similar smell after a single season in Knoxville—the smell
of the hybrid Chinese chestnuts growing in our backyard. These *dasodaquali*
cousins resided there because of an earlier Knoxville master gardener's attempt
to repopulate the region with chestnuts after the blight that began in 1904 and
swept from New York to Alabama at a pace of nineteen miles per year.[37] Our
backyard offered a distorted glimpse of the world Ageyutsa mastered.

Through the late summer and early fall, the *dasodaquali* grew nut-filled
burrs that would begin to fall around the first frost. First wrapped closely to her
mother's back and then mirroring the gathering activities of her mother, her
second mother (*taline etsi*), her older sister, and her slightly older brother, she
toddled and then walked among the trees placing *dasodaquali* burrs, acorns,
and black walnuts in baskets for processing. Whenever Ageyutsa fell on the
dasodaquali burrs, red needle-like pinpricks emerged on her legs and palms.

Smell played an additional seasonal role in Ageyutsa's relationship to *dasodaquali*, as fire entered Ageyutsa's forest curriculum. Just as ancestral Cherokees used a process of spot-clearing with fire that aided the repopulation of
pitch pine, oak, walnut, and *dasodaquali*, 200 years later Ageyutsa watched
women and men carry out those "land management" processes introduced
by her ancestors, which contributed to her education.[38] One day, she would
in turn pass this knowledge down. During the fall harvest, Cherokee people
burned the forest undergrowth where chestnuts grew to harvest them more
easily.[39] During this time, Ageyutsa just needed to stop and listen to hear the
burrs raining from their branches to the ground. If she spent much time in the
woods, certainly one of these burrs pelted her head. With only two trees in my
yard, the necessary number for pollination, and only five years at that particular
house, the number of times a burr struck me while walking or mowing the yard
are too numerous to count. An area of thirty square miles before the chestnut
blight would have contained 2.25 million trees, around 10 percent or 225,000 of
them *dasodaquali*.[40] Ageyutsa certainly noticed the wafting smoke at harvest
time and faced far more shellings than I did when she gathered those nuts.

Burning undergrowth provided visual and olfactory signals of classroom
changes and performed a public health measure on behalf of Ageyutsa and
her counterparts, thus enabling a more accessible and necessary education
for all Cherokee people. In turn, Cherokee people including Ageyutsa used

dasodaquali leaves for the treatment of sores. Her *etsi* saved dried leaves for a year and then mixed them with a sap to create a cough remedy.[41] Clearing out the undergrowth also enabled Ageyutsa to master a necessary and universal curriculum, one learned by women, men, and children—identifying the tracks of animals. Ageyutsa's "keen[ness] and precision" enabled her to assess the level of danger that animal neighbors might contribute as well. By sight, Ageyutsa could track her other-than-human relations, including bears, wolves, and deer. Her grandchildren would learn to identify the tracks of cows, pigs, and horses. Although Ageyutsa's teachers may have set and monitored the fires, their actions contributed to a fuller range of educational experiences and contributed to the well-being of the community. Fires consumed a "number of Serpants, Lizards, Scorpians, Spiders and their Eggs, as also Bucks [bugs], Ticks, Peties [reptiles], Muskitoes, with other Vermins, and Insects in general very offensive, and some very poisonous, whose Increase would, without this Expedient cover the Land, and make America disinhabitable."[42] Ancestral Cherokees and their kin "used fire to modify more extensive tracts of land, to build political centers and villages, and to grow maize."[43] Controlled burns literally and figuratively enabled Ageyutsa to see more of what she needed to learn in her thirty square miles.

When those *dasodaquali* burrs dropped, they provided a food source not only for Ageyutsa and her community but also for a variety of critters that ranged and resided in those thirty square miles with her. Ageyutsa competed with the 750 white-tailed deer inhabiting the area, whose tracks she would learn to identify, and the 120,000 gray squirrels and *dewi* (flying squirrel) scurrying from tree to tree above and on the ground.[44] That Cherokee *ageyutsa* wasn't the only living thing to rely on the *dasodaquali* and reckon with its height. *Dlaiga* (blue jay); hairy and downy *tsiguenalsa* (red-bellied woodpecker); owls; *tawodi* (hawk); and eagles all lived year-round among the trees. *Duwa* (warbler), *kawogv* (wood thrush), and *tsiyadvga* (black-throated blue warbler) also moved through the region. Winged teachers offered lessons on seasonal change while providing classroom materials for advanced study with specialized, feathered textile teachers.[45]

Ageyutsa, like most of the other *diniyoli*, likely learned to process deerskin for the long shirts commonly worn by women and the breechcloths and capes worn by men. Because hunting took place close to home during warm months and processing would more likely have occurred there, Ageyutsa likely witnessed and understood every step, from butchering for meat to the creation of clothing. Occasionally, Ageyutsa, but more often her brother, may have been called upon to assist. Ageyutsa knew that cutting called for precision to "maximize hide size."[46] Processing hides was a multiday process. It required scraping the meat away from the hide. If the hair needed to be removed, the hide needed to be soaked in water before it could be easily scraped away. Because of this, she likely took care to select a favorite bone of a deer's leg or a mussel shell scraper that best fit her hands to assist with the initial steps of hide processing. Because hide processing produced food, shelter, and clothing, everyone had a stake in the processing. Ageyutsa couldn't have escaped helping her brother carry the hides to family members to place in a cone-like shape over a slow-burning fire filled with corncobs. Smoldering corncobs maximized the smoke absorbed by the skins, providing water resistance and repelling bugs.[47]

This was a universal curriculum for most *diniyoli*, especially older boys, who would need these skills when they joined hunting parties and had to process deer farther from home, but ceremonial cycles and community dignitaries often required special attire. When Ageyutsa reached eight winters, she aspired to learn from more specialized teachers how to produce ceremonial wear. To secure her place, she had already developed a keen eye in the woods. Gathering feathers was an essential step in the process of producing feather capes. Any *diniyoli* could easily grab up the *gv na* (wild turkey) feathers that formed the bulk of the feathers used in capes, but Ageyutsa's vigilance also led her to collect the most colorful *tsi yes sdi* (Carolina parakeet) and most unusual feathers. She gave her most exotic feathers away. She gained favor through her generosity with what was one of her greatest loves—feathers. She held feathers up to the sunlight and watched them shimmer. It was all of this that provided her a front-row seat for special tutorials with the expert teachers in the community.[48] Feather cape making is "slow and repetitive," and acquiring the rigor and focus necessary may not have been the desire of all *diniyoli*; Ageyutsa had watched and knew what she was in for.[49]

Since she was six winters and first really noted how the Beloved Woman waved her *sa sa equa* fan, Ageyutsa had marveled at the educational possibilities at a distance and looked for ways to make herself useful. She asked her *etsi*, *elisi*, and *taline etsi* whether they knew how to make feather capes. They all possessed some skills, but they told her Asgeyvligei, an old woman, was the best feather cape maker in the community. By the time she was seven winters, she had already helped to gather feathers, watched, and knew that feathers must be culled and sorted and the quills soaked in water to soften and prevent them from splitting. By the time she was eight winters, she paid attention when someone requested a new feather cape. She showed up at exactly the right moment to assist in culling, sorting, and soaking the feather quills. She sat within eyeshot, trying to impress her potential mentor, practicing and demonstrating her commitment to learning the ancient knots for tying on the feathers. At first, Ageyutsa likely sat apart, picking up culled feathers and attempting to tie them to practice netting. Until her teacher embraced her as a student, she would not be permitted the time she needed to follow the thread path and figure out how to make netting. She would still have other responsibilities to fulfill for other women in her family, and so she stole these moments at the periphery, watching, learning, fine-tuning her basic skills, hoping to be invited closer.

When her prospective *dideyohvsgi* (teacher) did take notice, she might have administered a test immediately. Not a test of skill. *Dideyohvsgi* had already witnessed Ageyutsa's promise and interest out of the corner of her eye. She likely asked her to begin tying feathers, the most cumbersome and time-consuming task. It would likely have taken Ageyutsa more than an hour to tie twenty feathers, gaining in the process a swollen and sore thumb. (*Dideyohvsgi* could easily tie more than eighty in an hour, but being faster didn't lessen the physical discomfort.)[50] If Ageyutsa was truly committed to her education, this would be the test. And, in a couple hours' time, Ageyutsa's siblings might come by and tempt her to join them in the woods. Two tests in one. Was Ageyutsa committed to the craft, physically, mentally, and socially? But even if she was lured away by her siblings, the cape would not be completed that day. A single short feather cape would take almost two moons, working nonstop, to complete. The work and her lessons would wait, and her teacher needed a break, too.[51]

In contrast to cape making, which was an advanced curriculum, Ageyutsa and all her siblings and friends learned pottery making and basketmaking. Whether for carrying water, cooking, or gathering nuts and berries, mastering these curriculums were pragmatic and necessary. This learning likely occurred as part of the day-to-day rhythm. Ageyutsa may have been "given small bits of clay at an early age for play and may have [made her] own toys out of clay." She likely aided "adults with pottery tasks and contributed labor to those tasks. Playing, learning, and working [were] so intertwined that it may not be possible to distinguish these activities." Ageyutsa certainly learned "to make pottery in the context of both playing and working."[52]

Ageyutsa used and was given the materials surrounding her to produce all that she and her kin needed. Nearly every act of learning and creating, including vessels, were collaborations between the student, her teachers, and the ancestors who contributed their knowledge to the process. Pottery making was and is epic learning. By extension, learning and the creations produced from learning were collaborative and relational.[53] It is easy to imagine the educational process associated with pottery approximated, as it related to dozens of other activities including farming, bread making, construction of fishing weirs, and basketmaking.[54]

This collaborative model of learning created a failsafe for knowledge and archived it within families and communities, but it did not preclude individuality or innovation. Kinship systems built around women protected *diniyoli* and archives from major disruptions. Even if a child lost their biological mother, they were never motherless. Even if a family lost one teacher, communities preserved knowledge bases within intergenerational households. If social networks expanded or circumstances changed, Ageyutsa and her teachers could "use their growing knowledge to adopt new ways of doing things," just as ancestral Cherokees elsewhere had when they began using shell instead of just limestone to temper pottery, which kept it from expanding or cracking during the firing process.[55] Additionally, circumstances beyond a community's control could lead to changes in learning and teaching. These included "migration, shifts in the organization of production, consumer preference, natural disasters, disease, or warfare."[56]

As *diniyoli* grew up, the play and work remained intertwined, but it's also possible that students developed new attitudes toward the educational skills they had long since mastered. Some likely completed the work quickly and efficiently so they could free their time for other activities they enjoyed more. Some potters may have so loved digging the clay and seeing each project reach completion that they were compelled to do so again and again.[57] Others likely enjoyed the company of kin and friends engaged in tasks, so that work was less about the final product and more about the relationships it strengthened and renewed. Some like Ageyutsa may have understood its necessity but secretly disliked the particular task. Based on the ubiquity of pottery sherds found at Cherokee archaeological sites and the chronological demarcations assigned to styles of pottery by archaeologists as they piece together Cherokee history, there is no doubt pottery making was part of the required curriculum for Ageyutsa, but the motivation for completing the task may have been as diverse as the girls themselves. But the full range of this required curriculum is only partially evident because of differences in durability of materials.

Ancestral and historic Cherokee women's basketmaking provides ample evidence of the ways women (and men) "sometimes by choice but often by necessity" modified their approaches to basketmaking.[58] Over time and depending on the conditions they faced, Cherokee women have used river cane, white oak, honeysuckle, and red maple to construct baskets and mats. Cherokee people used baskets for a range of purposes, including gathering, storage, sieving, and food preparation. Women wove mats to act as insulation on the walls of winter houses and for seating and bedding on the ground.[59]

Handling each of these materials requires an education unto itself. River cane grew in immense stands, canebrakes, along rivers. Although cane can be harvested year-round, fall and winter are preferable. After it is cut, it can be kept fresh by submersion in water. As their mothers and grandmothers continued to harvest cane from the brake, older children placed the cane in rivers and streams for them. Then women prepared the splits, which required sharp tools of rock or shell and "a lotta practice."[60] Because of its difficulty, splitting cane is often the last step many basket weavers learn. Split-making is only part of the curriculum, which includes tasks that younger and less experienced basket makers could almost certainly assist with. Over time, basket makers have used various color dyes made from pokeweed, white and black walnuts, sumac, bedstraw, and bloodroot.[61] These have to be gathered and processed as well. Young *diniyoli*, boys and girls, probably mastered pieces of this curriculum.[62] By the time someone completed a basket or mat from start to finish, they would have mastered a range of subskills and received support from those less skilled than the person who completed the basket. Just as Ageyutsa had once gathered plants or nuts for dye, her completed project called upon the collecting of those same materials by those young people who might one day make baskets, too. Each basket represented contributions from multigenerational hands and hands over generations. While Ageyutsa performed this work, she paused when she saw a flock of *tsi yes sdi* nesting and resting on the cane itself. She couldn't help it; she had to scan the ground for their colorful feathers to collect.

For a period in their formative years, boys' and girls' curriculums included significant overlap in what was learned, but as Ageyutsa became an *ata* (teenage girl) and her *dinadanvtli* (brother) an *awina* (teenage boy), their daily rhythms had diverged. When they were babies, *selu* surrounded them in the agricultural fields of their mothers' creation. Both had toddled down the aisles with seeds, gathered nuts and foraged for flora in the woods at their mothers' heels, watched them prepare food, and responded to requests to provide what was not at the ready—more water for cooking—a chore that Ageyutsa's ancestors did far less of before fired portable pottery capable of withstanding a cook fire to boil water became ubiquitous.[63] While she was sneaking away to cull feathers, her *dinadanvtli* followed her older brother into the woods "when the sap's down" to "scout wood." While she was running her hands along netting to get a feel for tying feathers, her brother was envisioning how to transform the "rough piece of wood" into a bow.[64] As an *ata*, Ageyutsa watched her younger *dinadanvtli* continue to perfect his skills with the bow and arrow. At eight winters, he brought home his first deer from the woods beyond their town. At thirteen winters, his uncle invited him to join the men on a winter hunt. Even with all the work before her, Ageyutsa missed him when their lives diverged.

Different curricula provided different tactile experiences. Ageyutsa loved watching the less-used iridescent feathers of birds sparkle when capes moved in a particular direction under the light, but her *ulv* (sister) preferred the feel of the clay needed for pottery between her fingers. However, most *diniyoli* loved the *ama* (water). *Ama*, a part of daily chores, also had a deeper educational meaning.

Ageyutsa's mother had gone to water for ceremonies before Ageyutsa arrived in the world to keep both healthy and protected. Before Cherokee people walked in the world, Granddaughter Water Beetle had dived to the deep to bring up mud, which Grandfather Buzzard dried and made habitable. Between the power of water and fire, both of which are sacred, "the first place must be given to *ama*, without which life was impossible."[65] At four days old, after leaving the water of the womb, Ageyutsa's kin took her to *ama* so the priest could lift her up to the East and offer a prayer for her "health, long life, and future prosperity."[66] Going to *ama* had layered meanings—it was powerful, sacred, prayer, a source of life, a highway of connection to other communities—but it was fun as well.[67]

Mollusks, like the *equoni* (river) itself, provided a holistic curriculum. When the river ebbed, aquatic mussels and clams could be easily scooped up in baskets. One of the ways Ageyutsa's educational experiences sat on the cusp of change throughout the Mississippian world was her use of grit-tempered pottery as many of her regional neighbors shifted to the use of shell.[68] But Ageyutsa, like her adult counterparts, applied her critical thinking skills to develop a full range of multiuse possibilities for a variety of faunal materials. *Diniyoli* gathered, ate, and fashioned tools, spoons, and bowls from mollusks. While gathering feathers, nuts, herbs, and berries, *diniyoli* may have popped small terrestrial *eloqua* (snail) in their mouths and sucked out the meat for a quick snack.[69] They may have repeated this process with aquatic snails while laboring near creeks and rivers. *Diniyoli* also gathered larger mollusks in baskets to take home. Once gathered and transported, *diniyoli* and women roasted the larger mollusks to open the bivalves and then removed their meat, which could be smoked for later consumption or added to soups for flavor and some nutritional benefit. Perhaps *diniyoli* identified and set aside some shells to use as scrapers. Ageyutsa had learned long ago, when she had inefficiently struggled with both hands to use an adult's scraper, that tools matter. With her keen eye, she spotted various shells that would suit her hands and make an excellent scraper.[70] Because mollusks came in a range of sizes and shapes, Ageyutsa and other *diniyoli* learned to identify which kinds were best suited to specific purposes. But as *diniyoli* scooped up, snacked on, and toted mollusks, they also ran their fingers along the concentric lines that documented the moments the mollusks grew. *Diniyoli* may have wondered about the lumps in some shells caused by mud or debris during growth or about the sheer diversity of shell size.

Early students and teachers first witnessed the concentric patterns in the world around them and then embedded those same patterns into their ceremonial, artistic, and philosophical relationships to other earth dwellers and the natural world.[71] When Cherokee people danced the clamshell dance, they may have moved in the direction that the mollusks directed.[72] Did Ageyutsa take this for granted, or had she learned another deeper lesson from the shells of the snails and clams that she had gathered for her grandmother, *elisi*? Did she reflect upon the ways the spiral and curvilinear directions were ubiquitous in her world?[73] Did she possess some deeper understanding that the aquatic mollusks with the spirals on their shells filtered the rivers she played, worked, and cleansed herself in? She may have linked the design to how her prayers traveled to the sky on smoke spiraling upward from the fires around which she performed the clamshell dance, which were also meant to purify and balance her world.[74] She may have made connections when she witnessed elders displaying older shell gorgets or referencing images bearing this same spiral image.[75] When she made the connection, she may have noticed the pattern more and more often: snakes wound into a spiral, whirlpool formations in a river.[76] Elders may have shared stories of regional caves delicately marked with spiral images.[77] She may have witnessed these motifs throughout the region on open-air rocks marked by her ancestors. If the spiral shells of mollusks evoked layers of learning, what did Ageyutsa learn and intuit about even larger faunal neighbors whose classroom space she shared?

Unlike mollusks, other earth dwellers shared closer kin ties to her. As a result of these faunal relationships and learning, Ageyutsa mapped a much larger world. Through those other-than-human lineages, their history entangled with the Cherokee people, and the Cherokee people's continued reliance on their existence, she learned equally important curricula and local and international narratives. Rabbits remain the tricksters of Cherokee society.[78] Ageyutsa may have lived at a time when more than seven clans still existed.[79] Three of the seven Cherokee clans—Bird, Wolf, and Deer, which linked Cherokee people across towns to one another—also linked people to their other-than-human kin. *Yona* (bear), who had once been more closely related kin, still moved through the world with Cherokee people and could communicate with them if they chose to.[80] *Yona*, like mollusks, represented similar and yet distinct curricula that Ageyutsa and other *diniyoli* mastered at various points of their educational continuum.

Yona kin connected Ageyutsa to the larger world of humans as well. Her distant linguistic Iroquoian cousins shared narrative histories of *yona* with similar elements. Ageyutsa's Southeastern counterparts, including the Muscogee (Creek), Alabama, and Natchez peoples, shared other narrative historical parallels.[81] *Yona* moved between and semiannually resided in powerful spaces that permeated how Cherokee people mapped the world. Like the *dasodaquali*, *yona* also linked Cherokee people to much larger geographies. Areas that stretched from northern Canada to central Mexico accommodated *yona*, but a sleuth of *yona* ranged in smaller areas. Through her own observations or from those of her ancestors, Ageyutsa may have realized that female *yona* stayed much closer to home than males, their ranges three to eight times smaller. Did she see this knowledge as parallel to her own experiences of and movements in the world?

Ageyutsa learned to spot tracks, but she also studied *yona* and their cubs as they sauntered through their shared landscape. She watched them swim and play in some of the same waterways she visited. She watched them stand on their hind legs before climbing into tree stands. She watched them forage for berries and plants, including some of the same ones she gathered. Some of the *diniyoli* she knew became experts in tracking the *yona*. They knew where the *yona* communed and rested. She knew a distant kinship existed with the *yona*.

Yona, like Kanati, the first Cherokee man and Selu's husband, relied on caves for their well-being. Kanati rolled a stone away from a cave to release game for Cherokee people to eat, until his mischievous sons accidentally released all the game and forced Cherokee people to take up hunting. *Yona* relied on caves for torpor, but according to Cherokee narrative history, *yona* also used caves to commune with one another, store food, and occasionally interact with humans. Ageyutsa's *edutsi*, uncle, told her about "Bear Man," a *yona* who took a human hunter into a cave to attend a *yona* council. The space itself opened from a smaller entry hole into a room that resembled a Cherokee council house. There the *yona* discussed food shortages. Two *yona* in attendance announced a possible solution to those shortages. They had explored and discovered another mountainous area filled with *dasodaquali* and acorns.[82] The *yona* celebrated. Like their human and earth dwelling counterparts, *yona* relied on *dasodaquali* and adjusted their exploration and living patterns to the prevalence of those trees. Her *edutsi* told her that when the men hunted, they sometimes had to explore unfamiliar spaces when food was scarce.

Ageyutsa's knowledge of *yona* extended beyond shared narrative histories and place making. Although white-tailed deer remained the key provider of meat to Ageyutsa and possessed much closer kin ties to Cherokee people through the existence of the Deer Clan, the *yona* possessed a "different relationship to people than other animals" and provided a curriculum to *diniyoli* that had to be mastered by adulthood. "Native peoples dined on bear meat and fat when [eating] family meals, hosting visitors in their homes, participating in celebratory and ceremonial feasts, and other occasions."[83] This required mastering the best cuts for processing *yona* and acquiring the right tools to do this efficiently. Although most of this skill acquisition may have fallen to her brothers, Ageyutsa learned how to render *yona* fat and the other recipes that used *yona* fat for seasoning. She also used *yona* fat to condition and beautify her hair and to create a concoction to repel mosquitos. As she matured, she applied these treatments to younger children, thus providing their earliest lessons of a skill they, too, would be expected to learn and pass on. She may have first watched and then assisted her *elisi* in creating makeup and preparing ointments and medicines. She watched her elders ritually prepare *yona* oil in advance of burials and for the accompanying ceremonies.[84] Ageyutsa watched the boys excel in processing *yona*, and likely she could replicate some, if not most, of their actions if necessary. But she also learned a separate curriculum of food preparation and cosmetic and medicinal production that her male classmates bore witness to when they were young, at the heels of their mothers and grandmothers. If particular students, including Ageyutsa, obtained mastery of skill simply through watching, with little need to carry out the tasks themselves, these students may have crossed into adulthood with curricular mastery that defied some of the gendered expectations placed upon them. Polymaths, who excelled in multiple subjects, were likely the norm as opposed to the exception. And fauna provided one arena of displaying the wide range of skills *diniyoli* acquired.

Cherokee clans also reinforced the relationships between humans and earth-dwelling counterparts who made places together. When the *yona* council ended, the *yona* and the man who accompanied him left and traveled to another cave, where they dwelled together. The longer they lived together, the more the man became like the *yona*. Ageyutsa learned that a clan of Cherokee people, known as the Anitsâgûhĭ, went into the mountains and turned into *yona*. The Anitsâgûhĭ moved to the mountains because a boy who had also communed with *yona* suggested it as a solution to overcome the food shortages and the trials they faced. The Cherokee Blue Clan is thought to be made up of remnant members of the Anitsâgûhĭ.[85] Ageyutsa overheard her *edutsi* tell a group of boys this story when they narrowly escaped a *yona* after they had tracked too close to her cubs.[86] Her uncle intended to reinforce the close relationships of humans to bears historically but also to remind the boys of the powerful and potentially dangerous outcomes of getting too close to *yona*.

These narratives of caves, transformation, and animal kin linked Cherokee people to their wider ancestral Mississippian cousins. Ageyutsa knew who she was, but she also understood that people become who they are in relationship to those they live with, just like the bear and the boy. She was AniKituwah, the people of Kituwah. This understanding rooted her to a place, but it also connected her to a Mother Town located in what is today North Carolina, that continues to occupy a central place in the origin stories of Cherokee people. Living at Kituwah also linked her to her ancestral past. People have been living at Kituwah for 8,000 years. She was living not only at the spiritual heart of what would become a Nation but also in an educational center. Kituwah nurtured the children and the sacred fire that other Cherokee towns emerged from.[87] Kituwah linked people to an unbroken lineage of place but also became a new home and refuge for others. Everything and everyone was a part of her learning and what she would become.

Ageyutsa's great-grandchildren entered a world different from hers, but there were pedagogical and educational continuities. Despite some material differences, core pedagogical practices likely remained relatively consistent and stable. "Learning frameworks" continued to include "self-teaching by trial and error, observation and imitation, verbal instruction and explanation, or hands-on demonstration."[88] Learning continued to be rooted to place and to draw upon knowledge compiled over many generations and stored in human and geographic libraries across the region. Women provided the first, most sustained, and most universal education to all *diniyoli*. Archives included wampum, feathers, mnemonic devices, *edutsi's* and *elisi's* stories and knowledge, and the land itself. Ceremonies reinforced the most basic lessons imparted by mothers, grandmothers, and uncles, but they also provided more formal vocabularies for those lessons and introduced the community's youngest members to official legal codes and advanced curriculums. It was there Ageyutsa saw her first feather cape, which became one task among many that occupied her time. But it was a task she chose and that chose her. Place situated Ageyutsa, and it would do the same for her great-grandchildren. Her relationship to Kituwah enabled her to "simultaneously locate [her] experiences and memories in the physical, geographical world, thus becoming a tangible reminder of [her] people's normative code for living."[89] Kituwah wasn't simply a place; Kituwah was her teacher, her home, her classroom, and the school supplies for those around her. She was of Kituwah.

Ageyutsa's granddaughters still had to learn the primary curriculum shared by boys and girls alike. They learned to speak by listening to their mothers'

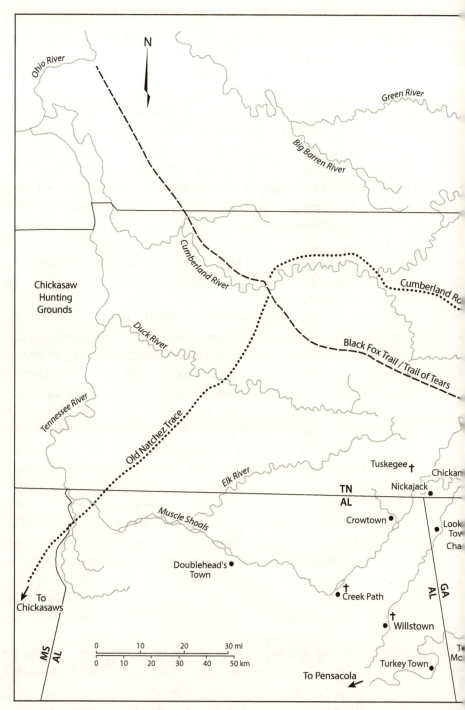

Lower towns and Chickamauga towns.

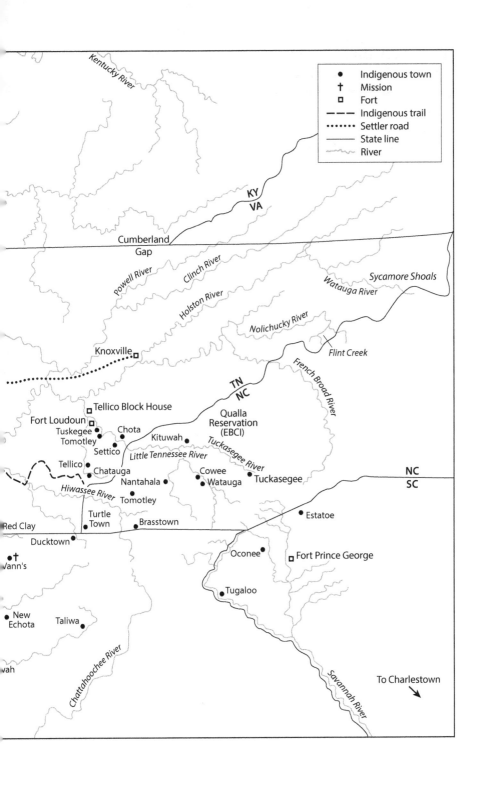

words and conversations. They learned who they were through their relationships to others and to the place they lived. They had to find their way to the
skills they most desired to learn and seek out teachers whose skills they wished
to watch and replicate. By the time she reached adulthood, the community no
longer called her Ageyutsa; she was Gatherer of Feathers. Her grandchildren
would share strong ties to their community and to pieces of the wider Mississippian world, but they would also encounter practices and people quite different
from their Mississippian counterparts. They would hear new languages, see
new flora and fauna, witness new ceremonies, and watch patterns and aspects
of their lives change even as other expectations and daily practices remained
the same. The old systems of education flourished but with glimpses of other
educational possibilities.

CHAPTER 2

Overhill Towns
Climber of Trees

By the first two decades of the eighteenth century, Ageyutsa's metaphorical grandchildren residing in the Overhill towns in what is today east Tennessee—girls named Pretty Girl, Kind Girl, Lovely Girl, Dance Leader, and Climber of Trees—lived in a changed and transforming world with small numbers of new permanent international neighbors, many of whom rarely came in contact with Cherokee communities.[1] Those newcomers, almost exclusively men, first spoke Spanish and then French, German, Dutch, and English. Many of them were transient traders, and their numbers remained low. Although the economic systems introduced by these individuals impacted international diplomacy and trade beyond Cherokee communities, day-to-day life and education remained somewhat unchanged in the first decades of the eighteenth century. As the girls' names indicated, they still participated in ceremonial dances and climbed the oaks, walnuts, and *dasodaquali* (American chestnut) trees. Their physical classrooms bore remarkable resemblance to those of Ageyutsa, their ancestral grandmother, *elisi*, who had resided wholly in the Blue Ridge and whose grandchildren spoke a different dialect of their language.[2] But their communities existed to the west of their Cherokee-speaking kin spread among other regions.

Climber of Trees lived on the borders of the Blue Ridge Mountains and valley where *dasodaquali* dominated, tulip poplars stood tall, and oaks presided at higher elevations. Cove hardwood communities of trees, including basswood, sweet buckeye, and sugar maple, interrupted the dense forests of giants. If Climber of Trees looked to the highest elevations, she saw spruce and firs reaching toward the sky, but even those heights held balds (spots with less tree growth), filled with ferns and grasses and *dvlasuga* (native rhododendron) that produced white, pink, or light purple flowers from *anyni* (March), when the animals begin to shed their winter coats (March), to *galoni* (August), when the birds shed their feathers, peaking in *dehaluya* (June), when the weather gets hot.[3] Like Ageyutsa, Climber of Trees likely learned not only to identify but to know the uses of the dozens of species of trees and plants that shared the region with her.

Climber of Trees at Chota. Artwork by Roy Boney Jr.

In addition to seeing much of the same foliage as her grandmother did, Climber of Trees attended an architecturally similar school. She learned to listen and speak in agricultural fields cultivated and tended by intergenerational groups of women in the community. Ageyutsa and Climber of Trees both lived in communities with a sprinkling of paired winter-summer homes.[4] In the winter, smoke from hearth fires in the *osi*, winter home, carried conversations and prayers up to the sky, warmed kin and community, and heated meals. Through her knowledge of the language, she understood the word *osi*. It not only conveyed ideas about whether a person had a balanced relationship with themselves but was also the place where one lived.[5] Year-round, the council house fire remained alight. She moved freely along the paths between homes, which were spaced about twenty-five to fifty meters apart.[6] After visiting a neighboring Cherokee town with her *edutsi*, uncle, she asked about Kituwah and learned that houses had been even closer together. Even if the lesson was not explicitly stated, through language and community design she likely intuited that her community arranged their neighborhoods toward the central ceremonial space to reinforce "a community-focused ideology."[7] Homes enveloped the areas around the council house and stickball field. Home layout and the centrality of community spaces encouraged Cherokee people living in the community to connect with one another.

In agricultural classrooms, Ageyutsa had received a wide array of lessons about women's health and well-being, but she also learned about vulnerabilities that existed regardless of the care one took. More than five generations later, Climber of Trees received many of the same lessons. They both knew that, like their mothers, once they started menstruating, they would rest and perform minimal labor during that time. They learned about the power of blood, both men's and women's, to upset the balances that sustained the community.[8] The practices related to the power of blood would take on particular importance as Cherokees adapted to the presence of settlers, including violence and the spilling of blood resulting from colonialism. Girls learned how women spaced their pregnancies apart to nurse properly. Polygamy, which often involved a man marrying sisters, maintained the power of women's households. The children of these women, whether they partnered with the same man or not, would be siblings regardless, and the women already acted as mothers to all the children in the household. Polygamy, rather than detracting from women's power and social relationships, reinforced existing economic and social relationships.[9] Women avoided sex with spouses to maximize postnatal health and avoid back-to-back pregnancies. For Cherokee families that practiced polygamy, women benefited post-pregnancy from other wives' sexual presence, thus enabling them to heal, have a manageable number of children, and properly tend to their children's needs. Collectively, women mothered lots of children since they acted as caregivers to all of their clan kin's children, but individual Cherokee women generally had fewer than five children even when they married more than once, thus keeping a household size under eight people.[10] While living at Chota, Climber of Trees likely bore witness to these responsibilities firsthand when a mother died while still nursing.[11] She would have watched as the baby's *taline etsi* (second mother), took on that role, nursing the baby at the perimeter of the fields.

Maternal health and the patterns it produced reinforced the lesson driving home the power of kinship. Climber of Trees held those babies, too. Side by side with her *taline etsi*, Climber of Trees learned to nurture children. She assisted with swaddling and, like the other mothers, drew no distinction between her biological siblings and her maternal cousins, who, by the rules of kinship, were her brothers and sisters. She also learned that any baby who lost their biological mother must be treated better by all adults than a child who still had a biological mother.[12] There was no such thing as an orphan; it was up to kin and the community to nurture those who lost a key provider and teacher. Ageyutsa had received all of these lessons as well.

More pragmatically, like Ageyutsa, Climber of Trees learned everyday health and wellness routines. She developed routines for rubbing bear fat into her hair to keep it shiny and healthy and on her skin to protect from mosquitoes. Her *taline etsi* may have reminded her that after working in the fields, they would need to prepare the bear oil base for medicinal ointments, paints, and makeup.[13] Just like going to water was fun *and* had deep ceremonial associations for Ageyutsa, for Climber of Trees these activities also had aesthetic, medicinal, and spiritual purposes.

Despite routines practiced over lifetimes and multiple generations to cultivate well-being, she also learned of women's vulnerabilities. She received lessons on the roles of the elder women who kept watch over the fields from a platform in late summer. Like Ageyutsa had experienced, when Climber of Trees' daily labor in the fields was complete, those old women remained behind to guard a sacred community food supply and, in doing so, put themselves in danger. She had heard stories of women taken captive from other towns during raids by Northern Indigenous peoples, including their linguistic Iroquoian kin turned enemies.[14] Because fields stood at the perimeter of the community, these sentinels were often alone and at risk of attacks from war or hunting parties who might move through the area.[15] Despite the risk, the women on the platform also served as an early warning to the community of potential human or nonhuman threats. Selu, the Corn Mother, had foreshadowed the danger that lay ahead for her when her sons plotted her death; generations later her grandchildren, these elder women, risked their lives for the sake of corn once again and for the generations of Cherokee *diniyoli* (children) who would come after them.[16]

Separated by generations, Ageyutsa and Climber of Trees shared the same annual school calendar, which was broken into two major seasons—winter and summer, with the New Year arriving in tandem with the autumnal equinox. Cherokee people associated women with summer and men with winter. Although men and women contributed to both, the bulk of active labor fell to one group. Summer, including the spring planting, harnessed the entire community's labor to prepare the fields. For a short period, men joined the classrooms headed by women. Collectively, they cleared the fields so that they would all harvest the rewards during the summer, thus reinforcing the community-focused ideology and gender complementarity embedded in architectural design. Women and girls maintained the fields and their personal kitchen gardens. Kitchen gardens, grown adjacent to homes, produced smaller types of corn that reached maturity more quickly than those grown in community fields. Women continued to grow and store food at the matrilocal level and along a slightly different growing timeline.[17]

Winter, the season associated with men because the community relied more heavily on the meat provided by hunting, also shifted the classroom spaces attended by children. As winter warned summer of its arrival through early morning frosts, Climber of Trees would see the *dasodaquali* trees' long, spindly, creamy white flowers and smell their distinct odor wafting through the air. The smells of burning served as the olfactory school bells, signaling to Ageyutsa and her granddaughter Climber of Trees that it was time to gather the *dasodaquali* nuts. Only when the trees began to pop and the snow spirits were in the wind and the time of frost shining in the sun arrived did the girls sleep indoors and spend some time in the *osi*.[18] Climber of Trees may have thought it ironic that the season associated with men was also a time when many of those men were absent. And at the same time, she likely spent more intimate time with elder men than perhaps at any other time of the year. While physically capable men, teenage boys, and a few women departed on hunting trips that could last months at a time, the town underwent a demographic shift, and the schooling available likely shifted with it.

Whereas in summer the community moved, gathered, and orbited around the town house and town center, households of mostly women and children gathered in winter around indoor hearths to complete daily tasks and socialize.

Elder men of their clan, especially uncles and great-uncles, who normally spent most of their time mulling over important issues in and around the usually male-dominated council house, may have spent more time within households, where women prepared and served meals with children underfoot. Did Climber of Trees witness her mother and aunties taking this opportunity to bend their ears? Probably. Over the course of planting, harvesting, and gathering, these women formulated their agendas concerning community and diplomatic concerns.[19] Climber of Trees watched women, acting as household delegates, prepare their agenda items for women's councils, a political body often directed by Beloved Women who brought issues of importance to the community council meetings. When the community reconvened collectively, the women would be ready.[20] During the winter months, Climber of Trees watched women wield and exercise power in more intimate spaces.

The intimacy of indoor spaces may have shifted teachers' subject matter as well. In the council house, headmen and medicine keepers may have regularly alluded to the histories of those honored and Beloved Men buried at their feet and in their vicinity. In the *osi*, different deeds may have been invoked. Women may have taken the time to remind *diniyoli* of the women who came before them, who were buried closer to their home hearths, and the contributions they made. Did women tell stories to invoke the legacies of their own female ancestors buried underneath those household structures to strengthen their appeals to elder men who may have been seated in their midst?[21] Did they use this time to air concerns about community balance? Climber of Trees likely received an interesting education on how women used power and authority within their winter homes to set the larger political agenda for the community. Despite this being the time of men, as the community prayed and sent up smoke so the men would return with bounty from the hunt, it was also a time for women to recenter their public concerns in more intimate spaces.[22]

Seasonal cycles, marked by lunar cycles, like the history that Ageyutsa and Climber of Trees learned, reminded them that though Cherokee people shared "a remembered sadness of dislocation and depopulation," they also adapted to change.[23] For Ageyutsa, perhaps community members recounted their split from their Iroquoian-speaking cousins to the north and travels through dark and cold lands to arrive reborn at Kituwah. For Climber of Trees, histories of sickness to the north and south that followed the Spanish entradas through the region may have formed part of the origin story for her own community, forged when many ancestral Cherokees living in mountainous regions benefited from their remoteness from Hernando de Soto's destructive path. She knew Cherokees had suffered, but less so than other Native nations, from the diseases that often preceded and certainly followed Spanish invasion. Cherokees arose demographically stronger than many communities and settled many places formerly controlled by their Muscogee neighbors.[24]

Despite a relative demographic stability compared with that of their Indigenous counterparts in the Native South during the preceding 150 years, all *diniyoli* learned a history of relocation and loss.[25] Knowledge of clans included lessons of displacement; Climber of Trees, like Ageyutsa, knew the story of the Blue Clan, remnant members of the Anitsâgûhĭ. Like Ageyutsa, she had heard of the multitude of clans who had merged into seven. They removed to the mountains because a boy, *atsutsa*, who had communed with bears suggested relocation as a solution to overcome the food shortages and other trials they faced. But unlike Ageyutsa, Climber of Trees may have had firsthand knowledge of the recent past that had led some people to immigrate to the enchanted town of Agustoghe, accessible only through a spiraling whirlpool in the river.[26] She understood that Cherokee women through women's councils exercised a unique authority related to decisions to relocate.[27] At the Green Corn Ceremony, which signaled the beginning of the winter season, she heard the "poetic strains" of songs and the words of elders.[28] The language had gradually changed as the people separated through time and geography from their Iroquoian-speaking cousins and as a result of the linguistic influences of their newer neighbors.[29] In those verses, the lyrics spoke of immigration into a strange country; those unintelligible strains were almost certainly more understandable to Ageyutsa than they were to Climber of Trees.[30] But more recently, her mother, even before the public discussions at council meetings, told her about communities that had suffered from the violence of the slave trade and disease. She knew the women in those communities had made the decision to reduce the size of their community fields and rely more heavily on foods gathered in the woods, in case they needed to move quickly.[31] Women anticipated the changes they might face and adapted to those realities.

Even some of Ageyutsa's predecessors had faced new circumstances that led communities to innovate and consider new security and architectural curricula. The elders who taught the *etsi, taline etsi,* and *edutsi* of Climber of Trees likely told of the tumult that had existed between communities to the south and west that pitted Mississippian chiefdoms against one another, securing allies where they could and coalescing when necessary.[32] They may have explained to Climber of Trees why their Cherokee counterparts at Toqua, even before de Soto's march through the region, constructed palisades around the community, an anomaly then and in the years that followed but certainly an appropriate adaptation to meet changed conditions in the area.[33] As the Mississippian world destabilized further and more centralized hierarchical chiefdoms dispersed, Cherokees "learn[ed] from mistakes, meaning the corrective consequences that emerged after some colossal failures in landscape and cultural learning" that had supported those systems.[34] Instead they preserved the meaningful parts of the culture and embraced systems of egalitarianism and kinship to manage those changes.

Both Ageyutsa and Climber of Trees lived close to rivers, enabling their communities to conduct water rituals at each of the twelve new moons and enabling individuals and families to start their days by going to water, a daily cleansing and purification ritual to seek protection, sing a song for wellness, and acknowledge the sun touching the tips of the trees to the east.[35] When Climber of Trees entered the water of the Little Tennessee River, it was likely warmer than what Ageyutsa had faced in the Tuckasegee, a far narrower body of water at Kituwah, which sits at a higher elevation. But in winter, *uyvtla ama* (cold water) is *uyvtla ama*. Both girls likely shivered as goosebumps arose on their skin, regardless of which *equoni* (river) they entered in the winter.[36]

Not only did the rivers in both communities provide a ceremonial and educational starting point for each individual's life and each community's day, but they also served as roads, grocery stores, fitness centers, and playgrounds. Before their own memories formed but collectively remembered by the community, Ageyutsa and Climber of Trees were both taken to a medicine keeper to be ceremonially plunged in the river. A baby's first lesson paralleled the story of Granddaughter Water Beetle, who plunged into the water's depths and brought mud to the surface to form the land on which all Cherokees reside today.[37] Despite their size, babies would contribute to a livable world for other Cherokee people. The ceremonial power of water formed a single facet of their relationships to Long Man, another name for the river.

Water served as a powerful force in the lives of children, but it also nourished their athleticism. Mothers taught their babies to swim "before they can walk, which greatly encreases their Strength, and of Course their Growth."[38] By the time Climber of Trees matured, she would be an "able and strong swimmer who could simply swim across many streams."[39] When *diniyoli* went to water each day, they may have hauled water back to their homes in ceramic bottles, gourds, or tightly woven baskets to begin meal preparation for the day. When the river was low, Climber of Trees joined other *diniyoli* to gather aquatic snails and mussels in baskets, like Ageyutsa had. Volunteering to gather mollusks and water possibly served as an excuse to see friends, splash around, and see who arrived by canoe on the Little Tennessee River from neighboring towns or farther abroad.

Over a century later, mollusks remained central to the everyday education of Cherokee girls. Both Ageyutsa and Climber of Trees lived along rivers teeming with mollusk biodiversity. Modern-day North Carolina, where Ageyutsa lived, was home to just under a hundred different kinds of freshwater mollusks. Using the artificial boundaries of the modern state of Tennessee, Climber of Trees lived near 130 different kinds but likely saw different mollusks transported by visitors and kin from other places. The fast-moving waters of the Tennessee and Cumberland Rivers boast far more mollusk diversity than the Mississippi to the west and the Conasauga to the south. Climber of Trees and other community members likely hauled river mussels home to process for the community's needs year-round. In the *osi*, Climber of Trees likely sat toward an exterior wall on a river cane mat she had helped weave, separating the meat from the shell. The hearth stood just a few feet away, providing the heat necessary to steam open the valves.[40] In the center of a fifteen-square-foot area, she placed a rock on the mat to aid her as she processed the shells into a fine or coarse powder and then separated it through cane basket sieves she had also helped create.[41] She encouraged her siblings to aid her with the tasks they could manage. What the younger *diniyoli* likely provided was nonstop audio of the sounds of shells tinkling against one another as little hands moved them across the mound, stacked them, and then let them tumble as they fell out of little piles. Shell-processing, like *dasodaquali* harvesting, had sensorial lessons associated with them.

All these shells would flake apart as Climber of Trees broke them down for pottery temper. The white powder and glittery dust must have covered her palms and accentuated the lines in her hands as she worked. Did the concentric lines on the surface of the mollusks remind her of similar patterns highlighted on her hands and fingerprints? Perhaps she had commented on this to her mother the first time she noticed this phenomenon when she was younger and it had led to historical narratives of the "concentric relationships" that connected her to her past and linked her to the faunal world around her, just as it had for Ageyutsa. As her younger siblings made similar discoveries as they aided her, her mother likely repeated the lessons for them. Even as the tactile experience prompted serious lessons, as the powder moved from surface to surface and ended up on clothing, skin, and pottery, it must have produced giggles and conversations and inspired artistic expression as *diniyoli* used that white powder to paint each other or create ornamental designs on surfaces. Maybe, like schoolchildren hundreds of years later who use their handprints to create turkeys for Thanksgiving crafts, *diniyoli* put their powdered handprints on surfaces, which have long since faded from existence. After processing the

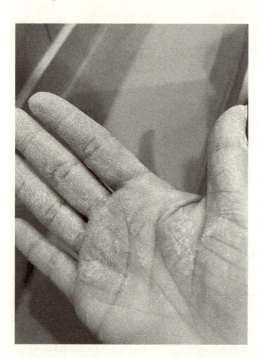

Shell dust on my hands.
Photo courtesy of the author.

shells, Climber of Trees returned to the river with the *diniyoli* to wash up. It was a circuitous path of gathering mussels, processing them, and then returning to their environment as one final reminder of how all processes and relationships spiral.

The river, like fauna and so many other physical spaces, provided a holistic lesson plan and connected her to other classrooms. Like Ageyutsa, who could hear the sounds of the Tuckasegee River from her home, Climber of Trees lived on a bend of the Little Tennessee River, a highway that connected Chota to the towns of Tuskegee, Tomotley, Toqua, Citico, Halfway Town, and Tallassee.[42] If Ageyutsa had traveled to the edges of her thirty square miles by river, she may have visited Judaculla Rock, a soapstone rock, with nearly 2,000 petroglyphs marked on its surface. Tsul ka lu (Judaculla), also called the Slant-Eyed Giant, met and courted a Cherokee woman in a local town. The woman's mother disapproved of the courtship and marriage and was horrified by his appearance. As a result, instead of living with the woman in her home, they moved to his farm. When the giant made one eight-mile step to his farm, his footprint created the scratches on the rock. This story, the place, and the rock all embedded important knowledge for women. The river enabled them to travel to other significant educational sites, but it also transported those bringing information, trade, and kin to the community as well.[43]

Two rivers, rather than one, provided *diniyoli* residing at Chota more traffic from Cherokee neighbors, Occaneechi trade middlemen, and European merchants who by the first decades of the eighteenth century operated "on a great scale." As a result, "substantial independent traders" moved through the region intermittently. Through these traders, Climber of Trees likely learned about cloth and saw glass beads for the very first time.[44] She may have overheard the traders remarking that breechcloths and long shirts could more easily be produced or altogether replaced with clothing made from fabric as opposed to deer hides. She listened to women debating the merits of cloth. Older brothers may have commented that they would no longer need to process deer hides for clothing and could instead focus on processing hides in order to participate more directly in the growing deerskin trade. When the cloth arrived, women likely debated the quality of the materials and expressed preferences for colors or features. Climber of Trees, unlike Ageyutsa, who likely never imagined processing anything other than animal hides for clothing, watched as this cloth began circulating in her community, lessening some families' reliance on deerskins for clothing and turning their attention more fully to trade.[45] She also watched as women in those families, instead of younger men and older boys, assumed the responsibility for processing those hides.[46] Of course, like Ageyutsa, she knew how to process the hides if she had to, but she dreaded the thought of that constant labor or her *taline etsi*'s absence with hunting parties.

This subtle shift among some families created unease. Climber of Trees wasn't the only person less than eager to take on deer processing at the expense of other responsibilities. She heard her uncle, *edutsi*, remind a group of boys, eager to track deer for trade, of their responsibilities to say a prayer for a pardon on behalf of the deer they killed. He warned the boys that if they failed to do this, disease could harm the boys or their families.[47] She also overheard her *edutsi* express worry to her *elisi* about the months when the water might freeze if the hunters failed to perform the proper prayers. She asked her *edutsi* what prayers she should offer; she had not learned any prayers for this circumstance. Her uncle thought for a long time, seven moons, before he offered her an answer. She also wondered how she would be able to fulfill all of her other responsibilities.[48]

Watching those materials slowly circulate in her community also led Climber of Trees to ponder new questions. She was intrigued by the colors of the fabrics and wondered about the dyes used. She pondered what plants the botanists and teachers living across the waters gathered to produce the colors in the fabrics. She also listened as women visiting from other communities discussed which traders and diplomats brought the best presents and materials to their towns.[49]

Climber of Trees, like other *diniyoli*, even those living in "remote and small" villages, could "boast of traders, white men of English, Spanish, or French, or even of all three, nationalities" passing through their communities in the first decades of the eighteenth century.[50] Multilingualism was not new—one of the Long Hair Clan women spoke Muscogee, Cherokee, and the Mobilian trade language—but some of the languages Climber of Trees overheard were.[51] She watched as some of these first interactions relied heavily on sign language.[52] But as the visits increased, a select set of adults around her worked on their proficiency in these other languages: French, German, English. Polyglots existed in the community already. Some of these same individuals began mastering even more languages. But others who had previously been uninterested in language acquisition felt intrigued by these new sounds. Men engaged in international affairs made up some of the multilingual speakers, but the women who served food, mended clothes, and accompanied groups of men on outings also gained varying levels of proficiency in these other languages. And, like *diniyoli* in the fields with their female teachers, many of these early visitors who had come from across the ocean mastered the same fundamental Cherokee curriculum as them—the Cherokee language.[53]

For *diniyoli* and outsiders alike, mastery of the Cherokee language served as the prerequisite for the world of Cherokee literacy. As learners advanced their listening abilities and honed their memory-building capacity, which *diniyoli* had trained since birth to do, and improved their vocabularies, a wider volume of the oral canon became available.[54] If *diniyoli* knew their history, allusions to the past offered by speakers in ceremonies and speeches served as cultural touchstones and historical shorthand that outsiders may not have fully understood. Students tapped for more advanced training, like nephews and nieces of the town headmen, attended school with select elders to learn "the lore and duties, and those destined to [be medicine keepers] were apprenticed to [medicine keepers]."[55] Additionally, Climber of Trees learned (as had Ageyutsa) that within her own family, "besides serving as an instructor in practical learning and a transmitter of ceremonial knowledge, [her] mother's brother was also responsible for [her] health. If [she] became ill, [her] mother's brother either attempted a cure himself or selected an appropriate medicine man [or woman]."[56] Medicine women specialized in conditions related to women's health, including but not limited to menses and childbirth. But just as Ageyutsa had demonstrated generations earlier her commitments to feather capes, others could demonstrate their commitment to select skills and literacies, like reading wampum belts or orating the ceremonies for community and kin.

Itinerant residents to the region introduced new, albeit specialized, possibilities for literacy. The traders and isolated missionaries who first passed through Chota and Tanasi around 1717 brought two sorts of literature with them: ledgers to inventory trade goods and debt, and Bibles and hymnals for recitation and song. This literature provided a "palpable sign [of her community's difference] from" those men.[57] Climber of Trees may have never been able to lay hands on the materials, but she more than likely saw them from a distance or overhead conversations emanating from their subject matter. It's possible that in her wonderings about the absence of women among these outsiders, she also considered whether only non-Cherokee men carried these particular types of literature. She may have drawn parallel connections between these outsiders and the speakers designated by her own community, who were almost always men "trained in dramatic performance and steeped in the ritual knowledge needed to conduct and participate in political ceremonies."[58] Did her exclusion make it more enticing to consider gaining access?

Literacy might have intrigued her because she had heard of her community's wider history of literacies. If she had traveled the nearly 100 miles to Tsulkalu Rock, she may have already read part of the educational landscape she shared with Ageyutsa. These bound materials circulating in her community may have prompted local teachers to recite portions of her history she had never heard before. Sitting in the council house, she listened to elders recall when her "ancestors . . . first came on this land that the priests and beloved men was writing but not on paper as [the Europeans did] but on white deer skin and on the shoulder bones of buffalo for several years but the proudness of the young people being so great that they would not obey the priests nor learning but let their minds run after hunting of wild beasts, that the writing was quite lost and could not be recovered again."[59] Hearing this, she pondered her *edutsi*'s anxiety about hunting for trade as she learned about other intellectual losses and their connection to deerskins. But if she knew about Tsulkalu Rock, perhaps she knew that other types of literacy were still a part of the Cherokee world. If she had seen Tsulkalu Rock or had it described to her, maybe she envisioned the designs she and her mothers and sisters incised into the soft clay of pots before firing or thought of the designs within caves described by elders.

What did she make of these teachings about the past during a time of exciting change? Climber of Trees was a young person. What responsibility did she bear in her community's ongoing adaptation, and what was her responsibility to continually renew its future as her grandmother and their grandmothers had done? She remembered her *edutsi*'s words that *diniyoli* teach adults how "to teach them things like the old way."[60] She talked with other young people about her suspicions of these newcomers and how they used their written materials to challenge their teachers. *Diniyoli* pondered the different intentions of these two types of materials. *Diniyoli* watched traders write and tabulate in their ledgers and listened as Christians recounted stories from bound pages. Traders put thoughts down with their writing implements, later retrieving and recounting what they saw on the page. On the other hand, Christians largely took words out of the Bible. Climber of Trees may have observed the distinction. Was she intrigued by the writing implement itself? Climber of Trees may have gathered feathers, not to garner favor with elder cape makers but to sit with friends reverse-engineering writing implements and devising inks using their knowledge of dyes used in basketmaking. *Diniyoli* witnessed traders challenging the memory accounting records of Cherokee hunters engaged in the hide trade.[61] Her *edutsi* also told her about how traders used information they wrote down in those ledgers to come back and take things from the kin of the recently deceased.[62] This behavior violated Cherokee morality.

Climber of Trees also noticed that many adults shared the same concerns, but sometimes her *etsi* and *edutsi* worried about different things. Climber of Trees silently castigated the older boys eager to enter the world of the deerskin trade, because she preferred other activities to deerskin processing. She knew the outcome of Selu's final lesson to her sons, who failed to follow her instructions. She resented the older boys who half-heartedly completed their tasks in the community in order to participate in hunting. This reinforced the lessons she learned on the importance of women's labor and wisdom to Cherokee society and her own place within it. Elders, like her *edutsi*, lamented that the deerskin trade had cost their ancestral community forms of its literacy. She also overheard men discussing how relationships with their old neighbors were changing. No one had any love for the Muscogee, but elders reminded people that the violence was different now, more frequent and more deadly, and that many Muscogee towns had relocated to escape slave raiding.[63] Climber of Trees often felt like all of this served as a call to intellectual arms. Maybe she could help reclaim forms of literacy for those who might come later.

Other times, Climber of Trees thought she needed to attend more closely to the teachings of local leaders and teachers as they, too, made sense of their past, present, and future. Climber of Trees had heard the stories recounting the fate of the priestly class who maintained a special status above others but who later abused that power.[64] She had learned about their supposedly superior knowledge, but she also knew they mistreated members of the community, often women. Some people discussed the similarities in some of the traders' behaviors toward women in the community. People linked the priests' use of writing on bones and bark to their larger abuses of power and violations of community norms that had led the community to castigate and kill them.[65] She reminded herself of the fate of the priests who had possessed this knowledge, and then she scoffed at these outsiders and their writing.

But sometimes she wondered.

Community members may have also witnessed the few Christians challenging the legitimacy and role of Selu in favor of a woman named Eve, a woman blamed for being a temptress and bringing sin into the world. Climber of Trees heard the resentment in her *elisi*'s voice as she talked about what Christians were saying. In turn, Climber of Trees resented the denigration of her mothers' and grandmothers' labor and of elder women's significance and authority in Cherokee society.

In more recent history, Climber of Trees learned about the devastation and disruptions caused by the Indian slave trade and at least some Cherokee people's intimate connections to it. Throughout the late seventeenth century, Westos dominated the Indian slave trade through their alliance with the Carolinas. As Climber of Trees grew up, tensions simmered between Cherokee people and their Southern Indigenous neighbors and the European newcomers residing in South Carolina. Through Indian information networks, Climber of Trees heard stories of women taken as captives to labor in fields, not for their own economic independence and in relationship with Selu but on tobacco and rice plantations.[66] She had heard the stories of the Shawnee living along the Savannah River attacking a Cherokee town, slaughtering elder men and selling women and children into slavery during her *edutsi*'s childhood.[67] She may also have understood that her own region's rise to prominence occurred as a result of Cherokee trade relationships with Virginians and their own use of force, including when Cherokee people allied with the Westos against the Guale in the 1680s and stepped into the vacuum left after the Westo "monopoly shattered."[68]

As a member of the community, she participated in ritual rebirth ceremonies to adopt kin and neighbors who had been taken captive but later returned. She may have heard stories of those lost to the slave trade, including Caesar of Chatuga, who in the years that followed would return from captivity proficient in English.[69] She may have mourned and despaired at the "bondage, sexual vulnerability, and forced labor" endured by other Cherokee girls subjected to the slave trade.[70] Did these ceremonies offer a warning about perilous places beyond her thirty square miles? She knew that those taken sometimes returned. She witnessed the rituals attached to those returns. She also witnessed the adoption ceremonies carried out by elder women to bring those who had formerly been strangers into kinship with Cherokee people.[71] Did she draw distinctions between those who returned from captivity and those who had not previously been members of the community but who were also adopted through similar ceremonies? For Climber of Trees and others, the ceremonies likely reinforced a social reality—that the people taken captive didn't return as the same people who had left.

Regardless, she learned that captivity and social death required ceremonies, perhaps a similar lesson learned by Ageyutsa. Ageyutsa and Climber of Trees both encountered captives, *atsi nahsa'i* (slave, one who is owned). But whereas "one who is owned" formerly meant captives taken in war and could also refer to the dogs who stayed close to fires, food, and children and who were sometimes carefully and lovingly buried in graves at Chota, it increasingly meant those who came from across the ocean with skin even darker than her own.[72] Many times these people spoke many languages, too.

Climber of Trees may not have been privy to details of political realignments, diplomacy, or the fear experienced by tribes and settlers alike during the peak years of tumult over the Indian slave trade, but she learned the new community lessons generated by those experiences. By the time she was reaching young adulthood, men named Slave Catcher, a title that indicated a low-level military rank, lived in towns across the Cherokee country.[73] But men with this name also existed in a larger world that increasingly attached profit to catching and returning enslaved people.[74] Just as some women may have disliked the shifting labor responsibilities attached to processing hides, Climber of Trees observed women who continued to assert their legal matrilineal rights to determine the fate of captives and saw men usurping the established legal rights of those women by laying claim to captives to manage new international, political, military, diplomatic, and economic relationships with European settlers.[75] Enveloped in history and political science curriculums, she witnessed historical and legal precedents in flux.

Climber of Trees continued to learn that Cherokees were Aniyuniwya, "The Real People," "The Principal People," even as European outsiders debated Native American religious and racial origins.[76] Local leaders most in contact with the Europeans deliberated and ruminated with these new arrivals on the explanations for this human diversity and the belief systems that governed this diversity. Despite these discussions among leaders, local priests and headmen served as mediators of these debates and their conclusions to the community. Some leaders and community members likely dismissed these outsiders' views because the outsiders' worldviews dismissed Cherokees as lesser peoples than

Europeans. Others retold older stories through new political, diplomatic, and international lenses.[77]

As men debated human origins, Cherokee women observed and evaluated the behavior of traders, which led to distinctions. In witnessing the rude behaviors of traders, they likely scoffed at a religion that appeared to produce worse humans than their own religious traditions did. Even though many of these conversations may have been beyond her understanding, Climber of Trees no doubt saw the "debauched" and "wicked" behaviors of traders who passed through her community.[78] If she also witnessed the unscrupulous tactics used by traders and their ledgers to undercut the economic power of Cherokee hunters, she may have scorned the ideas offered by these men that circulated among her community.

Local teachers mediated many of the interactions with outsiders, and even though her *etsi* and *taline etsi* may not have been central negotiators, they were always within earshot, preparing and serving food, mending clothes, and weighing in on the quality and types of goods provided by traders. Just as Cherokee headmen developed preferred relationships with traders "personally known and acceptable" to their people, women also had vested interests in these relationships.[79] Women witnessed and experienced outsiders' debauchery firsthand and in uniquely gendered ways; they shared this information among themselves and would come to perhaps different conclusions about which traders their communities should tolerate.

The same Cherokee epistemologies that were flexible enough to account for the presence of new peoples allowed for an adjusted vocabulary that helped make sense of and tolerate—or even welcome—new animals. Like Ageyutsa before her, Climber of Trees had knowledge of Cherokee clans that reinforced the close relationships between humans and their earth dwelling counterparts who made places together. She knew what animals provided in the form of sustenance and raw materials but also the dangers they posed. She knew living too closely with *yona* (bears) and away from one's community changed a person, and only through ceremonies could one reemerge into the community. Clans reinforced the permeable boundaries that existed between humans and animals; there was little "difference between [humans] and animals."[80] Cherokee clans traced their matrilineal origins to a single ancestor, and often those ancestral origins tied to "trees, plants, animals, birds, and the elements."[81]

At some point, in consultation with their mothers and uncles, some individual Cherokee women chose to marry outsiders. From the wives' perspectives, these husbands remained transitory. Traders came and went. During the winter months, Cherokee hunting parties predominantly composed of men (and husbands) often stayed away for months at a time. The absence of husbands, whether traders or hunters, strengthened women's everyday economic and political authority. It also privileged their position as educators. Headmen and priests certainly continued to reinforce advanced curriculums through ceremonies and community gatherings in the council house, but women and children dominated the learning environments of the everyday. Regardless, even when men were home, women and children outnumbered men. In winter, women's voices would have been the most abundant and perhaps more influential.[82] Yet, for those *diniyoli* whose households occasionally contained an intermarried European trader, the homeschooling curriculum changed. Those fathers spoke to their children in French, Spanish, or English. Fathers might tell their *diniyoli* stories of their family, religion, or national origin. These *diniyoli*, boys and girls, learned specific information about lands beyond the ocean. This information, coupled with invitations from familiar traders, would lead some Cherokee headmen to visit those places in the years to come.[83]

Teachers at every level adjusted their curriculums to explain the presence of and information offered by new peoples. As isolated seventeenth- and eighteenth-century traders and soldiers introduced racial ideologies and hierarchies, Cherokee people adjusted their worldview to accommodate this new demographic and historical reality. Captivity was not new to Cherokee people, but a new racialized slavery took hold throughout the region, solidified in colonial laws as settlers gained footholds in the region.

Climber of Trees' grandchildren's and great-grandchildren's lives faced disruptions and changes to many of the educational frameworks that had formed the intellectual connective tissue from Ageyutsa to her granddaughters. Chota and Tanasi would undergo major architectural shifts as they slowly adopted the hewn-log cabins common to settlers. As the deerskin trade increased and then plummeted, shared hunting grounds became more volatile and violence escalated. European settlement expanded as well, bringing far more non-Native people, men, women, and children, into Cherokee people's backyards. Growing populations alongside more trade increased the number of violent outbreaks experienced by Cherokee people. By the American Revolution, key elders were lost, including men like peace chief Keahatahee, a Beloved Man at Chota and *edutsi* to Sequoyah, one of Climber of Trees' grandsons.[84] During the American Revolution, American militia from the Carolinas and Virginia, like British forces in previous battles, laid waste to Cherokee towns and targeted cornfields. Chota declined after 1783 due to Revolutionary War damage, smallpox, and targeted deprivations. By 1789 and because of the Treaty of Tellico, Chota served as the boundary line of white settlement.[85]

But in the meantime, Climber of Trees' childhood shared similarities with that of her ancestral grandmother Ageyutsa. Her formative education was provided by women in the fields and community spaces in the towns. All *diniyoli* learned to speak and toddle in the agricultural classrooms of multigenerational teachers. Climber of Trees trained her ear to the same sights and sounds in her environment that Ageyutsa had. Their learning landscapes shared similar geographical sites that included mounds, paired summer and winter homes, central hearths, and flowing rivers filled with mollusks.

Nevertheless, Climber of Trees experienced a changing educational world based on the intermittent presence of peoples arriving from across an ocean and on the interactions of mostly men in the community with these newcomers that occurred through trade beyond the bounds of her thirty square miles. Those interested in languages rose to the challenge of learning new tongues. Local teachers reemphasized or reintroduced older curriculums related to their community's prior literacies to remind community members of their own internal intellectual capabilities. Teachers used stories of literacy to impart lessons to children on why they should attend to the teachings of elders, but some of those same ears understood that new literacies also presented new ways forward. *Diniyoli* presumably pondered the discrete uses of literacy presented by traders and early missionaries. *Diniyoli*, like Climber of Trees, likely formulated a range of new imaginings. Unlike Ageyutsa's teachers, who likely described their own experiences and the educational landscapes they might have visited, Climber of Trees' teachers needed to translate languages, worlds, and peoples that no one among them, not even their ancestors, had encountered. New and modified curriculums emerged even as some curriculums remained largely unchanged.

But for Climber of Trees' granddaughters, the world would be a very different place.

Ayohka, cocreator. Artwork by Roy Boney Jr.

CHAPTER 3

Wills Valley

Ayohka

An approximately 250-year-old *atsina* (cedar) tree guards the mouth of a cave that runs more than a mile deep. The *atsina*, "held sacred above other[s]," remains green throughout the year, defying the patterns of life common among deciduous trees.[1] When plants and animals first entered the world, Creator tasked them with staying awake and remaining watchful for seven moons, but only the *atsina*, pine, holly, spruce, and laurel remained awake. Because of this, Creator endowed these trees with powerful medicine and year-round color. The *atsina*'s balsamic fragrance wafts through the air. This particular *atsina* still stands today in a town briefly known as Willstown.

Located in Wills Valley, Willstown, renamed Fort Payne during the removal era, resides between Lookout and Raccoon Mountains on the Cherokee Trace. When I was there for the first time in October 2015, the trace looked down at me covered in a cornucopia of autumnal colors. It runs southwestward from Tennessee to Pensacola and New Orleans. Like the *dasodaquali* (American chestnut) in the early fall, the *atsina*'s distinctive aroma matters and provided an education to Cherokee people living in the region. Beyond its use in ceremonies and medicines, Cherokees used hollowed-out *atsina* to create a barrier around the sacred fire built on mound sites where council houses were built. One of these sacred fires burned at Kituwah and there the hearth remains. The *atsina* at Willstown overlooks a spring-fed pond that flows from inside the cave, a waterway that for Cherokee people connects realms of the world.

It was here where the landscape demanded that I consider far more expansive classrooms than I had originally conceived of for this project. It was here that I felt compelled to journal about my experience entering the cave for the first time, journaling being a practice I had given up more than a decade earlier. It was here that I sat with the implications and significance of Indigenous towns in a way that Josh Piker suggested we should in his book *Okfuskee* but in ways, perhaps, he had not conceived of either. I thought about the *usdi atsina* tree bearing witness to what must have been painful and impassioned debates over removal. I brought my daughter back to this area three years later, and she entered caves and ascended bluffs with me. Combined, these old archaeological

Atsina (cedar) tree. Photo courtesy of the author.

and Mississippian spaces, this young Cherokee region, the presence of my Cherokee daughter, the removal era, and this *atsina* tree pushed me to ask different questions and shift my perspective. I thought about the generations of girls who had traversed these spaces before my daughter. One Cherokee girl, about whom books have been written and yet very little is known, grew into childhood. Ayohka, the daughter of Sequoyah—the first student of the Cherokee language—was likely born in the area, or moved here shortly after her birth, and lived here until her parents removed to the West sometime around 1826.

It was here where a new generation of Cherokee young people, like Ayohka, matured, learned, and bore witness to rapid educational and intellectual changes that led a nation to become a Nation during the Long Removal Era. *Diniyoli*, children, including Ayohka, visited, rested, collaborated, and learned in the valley canopied by *atsina* and *dasodaquali*. Many of the key elements of a flourishing educational landscape existed at Willstown where Ayohka and the *atsina* matured. However, this educational landscape was different. Climber of

Trees' descendants pushed south into the area around Wills Valley, formerly Muscogee lands, what is today northern Alabama, for a variety of reasons, ranging from actively resisting Euro-American colonial intrusion, becoming refugees in the wake of land cessions, to seeking new opportunities.

Ayohka and the *atsina* flourished in a Cherokee educational landscape that included intellectual discord over who should educate Cherokee people and what the curriculum should entail. Tensions increased among those committed to older pedagogies and curriculums and those open to new systems, particularly the schooling introduced by missionaries. Most Cherokee people did not see choosing new possibilities as an outright abandonment of others, but that did not mean these choices lacked consequences.

Over the Long Removal Era, education continued to exist as it always had in many families and communities, but it was no longer a universally available education shared by all Cherokee people that began in local fields taught by intergenerational groups of women. Some towns still stood as educational centers rooted in older forms of knowledge transmission, others embraced new educational possibilities, and still others featured elements of both. Many of the people versed in older curriculums continued to nurture those in their families when they moved to the area from places like Chota and Tanasi, but many of those people were already familiar with other educational possibilities.

Ayohka emerged into a Cherokee world facing a second removal crisis at the behest of a young United States and a world grappling with the role of language, literacy, and debates over standardized curriculums. Even as these contexts informed her world, she was born to parents struggling to make sense of how their own worlds were changing and how they would exist within those worlds. But those same parents had a strong command of the histories and literacies of Climber of Trees' generation. They provided Ayohka with an intellectual and educational path forward, intimately tied to older pedagogical models but built with a distinct eye toward the future.

Beginning in the late eighteenth century, Overhill towns, especially Chota, began courting missionaries for their educational services. They did so in a time when most colonies relied heavily on churches for most of their schooling.[2] Attakullakulla, born around 1715 and raised in the Overhill towns, had traveled as a delegate to England in the 1730s, spent time in captivity among the Ottawas, and then rose to local power at Chota. In the 1750s, he had questioned the legitimacy of treaty negotiations with colonial officials that didn't include women. A decade later, he offered protection to a missionary named John Hammerer if he agreed to instruct people at Chota.[3] Around 1783, Reverend Martin Schneider visited Chota and the neighboring towns. Even then, Chota

remained "one of the largest Indian towns on the River, which consist[ed]
upwards of 30 Houses besides the Hothouses," where women still performed
dances.[4] Again, community members wanted the missionary "to come and
live among them . . . to be instructed."[5] Those still residing at Chota continued to perform the Green Corn Ceremony in 1792.[6] By 1799, only five houses
remained at Chota, but one of those residents was the Beloved Man Arcowee,
who educated visitors on the significance of fire and water to all people, not
just Cherokees, and suggested the Great Spirit was the Christian God. Even
as Arcowee acknowledged the need for Cherokee people to learn to read, he
also insisted on using old ceremonies, including smoking a pipe together with
outside visitors to let his prayers reach skyward and to legitimize their relationships.[7] Another Overhill holdout held fast to his home, not just because of the
graves of his fathers but also because his wife and some of his children were
buried there; possibly, like burials at Chota, their remains were placed around
the perimeter of her home and that of her children.[8]

This new generation of learners very often stood between the educational
pasts and a range of educational futures. Ayohka's father, with her assistance,
would first imagine and then bring forth the Cherokee written language, igniting
even more Cherokee educational possibilities. They did so in a moment when
educational leaders in the young United States, like Noah Webster, who promoted standardized spellings and definitions, worked to "Americanize Americans."[9] As these bursts of educational possibilities took form, Cherokee people
evaluated the degree to which mission schools presented tangible possibilities
through the realities of geography, politics, resources, and reciprocity. Unlike
the mission schools, missionaries, and the private tutors offering new curriculums with significant barriers to entry, what Ayohka and her father offered
was an educational technology universally accessible to all Cherokee speakers,
regardless of age, location, or class. It privileged students already rooted in the
most basic Cherokee curriculum—the Cherokee language. Ayohka's education
served as a bridge directly linking the educational possibilities taking shape
around her to the worlds of her grandmothers before her.

Like so many *anigeyutsa* (girls) and *anitsutsa* (boys) who received instruction
based on those Cherokee best practices, their educational attainments would
be overshadowed by their male and female counterparts who excelled in the
English language educational settings offered by missionaries. Because of the
educational space created by her family, Ayohka's intellectual accomplishments
provided an important educational trajectory for generations of *diniyoli* like
her and a clear embrace by her family of one of the possible educational futures
available and debated during her childhood.

Ayohka's grandparents and parents represented the generations of those Cherokee people who came of age during the seemingly unending violence born out of aggressive colonial expansion; they watched the birth of the United States. Ayohka's *digvgilisi* (grandmothers) and many of her aunts and uncles had previously resided in the Overhill towns along the Little Tennessee River. Wurteh, Ayohka's paternal *elisi* (grandmother), raised her father, Sequoyah, near Tuskegee on the Little Tennessee River. That same river linked Chota to Tuskegee and Climber of Trees to girls like Wurteh. Although ancestral Cherokees had occupied areas in and around Tuskegee for thousands of years, the iteration of the town where Wurteh resided and would later educate her son flourished (and later fell) in relationship to the development of local forts.

Similarly, Ayohka's maternal *elisi*, who gave birth to her daughter Sallie around 1789, grew to adulthood and raised her children in the town of Toqua, sometimes spelled Toquo. Toqua and its use of palisades to adapt to changes before girls like Ageyutsa or Climber of Trees were ever born set it apart from other Cherokee towns. Yet, Toqua also contained two mound sites, a geographic, ceremonial, and educational site/sight that Ageyutsa would have recognized as classroom fixtures that signaled their lengthy histories to their residents.[10] Sallie's mother, Ayohka's *elisi*, grew up in a town with thirty-two structures, including a council house. She waded into the same waters as Climber of Trees and Wurteh to gather mollusks and fresh water. Generations of girls, from Climber of Trees to Wurteh and Sallie's mother, shared an incredibly similar thirty square miles of classroom space.

Despite those similarities, Wurteh and Sallie's mother, unlike Climber of Trees, shared a recent and overlapping history of pronounced violent contact with European colonists. If Sallie was born in 1789, her birth coincided with another rebuilding of Toqua after three attacks by American soldiers during the Revolution, including in 1776, 1780, and 1788. Sallie entered a world familiar to her mother's own childhood, one punctuated by destruction. And yet, Sallie's mother and therefore Sallie likely also learned a community history that had included sixteen building stages by ancestral Cherokees and a firsthand knowledge of the rebuilding that happened in 1777, 1781, and 1789. Rebuilding was an older pedagogical lesson and yet an eternal one at a place like Toqua. This rebuilding of Cherokee towns again and again reinforced older pedagogies that assisted young people in orienting themselves not only to their community but also to their knowledge of the cosmos.[11]

It was this same history of war and resistance that had led many of the kin and neighbors of Wurteh's and Sallie's mothers to relocate first to the Chickamauga towns south of Chattanooga during the American Revolution and then farther south to the area around Willstown when John Watts, leader of the Chickamauga after Dragging Canoe died, moved to the area. The Chickamauga warriors waged war on the Americans and continued to do so even after most Cherokee towns had sued for peace. This relocation represented a break with the past and a desire to continue. The Chickamauga moved to the area to "innovate" because "it was necessary to do so in order to keep their way of life intact. Not unchanged, but intact."[12]

Ayohka's father, Sequoyah, also known as George Gist or Guess, was born around 1765 in Tuskegee on the Tennessee River in the Overhill region of the Cherokee nation, approximately four miles from Chota, where girls like Climber of Trees grew to adulthood. Like generations of Cherokee *diniyoli* before him, he received his primary education from his mother and his Paint Clan kin. He lived, grew, and learned within a world that was still heavily governed by matrilineal law. The absence of his father serves as evidence of his matrilineally centered world where husbands and fathers were only peripherally important to their children's everyday and long-term well-being. The existence of his English name, a name shared with a man known to Cherokee people, may have been his mother's and his community's attempts to remind the non-Cherokee Gist of his continued economic, political, and social ties, responsibilities, and obligations, not to a single child but to a kin network and town. The realities of war meant many men were absent throughout this period. Rather than the seasonal absences of Cherokee men to hunting and intermittent raids that girls like Climber of Trees experienced, the absence of men and the precarity of their return produced a different educational experience for several generations of children born and raised in the Overhill region from 1750 to 1790.

Throughout this period, as Cherokee men increasingly made difficult decisions to wage war against colonists, mothers, including women like Wurteh and Sallie's mother, remained closer to towns raising and educating their children, "managing [their] little property, and maintaining [themselves by their] own exertions."[13] Once their children were old enough, families continued to sustain themselves to varying degrees with the assistance of their children's contributions. Like other young boys, Sequoyah had aided his mother when she needed to clear the grounds for planting. Like Ageyutsa and Climber of Trees, he likely trailed his mother down rows cleared for cornfields to drop in four to ten grains. Many *diniyoli* still did so.

Even though they may have remained closer to home given the increasing settlement in the region, many Cherokee women still traversed their landscapes with competence and comfort. They could jump from canoes, depart for shore, and navigate their way home alone for miles, if they needed to.[14] If war arrived at their doorsteps, they could disappear into the thirty square miles that often separated concentrated towns from one another with their children and sustain themselves through foraging until they could safely reconnect with their communities. With or without husbands, they could call upon their male kin, uncles, and brothers to serve as male caretakers to their children.

Sequoyah and Sallie watched as their mothers adapted to economic changes around them that Climber of Trees may not have imagined. Sequoyah's mother, like Ageyutsa and Climber of Trees before her, was a woman in charge of her economic autonomy. Throughout the region and because of the willingness of Nancy Ward, the War Woman of Chota, to learn about raising dairy cows and butter making from a white woman, women like Wurteh diversified their economic practices. Climber of Trees likely heard about *waca* (cow) from men who traded in Charleston and may have seen *sikwa* (pig), but she might not have dreamed of her granddaughters keeping these animals close at hand. She might also have lamented the need of some women to do so because of the overhunting of deer.[15] Cherokee women's willingness to expand their economic practices also meant their children witnessed and then learned the skills necessary to sustain those endeavors. Sequoyah's mother traded goods with hunters and farmed, both familiar endeavors to her ancestral counterparts, but this new generation of women also maintained dairy cows, horses, and pigs and exposed their children to all these practices. Likely because of his mother's trade with hunters, when Sequoyah was old enough, he had a good eye for deer hides thanks to his mother's tutelage. Not only did Sequoyah contribute meat to his clan kin as a properly educated Cherokee man should, but he also provided quality materials for his mother when she manufactured deerskin clothing, even though cloth was ubiquitous.[16] Like children before him, he learned how to process deer to maximize their hides. Unlike his predecessors, he used metal tools obtained through trade with Euro-Americans to complete the process, not the shell scrapers of previous generations.

In addition to the pens of pigs and a few chickens adopted by Cherokee women and still frowned upon by men, the women in the community of Sequoyah's and Sallie's mothers planted *nuna* (sweet potato) side by side with *gu da ge wi* (wild potato). Their familiarity with peaches and watermelons points to the other changes experienced by the grandchildren of Ageyutsa and Climber of Trees as trade networks changed throughout the Southeast, power shifted, and other Indigenous and enslaved Black people brought new food sources to the region.[17] What was unknown to Ageyutsa and still novel to her grandmothers was more rooted for Ayohka.

Sequoyah and Sallie also came of age as new architectural teachings took root. As an *atsutsa*, Sequoyah constructed small houses with sticks.[18] Like their mothers, Sequoyah and Sallie were a part of the last generation to witness the consistent rebuilding of towns in Cherokee homelands. From 1750 to 1775, Cherokee people, at uneven rates, began constructing hewn-log cabins more like settlers in the region, altering long-held architectural practices and important educational landscapes. Regardless of those changes, as he grew, Sequoyah constructed the buildings his family needed.[19]

Like their mothers, Sequoyah and Sallie spoke only Indigenous languages, even though their worlds increasingly became intertwined with the growing dominance of English-speaking British and then Americans living in the region. They lived in communities that continued to expect outsiders to conform to their linguistic world. Within Cherokee communities, French, German, Dutch, Scottish, and English men had acquired varying levels of Cherokee language proficiency and had resided with families and fathered children. Even as Euro-American outsiders increasingly judged women like Wurteh as "untaught and illiterate," she existed in a world where she could continue to educate and raise a child whose efforts, alongside her granddaughter's, would one day maintain and simultaneously transform Cherokee educational history.[20]

Wurteh and her male kin raised Sequoyah to adulthood at a time when Cherokee masculinity, although pressured by outside expectations, still worked toward social balance and community well-being. In many parts of the nation, one's contributions to the community mattered more than the gendered nature of that work. At some point, Sequoyah suffered a leg injury; it's possible that the affliction was congenital.[21] If the latter was the case, he may have avoided some Cherokee masculine pursuits, especially stickball, which would have aggravated the leg. Instead, he embraced others, like more solitary trading and hunting pursuits. It may have also led him to stay closer to home than other *anitsutsa* his age.[22] He may have stayed closer to Cherokee women and children for a bit longer than many of his counterparts. Yet, Sequoyah also benefited from the models of diplomacy and governance offered by his male clan kin at Chota. Cherokee classrooms and teachers made room for children like Sequoyah to contribute in the ways most fitting for him.

Despite Sequoyah's and Sallie's exposure to educational continuities, their family histories included knowledge of the ravages of the eighteenth century that led to the rise and fall of places like Chota and Tanasi, the violent deaths of many of their clan kin, and the movements of others to the South to continue resisting encroachment.[23] As children, they may have also heard of other changes in Cherokee educational history. Sequoyah and Sallie likely knew about the Anikutani, the priestly class who abused their power and whom, as a result, the community rejected.[24] They also heard the stories and bore witness to the writing that young people before Sequoyah had failed to learn.[25] Wampum belts, eagle feathers, and swan feathers were not a literacy of the past to Sequoyah and Sallie; they were a part of the present.[26]

The demographic and geographic shift from the Overhill towns to the Chickamauga towns and Lower towns overlapped with shifts in political and educational power. Although Willstown was a new geographic center, many of the people who resided there were themselves arbiters of political power who connected to older spaces like Chota and Tanasi. At the same time, these shifts left questions as to where future core political centers would exist. In 1809, a council held at Willstown created the Cherokee National Committee comprising high-ranking chiefs, an additional step on a road toward centralization.[27] Increasingly, political power mapped onto educational access. Leaders like Attakullakulla and Arcowee at Chota had long courted missionaries willing to offer English language education, but war, dislocation, and land losses had stopped those efforts in their tracks. In the short term, the political and geographic realignments happening in the Cherokee Nation produced educational gatekeepers tied to new forms of wealth, especially Cherokee men and women who had adopted plantation slavery, including Nancy Ward, Beloved Woman at Chota.[28]

Economics acted as the first gatekeeper to new educational possibilities. It had often been the trade and intimate relationships forged between Cherokee women and European traders and soldiers that brought limited language and new cultural educations into Cherokee communities in the previous century. In the new century, these benefits went to families who could afford private tutors for their children and/or had access to Christian missionaries. Moravians finally bore fruit in 1801, when James Vann, the adult child of a Cherokee mother and a non-Cherokee merchant father, granted use of a tract of his plantation to the Protestant denomination to establish a mission school in what is today Chatsworth, Georgia.

In between the Moravian missionaries' trips to Chota in the late eighteenth century, Moravians had organized the Society for Propagating the Gospel among the Heathen in 1787. One of the first orders of business was establishing a mission among the Cherokees.[29] James Vann's patronage on behalf of the Moravians with Cherokee leaders in council made this a reality.

When they initially pitched their educational services to Cherokee leaders, Moravians committed themselves to learning the Cherokee language. When John Hammerer, a Lutheran, visited the Cherokees in the 1760s, he wrote that he intended to learn the language. When members of the Society for Propagating the Gospel sought advice on first steps to establishing a mission among the Cherokees, a missionary to Northern tribes suggested they first seek a Cherokee primary education: "Learn their language. . . . This would give opportunity to become acquainted with them, win their confidence."[30] When Hammerer's Moravian counterparts arrived on a tour of Cherokee country in 1799, just a few years before they would open Springplace Mission at James Vann's plantation, Steiner and de Schweinitz had not taken the earlier advice, did not have an interpreter, and used sign language to communicate.[31] These initial commitments to learning the Cherokee language gave way to a consistent pattern of reliance on translators and the need for English-speaking Cherokee converts, enslaved bilingual Black people, or students.

As for the education offered by the Moravians, it reinforced their early abandonment of Cherokee language learning and exposed the Faustian bargain at the heart of schooling for Cherokee people in its earliest years. The Moravians' curriculum focused on ciphering and writing, grammar, and the "fundamental Doctrines of our holy Religion."[32] For Cherokee people open to schooling, English language education was a means to protect Cherokee interests; for missionaries, it was the path to converting Native people. Conversion was only one of the potential educational minefields that many Cherokee people sought to avoid.

Cherokee children themselves offered an education rooted in matrilineality, which the missionaries often failed to master. In 1805, Ishkitihi, a student at the Moravian school, informed missionaries he had two mothers. Ishkitihi also told missionaries who his brother was. Confused by this description of his clan kin, the missionaries noted he had a different mother from that of his brother. Cherokee women, unnamed by the Moravians in their notations, were instilling in Ishkitihi the knowledge that all his female clan relations had responsibilities to him, just like his biological mother did, and that all their biological children were his siblings who had responsibilities to him. Ageyutsa and Climber of Trees would have clearly understood the lesson Ishkitihi was trying to convey.

Ishkitihi's family was steeped in many of the same learning systems that had endured despite the vast disruptions of war. Matrilineality and matrilocality served as the educational foundations of Ishkitihi's family and would continue to play a role in the lives of children born in the years ahead. Ayohka's parents and *digvgilisi* witnessed the colonial and then federal arguments, negotiations, and pressures to adjust their lives according to Euro-American middle-class values and norms. Sallie's mother had lived near Nancy Ward at Chota. After receiving first the status of War Woman after the Battle of Taliwa in 1755 and then the status of Asgeyvligei (Beloved Woman) as she aged, Ward periodically organized women to advocate for their economic rights as the political actors they had always been. Sequoyah's mother's willingness to adopt dairy cows even before the United States implemented its Civilization Policy in the 1790s suggests that like other Cherokee women, she embraced the pieces of her counterparts' lives that made sense to her and contributed to her family's overall well-being. In contrast to Nancy Ward, there is no evidence that Sallie's mother ever adopted slavery as an economic practice.[33]

Cherokee and African-descended children raised and educated at the Vann plantation provide an extreme example of educational reforms colliding with attempts by isolated women to hang on to Cherokee-centered curriculums. Vann embraced an acquisitive approach to farming that deployed the violent oppression and forced labor of enslaved African-descended peoples. But whether located on a plantation or in proximity to a community, the missionaries uniformly relied on the labor of enslaved people to sustain missions.

For Cherokee people who neither owned nor benefited directly from the labor of enslaved people, they still received lessons on the roles and relationships of enslaved people to missionary-provided educational institutions. When Cherokee people sent their children to these mission schools, children often performed labor to sustain the schools as well. If Cherokee students performed similar labor to that of enslaved people, families invested in these new racial hierarchies of labor objected.[34] For other Cherokee people who saw labor as something that all people did because it was one's responsibility to the larger community, to labor alongside African-descended people may not have seemed unusual. Children attending schools at plantations were on the front lines of an educational realignment that corrupted older ideas about race, gender, labor, and class. Students at these schools learned distinctions that their grandparents might have rejected or might not have confronted very often in their day-to-day lives.

A portion of the more than 100 enslaved people at Vann's plantation were children; the Moravian missionaries benefited from labor of enslaved people as well. Children living at the Vann plantation, Cherokee or enslaved, learned from one another. The Vann children, Joseph, and Mary, played with enslaved children. They attended many of the same ceremonies, including dances and ball games, and Cherokee children likely caught glimpses of "a black lifeworld rooted in memories of Africa."[35] For Ageyutsa and Climber of Trees, this would have been a remarkable change.[36] Children at the Vann plantation and Springplace learned that Black mothers, possibly their own, had few rights to their own children. Moravian missionaries took the child of an enslaved woman named

Pleasant away from her to be raised by another woman.[37] Withholding children to produce compliance from enslaved people was another part of Springplace's curriculum. This must have produced confusing lessons for Cherokee children rooted in matrilineality. Although initially it was the missionaries and the Vann family who controlled enslaved mothers' access to their children, over time mission schools and their officials would play an even greater role in limiting Cherokee women's access to their children.

Even as racial hierarchies took root, ideas about access to education and identities determined solely by race remained fluid. After Peggy Vann, Joseph Vann's wife, converted to Christianity and learned to read and write in English, she taught enslaved children to read the Bible to aid in their conversion, using Webster spelling books purchased by her husband to facilitate their learning.[38] Christianity, literacy, and enslavement were bound together for children at Springplace. At least two Cherokee men, Sour Mush and Ou see kee, advocated for a mixed-race Cherokee woman whose Cherokee mother had been killed in front of her during the American Revolution and who had been forced into slavery as a child afterward. Five years after Sour Mush called for the Moravians to begin their school's operation, he also made clear that matrilineality still operated with force of Cherokee law when he testified on behalf of Nancy, the Cherokee child, now a woman, who had spent her life in slavery.[39] Men like Sour Mush advocated for new educational possibilities even as they adhered to much older educational norms. Intended or not, a new generation of children, mostly those taught at mission schools or in schools in the United States, would abandon those older educational and political commitments to matrilineality articulated by men like Sour Mush in favor of notions of citizenship and belonging determined by the laws produced by a subset of Cherokee men informed by race.

For those undeterred by these conditions but who lived farther away and were unable to arrange lodging for their children, they initially had few options. Elite Cherokee families employed private tutors and with the right benefactors sent their children north to schools like Dartmouth, Harvard, and Cornwall's Foreign Mission School, founded to provide education to "heathen" youth.[40] Presbyterian minister Gideon Blackburn oversaw the opening of his first boarding school on Hiwassee River that served the bilingual or English-speaking children of elite families in 1804. He opened a day school on Sale Creek in 1806 near the plantation of Richard Fields, the same year Chickamauga leader Doublehead encouraged all Cherokees to be model "red men" at an international gathering of Native leaders at Willstown.[41] In order for teachers like Blackburn to maintain their support, they had to show results.

Blackburn inflated his attendance numbers and the number of students he taught to read and write.[42]

As plantation owners like Fields and Vann served as benefactors for some schools, calls for education by national leaders occurred under the shadow of violence, internal political differences and power struggles, and active dealings with the federal government to continue the dispossession of Cherokee people. This couldn't have been lost on people like Sequoyah or his wife Sallie. Ironically, in 1807, a year after Doublehead called for Cherokees to embrace key features of the Civilization Policy, Cherokees killed Doublehead in the home of Dr. Black, a teacher assigned to one of Gideon Blackburn's schools.[43]

Regardless of where children received their education, schools didn't insulate them from violence; often, schools facilitated it. Springplace and Brainerd used whippings, the same punishment inflicted on enslaved people, to discipline children for infractions. Rather than carry out the deed themselves, the Moravians often recruited James Vann, a man physically cruel to every person in his orbit, to whip the children.[44] Blackburn required children to keep their eyes focused on the books. For children attuned to the sounds, sights, and textures of the world around them, key to Cherokee-centered educational obtainments, this may have been a challenge. Blackburn's "rigid discipline" for infractions included whipping.[45] Even if children did not witness Vann's violence, they could hear the violence in their beds at Springplace.[46] Sound remained a part of Cherokee education, but at Springplace it was not the sound of processing mollusks or of *dasodaquali* nuts falling to the ground as it had been for Ageyutsa and Climber of Trees and may have remained in places like Willstown; rather, it was the sound of women being hit, enslaved people being whipped, and children being threatened. Violence was an educational sound at Springplace.

In addition to the new curriculum of corporal punishment and domestic violence, the curriculums of all schools relied heavily on Christian teaching. Students enrolled at mission schools received daily doses of prayers and sermons. The Baptists relied on printed catechisms.[47] Sermons, along with parent conferences, included polemics on the fall of Adam and Eve and the concept of original sin.[48] For those with little familiarity with Christianity, the concept of original sin must have seemed quite at odds with Cherokee cosmology. Adam and Eve's choices ruined the world, whereas Selu and Kanati's children made choices that made the world more challenging but did not bring sin into it. Missionaries told of a world perpetually out of balance, which offered people no ability to make amends for bad acts individually or collectively, instead one could only hope for God's mercy. Finding one's way back to the right path remained perpetually out of reach, and some clan members would have found this notion unsettling, particularly those who weren't living at or near places like Willstown where restorative ceremonies still occurred. To others, aware of the disease, violence, death, and displacements of the previous half century, this world perpetually out of balance may have resonated as truth.

For a small pocket of Cherokee people, Christianity filled a void. For example, for Peggy Vann, the Moravian missionaries and Christianity likely offered a refuge from the daily isolation from her clan kin who did not live with her in her husband's home and from the violence of her husband.[49]

Beyond the Vann plantation, kin may have been educating children, but communities no longer offered a collective education across the geographical landscape. And in the case of children attending school, it was likely that at least one parent was the product of intermarriage and already had less concentrated exposure to older curriculum and to different philosophies of education. These new teachings may have been part of the primary education they had already received at home. For example, "half-Indian John Lowery," brother of George Lowery, who would later serve as assistant chief to John Ross, asked the Moravians to perform a marriage ceremony for his daughter Betsey. He may have learned about Christian marriage ceremonies first from his non-Cherokee father and then from the missionaries. The Moravians, still in the early tentative years of their relationship with the Cherokee Nation and with Cherokee people, resisted performing a ceremony "according to the custom of the white people."[50]

Language remained at the center of educational conversations. Most Cherokee people who sent their children to school did so because they wanted them to learn to speak and write English. Families likely disagreed with the degree to which English should replace Cherokee. Missionaries initially saw the Cherokee language as a key part of their goals as well. Some came to see the Cherokee language as a "wretched language"; others saw it as an evangelical opportunity.[51] Men like Presbyterian minister Gideon Blackburn ignored the role the Cherokee language might play and instead put their efforts into using English-speaking Christian Cherokees to force the language shift of their Cherokee-speaking counterparts.[52]

By the time Ayohka was born, her father had already been imagining and articulating a range of Cherokee futures. He had already married and had children with a previous wife. He was a veteran of the War of 1812 and had negotiated a treaty that once again dispossessed Cherokees of millions of acres of land, offered the possibility of what became second-class American citizenship to some Cherokees, and encouraged removal of discontented Cherokee men and their kin west of the Mississippi but also led to the availability of pensions for widows, orphans, and soldiers disabled in the War of 1812, which would personally benefit Sequoyah and Sallie for years to come. These contradictory and multifaceted options point to the range of debates playing out among US officials and Cherokee people at the time of Ayohka's birth.

In addition to the penalties imposed on English-speaking Cherokees by other Cherokees at the treaty negotiations in 1816, Sequoyah and Sallie's residency in Wills Valley meant Ayohka's entire family was at the center of debates about educational pasts, presents, and futures. Ayohka's parents came of age and grew into adulthood during a time when older educational standards still existed. They may have aided or witnessed women and children continuing to clear woods using fire.[53] As late as 1822, Turkey Town, a Chickamauga town of about 100 residents, only one of whom spoke English, still operated a council house. It was also a town that had residents who modeled older standards of multilingualism. The Boot, who was Cherokee but was raised among the Muscogee, spoke Cherokee and Creek.[54] Cherokee people throughout the Nation thought "nothing of going sixty or seventy miles to see a Ball-play—at which they bett high." Some communities still centered around the town house and its male leadership and teachings, but others had abandoned these or, through the less concentrated towns organized in the second half of the eighteenth century, lacked access to them.[55] Willstown, "bounded by mountains," contained a council house, "extensive corn fields," and woods filled with "Oak Hickory, Chestnut, and Walnut." Cherokees also continued to hold at least one dance in which women chose their partners; "in this the Ladies have absolute command."[56] Children still witnessed the eagle tail dance and in some communities watched their mothers and older sisters prepare black drink for ceremonies. Some communities renewed the fires each spring.[57] In towns like Willstown and Turkey Town, strong commitments to scaled-back, Cherokee-centered curriculums and older educational leaders remained.

These curriculums were still in effect when Ayohka was a small child in Willstown. Women's centrality as teachers and leaders still existed but faced pedagogical challenges from a range of sources. The Green Corn Ceremony and dances in which women had "absolute command" continued to reinforce the central role of women's agricultural production, the role of Selu, and some notions of egalitarianism. In places like Willstown, the presence of extensive cornfields suggests women there were still farming and therefore educating collectively and within families. Yet, for those not living in or traveling to locations that celebrated the Green Corn Ceremony, they missed opportunities to hear the advanced curriculums offered by community leaders, men and women, that accentuated the role of Selu in their collective history. Even as women in all communities continued to maintain kitchen gardens, the move by many Cherokee people away from shared towns and community fields deprived children of the formerly universally available primary education taught by teams of intergenerational Cherokee women from all the clans. This left individual households of women in a single lineage with an outsize responsibility of remembering and drawing upon what had been a shared community archive.[58] All families contained part of the curriculum, but women no longer provided universally standardized, team-taught, community-wide classrooms in agricultural fields across the Cherokee Nation.

When missionaries faced a language labor challenge, they often turned to free labor. This led missionaries to make strategic evangelical choices early on; the Moravians focused their educational efforts on the students of elite, mostly bicultural Cherokee families.[59] The Presbyterians, largely under the auspices of the American Board of Commissioners for Foreign Missions, initially did the same, whereas the Baptists and the Methodists, later arrivals among the Cherokees, reached out to more remote, monolingual-speaking communities. Both of the latter denominations ordained and employed Native preachers who were often Cherokee speakers.[60]

In addition to language and language labor, physical labor was a central issue in the middle of educational debates. As concentrated towns broke apart into individual homesteads, challenging the efficacy of older systems that bound women's educational centrality to their labor, children's labor at the missions no longer exclusively supported their families or their neighbors but rather supported the educational institution's self-sufficiency. The farming carried out at schools produced crops for use at the mission, but it could also be used by the missionaries to increase goodwill among Cherokee people when food shortages occurred. In 1824, some Cherokee communities faced a famine because of a drought. The Moravians' gardens produced food, which allowed them to offer temporary relief to some families.[61]

Even as walled classrooms governed by missionaries began to dot the landscape, many Cherokee people remained committed to as many of the pedagogies of their grandparents that they could support. In the fall of 1824, Cherokee people continued to rely on old practices, gathering chestnuts and using controlled burns that "brought more useful animals, within range, and many turkeys and some deer were secured by the Indians."[62] The same year, communities experienced a smallpox outbreak, which some Cherokee people blamed on Uktena, a powerful horned snake with a crystal in its forehead. Cherokee people sought refuge at Taloney, where some conjurers still resided, to combat the danger of Uktena. There they participated in the "Physic-Dance," a dance that Climber of Trees would have been familiar with, to restore balance.[63] The dance lasted seven nights and included a tea, prepared by Cherokee women.[64]

Around the same time Ayohka was born, the federal government began funding its Civilization Policy, which had already been underway since the 1790s. The Indian Civilization Act provided $10,000 annually to fund projects already begun in the Cherokee Nation. This coincided with the creation of the American Society for Promoting the Civilization and General Improvement of the Indian Tribes within the United States. In addition to "secur[ing] for these tribes instruction in all branches of knowledge," the society also included a call to study Native nations' histories, government structures, religions, and geographies.[65] Missionaries no longer needed to rely solely on the financial largesse of their benevolent societies or wealthy Cherokee patrons like James Vann at Springplace for educational funding. They could receive funds directly from the federal government. For federal officials, this policy meant that Cherokee men should usurp women's control over agricultural spaces and assume the role of a male head of household governing his wife and children, convert to Christianity, learn to read and speak English, and abandon a more exclusive focus on growing corn in favor of wheat, rice, and cotton. Missionaries from the Northeast, beneficiaries of these dollars, increasingly adhered to the belief that children were pliable but needed to be molded and shaped into responsible citizens by adults.[66]

The Civilization Policy sought to mold and shape Cherokee people of all ages, not just children. Federal Indian agents and those they employed through contracts provided varying levels of adult education. Benjamin Hawkins, a federal agent, had years earlier established a demonstration farm (and a plantation that relied on the labor of enslaved people) within the Muscogee (Creek) Nation, modeling not only the domestic, social, and economic reorganization expected of Native people but also a system built on a racial hierarchy profiting off the labor and lives of Black men, women, and children.[67] Intermarried families, open to many of these changes, discussed converging on a single area in order to consolidate power within the Nation.

Class divides, often based on intermarriage and community affiliations and increasingly tied to educational access and Christianity, shaped many of the educational debates. By the time Ayohka was born, missionaries and elites increasingly viewed Cherokees who lived in towns "as indigent and degraded," as opposed to their counterparts living on farm sites at a distance from their neighbors.[68] As people reorganized, the collective knowledge base fragmented and became far less universal. An educational vacuum existed in many newer areas without the familiar classroom landscapes that had reinforced the curriculum or the diverse groups of Cherokee women who had gathered daily, imparting shared educational lessons.

Because of her parents' and grandmothers' ties to the Overhill towns, Ayohka likely spent time in their homelands before her parents permanently relocated to Wills Valley. Sequoyah moved back and forth throughout the region. Sallie remained tied to the Overhill towns until at least the time of the 1817 treaty negotiations her husband helped with after the War of 1812 and which cost Cherokee people, including Sequoyah and Sallie, their continued claims on and rights to their birthplaces. Ayohka might have traversed the region with both of her parents. Through this movement, Ayohka may have seen far more than Ageyutsa's and Climber of Trees' thirty square miles. Her geographic knowledge may have been more expansive but far less intimately tied and deeply rooted to a community center as it had been for Ageyutsa or Climber of Trees or even her grandmothers. For most Cherokee girls, the "map to the next world [was] in flux" and "could take many forms and shapes."[69]

The infusion of money by the federal government to support missionaries' educational efforts added even more curricular options to the Nation. From 1817 to 1835, the American Board of Commissioners for Foreign Missions established missions at Brainerd, Taloney (later called Carmel), Creek Path, Hightower, Willstown, Haweis, Candy's Creek, New Echota, Amohee, Red Clay, and Running Water.[70] The Baptists arrived in 1817 and by 1825 had established schools at Cowee, Tillanoocy, Eastatory, Peach Tree, and Tinsawatee.[71] In the Valley Towns, the Baptist teacher introduced the Lancastrian method, a teaching method prominent in the nineteenth century, whereby older or more advanced students used dictation to teach younger or less skilled students.[72] The Methodists, who operated day schools, entered Cherokee communities in 1822 and by the end of that year had thirty-three converts.[73] Educational options exploded in tandem with Ayohka's childhood, and yet older curricula flourished in her orbit.

Her parents witnessed the competition between their communities and the missionaries over the continuation of Green Corn Ceremonies. Recognizing the central economic and agricultural importance of Green Corn, just a year and a half after their arrival in December 1817, the missionaries at Brainerd simply "thought it best to have something like a vacation at [the time of Green Corn], & give liberty for all the children to visit their friends, if they choose, for three weeks."[74] Rather than challenge the centrality of the Green Corn Ceremony when they first arrived in the region, missionaries at Brainerd offered students and families a vacation to offset what would have looked like a massive departure of students in their next official report. Still, many students remained behind and observed Brainerd missionary Brother Chamberlain leave on horseback on a "visiting & preaching tour" and, ostensibly, a recruitment tour to the westernmost portions of the Cherokee Nation.[75]

In just a few short years, missionaries' attendance accommodations for Green Corn Ceremonies fell away. Excused absences for the "season of the year" when "green corn and watermelons are plenty—a sort of feasting time" for communities disappeared. By 1822, students likely heard missionaries deride their mothers, aunts and uncles, and grandparents living in the Upper towns whom the missionaries regarded as "ignoran[t] and superstiti[ous]" because they "still adhere[d] to the old custom of a sacrifice and dance, before they eat green corn or beans." And yet some Cherokee people continued to educate the newcomers and provide models of older educational practices for young people at mission schools. When a newer missionary offered beans to those employed in the fields in advance of Green Corn, Cherokee adults "remonstrated" with him and "accuse[ed] him of great wickedness." When the missionary sat down to eat in front of them, they "refused to partake and left the field."[76] Even children attending Brainerd still witnessed competing educational standards.

Boys who attended mission schools experienced the pull between old and new curricula in particularly gendered ways. Boys listened to missionaries critique Cherokee men's consumption of alcohol and the "intemperance which generally attends" stickball games.[77] Male students gravitated toward stickball as the *anitsutsa*, boys, before them had. Some even asked permission for an excused absence to play stickball, but none of the scholars "could ever be permitted to attend." Because of the missionaries' position on stickball, the boys who sought dual enrollment opportunities in ancient curriculums and missionary-provided education faced only one choice—to skip school. And afterward they faced "examin[ation]" by teachers when they returned, along with discipline because of their absenteeism and a castigation that included morality lessons related to the "demoralizing effects" and "evil" of ball play and the "evil of going from school without permission." The Brainerd missionaries expelled an English-speaking child who had sought permission to attend a stickball game, was denied permission, and then went anyway. His "ability to read the word of God" and his knowledge of school rules made the case against him even stronger in missionaries' minds—he knew better. And the nature of the event—ball play—sealed his disciplinary fate. Despite evidence of his academic capabilities (mastery of English, ability to read the Bible), it was his disobedience to teachers, the threats that disobedience made to the "social welfare" of the school, and the boy's clear adherence to older curriculums that resulted in his expulsion. For *anitsutsa* committed to the more limited, Cherokee-centered curriculums that still flourished in their neighborhoods, regardless of their intellectual strengths, they faced ridicule, shame, and expulsion from Brainerd missionaries for pursuing them. Mission schools sought children who obeyed missionaries and abided by Christian principles, not autonomous actors guided by Cherokee cultural expectations and standards who wanted to learn English.

The shame inflicted on those boys who attempted to balance their commitments to dual curriculums spread to other places as demand for missionary schools increased from some families and as missionaries felt more confident and stable within the Nation. As some Cherokee people converted and bore witness to the increasingly judgmental positions of missionaries on the continuation of competing academic calendars and standards that events like Green Corn represented, their evangelical zeal extended from more private, individualized shaming within the church and school into the public sphere. In Etowah, about sixty miles northeast of Brainerd, Cherokee Christian converts spiritually harassed their neighbors. For Cherokees who adhered to older educational calendars and cosmologies centered on balance, which assured that people moved on to the Darkening Land after death, Cherokee converts suggested their Cherokee neighbors would experience perpetual turmoil in the afterlife due to Adam and Eve's sin. When local town leaders appealed to centralized national leaders—like Charles Hicks, who was a Christian convert—to protect them from the harassment of other converts, they found little support.[78] This was the intellectual and educational maelstrom that framed Ayohka's formative years. That tumult was picking up speed as Ayohka came of age.

Sallie and Sequoyah were intimately aware of the continued power of language and literacy within their communities. Increasingly, those wielding national political authority had never mastered a Cherokee primary education any more than the missionaries had. At treaty negotiations following the War of 1812, "about three-fourths of [those selected as treaty negotiators] not only understood the English language but had become so accustomed to thinking and speaking it, that they frequently used this language in their private discussions." Despite being in the minority in some specific political arenas, Cherokee-speaking and -thinking negotiators still exerted their authority by demanding "that at such discussions in which the ones who did not understand English also had to take part and had to use their mother tongue," the English-speaking Cherokees who had "promised more plainness but frequently forgot" would be fined "for every case of infringement."[79] Ayohka's father participated in treaty negotiations in 1816 and may have been one of those negotiators who expected the uneducated to conform to older educational standards or face a penalty. If the English-speaking Cherokees intended to impose English on their counterparts, as teachers like Blackburn had hoped, others like Sequoyah intended to push back.

As he was negotiating treaties and parenting Ayohka, he also diligently labored in fits and starts on the syllabary. Sequoyah took several approaches to the syllabary. First, he tried to create pictographs—echoes, perhaps, of the literacy of Tsulkalu Rock or tied to mnemonic devices. Next, he attempted to create signs for each word. Then he experimented with several other methods.[80] At some point in his process, people accused Sequoyah of witchcraft; others simply questioned the value of his work.[81] These objections may have connected to his early efforts, which used pictographs or signs. Cherokee people versed in older educational systems may have equated those designs with the knowledge rejected when their grandparents cast out the Anikutani for abusive practices. As Ayohka toddled around as her mother worked her field and prepared food and manufactured clothes, her father perfected his syllabary. Like Climber of Trees had done with the mollusks she steamed open in a corner of her home with her siblings, Ayohka *usdi* sat next to her father, watching, listening, and working with a needle on a discarded whetstone, learning a new skill. Listening and watching, two of the oldest pedagogical skills available to Cherokee people, are also the skills that elevated her from student to co-collaborator.

Sequoyah was an older man when he hit his creative stride. His hearing was not what it used to be. But Ayohka's hearing was fine, as was her mother's. They acted as his ears, listening intently to speakers and discerning the sounds that Sequoyah missed. Just as he had spent his childhood and young adulthood looking for ways to aid his Cherokee mother, Sequoyah honored Wurteh by inviting his wife and child into his intellectual endeavors. Without them the syllabary might not have reached its fruition when it did; without them, his sense of urgency and purpose might have faded. Was it Ayohka's curiosity, her mimicking of her father's under-the-breath sounds, his furious scratches on whetstone or paper when it was available that Ayohka *usdi* copied that made him smile in his moments of frustration? Sequoyah didn't have to teach Ayohka the syllabary; she was a part of his Cherokee educational world, as Cherokee children had always been since time immemorial.

When guests visited the house, she recited her father's syllabary from memory—not from rote memory but from the deep listening to speakers in her community and her family, from remembering those voices, from watching her father in their shared domestic space add symbols to sounds.[82] She, too, "marked them [in her] Own mind."[83] This was cocreation.

For a moment, she was the only child literate in Cherokee.

She was the first.

Like Grandfather Buzzard knew about Granddaughter Water Beetle, Sequoyah understood about Ayohka *usdi*. Just as his mother had taught him. Nurture children's talents.

Ayohka wasn't a student, she was a cocreator of Cherokee futures.

Sequoyah embraced fatherhood as the Civilization Policy actively sought to reeducate Cherokee men about their roles as men, as fathers, as husbands. In 1808, in communications to Cherokee men about the changes necessary for their full integration into American society, Thomas Jefferson made sure that Cherokee men knew that Cherokee women would also have to radically re-alter their ways. "But are you prepared for this? Have you the resolution to leave off Hunting for your living, to lay off a farm for each family to itself, to live by industry, *the men work their farm* with their Hands, raising stock or learning trades, as we do *and the women weaving Clothes for their husbands and children? All this is necessary before our laws will suit you,* or be of any use to you however let your people take the matter into consideration" (emphasis added).[84] Sequoyah had heard and embraced pieces of this, and so had his wife Sallie. He had taught himself blacksmithing and silversmithing. The former was a profession consistently needed in the early decades of the nineteenth century and one often occupied by white men on work permits from the United States.

Cherokee men from all walks of life took heed of what this meant for their sisters and daughters. As elite men like Vann, Major Ridge, and John Ross sent their daughters to mission schools and academies like Salem Academy in what is today Winston-Salem, North Carolina, Sequoyah and Sallie provided a very different education for Ayohka.[85]

As some men adopted farming and asserted themselves as male heads of households, the hope was that women would turn to domestic tasks, which many Cherokee women had already done without the Civilization Policy. Domesticity was one layer of reeducation. Altered from its previous form, a version of Thomas Jefferson's earlier admonition took center stage again in 1820 in a report submitted to the Secretary of War.

> They require only education, and the enjoyment of our privileges, to make them a valuable portion of our citizens. Let this education then be given them, particularly to the female Indians. It is essential to the success of the project of the Government, that the female character among our native tribes, be raised from its present degraded state, to its proper rank and influence. This should be a primary object with the instructors of Indians. *By educating female children, they will become prepared, in turn, to educate their own children, to manage their domestic concerns with intelligence*

and propriety, and, in this way, they will gradually attain their proper stand-
ing and influence in society. . . . Thus educated, and the marriage institution,
in its purity, introduced, the principal obstacles to intermarriage with them
would be removed. Let the Indians, therefore, be taught all branches of
knowledge pertaining to civilized man; *then let intermarriage with them*
become general, and the end which the Government has in view will be
completely attained [emphasis added].[86]

Not only did these efforts incite Indigenous men to usurp their wives', sisters',
and mothers' places as the agriculturalists, but the education of women also
encouraged Cherokee families to undermine their daughters' sexual decision-
making and the ability to establish and end intimate relationships as they saw
fit. For Cherokee people to be civilized and educated, the report made clear
that Cherokee women must marry, have sex with, and produce children with
white men. These positions on marriage, and by extension divorce, undermined
hundreds of years of Cherokee educational practices. It also made marrying
Indigenous men and raising children with them acts of educational resistance.
In keeping with this educational mission, officials castigated Cherokee women
who divorced.[87]

Whether it was commitments to older educational systems or opposition
to explicit policies like this, Cherokee people resisted. In a nod to Christian
beliefs about heaven, a Cherokee man objected to mission-provided schooling
and articulated what a Cherokee heaven might look like.

Why have white teachers in the country? Their teachings are not correct
and not suited to the Indians who have been better instructed by their
ancestors. Some time ago, he himself had been 4 days in a seemingly dead
condition. During this time, he made a visit in heaven and found everything very nice; corn growing without labor, plenty of deer of unusual
size, and everyone fat and happy and in one continual round of pleasure.
Their faces were like the full moon. He had found there all the Indians
who ever lived on earth, but not a single white person.[88]

Cherokee heaven resembled the educational world where Selu and Kanati had
resided and taught their children. Women also participated in the discussions
and voiced their concerns when missions sought to relocate to their communities. In an 1822 Turkey Town Council, men and women attended to debate the
merits of a mission school.[89] Women also spread rumors about missionaries,
suggesting that the continued power of women to organize their political views
across towns and fields still existed.[90]

The skepticism or hostility expressed by these Cherokee women and girls (most often referred to in missionary records as nameless "Indian women") who were committed to older educational systems may have also been informed by their individual experiences with missionaries. Missionaries chastised Cherokee women for their "loud displays of pleasure and laughter" and made women's quiet a condition of their visits.[91] Missionary dismay with these women spilled onto the pages of their journals and into their interactions with the women themselves. When a mother returned to take her child home because she had heard that her child cried for her at bedtime, missionaries attempted to reassure the mother that other children cried far longer. When this did not assuage her and she took the child home anyway, missionaries described her as returning to the "regions of darkness."[92] Missionaries also aided and abetted "half-breed" fathers in their efforts to take control of their children's custody without the Cherokee mother's consent. Girls who "were unwilling to go with their father" were forced to do so.[93] As enslaved women at Springplace already knew and Cherokee women were learning, missionaries would not advocate for women's matrilineal rights to their children if doing so threatened their own interests or their larger charge as Christian missionaries.

Families that shifted to bilateral-headed households, where fathers played a greater role than in the past, made choices about their parenting. Some sent their children to schools to learn the English language, in part so that their children could uphold and protect other features of Cherokee education.[94] Sequoyah's choice to step into his role as a father and then partner with Ayohka to demonstrate the efficacy of the syllabary in 1821 upheld older models of intergenerational teaching and learning. Her family's choice to educate her among her community at a time when school options were proliferating served as another educational continuity and, after 1820, an educational resistance.

Ayohka's childhood illustrated the willingness of families to accommodate some features of the Civilization Policy while actively defying others. Sequoyah simultaneously thwarted and aided Christianity's efforts. On the one hand, his invention kept the Cherokee language from becoming one of the written languages created by non-Native Christians to missionize Indigenous peoples. On the other hand, his invention hastened the efforts by Christians to print Bible translations and thus advance "the most systematic program of educational intervention in global history."[95] Missionaries credited this with teaching many to "read the word of God; the perusal of which proved the means of salvation to some who had never seen a missionary."[96] Sequoyah never converted to Christianity and supposedly "lamented his invention when he saw it used for circulating the New Testament. But he could no more recall his alphabet than

Erasmus his Greek Testament, when it had been launched upon the world."[97] Indeed, just as Sequoyah could not control what Cherokee people used his language for after learning it, neither could the missionaries whose teachers taught people to read and write using religious materials.

What Cherokee people wanted from the syllabary and how they intended to use it mapped onto educational systems provided by their larger kin and community connections. In 1823, the American Board of Commissioners for Foreign Missions school opened at Willstown.[98] This no doubt raised concerns for those committed to matrilineal kinship systems and older cosmological understandings of the world who resided in the area. Missionaries expressed anxieties over rumors spread throughout the area that they were encouraging Cherokees to move west.[99] The missionaries also reported that Cherokees executed a witch in Willstown, whom they described as an "inoffensive old man."[100] In December, the missionaries reported that congregants traveled fifteen to twenty miles to attend evening services at the Willstown mission. Sometimes the numbers of attendees reached sixty to seventy.[101] In a single year, Willstown Cherokees faced continued coercion to remove west, the arrival of missionaries, and the descent on their town by other Cherokee people from the larger region curious about the missionaries' evangelizing efforts. Many Chickamauga Cherokees and their descendants had moved to the region to resist these pressures, yet by the early 1820s the pressures had arrived at their front door once again. Even as Willstown served as a site for the trials and tribulations that plagued all Cherokee people and contributed to serious social upheaval in the Willstown area during the Long Removal Era, it fostered the use of Sequoyah's educational tool.

Some students of missionaries did convert to Christianity; some of Sequoyah's pupils used the syllabary to transmit older teachings and ways of knowing and did so on the landscape itself. Big Rattling Gourd sought out Sequoyah to help him record the speeches of past leaders that he had memorized.[102] National political leaders may have quelled Whitepath's 1827 resistance to the Cherokee Constitution (ratified in 1828), whose rejections were based in part on its infusions of Christian language, but a year later in 1828, Willstown residents literally went underground to document their lives and values.[103] In caves near Willstown, Cherokees wrote letters of events on the walls. Instead of reporting on the "civilized" accomplishments of Cherokee people, these Cherokee language writers authored pieces on more cosmologically significant events. One writer referenced three lives lost that needed to be replaced.[104] Another cave writer recorded the details of an important stickball game, a game that had threatened to bring turmoil back to the Nation and a game the missionaries sought to prohibit. One of these writers included Sequoyah's older son Teesee, who remained in Wills Valley after Sallie, Sequoyah, and Ayohka moved west. Sequoyah's time in Willstown and the thirty square miles beyond it contributed to his scholarly efforts and certainly provided the venue for those efforts to be disseminated to other Cherokee people.

As removal pressures by settlers, government officials, and, at places like Willstown, new Cherokee residents to the area continued, the desire by some Cherokee people to move west to escape hostile conditions intensified, eventually enveloping Ayohka, her family, and her community. Unlike the uniform strategy of the Chickamauga to fight back militarily in the 1790s, the response to pressures to civilize or move west of the Mississippi was anything but uniform among Willstown residents. The Glass, a Chickamauga who had lived in the area, had already moved west a decade earlier.[105] A number of warriors from Willstown traveled to the west in 1817 to assist Arkansas Cherokees in battles against the Osages. This included Willstown residents Turtle Fields, John Huss, and John F. Boot.[106] Although Sequoyah signed up to remove west of the Mississippi in 1818, documents suggest he either traveled back and forth or remained in the East for some time. By 1826, he had arrived in the West permanently, but his son Teesee and family remained in the Wills Valley region.

Once Sequoyah, Sallie, and Ayohka arrived in the West, the syllabary proliferated, and it did so among children and adults. One of his motivations for heading west was to introduce Western Cherokees to the syllabary. His first students and earliest adopters of the syllabary were "more obscure individuals of the Cherokees. . . . The most intelligent portion" dismissed its importance "until their senses gave evidence of the existence and utility of this remarkable invention."[107] Sequoyah offered his invention to all—girls Ayohka's age and adults like The Glass, who had removed west after the political fallout that had led to and followed the execution of Doublehead, an ally of The Glass, by Cherokee officials in 1808.

After he learned the syllabary, The Glass embraced the new skills and wrote a series of three letters to his kin and town connections in the East, which were published in the *Cherokee Phoenix*. In those letters, The Glass articulated older pedagogies that guided the lives of many Cherokee people in the West and reminded those living in the East of those curriculums. Like the writing in the cave that called for the balance of the three lives lost, these curriculums challenged newer written laws adopted by officials in both the East and eventually the West.[108] This enabled Arkansas Cherokees to communicate with their counterparts in the East, but it also enabled them to remind others of older educational expectations. The Glass grieved over what seemed the perpetual state of war in the West, although given his former status as a Chickamauga, he had been at war for more than two generations. In his grief, he called out to the clans of those whose clan kin had been lost in raids in the West. He also evoked the spiritual and political power of women whose children were lost to the violence. The Glass recorded, "Then the woman spoke: 'All of you have veered away from your clan-places! He has done evil to my son!'"[109] In his world, Cherokee women still had claims on blood law, and he used his literacy to elevate the role and voices of women, much like Attakullakulla had in the 1750s at treaty negotiations.

As one group of former Chickamauga warriors left, many previously tied to the Overhill towns left the Wills Valley region, and the political power that had resided there shifted eastward to New Echota. Increasingly, some of those committed to remaining in the East acknowledged the legitimacy and supported the positions of those leading from the capital at New Echota. Additionally, many of those men consolidated power, often, though not always, at the expense of their mothers, sisters, and wives. Others remained deeply committed to maintaining their homelands based on much older pedagogies guided by their relationships to land. And still others held fast because it was in their financial interest to do so.

Certainly, the Wills Valley area owes its temporary rise to prominence as a Cherokee region to the Chickamauga who sought fortification and refuge in the region as they resisted American encroachment. But Willstown's specific prominence and the place it occupied over a longer period of Cherokee dislocation ties directly to the educational spaces it opened for Cherokee people. Here, Cherokee people grappled with how best to move forward into the future. They entered caves; they embraced schools; they invented languages. It was a place where Sequoyah could be a husband to Sallie, where even if she was the wife who threw his drafts in the fire, he recognized her frustration, acknowledged it, and renewed his efforts without the violence that was taking hold in many marriages during this time.[110] Similarly, it was a place where Sequoyah could be a Cherokee father to Ayohka, as fatherhood underwent changes in the Cherokee Nation and in the larger United States—a fatherhood not committed to dominance or control but to social complementarity and an older democratic ethos. Wills Valley created an educational space for Cherokee people to experiment with educational futures. It was likely the place where Sequoyah and Sallie decided to take Ayohka west, perhaps because beyond the financial losses they faced or their own grief at abandoning the classrooms of their youth in the East, they worried that remaining might cost their daughter something more.

Did Ayohka turn to look at the mountains, listen to the *wagule* (eastern whippoorwill) and smell the *atsina* one more time, just in case she would never experience them again? Did she weep before turning her eyes toward the West and putting her feet on the path to begin the walk? Or had she already recorded the stories and images of this home in writing and in oral narratives to carry with her and give to those who came after her?[111]

Ayohka was a child of the Long Removal Era and the turmoil it laid bare. She was a witness to new pedagogical possibilities. She was the daughter of Sequoyah and Sallie. She was the granddaughter of Wurteh and Sallie's mother. And although she wasn't raised there, Ayohka was a child of the Overhill towns, like Climber of Trees before her. She was a bridge. She was a keeper of Cherokee educational pasts, presents, and futures. She was an explorer of new intellectual worlds. And by removing west when she did, that exploration continued.

CHAPTER 4

Skin Bayou District
Caroline Fields

Ayohka lived through and witnessed waves of removal to the West. Unlike Ageyutsa's and Climber of Trees' lives, her life was marked by educational dislocation. Ayohka moved at least three times before adulthood: first to Willstown, then to Arkansas Territory, and then to Indian Territory. Before barely becoming familiar with one classroom, she moved to another. The deep knowledge of place that existed among her ancestors in the East would take time to develop in the West. Students of medicinal practices and foodways had to overcome the loss of a third of the medicinal plants available in the East that did not exist in Indian Territory.[1] The landscape in the West provided a curriculum with variations on those in the East, some minor, others significant.

Dasodaquali (American chestnut) trees—a significant and essential part of the flora that marked the seasonal changes of classroom life in the East—were "seldom found" in the West.[2] If Ageyutsa or Climber of Trees had lived in Arkansas Territory or Indian Territory, they might have looked in awe at the volume of *tsi yes sdi* (Carolina parakeet) that "circled with rapid flight screaming loudly," leaving their colorful feathers to carpet the areas surrounding river canebrakes.[3] Ageyutsa might have imagined what capes would look like that integrated the long, distinct tail feathers of the scissor-tailed flycatchers, not common in the East. Climber of Trees and her siblings would have lamented the lack of mollusk diversity in the West.[4] Both girls would have noticed that the mountains and hills were too small and that the *wagule* (eastern whippoorwill) sounded different from the *squalequali* (western whippoorwill).[5]

Neither Ageyutsa nor Climber of Trees would have recognized the home structures or the architectural layouts of Ayohka's educational landscape. The absence of council houses and the paired winter homes would have been jarring, but maybe those structures didn't belong here. The bellies of mounds, now absent, may have been a required teacher and feature for those structures to be present. Families lived farther apart. Many communities lacked shared ceremonial spaces and easily traveled paths that connected kin and community. Who would help take care of the buildings and maintain the ceremonies if people lived so far apart? What might they have thought about Ayohka's

Caroline Eliza Fields on a hill above Dwight Mission, Skin Bayou District.
Artwork by Roy Boney Jr.

mobility? Would they have thought of their ancestral Iroquoian linguistic kin? Ayohka may have asked or considered similar questions when she first saw this landscape, at a time when fewer than 4,000 Cherokee people lived in the West.

Although the disjuncture created by removal starved Cherokee people of their older educational systems, the educational lives of girls in the West bore some similarities to those of their forebears in the East. Cherokee people who removed early, including Ayohka, first "lined" "both banks of the [Arkansas] river . . . with . . . houses and farms."[6] They relocated close to waterways as their ancestors had, and they encountered vast canebrakes.[7] When the 1828 treaty, signed by Ayohka's father, forced Western Cherokees to move again, they located along the banks of the Illinois, Arkansas, Grand, and Canadian Rivers and their tributaries. They lived in areas populated by oak, hickory, and pine forests, less hospitable to agriculture but interspersed by grasslands made up of dark, organic soils, "among the most important agricultural soils in the world."[8] In those forests, Cherokee people could forage for walnuts, hickory nuts, and hazelnuts. Cherokee women resumed using the hickory nuts to create milks and oils to prepare "many kinds of breads."[9] Girls in the West encountered some familiar faunal neighbors. Wild turkeys and white-tailed deer resided in the West too. Black bears lived intimately with Cherokee people in the southeasternmost corner of Oklahoma—at least until 1915—as they had in the East and as they had in the area that would become Cherokee County, Oklahoma, for more than 10,000 years.[10]

The Treaty of 1828, the first treaty negotiated separately from those still residing in the East, made explicit calls for educational funding, drawing upon the aims of the Civilization Policy. The treaty provided $500 to Sequoyah "for the great benefits he has conferred upon the Cherokee people, in the beneficial results which they are now experiencing from the use of the Alphabet discovered by him." Not only did this provision require the federal government to acknowledge Sequoyah's accomplishment, but it was also the first provision in a longer list related to education. The treaty provided $2,000 annually to the Cherokees, for a period of ten years, for Cherokee children to be educated in "letters and the mechanic arts," as well as $1,000 "towards the purchase of a Printing Press and Types to aid the Cherokees in the progress of education and enlighten them as a people, in their own, and our language."[11] Sequoyah assisted in negotiating the treaty that would lead to a new educational space in the West, a classroom centered on what would become the Western Cherokees' Lees Creek circuit court district. In 1841, after reunification, an act of the Cherokee National Council created the Skin Bayou District and portions of the Flint and Illinois Districts out of what was formerly Lees Creek. Skin

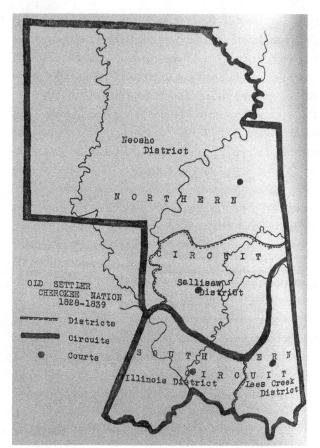

This map of the Cherokee Nation's Old Settler Districts was originally published in Thomas L. Ballenger's dissertation, "The Development of Law and Legal Institutions among the Cherokees," completed at the University of Oklahoma in 1939.

Bayou was home to Dwight Mission, which Caroline Eliza Fields and Caroline Matilda Fields would attend in the years to come.

The Western Cherokees established their capital at Tahlontuskey, near present-day Gore, Oklahoma. Tahlontuskey, which sat at the mouth of the Illinois River, served as the capital from 1829 to 1839.[12] The same year that Western Cherokees established a political center at Tahlontuskey, Dwight Mission, initially established at present day Russellville, Arkansas, and administered by the American Board of Commissioners for Foreign Missions, relocated to a site known as Kidron on Sallisaw Creek near present-day Marble City. And in a trifecta of educational offerings, in 1829, Sequoyah built his hewn-log cabin, near present-day Sallisaw, which still stands today. Educationally, what would become the Skin Bayou District provided a range of educational options for those arriving from the East.[13]

Because the Arkansas River served as the area's southern border and the Sallisaw Creek flowed from it, the area teemed with fish. Streams "abounded" with black bass, perch, crappie, and several kinds of catfish.[14] These families of fish also lived in the waterways of the Tennessee River that flowed through the Old Nation. Deer, antelope, bears, wild turkeys, black wolves, wildcats, quail, and wild fowl roamed the forests and prairies surrounding Dwight Mission.[15] Again, these same creatures had wandered the lands and served as food sources in the East. Hunting and fishing skills learned before arrival in the West were taught to a new generation of young people. And yet, the biodiversity of fish, game, and forage available in the East surpassed the biodiversity available to Cherokees in the West.[16]

Once the Indian Removal Act passed in 1830, many Cherokee families subjected to violence made the difficult decision to remove west against the wishes of Cherokee Nation officials, and education remained a point of contention. In 1834, Ayohka's older brother Teesee made the choice to move west. After a white man named Mullins stole Teesee's property and burned his home to the ground, he arranged to move with his family. Teesee's 1834 choice overlapped with the arrival in the West of a larger body of Eastern immigrants, including Caroline Eliza Fields's family.[17]

As more people arrived from the East, educational expectations changed. Officials in the East, eager to discourage western migration, accused Western Cherokees of educational misdeeds and took advantage of the educational critiques that those arriving in the West offered. In January 1834, leaders of the Western Cherokees launched a defense against accusations by Eastern immigrants that they were refusing to provide educational services. Western Cherokees offered several explanations for the lack of schooling. First, Western Cherokees had only one school in operation, and that school was at capacity. Until they could place all thirty of the children whose families were requesting schooling, they refused to grant individual access. Second, they wanted to avoid placing in schools the white children who were not entitled to educational services. This suggests that people claiming to be Cherokee to take advantage of Cherokee social services were exploiting the disruptions of removal even more or that Western Cherokees were resistant to providing Cherokees with intermarried white spouses who brought children to those marriages with the limited schooling options available. Both were likely true. Even as Willstown residents moved west, debates over education and schooling moved with them. The arrival of families like that of Caroline Eliza Fields changed the expectations for schooling in the West.

Notwithstanding their efforts, the Long Removal Era amputated parts of Cherokee educational pasts and futures. Removal thrust Ageyutsa's and Climber of Trees' granddaughters into geographic and botanical classrooms a world away from theirs. Forced removal robbed the educational system of its elders and its wisest teachers while it ripped others away from their laboratories, archives, and libraries. It disrupted courtships, marriage ceremonies, and the birth of babies, thus depriving Cherokee people of part of the next generation of students and teachers. It subjected women and girls to sexual violence, especially in the camps awaiting removal, and eventually it led to educational reprogramming. The violence of the Long Removal Era caused many to distrust their neighbors. Many Cherokee people turned to alcohol to cope with forced dislocation, which in turn fueled the internal violence provoked by removal. As devastating as the Long Removal Era was to older educational systems collectively, families and communities carried an abridged archive and pedagogical tools with them to the West. Removal also resulted in the merging of competing educational systems, since some of those who had moved west before mass forced removal did so because they objected to the educational changes happening in the East and had hoped to preserve features of the previous educational system they valued.

As Cherokee families and towns worked to reestablish themselves in the West, Cherokee families and officials prioritized education, including massive investments in the education of girls. The educational paths each girl followed depended on a variety of conditions, none of which were fixed over time. In the immediate post-removal period, deprivation led many Cherokee people to make educational choices they might not have made before, choices they later chose to abandon when conditions improved. As people reestablished themselves, class, location, and later race served as the most critical factors in determining a family's educational choices, especially as these related to schooling. For those less interested in schooling and more interested in older educational systems, language, kinship connections, egalitarianism, community, and the land itself served as the guiding determinants to reconstructing those older systems. Removal acted as a centrifugal educational force, sending Cherokee people away from a core part of their educational center—their homelands in the East. But as powerful as that force was, it did not eliminate other powerful educational foundations rooted in kin and the language itself. It did not erase the knowledge of the landscape that was transferable to the West. Nor did it erase Cherokee connections to kin who remained in the East, those still living, learning, and growing in a reduced educational landscape.

For some students, the West potentially breathed new life into older curriculums. For young boys, the prospect of hunting bison on the plains may have reinvigorated their interest in the tales of bison hunting passed down by great-uncles; it renewed questions by all children about the ceremonies that invoked their historical relationships to buffalo.[18] Western Cherokees taught others about those older dances.[19] Ayohka may have written down the vocabulary and sentences for those eager to learn these old curriculums revitalized in the West. The practical purposes of these old dances likely led children to listen more closely to elders when they described the buffalo dance.[20] Some aspects of older curriculums and ceremonies seemed more salient in the West than they had been the previous decades in the East. The move to the West, regardless of the conditions under which one made the journey, provided moments of educational wonder and possibility for its youngest members.

Removal, notwithstanding when it took place, continued to produce educational shockwaves. Missionaries associated with Cherokees in the West lamented the impact of the Treaty of 1828, which forced them to suspend their operations and relocate. Just before removal west from Arkansas into Indian Territory, Dwight Mission served 60 residential students and another 30 day-school students. Their counterparts in the East, operating six mission schools, counted 180 scholars.[21] Both groups of missionaries bemoaned the educational impacts of continued pressures on Cherokee people to remove. Missionaries in the West worried that without the removal of those remaining in the East, the mission stations in the West might fail, while in the East, "some of the schools have . . . been affected by agitation occasioned by the apprehension of being removed to the West."[22] Within just the American Board of Commissioners for Foreign Missions, removal produced competing attitudes among the missionaries, but their thoughts and emotions on removal failed to capture the full range of deliberations, calculations, and coercions faced by 16,000 Cherokee people. Those diverse assessments led Cherokee people to trickle westward until the forced deluge in 1838.

Caroline Eliza Fields's family was part of the trickle, while Caroline Matilda Fields's family arrived in the flood. Like Ayohka's family, Caroline Eliza's parents arrived in Indian Territory before universal forced removal began in 1838. The family signed up for removal in 1833 and arrived in the West by 1834. She was just five years old when her family moved; Ayohka had been around ten, just a few years older, when her family had moved not a decade earlier. Of the Cherokee families who signed up to move with their 306 boys and 265 girls under ten in 1833, women exclusively headed twenty-five of the families that arrived in Indian Territory in 1834.[23] Women who made the decision to remove west earlier than their counterparts may have done so as an act of educational resistance to an international institutionalized policy of schooling intent on reshaping Cherokee women's rights related to marriage, husbands, and child-rearing.

And yet, when girls like Ayohka and Caroline Eliza arrived, life in the West was not free from its own matrilineal and matrilocal modifications. When Indian agent C. C. Trowbridge traveled among the Western Cherokees in the early 1820s, he recorded Cherokee people's adaptations to federal policies. In addition to recording the vast knowledge of older educational practices among those living in the West, including the continued power of the laws of kinship, mothers still passed clans to their children and thus their Cherokee identity. Trowbridge paid special attention to how children were raised. *Anitsutsa* (boys), he noted, reached adulthood when "they could procure a subsistence for themselves.... Boys and girls are treated with the same affection & Governed with the same strictness in all families—the one being under the direction & care of the father and the other bound to obey the mother & receive from her the instruction necessary to their situation & sex."[24] Families in the West acknowledged the place fathers now played in the daily lives of their children, a role previously occupied by matrilineal uncles. Despite this change, Cherokee mothers still educated their children and exercised authority over their lives.

When it came to marriage practices, Trowbridge recorded uncertainty. The betrothal, he described, remained consistent with older practices:

> It was formally customary to place a kind of bench before the door of a house where young unmarried females lived. Young lovers who are desirous to ascertain the disposition of their mistresses toward them, were in the habit of killing a deer and carrying it to the house where it was thrown up on the bench in such a manner as to make a noise which awakened the attention of the girl within. If she came out and received the offering & added these to an invitation for him to enter the house, it was accepted & considered a favorable omen.

According to Trowbridge, a man still sent presents to the family of the woman he hoped to marry. If the family accepted the presents, the proposal had been accepted and he could "receive" his wife. In more ambiguous language, Trowbridge wrote, "She was compelled to submit to the will of her parents, whether she felt any affection for the lover or not. Her father's word was law to her and it could not be disobeyed."[25]

On the one hand, the change suggests exactly what non-Native and some Native reformers and educators hoped for: Cherokee women beholden to their fathers, their marital choices not their own. On the other hand, the semantic shift from parents making decisions ("She was compelled to submit to the will of her parents") to only fathers doing so ("Her father's word was law") indicates something less clear-cut. Decisions were being made behind closed doors in consultation with parents. That did not necessarily mean an unmarried woman's thoughts and feelings were excluded from the consultation. It also did not preclude a strong role for mothers in these determinations, given that earlier in his account Trowbridge made clear that daughters were "bound to obey the mother & receive from her the instruction necessary to their situation & sex." However, it did suggest that fathers were taking on the intermediary roles that uncles had previously exercised as spokespeople to those with different educational backgrounds, not unlike some of their counterparts in the East.[26] What Trowbridge's interviewees may have been implying (or may not have understood) is that families made decisions together, fathers provided the public declarations of the family's intentions, and once those declarations were made by "heads of household," men seeking marriage should not question them. Still, a troubling possibility existed for some girls: becoming economic and sexual pawns in systems no longer designed for their protection and autonomy.[27]

Additionally, if the last few decades had taught Cherokee people anything, whom women married—especially non-Native men—had consequences not just at the family level but for the community more broadly.[28] Western Cherokees may have been dealing with intermarried whites trying to take advantage of schooling opportunities meant for Cherokee children. Intermarried partners, especially men, "had more efficient access to the land and its resources after gaining the community's trust, thus speeding the processes of colonization."[29] Those who removed west under the treaties of 1817 and 1819 likely knew that intermarried white men had used their marriages and marital authority in the East to take individual allotments of land "through right of wife," thereby siphoning off communal lands from the larger body of Cherokee people who remained.[30] They also knew many of the Cherokee families who had taken 640-acre reserves under the treaties of 1817 and 1819, to secure their rights to lands in the East, had been violently and unscrupulously dispossessed of those lands within a few years. Some of these intermarried families did "find ways of building community with those they displaced." Some "also faced terrible experiences and laboured under oppressive conditions." Some "formed lasting alliances of kinship, love, and fierce friendship." But during the Long Removal Era, due to force, coercion, trickery, or other nonconsensual means, Cherokee people lost lives, lands, and livelihoods because of non-Indigenous appropriations of lands and territories.[31] In response to these conditions, the Cherokee

Nation passed a law in the East in 1829 requiring those who removed west or took reserves in 1819 to forfeit their citizenship rights.

Women's marital decisions, alongside those related to land reserves, remained educational battlegrounds. Despite missionaries' efforts to curb the practice, Cherokee women in the West still left dissatisfying marriages as they saw fit.[32] When they did so, the children remained with their mother. This situation also undercuts the supposed power of fathers. If mothers and daughters objected to the marital decisions that fathers were making on behalf of daughters, mothers would simply divorce those men and make decisions without them.

Reading Trowbridge's account holistically, mothers still exercised educational influence over their children, especially their daughters. What did this mean for daughters whose mothers and fathers had adopted the newer curriculums offered by missionaries and government officials? In those families, were girls more likely to be discouraged from marrying Cherokee men or Cherokee men of a certain kind? Cherokee boys in those families may have received strong educational messages about how their worth was defined in relationship to white men. In the years ahead, institutional affiliations, whether at missions like Dwight or the Cherokee seminaries, which would open in the 1850s, became the prime determinant of who married whom for a subset of Cherokee people.[33]

In the meantime, schooling and education remained both fragile and flexible in the West. Before removal to Indian Territory, an Arkansas village just a tributary away from Dwight led by Cherokee chief Takatoka had "from the first fostered a settled opposition to schools and the gospel and [kept] the people of his village with their children from instruction."[34] Ayohka's and her family's activities in the early years in Indian Territory document some of the educational changes that had seeped into the lives of Western Cherokees. Ayohka and her father had laid the groundwork for old intellectual traditions to move forward in time, through writings on cave walls in the East and in the thousands of pages of notebooks of ceremonial leaders and medicine keepers that would follow in the years ahead. Sequoyah's architectural choice in 1829 to build a notched, horizontal log building in the style of American settlers' homes ubiquitous across the Eastern United States supports the intellectual flexibility Cherokee people like Sequoyah used in making decisions. The community where Sequoyah grew to adulthood, Climber of Trees' world, ignored or resisted architectural changes for nearly the entirety of the eighteenth century, prioritizing building and rebuilding homes on the same spot and in basically the same style as what had stood there before.[35] It's possible that those structures, rebuilt again and again in the East, were not meant to be built somewhere other than in the homelands.

The new neighborhood layouts that abandoned multifamily towns with shared fields, both in the East and West, and the loss of some ceremonies may have also prevented Cherokee people from carrying out the educational protocols necessary for those structures to be built. New landscapes may have required new ceremonies and new architectural approaches to those educational spaces.

When leaders like Takatoka passed away, missionaries likely saw potential entryways into those communities through bilingual education. Once Ayohka and Sequoyah arrived in the West, they offered an alternative form of schooling. In 1826, the *Arkansas Gazette* reported on the accomplishment and noted that, for at least two years, the Cherokee people's interest in the syllabary increased, enabling "Cherokees in Wills Valley and their countrymen beyond the Mississippi, 500 miles apart to communicate."[36] The Glass, who had removed west early, sought out the education Sequoyah offered and wrote letters to the East in the years that followed. Teesee, Sequoyah's son, entered caves in Wills Valley to record other events in syllabary. Ayohka reached her teenage years close to her parents, as Sequoyah helped negotiate for a bilingual printing press in the Treaty of 1828. Once again, missionaries and Cherokee converts ultimately controlled the printing press. Because missionaries, in theory, hoped to reach a wider swath of Cherokee congregants, they may have recognized the need to adjust their curriculums in order to reach those resistant to some subjects potentially provided by schooling but not others.

As was the case in the East, language and language labor continued to pose challenges for missionaries. The missionaries sought translators who would relay messages about theology without question, but many of the bilingual translators often created discomfort and raised suspicions among the missionaries. Cephas Washburn, who relocated to the West from Brainerd and wrote an account of his time among the Cherokees at Dwight Mission in Arkansas, exoticized his interpreter and blamed him for his distraction from preaching: "The interpreter, a tawny son of the forest, took his seat by my side. I announced my text. The interpreter in strange tones repeated it to the people. I then uttered the first sentence of my discourse and stopped short. Again the strange sounds commenced, and my whole attention was attracted by them. When he ceased I had entirely forgotten the words I had spoken. I was again obliged to speak, but I knew it could have no connection with the foregoing sentences." Rather than a story of overcoming a new experience of using interpreters to gain comfort, Washburn described the difficulties of finding "competent interpreters" who could produce honest interpretations.[37]

Washburn based his distrust on an interpreter's challenge to his educational authority. When Washburn told an interpreter to tell congregants "that, in the sight of God, there are but two kinds of people," the interpreter interjected, "But I do not believe him. I believe there are three kinds; the good people, the bad people, and a middle kind, that are neither good nor bad, just like myself." The interpreter refused to abandon his view or spread without question a binary view of the world, rooted in good and evil. Instead, he insisted on a view of the world that accounted for human complexity, a teaching consistent with older educational frameworks.[38]

Despite benefiting from the older pedagogies embodied in women, some female missionaries shared these attitudes toward interpreters. When Cassandra Lockwood traveled to Dwight Mission, she rested at the edge of the Western Cherokee Nation, where she relied on a Black woman who was "the only person among [those within the town] who could serve as an interpreter." When Lockwood arrived at Dwight, Cherokee women often sold "quilts, lace, [and] muslin. Not one of these Cherokee women could speak or understand English and the girls of the school would act as interpreter." She echoed Washburn when she lamented the "difficulty . . . in giving instruction through an interpreter. It is very desirable to have a pious interpreter lest a different coloring be given to the truth from what is intended." She resented the "time . . . consumed in giving instruction in this way and the force of the sentences . . . lost by the unnatural pauses." And when she traveled out of the Nation, it was an "experienced Cherokee woman" who carried Lockwood's baby in a sling around her neck.[39] Black Cherokee women, Cherokee girls, and Cherokee women eased her transition and enabled her work, but it was Cherokee translators who likely resisted missionaries' efforts to undo some features of those educational foundations that Lockwood objected to.

In the years leading up to and immediately following forced removal, educational options resembled the options in the East; missionaries dominated schooling, but education remained available to everyone. In 1835, as the Cherokee Nation in the East was facing down the next stage of its removal crisis, the American Board of Commissioners for Foreign Missions operated three mission stations in the west: Dwight, Fairfield on Sallisaw Creek located near the Webbers' home, and Union Mission, which ceased operations that year. The Methodists operated three schools, and the Baptists operated one. That year, the Western Cherokees had assumed control of Fairfield.[40]

School demographics shifted quickly after the Treaty Party signed the Treaty of New Echota in December 1835. In that year, Dwight reported forty-four male "scholars," including five Muscogee students, thirty female "scholars," including seven Muscogee, and one Osage student. They also included the numbers in the infant school, only two of whom were Indian; the other twelve were white students, almost certainly a large number of the missionaries' own children. This also suggests that even Cherokee families kept their youngest children at home through their formative years. The numbers in January 1836 included thirty-seven male students and thirty-two female students. For at least one year while Samuel Worcester was in residence, the children received bilingual education. Since these numbers were not included in the report the year prior to or following this, the 1836 report stands out as an anomaly.[41] In 1837, the number of male students dropped to thirty-two, and the number of female students remained at thirty-two.[42] As forced emigration neared, female student numbers crept up.

Many of the families who had resided close together in the East sought out former neighbors and kin in the West. Some families communicated their spatial existence to outsiders much as they always had, in proximity to water—"on Little Sallisaw [Creek], on Lees Creek." But more recent ways of reckoning the center of their communities also took shape in documents immediately before and after removal. People also articulated (or were encouraged to orient) their locations in relationship to key leaders in their communities, men who had stores or established properties—"about 6 miles from John Benges, on Little Sallisaw"; "about five miles from [John] Benges on Lees Creek." John Benge served as a detachment leader during forced removal. Benge maintained kin and political connections to Western Cherokees, and his detachment landed at Mrs. William Webber's farm in Webber's Falls. The Webbers had lived in Wills Valley before their removal. William Webber, whose father's first name lent itself to the name of Wills Valley, had died the year before. Many Cherokee people who faced forced removal chose to organize their post-removal lives in the orbit of men like Benge and Webber. Others reported their spatial existence in relationship to existing institutions, including Dwight Mission—"about one mile & a half from Dwight Mission on Sallisaw," "about one miles a half from Dwight Mission on Sallisaw and now lived with Head Eater."[43]

When more people arrived, despite an opportunity to remake communities and their associated classrooms in a variety of ways, Cherokee people did not uniformly create concentrated towns along waterways, which would have enabled them to easily farm, commune, and educate their children collectively. Instead, they chose a range of spatial organizations that in many instances reinforced older classroom spaces, deviated from them, or created hybrid classrooms, with elements of old and new. In 1840, the Moravians passed one "field belonging to the Indian town & is called the town-field. It contains several hundred acres, but is not under cultivation. Each family has a lot of five, or six or more acres, which is separate from an adjoining lot by a narrow strip of uncultivated land. It seems that each family cultivates its own lot. As I passed this field to-day I saw a Cherokee man plowing with a single ox in his plow."[44] This particular town merged the old and the new.

The shared field harkened back to an educational system that Ageyutsa and Climber of Trees would have recognized. It created a shared space where families living in the community would have gathered for communal work that centered on corn. Even the presence of men to help clear the fields wasn't completely foreign, but the isolated work of a lone man without women overseeing their children and the other men assisting these efforts would have been a strange sight for both girls. And yet, the shared field made communal labor a possibility. If a neighbor showed up to the field, they likely would have assisted the lone man if he was in need, and plowing with oxen often required several people to do so effectively.

In other places throughout the Nation, many people chose newer dispersed living patterns common after the American Revolution. Isolating one's family came at an educational cost within an older educational framework. Dispersed living divided experts and the community library and archives across individual families and across the Nation. The telling of community narratives required one family to remember much more than living collectively and gathering for shared ceremonies had previously required. Students from previous generations eager to advance their learning could easily identify expert teachers in their communities. The educational access that girls like Ageyutsa had by watching the feather cape makers from afar, even as she completed other educational tasks, was made more difficult with these new spatial configurations. Even those Cherokee people without common fields and with individual family boundaries often chose to live near extended communities and kin. After he emigrated, Teesee lived "about a half mile from John Benges." Sallie and Sequoyah lived within walking distance, just "one mile from Benges."[45] Girls coming of age on dispersed homesteads had far less knowledge of the advanced training they might pursue if no one in their immediate families modeled those skills for them. And if they were sent to boarding schools, their access decreased even more.

Two clear poles of education had taken shape in the Cherokee Nation during the Long Removal Era. Elite Cherokee families, most of them the products of intermarriage, embraced schooling with zeal. Because many of these families used the labor of enslaved people for agricultural and domestic tasks, elite women looked to other spaces to educate their children. Many chose to educate young children close to home at first, but when their primary educational years began, parents would send their children to boarding schools, where they focused on mastery of basic spelling, reading, and arithmetic. Other families relied on older pedagogical practices and took advantage of schooling when it made sense and was accessible to them.

Even with the financial support allocated in the Treaty of 1828, Dwight Mission and the children to whom it provided schooling faced challenges. In 1834, the same year Caroline Eliza Fields's family arrived in the West, death plagued Dwight Mission.[46] And over the years, missionaries struggled to find "competent interpreters" or those they could trust to produce precise translations.[47] Reverend Jacob Hitchcock attempted to overcome this challenge by having a lithograph of the syllabary printed in Boston for use at the boys' school at Dwight. He intended to use itinerant "native teachers" to "aid Cherokee families in reading their own language." This occurred the same year Samuel Worcester was temporarily at the station to set up the printing press at Union Mission.[48] These efforts also reflected the desire by people in the West to have bilingual education available to their children and the missionaries' attempts to fulfill the wishes of families. The missionaries, as they had in the East, wanted to control the education of their own translators for this work. As in the East, they initially focused these efforts on boys, even though girls increasingly occupied schools in higher numbers and performed the unpaid language labor of their families and institutions.

When Eastern Cherokees forcibly removed arrived in the area, political structures existed, schools existed, and a somewhat familiar geography surrounded them. These individual and structural resources made Cherokees' transition somewhat easier. When the Moravian missionaries arrived in the West in October 1838 in advance of the mass of forcibly removed Cherokee people, they received respite at an inn run by Presbyterian Cherokee-speaking Native women, which they deemed up to their standards. They also took advantage of Stand Watie's hospitality, who had removed early with the Treaty Party, before traveling to Park Hill to meet with Samuel Worcester and Elias Boudinot.[49]

The Moravians were direct beneficiaries of multiple strands of Cherokee educational history and Cherokee educational commitments. The relationships they had forged with leading Cherokee families through their educational inroads in the East enabled them to travel west and receive accommodations. When they arrived in the Nation, they had not received a permit from the federal Indian agent to begin a mission. Not only did one of their congregants advise them to buy a home in a Cherokee's name in order to establish their residence, but he also assured them that any hostility or resistance toward missionaries by Cherokee people would be overcome by their desire for teachers.[50]

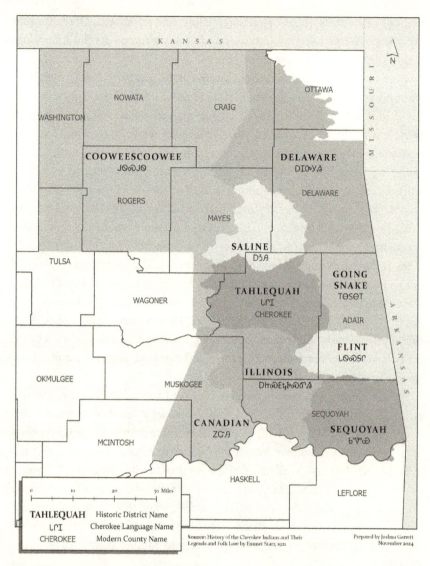

Political districts within the Cherokee Nation, 1851 to 1906. The National
Council renamed the Skin Bayou District the Sequoyah District in 1851.
Courtesy of Joshua Garrett.

The missionaries reported the "civilized" activities of many of the Cherokee people they interacted with, including the massive corn crop produced by Stand Watie and also Susannah Ridge's intention to move from her current location in order to build a flour mill and sawmill. They noted, "Only a small portion of the inhabitants here busy themselves with hunting, which here and there is still very good." Paradoxically, it was the generosity of Cherokee people's hunting that supplemented the missionaries—"half of a deer from Hicks", bear meat from Cherokee hunters—as they reestablished themselves.[51]

The missionaries also continued to desire the labor and rely on the contributions of Cherokee women, often—Cherokee speaking women—to flourish. Missionaries had benefited from the continuation of Cherokee women's economic independence when they sought rest at the tavern. It was their congregant's daughter who accompanied them to her father so he could advise them on how to circumvent laws that would have prevented them from establishing themselves in Indian Territory. And once established, they hoped to obtain the free labor of a Cherokee girl to serve as an assistant to Sister Vogler; they had to settle for Brother Copeland's daughter's help until they could secure a Cherokee girl. They preferred the free labor of Cherokee girls over the free labor of their own children.[52]

Immediately after forced removal, Cherokee people's most pressing needs were not related to schooling but to survival. They needed to recover from the arduous journey, but life in the West didn't offer people who were somewhat physically healthy that option.[53] The removal treaty provided only a year's worth of rations, so Cherokee people urgently needed to locate lands where they could construct homes and begin preparing the fields for crops.

When the Eastern emigrants arrived, they brought their own government, treaty negotiations, and missionary educators with them. In the years that followed, they would have to reconcile how to move forward as groups who had negotiated separate treaties, one of which remained contested until 1846, but also figure out how to combine resources and unify. Unlike the Treaty of 1828, the Treaty of New Echota in 1835 did not leave educational control to the federal government. It did, however, provide the budgets and a plan for a national public school system. That system would place new pressures on mission stations like Dwight in the years that followed. With the 1841 Public School Act, the Cherokee Nation began funding teachers and supplying materials to communities that provided a school building for a public school.

In the period immediately before forced removal, the enrollment numbers at Dwight Mission had remained somewhat balanced, though shifting slightly in favor of girls. After a fire destroyed the boys' building in December 1839, just as forced removal concluded, the boys' enrollments plummeted.[54] However, rather than seek supplemental schooling for boys, throughout 1840, families affiliated with the Moravians increasingly called upon them to establish a girls' school. The Moravians, too, struggled to keep boys enrolled. In 1841, "the boys' school commended with 18 scholars, 10 or 12 being absent. . . . The girls school commended with 33 scholars."[55]

Many families wanted to send their boys to school but instead chose to continue the "civilizing" educational practices promoted by missionaries and government officials, to displace women from their agricultural classrooms and insert boys and men in their place. Boys were "kept away by being obligated to assist in planting corn."[56] Another boy died when he was "struck by lightning while gathering strawberries with other boys."[57] Families may have kept sons closer to home due to labor shortages, but a sizable portion of the population no longer viewed their daughters as caretakers of the land and agricultural experts. They did see women as intellectual beings with an aptitude for new skills just like Wurteh and Ayohka.

Even after the boys' building reopened at Dwight in 1841, the numbers at the mission grew more lopsided in the years that followed. In 1842, there were thirty-six female students and only one male student listed. In July 1843, the school enrolled a total number of fifty students; forty-eight of those were girls and only two were boys.[58] In some cases, the education that Cherokee people sought for their daughters was quite specific. "[William] Henry brought Sarah Jane, his daughter, to live with us for awhile because Mother Martha especially wants her to be introduced to proper housekeeping. Her parents are willing to provide her clothing."[59]

In addition to instruction in how to manage a domestic space, schools provided a particular kind of academic curriculum as told through the materials and textbooks they purchased. Whereas in the pre-removal period, missions relied heavily on the Bible, hymns, and an occasional Webster's spelling book provided by a benefactor, the 1841 Cherokee Nation Public School Act changed the textbook offerings available at all schools, including Dwight Mission. The Cherokee Nation's superintendent of public schools purchased a variety of textbooks from the Northeast, which provided more robust secular academic offerings. In 1842, Dwight Mission received copies of *Mitchell's Geography, Introduction to the National Spelling Books, Primers, First Arithmetic,* and *Second Reading Book.* The classroom supplies included prisms, ream paper, slate pencils, and quills. In 1844, Dwight Mission secured copies of *The Rollo Code of Morals,* first published in 1841, which reinforced the mission's morals.

The Rollo series of books, written by Congregationalist minister Jacob Abbott, were one of the first series of books aimed at early readers, with the book's namesake as the central male character. In the books, Rollo learns at home and school, a notion that likely would have resonated with Cherokee girls. *The Rollo Code of Morals* reinforced a hierarchy that privileged men over women, husbands over wives, wives over children, and older children over younger children. Girls at Dwight, including Caroline Eliza Fields, learned that "there is a sort of gradation, in rank, among the children of a family. That is some are older, wiser, more prudent, and more careful; others are younger, weaker, more inexperienced, and more dependent. This difference of position and character gives rise to a variety of different duties." In the Rollo books, Rollo learns that self-discipline helps one avoid physical punishment, and that children should obey their parents to avoid having their meals withheld. Just a few years earlier, Cherokee mothers in the East had removed their children from mission schools if they even heard a rumor that their children lacked for food. The federal government and missions actively worked to teach Cherokee people, including the children themselves, they were "partial," instead of "part."[60] These teachings stood at odds with the older Cherokee-centered pedagogies that expressed an ethics of care that required providing nourishment for another and that viewed children as potential teachers to adults and as people called to tasks whom adults needed to nurture.

Additionally, the *Rollo Code* took aim, once again, at Cherokee people's sexual autonomy: "The most degraded, and miserable, and wretched, men and women, that are to be found in the world, are made so by the consequences of impurity." The book refused to name what these impure sins were, "which may be committed by the young ... [and] cannot be particularly explained to them, because our instinctive sense of modesty and propriety forbids mentioning them as well as practicing them."[61] When it came to perceived sexual improprieties, children and youth were told that they should instinctively know which behaviors were sinful. Girls at Dwight Mission received the message that the sexual autonomy exercised by many of their grandmothers when they entered relationships with their non-Native grandfathers was sinful.

Dwight Mission's church services reinforced similar ideas to its congregants. Each year the church reinscribed its covenant and its confession of faith in its records and among its members. Families attending church services at Dwight likely received constant messaging about their moral expectations. They may have been privy to the church trials held that led to the excommunication of some members and the suspension of others. The church also "withdrew

Christian fellowship" from some, the adult equivalent of withholding dinner from Rollo for not obeying his father. Those excommunications and suspensions nearly always focused on perceived sexual deviance: sneaking into someone's room at night or having sex outside of marriage. The church expected its members and its students to marry within the church and have their nuptials recorded by church officials, just as federal policy had endorsed decades earlier.[62] A school of Cherokee children likely heard this message loud and clear.[63]

Dwight Mission girls produced essays that indicated religious principles guided part of their intellectual pursuits. They may have been responding to the *Rollo Code*'s student prompts, but their work also reflected a diversity of interests. They wrote essays focused on behaviors ("Habits," "The Improvement of Our Families," "Meditation"), emotions ("True Happiness," "Hope"), and seasons (two essays titled "Spring"). Nearly all the essays infused Christianity into the content or made it the central focus, as was the case with the essay titled "The Bible is the best of all books."[64]

The girls may have taken comfort in the belief that they had individual control over part of their worlds, or that God did, in what increasingly became a world out of balance with past traditions and practices and with the death and dislocation wrought by removal. In the post–forced removal Cherokee Nation, which had deeply divided Cherokee people and resulted in a civil war among Cherokee people following forced removal, students learned new lessons about community and the perils that lay within communities. This new curriculum was gendered and class-dependent. Narcissa Chisholm, who resided in the southernmost area of the Cherokee Nation in the 1840s and attended Dwight Mission for a time, "learned to hate the singing of the katydids and the grasshoppers and the other noisy insects at night that prevented us from hearing the approach of the intruders."[65] Some girls began to listen differently and more attentively to the sounds of their environment, not to hear the difference between an eastern or western whippoorwill, but to listen for and recognize the dangers of their human counterparts in a place where new political and legal voids existed. During the Long Removal Era, the people to fear now included other Cherokees.

The post-removal period, filled with political violence, led the Cherokee Nation to pass a series of laws related to those threats. In October 1841, the Cherokee National Council passed a law enabling "neighborhoods" that "deem it necessary" to organize "patrol companies." Two days later, it passed "An Act prohibiting the carrying of [concealed] Weapons." In February 1841, the Moravians reported the execution of a young man in their neighborhood for murder.[66] Much of the violence during this period involved men.

Even if men were at the center of that violence, women were not free from it. In October 1841, Walter Foreman, a former student of the Moravians at Spring-place in the East, who had likely witnessed the everyday domestic violence perpetrated at the Vann Plantation and the associated curriculum, "stabbed his wife in the crown of the head, the point of the knife entering her tongue."[67] In late 1840, "a murder had been committed the night before not more than 1/7 of a mile from [the Moravians], at a house where several woman [*sic*] live and keep whiskey for sale & drinking is carried on to great excess & we frequently hear them hooping all night." The very next night another murder took place, perhaps in retaliation for the previous murder. During the violence, women sought safety at the mission.[68]

Missions like Springplace in the East or Dwight Mission in the West could foster or turn a blind eye to violence, but they could also provide a temporary refuge from it, as they had in the East for women like Catharine Brown, the first Cherokee Christian convert at Brainerd.[69] As some girls learned to fear their neighbors, families may have used schooling as a form of protection for their daughters. Instead of looking to elder women who had served as sentinels, pro-tecting fields and warning the community of potential danger, new generations of Cherokee people turned to missions for the protections formerly offered by educated and trained Cherokee specialists and kin. Because all girls faced greater threats of sexual violence and wealthy families increasingly relied less on women's agricultural labor for their economic well-being, elite Cherokee families may have viewed missions as places of refuge for girls when political violence was ripping through the Nation.

At the same moment that mission schools shielded some Cherokee girls from internecine violence, curriculums at the mission stations normalized other kinds of violence. Nearly all the children attending the Dwight Mission in the 1840s came from a core group of ten Cherokee families, all of whom were slaveholding and most of whom had marital and economic ties to the rest.[70] The *Rollo Code* included a section that reminded students when physical punishments were warranted and who could dole them out: "Some persons have a right to punish, and some have not. Parents have a right to punish their children, by nature, and by the law of God. Guardians have this right; and mas-ters are empowered to punish their apprentices, by the law of the land. Teachers have it by delegation,—that is, parents and guardians, by sending the children to school, delegate or commit the power to punish them to the teacher."[71] Caroline Eliza Fields and her counterparts, including fellow student Caroline Matilda Fields, learned that all these individuals had the right to discipline. One day many of the students would have the right to discipline and punish enslaved people owned by their families. Some of Dwight Mission's girls may have already known the names of the enslaved Black people they would one day inherit. Mary and Susan Gunter descended from John Gunter Sr., their great-grandfather, whose 1833 will contained specific instructions for

> Peggy, Peter, Winne, Sucky, Sucky's children Viney and Lucy, and all increase,
> Olivar, Nero, Judah, Amy, Old Lucy, And all increase,
> Bill, Andrew, Calvin, Polly, Peggy, And all increase,
> Tom, Bobb, Mary, Augustis, Daniel, China, And all increase,
> Aaron, Jacob, Cloe, Mary, and all increase,
> Sophy, Jack, Abram, Bolivar, Rachel, Bonaparte, and all increase,
> Enslaved people he owned and their future children, should be distributed amongst his children.

It also contained a provision dictating that one of his daughters would not receive her inheritance, which included Black people, until such time as she divorced her husband. One of his sons wrote a very similar will in 1842. In his will, in addition to distributing Bill, Grace, Bessie, Alfred, Jack, Rachel, Dred, Caroline, Sylvia, Sophia, Mary, Solomon, Suce, and Ara and his other property among his relatives in "ten equal shares," it required his daughters "be sent to school until they obtain a common English Education. Reading, Writing, Arithmetic, Grammar & Geography." Mary and Susan's grandfather Samuel owned twenty-two enslaved people at the time of the 1835 census. Their father George owned seven enslaved people.[72] In the Gunter family, race, economics, and education all intertwined in legal documents sworn before legal agents and God.

The education at Dwight Mission merged these curriculums as well. Rather than use the 1828 math book by Catharine Beecher, whose family had associations with Cherokee people, Dwight Mission used Joseph Ray's *Little Arithmetic* and *Large Arithmetic* while Susan, Mary, Caroline Eliza, and Caroline Matilda were students. The latter arithmetic book, "nearly identical in content" to Beecher's book, marketed itself as a text focused on the skills required to conduct business, including skills that privileged the financial worlds of the United States. Ray, unlike the Beecher family, steered clear of public statements on slavery.[73] Ray's text focused on a variety of weights and measures, including those needed by apothecaries, vendors of dry goods, surveyors, and tavern keepers selling alcohol. It also aided students in understanding how to work with "federal money," which included addition and subtraction involving dollars and quarters. Additionally, an entire section focused on calculating interest. Given the overwhelming number of female students at the school, it raises the question, Who was receiving the advanced math curriculum? Were these books set aside for male students, or were elite Cherokee girls receiving an advanced curriculum in business math that would enable them to continue to do as Cherokee women had always done—exercise control over their financial lives?

Based on the numbers of books alone and the assumption that neither Dwight Mission nor the Cherokee Nation had the budgets to order surplus books, a small subset of girls received a math education that would have enabled them to run a variety of businesses. Like Cherokee women of previous generations, some Cherokee women received an education that provided them with the skills to adapt to changing economic realities.

And yet, for these women, the changed economic reality in their families and in the Cherokee Nation more broadly included plantations and the labor of enslaved people. Enslaved Black people, possibly relatives of Bill, Grace, Bessie, Alfred, Jack, Rachel, Dred, Caroline, Sylvia, Sophia, Mary, Solomon, Suce, and Ara, made financing Mary and Susan's education possible. They made some measure of the girls' safety possible, even as the educational access available to enslaved Black people became more precarious.

In contrast to the situation in the mission stations in the East, which operated in close proximity to wealthy Cherokee-owned plantations and aimed to offer coeducation but often favored boys' educational opportunities, the girls at Dwight substantially outnumbered the boys in the years following forced removal. While Eastern missions like Springplace offered some degree of racial diversity, due to their proximity to or their assistance from enslaved African-descended peoples, Dwight's records make little mention of the presence of enslaved or free African Cherokees. Not only were girls at Dwight receiving the business training to operate their families' plantations if necessary, but they were doing so without the constant presence of and intimacy with the very people who would enable their continued prosperity.

Schooling often physically separated a subset of Cherokee girls from the people whose lives they would learn to properly quantify. In this educational context, women mastered the math necessary to buy and sell dry goods, wine, land, and people. For some of the girls, this curriculum likely transformed their relationships to enslaved people, "a relation that was, above all, economic at its foundation," and in Susan and Mary's case, an inheritance.[74] Even though this was a specialized curriculum for an elite group of Cherokee girls and boys, the general concepts that privileged measuring and selling property, buying and selling goods, and farm production would continue unabated.

Although the official position of the American Board of Commissioners for Foreign Missions was that slavery was a gross violation, missionaries agreed to remain mute on the issue. No slave owners at Dwight had Christian fellowship withheld from them, and their children certainly did not have schooling withheld.[75] In the years that followed, one missionary who had advocated for abolition before the Civil War and whose father had expelled slaveholding members from his congregation in 1852 created textbooks that reinforced the continuation and normalization of slaveholding.[76] Bilingual missionary John Jones, a staunch advocate of bilingual education who had angered Cherokee elites for his abolitionism, produced a bilingual arithmetic textbook in 1870 that devised word problems that invoked systems predicated on slavery: "A plantation in Cuba was sold for 7,011,608 dollars, and the amount was divided among 8 persons. What was paid to each person? Ans. 876,451 dollars."[77] Cuba didn't outlaw the slave trade until 1867, nor did it abolish slavery until 1880. Even when children in schools in the Cherokee Nation had little or no direct connections to slavery, the curriculum provided by the schools—and even provided by abolitionists—emphasized the profitability and perceived mathematical benefits of slavery to Cherokee children from all walks of life.

Added to the political and social melee, in November 1842 twenty-five enslaved people from Joseph Vann's plantation in Webber's Falls, just over twenty miles from Dwight Mission, staged an escape.[78] The Vann family had hosted the Moravians in the East at Springplace. The Moravians had documented the intense violence that was associated with the Vann family, directed at both Cherokee women and enslaved people. The missionaries did little to intervene on behalf of the victims in the East. In the post-removal period, laws toward enslaved people hardened.[79] The same year the Cherokee Nation passed its Public School Act, seemingly universalizing education throughout the Nation, it also passed "An Act prohibiting the Teaching of Negroes to Read and Write."[80] This move stood in contrast to the educational possibilities that had existed for enslaved children who lived close to schools in the East. Members of the Vann family, the same family that had inadvertently created access to education for enslaved people in the East, approved the law denying the next generation of enslaved people educational access and criminalized the act for Cherokee people. If the law had been applied retroactively, the Vann family would have been compelled to pay between $1 and $500 in fines ($40 to over $20,000 in 2025 dollars). By sending their children to schools away from their plantations and to schools that didn't rely on the labor of enslaved people, as most had in the East, elite families could not be accused of aiding in the education of enslaved people.

Ironically, the Cherokees' educational attainments in the East had served as a direct threat to Southern state governments and plantation owners eager to see educational access cut off to people of color throughout the South. Although not a stated reason for removal, some state and federal leaders must have seen the irony of a Native nation obtaining near universal literacy at the same moment it sought to curb the educational possibilities for enslaved people.[81] Now in the West, with pressures from settlers reduced, the Cherokee Nation pursued the very policies that might have limited Cherokees' educational futures had they remained in the East.

Dwight Mission's curriculum grew to mutually reinforce ideas about race, economics, and systems of violence in service to systems predicated on slavery; as it elevated one economic activity and provided Susan and Mary Gunter the math skills necessary to perpetuate it, the curriculum continued another long pattern of missionaries undermining other women's economic autonomy. Most of the Western Cherokees moved west under provisions contained in the treaties of 1817 and 1819 that enticed "poor warriors" with "one rifle gun and ammunition, one blanket, and one brass kettle, or in lieu of the brass kettle, a beaver trap," to compensate them for property they might leave behind.[82] While those policies were aimed at men, that did not stop some Cherokee women from deciding to move west: some alone, some with young children, some with enslaved people, some without their husbands. When those women arrived in the West, they often made economic demands to reestablish their economic livelihoods.[83] Cherokee men, on behalf of women, continually sought a gristmill in the West to aid women's labor and equalize what had been given through treaties to Cherokee people still living in the East. The federal Indian agent, in contrast, wrote to DC that instead of providing a gristmill, the government should prioritize a cotton gin, which benefited men's economic interests and those of slaveholders.[84] Officials eventually built a gristmill at Dwight Mission in Arkansas, but this forced women uninterested in Christianity or in interacting with missionaries—or forced missionaries unwilling to interact with them— into unwanted encounters.[85] Around the same time, Ayohka's father operated a saltworks in Arkansas, while Sallie was continuing to document claims for her personal property losses in the East. The degree to which Sallie or Ayohka visited Dwight Mission or relied on its services is unclear.[86]

Some missionaries in the West had entirely resisted interacting with Cherokee women as autonomous economic actors. When a Cherokee woman arrived at the Union Mission, which served the Osages, to trade chickens for coffee and sugar, the interpreter said the missionary didn't "deal with the females" and sent her to one of the female missionaries. By limiting women's ability to foster a full range of economic relationships, missionaries could limit Cherokee women's economic and, by extension, political power. When missionaries at Dwight began their efforts to teach Cherokees to read the syllabary, they focused exclusively on boys, just like the Cherokee National Council had done in the East. National authorities and missionaries both may have worried what Cherokee women might accomplish if they had full access to Cherokee literacy and economic opportunities.

The Long Removal Era had taken a toll on Cherokee women's more universalized economic independence, especially those removing from Wills Valley, where women continued to assert distinct property rights from their husbands.[87] Even in the wake of removal, the collective economic skills of women and their children continued to help them recover from forced removal. In 1840, the Moravians reported, "A few days ago, a poor widow sent us a chair, quite nearly made by her son, earnestly requesting us to buy it, to enable her to buy some corn. She has been in her time in better circumstances; but at the time, when many poor Cherokees were taken from their homes by military force and obliged to leave their little all, this poor woman was among the number."[88] Just a few decades earlier, Wurteh and Sequoyah had likely worked collaboratively to bolster their family's economic situation.

The girls at Dwight confronted the attitudes toward some of these women in the teachings they received. In an essay titled "Hope," one student wrote about a widow, a husbandless mother, not as Wurteh, Ayohka's grandmother, existed but instead as a woman desperate "when she can get nothing to eat [who] hopes to find some way to get supplied."[89] Certainly, some of these children understood the irony of casting Cherokee widows as desperate. Indeed, a few of their grandmothers had taught them how to adjust their lives to maintain their economic independence, regardless of the presence of husbands. Maybe learning how to calculate compound interest was one thread of this legacy. But even as some aspects of their family relationships had changed, some of these girls may have questioned the accuracy of depicting any Cherokee woman as disempowered, let alone widows who stood in contrast to the Cherokee women of means they likely lived with and learned from when school was not in session.

Beyond debasing widows, the education and classroom activities of missions sent seemingly conflicting messages about the role of alcohol in the community.[90] On the one hand, their math books included sections that focused on weights and measures related to the sale and distribution of alcohol, while on the other hand, missionaries emphasized that those who drank alcohol displayed moral weakness. Students learned that profiting from goods and services, including human beings, through certain kinds of business transactions was amoral, but in other instances partaking in some of those goods would debase them. At least one of the girls witnessed the effects of alcohol firsthand and passed judgment accordingly in her written work.[91] The community's role or responsibility and care of one another disappeared, and individual weakness took its place. Before, the community had held annual ceremonies like Green Corn, which established restoration for all as one of its purposes, in order to begin the new year renewed to one another for the sake of the entire community, but after forced removal the church became an arbiter of its members' sins related to drinking and whiskey selling and of its students' behaviors when it came to alcohol. The girls learned to judge drinking and expel members who couldn't control their drinking, all while studying math that taught them how to measure, quantify, and profit from it.

Lessons in economics abounded at places like Dwight. Many of the earliest professional opportunities created by the schools in Indian Territory, including the Cherokee public schools, failed to benefit Cherokee people; schools still relied heavily on the educational skills of non-Native people, especially, though not exclusively, men. Sophia Sawyer, a former missionary at Brainerd and an outspoken advocate for Cherokee girls' education, moved to Indian Territory at the invitation of John Ridge. He provided a school building for her to educate his children and others in the area. When Cherokee people extrajudicially executed Ridge in 1839, Sawyer moved with the Ridge family across the border into Fayetteville, Arkansas. There, Sawyer opened her own school serving Native and non-Native students. By 1844, the Nation employed eighteen teachers, all of whom were men and sixteen of whom were not Cherokee. More than 20 percent of them were missionaries. Three of the men were citizens by intermarriage. One of the two Native teachers was William Vann, who had been an early beneficiary of his family's support of the education provided by the Moravians at Springplace in the East.[92] The following year the Nation provided education to 654 students at eighteen public schools, including a school operating at John Benge's home in the Skin Bayou District. By 1847, white Arkansas and Missouri residents sought the professional opportunities provided by the Cherokee Nation public schools, occupying a third of the total positions. Over half of the teachers were missionaries. Two women obtained positions that year, one Cherokee and one a missionary from the Baptist Mission Station operating in the Cherokee Nation. The Bell brothers, both Cherokee Nation citizens, had close ties to mission education; a number of their family members attended Dwight Mission throughout this period.[93]

Although non-Cherokees still dominated the teaching positions in the early schools approved by the Cherokee Nation, religious and national, eventually the Cherokee Nation took steps to undo this trend. In 1846, the Cherokee National Council passed legislation for the construction of the Male and Female Seminaries, which would serve as schools for Cherokee Nation youth to train to become teachers. Caroline Matilda Fields, another Dwight Mission student, would be one of the Female Seminary's first students. Dwight Mission's earliest alumni would provide more than half of the students in the seminaries' first years of operation.[94] The class divides that existed in schooling would simply continue in the years ahead, bolstered by the Nation supplementing the educational opportunities of its wealthiest citizens.

Dwight Mission laid the curricular groundwork for what was nearly an all-girls academic environment. In the years to follow, the Nation would take up the mantle from Dwight when it opened the Male and Female Seminaries in 1851. Earlier federal policies had encouraged intermarriage of Cherokee women with white men, and the seminary provided schooling for Cherokee girls that would prepare them for intermarriage, but they also elevated a class of Cherokee men as suitable partners. Students who attended the seminaries largely married one another.[95] The Cherokee seminaries encouraged marriage within, although many of the girls continued to marry non-Cherokee men.

When the Civil War broke out in 1861, most of the families bolstered by the labor of enslaved people moved south with the enslaved people they owned, beyond the boundaries of the Cherokee Nation.[96] When Caroline Matilda Fields's daughter Elinor recounted her mother's move to the Choctaw Nation "to escape the unsafe condition that existed in the Cherokee Nation brought on by the civil war," she named the other elite slaveholders whose families had helped her family flee to the safety of the Choctaw Nation under the cover of darkness. She described the volume of goods they were able to transport by oxen and wagon and the gold they had on hand.[97] What she did not mention was the role that enslaved people played in making that move possible. Caroline Matilda kept Elinor at home and out of the public schools, where she would have been exposed to a potentially diverse group of Cherokee children whose educational experiences and comfort in English would have been markedly different. Instead, Elinor had a mother who could provide a primary education of equivalent or better quality than most schools and a Nation willing to provide advanced schooling that rivaled the education available to most girls throughout the United States at the time. Caroline Matilda homeschooled her daughter until the age of fourteen, when she enrolled in the Cherokee Female Seminary.[98] Both mother and daughter married men who had received their education at the Cherokee Male Seminary.

The political science education that Caroline Matilda imparted to Elinor enabled her to articulate a sophisticated and nuanced understanding of the events that tore Cherokee people apart again during the Civil War. As a result of her mother's teaching, Elinor understood "there yet existed a factional feeling that originated in Georgia between the Ross and Ridge Boudinot factions prior to the moving of the Cherokee from east of the Mississippi river to the Indian Territory, and caused the assassination of my grandfather, Elias Boudinot, Major Ridge and his son John Ridge on June 20, 1839, and as my father was a southern sympathizer the civil war furnished an opportunity for renewal of persecutions by the opposing faction."[99]

Caroline Matilda had also shared with her daughter her contempt for the Pin Indians, "a band of Indians that had joined the northern side" and "robbed" them of their stock and "much personal belongings."[100] Elinor analyzed the political roots of the Civil War with precision and succinctness, despite the personalized violence and brutality in her own family's history. And yet, it was Pin Indians, a group of John Ross supporters committed to older curricula, Cherokee language use, and averse to acquisitive wealth, who drew Elinor's sharpest critique. The people she had learned to judge and deride were those referred to in government reports in the decades ahead as the *poorer* classes of Cherokees: those most likely to have received sporadic public schooling, those most committed to Cherokee language use, and those most likely to foster community-centered agricultural models that didn't exploit the labor and bodies of enslaved people—people more like Ayohka and Sequoyah. Caroline Matilda taught her daughter to overlook political divides in favor of educational and class similarities. This lesson must have taken, because Elinor married John H. Meigs, the great-grandson of Chief John Ross. Even as class, linguistic, racial, social, and political divides still plagued the Nation in the post–Civil War period, the marriages of Ageyutsa's and Climber of Trees' granddaughters would provide a salve for some of those wounds while allowing others to fester. Ayohka's family traveled one educational path in the post-removal period; Caroline Eliza Fields and Caroline Matilda Fields traveled another.

For a period of time, there was something that linked all these girls together. Several of the essays written while the girls attended Dwight Mission, including those focused on seasons or the outdoors, seemed to whisper elements of older pedagogies, absent discussions of Christian morals and values. Both "Spring" essays directed their readers to flowers that will "spring up," to the birds that "busy their nests," and to the "mountains" that will "look so green." One of the essays reminded readers that when those flowers bloom, the smell would be "very sweet and the land will be filled with the odor." Even as spring had become a seasonal demarcation filled with understandings of generic flowers blooming, concepts that Ageyutsa and Climber of Trees may have scoffed at for their simplicity, at least one girl knew and noted that smell was a key tool for learning about and recognizing the curricular changes of the classrooms beyond school buildings.[101]

Caroline Eliza wrote the most unconventional essay and the most embodied. In an untitled piece, she wrote about children climbing a hill above Dwight. While climbing, she had fallen and hurt herself, but it didn't deter her from completing the climb. When she and her classmates reached the top, they "ran about picking up what we called our pretties. . . . When we were tired of picking up our pretties, we ran to the edge of a large rock and looked as far as we could, o, o, o resounded from almost everyone, it was a fine sight indeed for when we looked down at Dwight and saw some of the children playing in the big yard they looked as small as chickens. We could see a house that stands a mile away of Dwight."[102]

Caroline Eliza described a new generation of children in awe of and in deference to their physical environment. She knew there was something significant and profound about seeing more of her thirty square miles and gaining a sense of the scale and scope of that space. Was their collective sense of awe indicative of the shrinking world they existed in educationally, or an acknowledgment of the education they lacked? Who climbed that hill with Caroline Eliza? Most of those collecting "pretties" were likely her female counterparts. Ayohka might have climbed a hill not far from this one, maybe even this hill, when she first arrived in the area. She may have watched as her children, born later in the same decade in which both Carolines and the Gunter girls attended Dwight, gathered their pretties and helped her gather hickory nuts.

Rather than rely on "the gardener [who] would plant seed to make the flowers grow in spring" like the students at Dwight, Ayohka lived just down the road planting her own garden on this same landscape.[103] What did this new generation of elite Cherokee girls understand as their legacy and relationship to agriculture and growing corn? Did they consider themselves connected intellectually to their great-grandmothers Selu, Ageyutsa, and Climber of Trees? When they went home, did they see women overseeing vast fields of corn, beans, and squash, with the added crop of watermelons or a smaller version of those fields? Or did they witness enslaved people performing the work that was once their economic, political, and spiritual inheritance?

In that moment, on the hill above Dwight, Caroline Eliza and Ayohka shared an intellectual past and present filled with the violent disruptions of the Long Removal Era. They shared a childhood experience that bridged East and West. They shared the experience of migration from one homeland to another. These girls were filled with mixtures of grief, uncertainty, and educational promise but also with awe for the vast landscape before them, as they carved new educational paths for the girls who would follow.

Rachel Johnson and the *uktena* that she learned followed Cherokee people from the East during the Long Removal Era. Artwork by Roy Boney Jr.

CHAPTER 5

Oklahoma Indian Schools

Rachel Johnson

As the nineteenth century drew to a close, the Cherokee Nation continued to demonstrate its commitment to institution building, including an expansion of its public school system and social welfare services after the Civil War; maintained its advocacy for Cherokee Nation sovereignty in Washington, DC, against railroad impositions, timber theft, territorialists, and intruders clamoring for more land for white settlers; and defended itself against reformers worried about the morality, material conditions, and souls of Cherokee people. Despite these efforts, the federal government once again subjected the Cherokee Nation and Cherokee people to the fickleness of federal Indian policy when it passed the Curtis Act in 1898, which worked to break up the Five Tribes' communally held lands into privately held property, and imposed Oklahoma statehood in 1907.[1] During these years after the Civil War, the Cherokee Nation expanded its educational options, enabling most communities to avoid interactions with US federal and state officials and instead build up their local communities to suit their specific educational needs. Some communities needed bilingual-speaking teachers; others wanted only English-speaking teachers. Some still hoped to avoid schools altogether.

In what had formerly been the Skin Bayou District, which later comprised parts of the Illinois and Sequoyah Districts and would shortly become Sequoyah County, Oklahoma, former slaveholders sought to continue maximizing profits from their lands but without enslaved people's unpaid labor. To do so, they increased their reliance on tenant farming and land leases. William Penn Boudinot, who had married Caroline Matilda Fields, defended the hiring of foreign labor in the *Cherokee Advocate*, the Nation's newspaper, in 1877 for these reasons. Because of the high death rate among Cherokee men during the Civil War and the near century-long reeducation that encouraged Cherokee women to marry white men, the number of white men marrying Cherokee women from former slaveholding families to gain property rights and then cultivate large swaths of land only increased in the years after the Civil War.[2]

Alongside these evolving political and economic forces, environmental forces in the Cherokee Nation changed too. Hickory trees still grew, but walnuts and hazelnuts were often hard to find, and pecans were nearly absent.[3] River cane had fought back at places like Dwight when the mission was abandoned during the Civil War, but after the war river cane once again dwindled in the West, and in turn populations of *tsi yes sdi* (Carolina parakeet) and the *wa da lo ni* (passenger pigeon) plummeted as well. *Tsi yes sdi* and *wa da lo ni* relied on the canebrakes for shelter and food. The girls of this generation would be the last to feel the same wonder that Ayohka and Caroline Matilda and Carolina Eliza Fields and their grandmothers had felt when groups of *tsi yes sdi* with their magnificent colors screamed through the area. The name of the town of Pigeon Roost in the Choctaw Nation would need to be explained to future generations, who would never see the weight of *wa da lo ni* break the limbs off trees when they passed through in the fall. To explain their absence, some Cherokee children learned that the *wa do lo ni* "attempted to cross the ocean or were caught in a tornado and were drowned, because they left one day and never returned."[4]

The illegal settlers who arrived in anticipation of statehood at first strained and then eventually exhausted the grasslands that had produced the deep, rich black soil and sustained the farming efforts of Cherokees when they first settled in Indian Territory. In the decades ahead, this would have catastrophic results for all of Oklahoma but particularly for the plains regions stretching across the western portion of the state.[5] By the turn of the century, growing cotton in what had been the Skin Bayou District became untenable both economically and environmentally for individual farmers, and many moved away.[6] Even before statehood, resource extraction had begun, first through timber exploitation and then through oil and gas wells that would bolster the petroleum industry. By 1913, there were entire publications dedicated to noting the subsurface resources under Cherokee people's feet.[7]

Populations of non-Indians, Black and white, and some of Native descent, surged into the area when the promise of free or cheap land circulated in the United States from the Civil War through Oklahoma statehood. Cherokee descendants whose families had relinquished their political ties to the Cherokee Nation in the states of Georgia and Tennessee through the treaties of 1817 and 1819 flocked to the Cherokee Nation in search of these same promises. The federal government engaged in another push to remove those North Carolina Cherokees who had taken land reserves through the treaties of 1817 and 1819, only to be dispossessed by the state, to Indian Territory. Settlers working on railroads streamed into the Nation. The sudden population growth overloaded the administrative bureaucracy of the Cherokee Nation, led to a new phase in criminal legal reform, and taxed the Nation's jurisdictional integrity.[8] The surging population burdened the environmental resources in the twin territories, Indian and Oklahoma, the latter formed after the 1890 land run. This only increased the pressure on the Five Tribes to allot their lands.

For centuries, Cherokee mothers had birthed relatively few children because Cherokee people dwelled with large, intergenerational families; they exercised sexual and reproductive autonomy; and men left seasonally for hunting expeditions. In homes before and following removal, children were always afoot, but they may not have been the biological children of the women who parented them. The aftermath of removal and the Civil War led many families to open their doors to orphaned children. At the same time, the Cherokee Nation also cracked down on the bodily autonomy of women, which had enabled women to control the size of their families during the Long Removal Era. The Nation first passed laws in the East and then in the West that criminalized abortion and further eroded the legal rights of women.[9] However, when the Curtis Act passed in 1898, subjecting the Five Tribes to allotment, the terms included allocating forty additional acres of land to children of heads of household; allotment incentivized having more children, and a baby boom followed.

Intermarried whites tended to produce larger numbers of children in the years leading up to and following removal. Brothers who married into the Cherokee Nation in the first decades of the nineteenth century often married Cherokee sisters. The Fields and Gunter families, both of whom sent children to Dwight Mission, are two prime examples of the proliferation of families and family size in this period—and are two families from whom I and many other Cherokee people descend, and it was only through writing this book that I fully teased out these relationships. Growing families supported the fathers' farming aspirations and also led to reconceptions of extended families among some Cherokee people. The men could aid each other's commercial interests while their wives provided their claim to citizenship and property rights in the Nation. The right-of-wife provision that had enabled intermarried men to claim land reserves decades earlier took on new unstated variations during allotment. At the time of the Dawes Commission, more culturally conservative Cherokee families grew their families too, which stood at odds with the shrinking size of families in the larger United States and caused alarm among reformers who were preoccupied with the so-called Indian problem.[10]

One of these growing families was Rachel Johnson's family, who resided in the Illinois District at the time of allotment. Rachel was born in 1899, the second child of Samuel Johnson and Jennie Hopper Johnson, just a few miles from where two of Ayohka's sons had died in recent years. By 1910, Rachel's parents had five children. Rachel descended from families who had waged acts of educational resistance to schooling from the Long Removal Era forward. Her father, Samuel Johnson, had benefited from the intergenerational learning provided by his grandmother Lydia Justice, who had raised Samuel and provided his primary education. Lydia called Sam Oochilata and had stepped in to raise him while her daughter Aincy, Sam's mother, exercised her right to begin and end relationships as she saw fit. Aincy began and ended marriages to men by the names of Poorbear, Cochran, Hogtoater, and Johnson. Aincy later stepped back into her role as mother and grandmother, serving as the midwife at the birth of Rachel's younger brother, Albert. Even with Dwight Mission just down the road, some Cherokee women continued to educate their children according to older sex education curriculums.

Jennie Hopper Johnson, Rachel's mother, knew her own birth date with precision, "24th of November 1880." For Cherokee people living in monolingual communities at the time of allotment, possessing this information was extraordinary, and it may have been born out of death. Jennie's father, Martin Hopper, revealed in his allotment enrollment testimony that his previous wife, Jennie's mother, Nellie/Nannie, had died sometime around 1880. Perhaps that was the day of Jennie's birth *and* the day of Nellie/Nannie's death. Beyond recording dates with precision, Jennie recorded the continued presence and the loss of her mother in other ways.

Jennie gave her firstborn daughter the name Nannie. She might not have been able to bury her mother at the base of her matrilocal home like Climber of Trees might have done, but she could plant her mother in her daughter's future existence.[11] And since Nannie did not raise Jennie, it means it was Nannie's family, Jennie's maternal grandparents, who helped pass the larger knowledge of whom she descended from to Jennie, who then gave it to Rachel, who ultimately shared it with federal officials.

The language of this history was oral and written, in both Cherokee and English. Rachel's grandparents were all fluent in Cherokee, and people in her orbit were biliterate. Both of her parents were likely somewhat bilingual but more comfortable in Cherokee. Because of this, her father chose to use a translator to communicate with the Dawes Commissioners in 1901. Jennie Johnson, whose Cherokee name was Kahladi, could reconcile her family bilaterally.[12] She knew her parents' and grandparents' names in English and Cherokee, indicating a move away from matrilineality as a means of defining parentage and kinship for all Cherokee people but not necessarily an abandonment of other matrilineal practices. All her grandparents had been born in the "Cherokee Nation east," the more common way among those educated in older curricula and more culturally conservative communities to express continued Indigenous notions of sovereignty for what had become the states of Georgia, Tennessee,

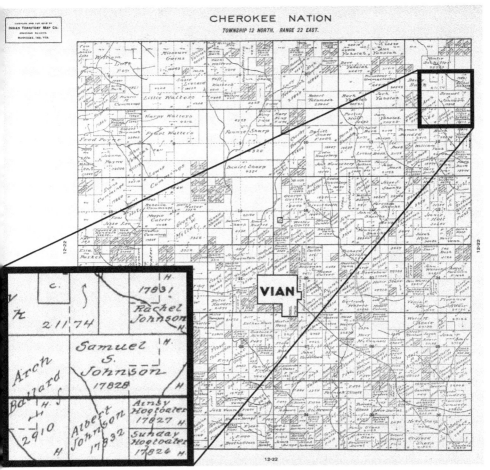

A map showing allotments in Township 12 North, Range 22 East, surrounding Vian, Oklahoma. The inset map shows a portion of Rachel Johnson's family's allotments, located in what is Sequoyah County, Oklahoma, today. There were additional family allotments not located on this grid. Courtesy Geography and Map Division, Library of Congress, Washington, DC.

Alabama, and North Carolina—the land terms used more often by those more exclusively educated in schools, those who were the products of intermarriage on both sides of one's family, and those living at a social, class, and linguistic distance from core Cherokee communities.[13]

Rachel and her siblings were born in a moment of bureaucratic educational transition. When Rachel was four, federal officials informed Cherokee people that despite their success complying with educational policies, enrolling students, and funding school buildings for 171 communities, there would be enough funds for only seventy teachers. Rural schools with lower enrollments, regardless of whether they were in compliance, were denied teachers.[14] When Rachel was five, tribal leaders waged a final unsuccessful push for the State of Sequoyah in order to maintain a state designed by and governed by Native people.[15] She was born in a moment where national leaders fought for control of the educational institutions their treaties mandated, that they built and supported, and that their families had passed through over the course of more than fifty years. When Rachel was six, the year most children started school, Cherokee Board of Education member O. H. P. Brewer, who had been raised in Webber's Falls, less than twenty miles from where Rachel was growing up, sat through a meeting with other Five Tribes officials and the newly appointed federal superintendent of education, J. D. Benedict. The purpose of the meeting was to create uniform school rules and regulations across all of the schools operated by the Five Tribes, erasing the nationally specific policies that had developed since removal to meet each Native nation's specific needs.[16]

At the same moment, the United States had also ushered in a second, more insidious version of the Civilization Policy, bent on assimilating Indigenous peoples and treating them as if they were equivalent to the immigrants arriving in droves from around the world.[17] In 1905, when Rachel was six, still two years before Oklahoma statehood, representatives of the National Education Association wrote, "A speaking and reading knowledge of English is one of the most effective instruments in assimilation; and as these children not only present an opportunity for the most effective work in assimilation, but are active agents in the same cause with their elders at home, it is plainly our duty to devise ways and means of bringing our language, and hence our ideals, within their understanding."[18] In short, the NEA encouraged educators across the United States to see children's English language acquisition as a mechanism to "educate" their parents and grandparents as well. The NEA, like some missionaries in Indian Territory who predated them, distrusted speakers of other languages, those who had the audacity to "foster [a non-English language in the home circle; and [to] encourage secretly, and often openly, the retention and cultivation of its vernacular."[19] This education policy also stood in stark contrast to the position of missionaries like Evan Jones who had embraced Cherokee language learning a hundred years earlier. It also promoted a plan that used children as intergenerational weapons against their elders to stamp out non-English speakers. For reformers, schools became the training grounds for intergenerational educational warfare, just as educating women in Christianized marriage and intermarriage practices had been during Ayohka's childhood.

This attitude and its accompanying approaches were not necessarily new to Native people. Even the NEA pointed out, "The problem of assimilating great masses of people with different tongues and customs is not a new one—not even in our country, where the Indian problem still confronts us."[20] Many immigrants were about to face similar assimilationist assaults that Native peoples had already made choices to resist, accommodate, or slowly adapt to over hundreds of years, work often carried out through Christian missionaries. The evangelism of assimilation had broadened beyond federally funded missionaries to include the national educational scene. This policy would combine imperialism and militarism in the educational curriculum targeted at Native peoples.

These shifts in educational policy were tied closely to ideas about race and ethnicity held by those in power. Miss Ida Mitchell, principal of Bryant School in Chicago, Illinois, and a member of the NEA, put it this way, "The changed character of our immigrants affects the teaching of English. So long as the Teutonic peoples came here, the problem was simpler than it is now that most of our immigrants are of the Alpine and Mediterranean races, whose languages and customs are more unlike ours."[21] According to Mitchell, the new immigrants were somehow different than the people who had arrived earlier, Mitchell's ancestors certainly included.

And yet the oldest inhabitants, including the Cherokees—descendants of Ageyutsa, Climber of Trees, Ayohka, and both Caroline Fieldses, whose ancestors had always been in what was then the United States—still presented a "problem." And they were not alone. African-descended peoples, who first began residing in what became the United States in large numbers in 1619 and had regularly outnumbered their white and Native counterparts in Southern states, presented their own "Negro problem" for white educators. For educators like Mitchell, the issue was less these new immigrants and more their relationships to acceptable definitions of Americanness that included cultural, religious, and linguistic expectations and their proximity to "slippery" definitions of whiteness.[22]

Within Oklahoma, the Five Tribes had a legacy of schooling and institution building that helped their citizens mitigate some, though not all, of the potential damage these new policies wrought for Native people there. Understanding Cherokee educational history post-allotment involves tracing a web of disparate educational offerings that includes subscription schools, common schools, mission schools, and federal Indian boarding schools. Allotment and statehood would have been enough for Cherokee people to navigate, but in the years following statehood, women and men faced additional local, national, and international changes that would impact the education imparted about and to Cherokee people. By the mid-1930s, these larger racial, linguistic, and class

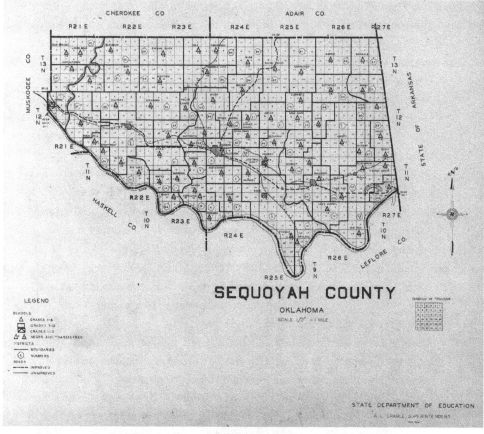

A map from 1936 shows the location of schools in Sequoyah County, Oklahoma.
Oklahoma State Department of Education, Oklahoma State Archives, Oklahoma City.

biases cast a shadow over how Cherokee people understood their relationships
to one another and to the wider public.

As a child, Rachel Johnson probably knew little to nothing about Ida Mitchell, her speeches, or the NEA, but she was learning about her family history,
Cherokee history, and federal Indian policy. Many of those educated in the
Cherokee Nation schools and communities built the educational and intellectual bridges for Cherokee people to cross over, but often those bridges required
tolls that only educational, racial, class, familial, and town connections could
pay, as Rachel would learn and understand.

Another Rachel, Rachel Eaton, is one of the more well-known beneficiaries
of Cherokee educational efforts. Eaton was the daughter of a Cherokee mother
and an intermarried white man, a common refrain for many elite Cherokee

people since the late eighteenth century. She was born in 1869, just after the close of the Civil War, attended Cherokee Nation schools, and later graduated from the Cherokee Female Seminary in 1887, which became Northeastern State Normal in 1909. Unlike many other Female Seminary graduates who married their Male Seminary counterparts and made a life in the Cherokee Nation, Eaton went on to attend Drury College in Missouri. She then departed from the trajectory of most women in America at the time, joining the one in fifty women who advanced their careers beyond their undergraduate degrees and pursuing a graduate degree at the University of Chicago.[23] Interspersed throughout her educational attainments, she taught in a variety of school settings, including in the Cherokee schools and at her alma mater, the Cherokee Female Seminary. She was elected superintendent of public instruction in Rogers County, Oklahoma, formerly the Saline District of the Cherokee Nation and the site of the Cherokee Orphan Asylum from 1872 until it burned down in 1904. There, she served for two years. Eaton's educational influence extended beyond the Cherokee Nation and Oklahoma as well. She taught at Lake Erie College in Ohio and served as dean of women at Trinity University in Waxahachie, Texas.[24] She joined the growing numbers of women in the workforce, numbers that would peak in the 1920s and not hit those rates again until women like my mother, born in 1945, straddling the Silent Generation and the baby boomers, entered the workforce in the 1970s.[25] In many ways, Eaton is an outlier, but the basic contours link her to Cherokee women's educational heritages in the post-statehood moment, and her experiences forecast educational trends emerging among middle-class white women in the United States more broadly.

The educational opportunities provided by the Cherokee Nation at its seminaries to its "most promising" students like Caroline Matilda Fields, her daughter Elinor Fields, and Rachel Eaton—often the wealthier bicultural students—continued to stand in contrast to the educational opportunities available to most rural settler families in the decades that followed statehood. A 1907 article in *The Oklahoman* stated that Native people preferred boarding schools and often neglected their district schools; it also made sure to mention that "all of these schools were maintained exclusively for Indians, the whites not being allowed to attend any of them. At the time there were no schools for whites, except a few denominational and mission schools, and a few subscription schools."[26] And yet, the Cherokee Nation's sustained commitments to schooling laid the groundwork for Johnson, Eaton, and white settler children.

When Oklahoma became a state, it inherited the progressive educational legacies of the Five Tribes and entered the United States at a time when reformers and elected officials believed in the power of schooling to tackle perceived social ills. In the years that followed, places like Pennsylvania instituted the use of "visiting teachers" to rural districts. Visiting teachers had a dual background in teaching and social work.[27] Because of the professional inroads that growing numbers of white women had made into both fields, visiting teacher programs exploited the ability to pay one woman to perform two jobs. Both inside and outside the Cherokee Nation, the free or reduced cost of women's labor continued to supplement educational institutions and expand opportunities for all children across the United States.

The Cherokee Nation's post-removal and post–Civil War commitments to educational and political institutions provided a professional landing pad for Cherokee people in the post-statehood period, as Eaton's résumé suggests. Cherokees who cut their professional teeth in Cherokee educational institutions had the background necessary to obtain a variety of offices in the state of Oklahoma. O. H. P. Brewer, a graduate of the Cherokee Male Seminary, had served on the Cherokee Board of Education for five years before Oklahoma statehood and as a delegate to the State of Sequoyah Constitutional Convention. After statehood, he served the State of Oklahoma in a variety of capacities, including the Oklahoma Textbook Commission in 1907 and later the School Land Commission.[28] Robert L. Owen, who was raised and educated in Virginia, obtained Cherokee citizenship through his mother, Narcissa Chisholm Owen, an alumna of Dwight Mission. He became one of Oklahoma's first senators after statehood.[29] His life had been marked by a different educational path.

Cherokee men like Owen and Brewer made decisions that shaped schooling in Oklahoma, the former Cherokee Nation, and the United States in the years ahead; Cherokee children traveled a range of educational paths impacted by those men's decisions, as well as by some decisions made by Cherokee women long before them. They attended school in diverse educational settings—federal Indian boarding schools, mission schools, normal schools—and some continued to receive teachings steeped in older curriculums. Bureaucratic processes muted Black Cherokee connections to the Cherokee Nation, which more closely aligned Black Cherokees' educational futures with African Americans in Oklahoma.

For numbers of Cherokee people, many of the same educational settings that had existed before statehood remained, but how and where Cherokee people chose to expend their educational energy shifted significantly, and much of this depended on where they lived. By 1918, just two years before the United States would see a demographic shift from a majority-rural to a majority-urban nation, educators added the "Rural Problem" to the list of "problem" demographics.[30]

This made rural Cherokee people and African Cherokee people doubly and triply problematic to educators and reformers and even to some of their civic-focused Cherokee neighbors.

Post-statehood, educational programs increasingly targeted rural women and girls, thereby acknowledging the vital importance of women's free domestic labor. Until the 1914 Smith-Lever Act, which established cooperative outreach extensions through land grant universities, rural communities had relied on the philanthropic efforts of organizations like the General Education Board.[31] Established in 1902 through a million-dollar contribution from John D. Rockefeller, the General Education Board not only funded schools in rural communities but also worked to educate adults in those communities in agricultural best practices. A year after the Smith-Lever Act passed, J. H. Downing, a "Cherokee of the progressive type," advocated for the education of "full bloods," likely a shorthand for those with restrictions on their lands, and he believed that education should start with canning clubs aimed at women to increase food for winter stores.[32] By 1917, the *Vian Press* published articles listing the name and contact information for the supervisor of home demonstration work in Oklahoma and steps for canning various kinds of vegetables in jars.[33] In 1918, the Department of the Interior issued "Directions for Making a Home Canner" in the Cherokee language to distribute to Cherokee readers.[34] By the 1940s, most women residing in Oklahoma, including Rachel Johnson (then Quinton) and her white neighbor Eva Duffield, grew, canned, and stored food.

Federal boarding schools provided a direct conduit for many of the educational programs pushed by reformers and those involved with the General Education Board. Once they were controlled by the Bureau of Indian Affairs, schools like Bloomfield Academy and the Sequoyah Orphan Training School, renamed in 1925, turned away from the academically rigorous parts of their curriculums that had existed prior to statehood and toward a focus on manual labor, the domestic arts, sports, and more rigidly disciplined structures, including military training for boys.[35] Boarding schools, including Carlisle Indian Industrial School in Pennsylvania, produced domestic workers and laborers in service to white families throughout the areas they were located.

Boarding schools also continued a much longer process of erasing Indigenous people's names, while the local and national press helped to exoticize and shame those who had Indigenous names. In 1916, the *Pawnee Times-Democrat*, printed in a Native community now within the boundaries of Oklahoma, reported on the "cumbersome" names of Native students at Carlisle, citing the longest and shortest names and lamenting that "the odd names have not entirely passed away." Numerous children's names were listed for all to read.[36] Although the point was likely to shame Native people and discourage the old naming practices, some Native people may have smiled that old educational practices were still alive and well at places like Carlisle. Rachel's mother Jennie, for instance, knew all of her names, in Cherokee and English, and she knew the names of the people who connected her to the Old Nation. Many Cherokee people involved in the allotment enrollment process may have scoffed at the irony as they recalled the numerous non-Native people with the same English names as Cherokee people who inundated the allotment process with their applications claiming to be Cherokee to gain access to land. Native names connected one to family. They distinguished people from others in their family. Abandoning or being forced to abandon older Indigenous naming practices that changed over time also erased a history of childhood, a documentary record of who those children were as autonomous actors in their youth.

Because so many Native political leaders transitioned to state political offices, the influences of those individuals were evident in private and public educational efforts. Elite and politically connected Cherokee women chose to channel their energies into a range of projects that continued to educate the public on the political histories and Five Tribes' contributions to the state. Rachel Eaton's history *John Ross and the Cherokee Indians* was completed in 1914, when Rachel Johnson was a fifteen-year-old student at Dwight Mission. Like Elinor Fields's description of the political history leading up to and following Cherokee participation in the Civil War, Eaton's work still stands as an important contribution to Cherokee political history. Others chose to focus on bolstering the relationships forged among the "aristocracy of the Cherokee tribe."[37] In 1899, the same year Rachel Johnson was born, a group of six young women from some of the same families educated at Dwight Mission during the Long Removal Era formed the Indian Women's Pocahontas Club, a club still in existence today. The group studied early Cherokee Nation written laws and quizzed each other on Cherokee political history.[38] Many of them attended the same Presbyterian church in Claremore, not a bilingual church with "full-blood" Cherokee people but an integrated English language church attended by local whites. Seminary alumni and students at Northeastern State Normal, formerly the Cherokee Female Seminary, gathered funds to erect a monument honoring non-Indigenous educator Florence Wilson, who had served as the assistant superintendent of the seminary for twenty-five years.[39] These groups of women acted as "loyal countrywomen" who made sure that key state political and educational leaders did not forget the legacies of the Five Tribes and their educational contributions to the region and the state, even if it meant elevating white women to do it.[40]

Because of the knowledge base possessed by Cherokee people and the initial political influence of elite Cherokee powerbrokers, early history books produced by the State of Oklahoma included fairly accurate Five Tribes political histories and included key biographies of Five Tribes leaders. O. H. P. Brewer's service to the Oklahoma Textbook Commission the year Oklahoma became a state set the stage for the inclusion of Cherokee history.[41] The 1910 *History and Civics of Oklahoma* included an image and biography of Sequoyah, images of the Cherokee capital at Tahlequah and the Chickasaw capital at Tishomingo, and a map of Indian Territory prior to the Civil War and again in 1880.[42] *The Essential Facts of Oklahoma History and Civics*, published in 1916, two years after Rachel Eaton completed *John Ross and the Cherokee Indians*, dedicated a section to each of the Five Tribes' removal experiences, another section outlined the Civil War and Reconstruction through the political history of the Five Tribes, and an additional section discussed the conditions that led other Native nations to be forcibly removed to Indian and Oklahoma Territories.

Despite an overwhelming amount of space dedicated to these events, the first section of *The Essential Facts of Oklahoma History and Civics* begins not with a history of the Native peoples who predated the Five Tribes but instead with European explorers; they mark the starting point of this Oklahoma history. The final subsection lays out the case that multiple claims had been made to "Ownership of Oklahoma" and that "the Indians really had the first right to it, at least in point of time. But when the claims were being asserted European people had little respect for Indian rights." This acknowledgment of Indigenous peoples' primary rights to land echoed the teachings of Beloved Man Arcowee at Chota to would-be Moravian missionaries in 1799. The textbook places the blame for Native dispossession at the feet of Europeans, as opposed to the United States government, which had only a few years earlier confiscated the Five Tribes' communal land base in favor of statehood and whose state citizens were actively engaged in the theft of Native peoples' lands at the time of the book's publication.

Despite the complexity present in the subsection on Indian Territory and Oklahoma's history, the textbook's final exercises and questions erased that nuance.

Questions. What Indians had their homes in Oklahoma? In what part of Oklahoma did they live? What real right did they have to the lands they occupied? Trace the title of Oklahoma, east of the 100th meridian, from the Indians to the United States. Trace the title to the Panhandle from Spain to the Territory to Oklahoma. What right did England have to

Oklahoma? How did the Compromise Bill of 1850 affect its boundaries? The Kansas-Nebraska Bill?

Written Work. Set forth in writing the reasons why Spain had a strong claim to the lands included in Oklahoma. State why in writing France had a better right to these lands. Give brief biographies of: Columbus, De Soto, Coronado, Champlain, Marquette, La Salle, Pike, Marcy, Irving, Catlin.[43]

These exercises didn't ask students to consider the long-term claims of occupancy and sovereignty of Native nations or the rights established by treaty; instead, they asked students to articulate the "real" claims of Europeans and Euro-Americans over time and to legitimate non-Native explorers who provided a through-line for these claims. Simultaneously, the textbook acknowledged the rights and occupancy of Native nations to the lands while the questions it posed to students sought to articulate the legal legitimacy of Anglo-Americans' claims to lands at the expense of Native nations.

By the early twentieth century, many of the educational institutions in Oklahoma that were available to Native people were direct descendants of the educational institutions built by Native nations or by the missionaries who served them in the period before statehood. The 1910 *History and Civics* textbook included an image and discussion of Bloomfield Academy, a girls' school established by the Chickasaw in 1852, which was operating as a federal boarding school by the time Rachel Johnson came of age. Like the situation with Bloomfield, in 1914, as allotment enrollment reached a conclusion, the secretary of the Interior assumed control of the Cherokee Orphanage, which had relocated to Park Hill after it burned down. It was later renamed the Sequoyah Orphan Training School. Not only did this process maintain the location of the school within the former Cherokee Nation at a moment when Native American children were being forcibly removed from their communities to distant schools, but its name also reinforced the legacies of Cherokee educational and intellectual accomplishments.

In contrast to the continuous schooling at Sequoyah, albeit under different administrative control, allotment and impending statehood disrupted Dwight Mission's operations as a boarding school for five years before it eventually reopened to serve Native youth in 1900.[44] Rachel Johnson attended school there in the second decade of the twentieth century, and her oldest children would attend the mission school as well. The landscape around Dwight likely looked remarkably similar to its earliest years; the hill Caroline Eliza had climbed in the 1840s stood firm. An old prominent tree still drew attention. While a number of buildings had changed, one of the oldest log homes in Indian Territory—built after Dwight's move to the territory in 1829—still stood on the property. Dwight also had continued the tradition of distributing Cherokee language materials throughout the Cherokee Nation and beyond. In 1904, the Reverend R. L. Schaubb resumed publication of the *Cherokee Gospel Tidings*, a Cherokee language religious publication.[45] The mission also published Cherokee language Christmas greetings, the Lord's Prayer, and a Ten Commandments card.[46]

As schools became more accessible, students continued attending at older ages than children of previous generations had. Compulsory education, thanks to people like O. H. P. Brewer in Oklahoma and advocated for by people like Robert L. Owen nationally, became the norm throughout the United States. Cherokee people made choices about where to send their children based on a range of considerations. The continued use of the Cherokee language by some of Dwight's adherents or the bilingualism of local public school teachers contributed to the decision-making of people to send their children to particular schools. A school's proximity to families informed the choices of others.[47] When Rachel Johnson attended Dwight Mission and later sent her oldest children there, it was a four-to-five-mile walk to her homeplace, a walk her son Breezy did on occasion when he attended. Because of changes to the landscape, the intrusion of roads, and the impacts of communal lands passing out of Cherokee control, the direct route to Dwight Mission is impassable today and is now eight to nine miles by car from where Rachel's house still stands.

Denominational allegiances probably informed other people's decisions about where to send their children. Familiarity and comfort with the teachers hired likely factored into decision-making as well. During the Long Removal Era, an entire Baptist church community had removed to Indian Territory early after its non-Native minister Duncan O'Bryant's popularity faltered when he signed the oath of allegiance to the State of Georgia instead of resisting, as most missionaries did.[48] It is unclear what led Samuel and Jennie to enroll Rachel at Dwight. Samuel's paternal family affiliations may have been a consideration. Rachel's later decision to send her five oldest children to Dwight would produce long-term educational differences between her oldest and youngest children.

The post-statehood educational world experienced by Cherokee children added new educational challenges on top of old challenges that remained. These changes played out as a new racial regime took hold: the assimilative Jim Crow era, in which federal policy encouraged all Black and Brown people to conform while simultaneously erecting legal barriers that prevented them from doing so. These changes also coincided with a range of international,

national, state-level, and tribal crises. As the creation of the Cherokee allotment rolls closed in 1914—when Rachel Johnson was fifteen years old—World War I broke out. The war aided the spread of a pandemic from Kansas to the world and into the heart of the Cherokee Nation. Native people deemed incompetent by federal officials were unable to manage their land allotments, including Rachel's family. In turn, they faced legal vulnerability and rampant exploitation throughout Oklahoma; and, in the glaring case of the Osages, recently dramatized in the film *Killers of the Flower Moon,* they encountered widespread violence and murder. A full decade before the Great Depression, Oklahoma's agriculture was in peril. These conditions conspired to create an educational world hostile to a subset of Cherokee children.

In turn, many Cherokee people wed to older educational systems pulled back from schooling and resisted the changes. When Hogan Markham, a Cherokee graduate of the Tahlequah Normal School, was young, he heard the educational resistances of at least one Cherokee woman voiced publicly to a politician giving a speech in Tahlequah. "[The politician] was saying 'Our Land and Our Country.' I was standing by a full blood Cherokee woman there and when [the politician] said our 'Our Land and Our Country,' she said, 'Not our land and *not* our country,' and I thought that was one of the saddest things I ever heard and it was true, too."[49] Markham's sympathy for those statements likely stemmed from his Cherokee educational origins.[50] The Cherokee Nation provided Markham's educational foundation, as it had for Rachel Eaton. And yet, he achieved success through schooling when other Cherokee people saw schooling become unmoored from their history, communities, and kinship responsibilities.

Allotment and statehood destroyed any semblance of a clearly defined Cherokee governing body, the type of unified political force that could interact with federal and state governments, for more than half of the twentieth century. Field agents acted as liaisons for Cherokee people on matters related to allotment, competency, medical care, and school-related issues. "Official" Cherokee leaders were no longer democratically elected, as they had been since 1828; instead, they were selected by the executive branch of the federal government, with the exception of the Keetoowah Society. The Keetoowah Society, intimately connected to the Pins, was a subset of Cherokee people committed to ongoing Cherokee governance who continued to select leaders internally. A group calling themselves Eastern Emigrant Cherokees stepped forward to claim local authority as well. Communal landholdings, which had been a bulwark against widespread poverty, were diminished. Schools, which Cherokee people and the Nation had fought to support and control, were no longer theirs. In the eyes of the United States, "competent" Cherokees, those assigned a blood quantum under one half, were now individual citizens, not members of a Native nation. The efforts by federal officials and reformers to solve the Indian problem had created perilous conditions for former Five Tribes citizens, which James Malone described in the *Chickasaw Nation: A Short Sketch* published in 1922.

As Rachel Johnson reached young adulthood in the 1920s, educational materials produced by Oklahoma officials and journalists to inform teachers and the public about the state of education reflected the national preoccupation with "the Rural School Problem" as defined by the educational divides among students. These articles appeared during the decade in which the United States officially became more urban than rural. Newspapers in the former Cherokee Nation printed throughout the 1920s contained articles reminding schools and teachers, and secondarily parents, of the role they played in monitoring the public health of their students.[51] In 1922, the state again sponsored a Health Tournament among schools, which reflected the rural/urban divides but also the diversity of schools available within the state. It subdivided the competition into city schools with more than 200 students; city schools of 200 students or less; rural schools; and parochial, private, and boarding schools. Students earned credit by "washing hands before each meal, weekly baths, brushing teeth twice a day, sleeping with open windows, and exercising outdoors."[52]

Although many of these concerns didn't specifically identify Native people—and in a place like Oklahoma where poverty was widespread, these concerns likely included all races of people—other reports vilified and damned Cherokee families for the very conditions Cherokee people had warned officials that allotment and statehood would produce. In 1898, D. W. C. Duncan, an Old Setter educated at Dartmouth, wrote in the *Indian Chieftain*, "The nefarious, tyrannical, Curtis law dishonors the social life of our people; it invades the domestic circle, abolishes the institution of marriage, it stigmatizes our happy homes as mere places of brutal cohabitation, it bastardizes our children, and reduces all the noble fathers and mothers of our country to the moral condition of pimps and prostitutes."[53] In the 1920s, federal and state-level government officials contrasted the wealth of the 1920s with the poverty faced by Native peoples to point out the disparities.[54]

In 1922, when Rachel Johnson's oldest child, Nelson Smith, was two years old, and a year after she married Sequoyah Quinton, "a survey of public education in the State of Oklahoma" described "full blood parents" as "markedly careless in the care of children." Respondents blamed close intermarriage among Five Tribes people for most of the cases of epilepsy. They categorized Cherokee people into three groups. The first category comprised town Indians who were leaders in communities and who sent their children to town or boarding schools or junior colleges in nearby states. The second were full-bloods and many mixed-bloods who lived in two-to-four-room log houses in the country that were not well-kept—untidy but not dirty—whose children attended boarding or district schools. They were eager to see their children "advance" but would remove them from school for important reasons. The third group included those who were "full bloods, or nearly so," who were not more advanced than so-called "pagan Indian people" and who "lived far from the paths of civilization" in one-to-three-room log homes in hills, with little furniture except beds.[55] Ironically, many of the homes critiqued in these reports represented the architectural changes ushered in by men like Ayohka's father, Sequoyah, homes that replaced styles in the East that had endured for a millennium and represented the continuing subsistence-level living in many rural communities. The homes described in the survey also bore remarkable consistency with the homes of white tenant farmers, which would be captured in photographs throughout Sequoyah County in the decade ahead.[56]

Public health was a major concern in the wake of the global flu pandemic, but the policing of public health and the judgments cast as a result fell most heavily on the economically vulnerable, those who were somehow different and less like the people who passed policy.[57] Economic vulnerability was widespread in Oklahoma, but Native-presenting people, Black people, and recent immigrants were those being targeted for assimilation, and these groups were often deemed "problems" nationwide. The same 1922 survey went on to state that children of the third Cherokee group, the "full bloods," were "often undesirable in public schools because of the previously mentioned diseases which follow lack of cleanliness."[58]

Federal boarding schools, even those formerly controlled by Native nations, advanced many of the same policies. Jack Brown superintended the Sequoyah Orphan Training School from 1925 forward. His educational lineage traced directly back to the first mission schools in the Cherokee Nation, and he knew his lineage well. He descended from the same family as Catharine Brown, the first Christian convert at Brainerd, and David Brown, one of the eight Cherokee men sent to Cornwall who later consulted Sequoyah on biblical translations using the syllabary. He was also kin to William Webber. Jack Brown first attended the Jay School, an all-Cherokee school housed in a one-room cabin with a single window and barrels for chairs and desks. All the students spoke Cherokee except for him. His family provided room and board to the local teacher when he was just starting school. After Jay, he attended Mackey Switch, followed by Webber's Falls at the age of twelve and then Sallisaw from the ages of twelve to fourteen. Brown attended the Cherokee Male Seminary beginning in the sixth grade.[59]

Jack's father and older brother spoke Cherokee, but he decided at the age of six that everyone should speak English. He made this decision in the same era that students like Luther Standing Bear (Sicangu Oglala Lakota) at Carlisle had no choice as to which language they would speak in their day-to-day lives at federal boarding schools. Unlike Standing Bear and so many others, Brown was free to make this choice because of the educational futures created by Cherokee people.

Like his schooling years, Jack's professional life included numerous educational institutions. He worked at the Cherokee Male Seminary turned Northeastern State Normal from 1907 to 1910, when it burned down. He served as a teacher and the military drill team leader to O. H. P. Brewer. From there he went to Armstrong Academy, a boarding school for boys in the Choctaw Nation established in 1845. He followed that with stints at two Presbyterian schools funded by the Muscogee Nation, first the Nuyaka Boarding School and then the Euchee School, which served both Euchee and Muscogee students. Then he moved to the Sequoyah Orphan Training School, where he served for the next thirty-one years of his career, until his retirement in 1956.[60]

Jack Brown represented Cherokee educational continuities and discontinuities. His position on Cherokee language stood at odds with David Brown's a century earlier and that of his predecessor at the Cherokee Orphan Asylum, Walter Adair Duncan, who had embraced the bilingualism of the home provided by the orphanage even as he encouraged English to be the language of the school. Yet, Brown remained committed to serving Presbyterian institutions like Dwight Mission, as his great-aunts and great-uncles had.

At Sequoyah, under Brown's leadership, medical officials also administered typhoid serums and vaccinations for smallpox and diphtheria.[61] Brown was likely aware of the violent resistances to vaccinations at the Cherokee Male Seminary in 1902 and the pushback by Cherokee people to the dehumanized medical care provided by doctors at the Cherokee Asylum for the Deaf, Dumb, Blind, and Insane, which had operated through statehood.[62] As superintendent at Sequoyah Orphan Training School, he oversaw the doctors and nurses assigned to the school who evaluated children for syphilis and gonorrhea, which may have included blood tests but more than likely included invasive inspections of the children's bodies.[63] Given his family's entrenchment in Presbyterianism's benevolent authoritarianism, he likely believed superintendents', medical practitioners', and his own authority overruled the concerns and objections of students or patients.

These concerns over disease within federal and public schools masked another justification for discrimination against "full blood" students. Most "full blood" families likely faced continued restrictions on their allotted lands, which exempted them from property taxes. In 1922, of the 36,432 documented Cherokee "members by blood," 9,000 were counted as full-bloods. Schools enrolled a total of 10,318 children, which included 322 in government schools, 179 in tribal schools, 250 in other schools (most likely parochial private schools), and 1,545 not in school.[64] Reports reminded Oklahomans, "Inasmuch as the land in the Indian Territory part of Oklahoma belonged to the Indians, the Federal Government gave the new state $5,000,000 for the Common School Fund in lieu of sections 16 and 36"; it calculated this by "figuring the number of acres of land in these sections in Indian Territory at a value of $3.53 an acre." State reports regarded the problem of Indian education as one of taxable land.[65] By 1930, officials claimed those funds were depleted and increased the allocations from thirteen cents per day per student in attendance to twenty cents per day.

Cherokee people who lived on allotments were exempt from property taxes, and despite their collective, albeit forced, contributions of land, wealth, and institutions to the state of Oklahoma, many politicians, educators, and educational administrators charged that Native people were a drag on educational coffers. In his 1927 annual report, Jack Brown assured federal officials, "Our community is in no way opposed to the intermingling of the White and Indian races. In the state of Oklahoma an Indian is lawfully on an equal with his White neighbor." Although this equality was legally true based on the efforts of Five Tribes officials alongside Oklahoma officials to define "the term 'colored' . . . to mean All persons of African descent who possess any quantum of Negro blood, and the term 'white' shall include all other persons," in practice many Native people continued to face discrimination based on race well after statehood.[66] Brown also stated in his annual report why the school existed: "The public schools are crowded and the Indian children because of their timidity are not given a fair show with white children."[67] Brown laid the blame for Cherokee children's lack of success in public schools on their demeanor when he could have easily called out the behavior of the school administrators, teachers, and students for their treatment of timid students. What Brown omitted mentioning, likely because federal reports failed to ask or perhaps because his social distance blinded him, were the declining conditions in many Cherokee communities throughout this period.

By 1930, it was clear to federal officials who held hearings in Oklahoma that many Native children were not enrolled in school at all. In Adair County, a Keetoowah estimated that 50 percent of the children in his community were not enrolled in school. Cherokee witnesses outlined many conditions that limited their access to schools: lack of clothing, the cost of books, and the distance to travel for schooling in rural areas. Sometimes Native children entered the school system at later ages but arrived lacking the English skills to achieve success, while some families preferred sending their children to federal boarding schools because they were year-round and provided clothes and books. Person after person said their communities wanted schooling. Only when pressed did one witness finally say what was under the surface of all the other witnesses' testimonies: "Mr. Wolfe (on behalf of the Keetoowah): The white teachers do not want those Indians to go to school because they are too dirty. They have not got enough clothes to go there. Another thing is they haven't got enough to eat to take to school with them. What are they going to do? That is one reason. I know it because I have been through there everywhere. I know pretty nearly everybody. I know pretty nearly every man in the Cherokee Nation."[68] The economic fallout of allotment conspired with new attitudes about public health to make educational outcasts of Cherokee children who had parents with land restrictions.

As a child, Rachel Johnson would have fallen into the second category of Indians in the survey of public schools, a full blood who lived in a two-to-four-room log home in the country. As an adult, Rachel lived in a more modest home than the one in which she grew up, but house size was only one indicator of the conditions created by allotment. When Rachel began raising her children, officials might have placed her somewhere between types two and three, those full-bloods seeking education but who pulled their children out of school should they need to and those living in one-to-three-bedroom homes with dirt floors. She played the piano at the Sycamore Church just down the road from her allotment, which she walked to every Sunday. She and her husband Sequoyah Quinton were both classed as "full-bloods," an indicator of lineage and cultural values but increasingly a designation tied to a family's restrictions on their lands. Both were bilingual; Sequoyah was biliterate. For a period of time, Rachel lived in a modest log home with dirt floors, no electricity, and an outhouse, but so did many of her white neighbors. Aincy Hogtoater, Rachel's paternal grandmother, lived with her after statehood.

Nelson, my grandfather, Rachel's only child with Kiah Smith, was her only child who qualified to attend the Sequoyah Orphan Training School. Attendance requirements included being an orphan and having restricted status, meaning the student's parents had blood quantum higher than one half and were deemed incompetent to buy, sell, or lease their allotments. Nelson was not an orphan by a Cherokee system of matrilineality and was being raised in a home with two parents, but his biological father, Kiah Smith, was not in the home with him. This murky definition of "orphan" was a holdover from policies instituted by the Cherokee Nation at its orphanage before statehood and that converged with officials' views (and the systems they created), which held that children were at a marked disadvantage without their biological parents, especially their fathers.

Rachel's husband Sequoyah Quinton served a year in prison—first at Leavenworth and then at Muscogee, for embezzlement—leaving Rachel a single parent caring for four children ages ten and under. For some Cherokee families, prison sentences—in the Cherokee National Prison, which opened after the Civil War until allotment forced it to close, or in federal prison in the states—introduced a new reason that men might be away from families for months or years at a time. There were no universal ceremonies shared within the Nation to restore these men to their communities when they returned from prison, unless they participated in Green Corn, but there were medicines and rituals to help them evade capture.[69] But in core Cherokee communities, one's return to the community after completing a sentence served as restoration enough. Sometimes the men who returned were not the men who left, something Climber of Trees surely would have understood when captives returned. Many churches no longer held hearings to evaluate parishioners, but some communities still withdrew Christian fellowship from those convicted and sentenced to prison. Even if they shared Christian fellowship on Sunday, some Cherokee people no longer abided by the same communitarian ethic that called them to open their home and share resources, as Ageyutsa and Climber of Trees' communities had, but some still did. Although reformers and some Cherokee people judged others by their loved one's time in prison, Rachel's Cherokee community supported her during this time.

Rachel's family was closely linked to the Keetoowah, Cherokee people committed to the ceremonies revitalized by Red Bird Smith held at the stomp grounds near Gore and Vian, who were derided in *The Red Man*, a periodical published at the Carlisle Indian Industrial School.[70] The fathers of Rachel's children were Keetoowah. She may have met Kiah Smith, Nelson's father, at the cornstalk shoots her father Samuel Johnson had participated in when she was young. Kiah Smith was the seventh son of Redbird Smith and Lucy Fields Smith. Redbird Smith, a former Cherokee National Council member, in his capacity as leader of the Keetoowah, had actively protested allotment. Smith's resistance led to his arrest and near-lynching before statehood. After statehood, Smith remained committed to community-centered education and values that privileged working together. Smith died in 1918 as a result of the flu pandemic.

Lucy Fields Smith was the daughter of Richard Fields, a former judge for the Cherokee Nation, and Eliza Brewer. She descended from both Western Cherokees and those who had faced mass forced removal, and she was distant kin to both Caroline Fieldses. She knew her parents' and grandparents' English and Cherokees names. Some credited Lucy with all that Redbird accomplished.[71] Lucy likely prepared huge meals for community gatherings and stomp dances, helped her daughters and granddaughters make their shell shakers, mended clothes, gathered water, and raised ten children to adulthood. She said prayers when she sent her two youngest boys off to war. Lucy's daughter, Kiah's sister, married one of Ayohka's great-grandsons.[72]

Ageyutsa and Climber of Trees would have undoubtedly recognized some of the values and symbols embedded in the teachings espoused by Smith and other Keetoowahs (Ayohka certainly would have), but they might have questioned some of the changing attitudes toward women and the absence of any Beloved Women or War Women in leadership positions. The girls would have recognized the significance of the fire that burned at the stomp grounds located throughout communities in northeastern Oklahoma, including near Vian, where Rachel was raised and where she was raising her children. And they certainly would have understood an elder woman like Aincy's presence in the home with young children underfoot, but they might have been confused. Was it Aincy's home? Why was the daughter of Aincy's son in the home? Or was it Rachel's home? Or was it the home of Aincy and Rachel, a strange violation of matrilocal practices? If it was Rachel's home, why didn't Aincy have a home of her own? Whose home was it? Ayohka might have understood. Aincy and Rachel understood, but this would have been foreign to Ageyutsa and Climber of Trees. Lydia, Aincy, Rachel—all the women in Sam and Rachel's orbit—created a Cherokee-speaking home that they would have recognized. Aincy and Jennie reinforced the language lessons Rachel provided for her children at her breast, so it's possible Aincy and Rachel could have communicated with Ageyutsa and Climber of Trees. These women weren't alone in the lessons they imparted to the next generation.

Maggie Fry, born a year after Rachel, grew up in Vian too. Her parents' and grandparents' lives intertwined with the Cherokee Nation's governmental systems. Her grandfather had served on the Cherokee National Council. Her father, bilingual in Cherokee and English, worked as an interpreter for the courts and served on the council too. Her grandmother received her education at a neighboring Native nation's seminary but picked up her medical training within the community. She served as a territorial midwife and often doctored people in emergency situations, including gunshot wounds and train accidents. Maggie never attended Indian schools. Instead, her parents sent her to a boarding school in Muscogee. Her education outside the Cherokee Nation set her apart from many of her counterparts, but she still received a dose of education from her family and the community itself. Despite being an English speaker, she attended stomp dances at the Stokes-Smith grounds knowing that she could not communicate with anyone there, which suggested how linguistically divided the Nation was after statehood.[73] She also was taught the cause of Oklahoma statehood, but it was not the version offered by the textbooks in public schools or by women like Eaton in the years following statehood that focused on political history.

Maggie was taught that statehood occurred not because the federal government violated its treaties and ignored the land rights of the Cherokee Nation but because a member of the Cherokee Starr family shot and killed a "deerwitch" in Tahlequah in the years leading up to statehood.[74] A "deerwitch," also known as Deer Woman, is a powerful woman educated in ancient cosmologies and medicines. She possesses features of both deer and woman and the physical and intellectual attributes that link her to the first ancestors of one Cherokee clan. Deer Woman, like Uktena, possesses power capable of good or ill. She often acts on behalf of those wronged, especially women and children. In the teaching Maggie received, killing a "deerwitch" results in a change in government. Part of Maggie's lesson was that if you kill a powerful female figure, a keeper of ancient knowledge, your leaders no longer deserve to govern. For Maggie and probably many others, the Cherokee Nation ceased to exist as it had because it slaughtered older curricula and disrespected the power of clans and the central place of Cherokee women.

The education provided and endorsed by the Cherokee Nation had laid the groundwork for Cherokee people to draw distinctions among themselves based on race, class, houses, land restrictions, and language. But the national and state conditions post-statehood and the legal distinctions produced by allotment, coupled with the schools Cherokee children attended, deepened the fissures and produced a subset of elite and mostly white-presenting Cherokee people who distinguished themselves from "Indians." The Indian Pioneer Papers gathered through the WPA projects in the 1930s lay these distinctions bare. At the same time, the elite English-speaking Cherokee women called upon to bear witness to Cherokee history and culture told a story of deep divides, remarkable continuities, and shared knowledges across the Five Tribes. Lucinda Hickey learned about the game of stickball from a Choctaw girl.[75] The continuities Hickey and other women described bore witness to the educational threads provided by women that stretched back to Ageyutsa.

Although the gendered labor remained similar in Cherokee families, the legacies of enslavement meant that some Cherokee girls had access to different teachers. In the Pioneer Papers, Lucinda Gott Hickey, like Elinor Fields, described living in the Choctaw Nation during the Civil War. Whether it was the conditions of the war that had leveled the class playing field or whether her mother had maintained key aspects of domestic labor, as opposed to farming all of it out to the enslaved women in her midst, Lucinda shared that her "mother raised sheep and cotton, and our clothes were made homespun." Lucinda's mother "would card the wool and weave it into cloth." "With the help of four negro women slaves, given to her by her mother who brought them from Georgia," they picked cotton seed out of the cotton by hand and then wove the cotton into cloth. "These materials were dyed with dyes made by boiling roots and barks. Our clothes were all made by hand. . . . We knitted our stockings, gloves, and scarfs. One time I knitted a pair of stockings for a girl who could not knit and she gave me six hens and a rooster for my pay."[76]

The education Lucinda received from her mother was both explicit and implicit. She learned the skills that were taught to her and also how to capitalize on those skills. Her mother imparted secondary lessons related to Black women's labor. In her retelling, Lucinda attributed her learning to her mother, even as she acknowledged the abilities and skills of other women in her midst. Lucinda simultaneously acknowledged Black women as laborers but erased them as teachers. It's more than likely the enslaved women provided a portion of this education to Lucinda's mother and to her too. Elinor recounted recipes for corn preparation that those same Black women reinforced.[77] Both women described the continued significance of agriculture to the women in their orbit and to the work Black women completed with their hands to produce items used by the larger community. Like many of the women who attended Dwight Mission during the tumultuous years following removal and leading up to the Civil War, Lucinda benefited from the labor and knowledge of Black Cherokee women, white Cherokee women, and other Indigenous girls.

Language learning, still tied tightly to generations of women, could come from other sources as well. Unlike Rachel Johnson, who learned to speak Cherokee from her grandparents and parents, Lucinda Hickey learned some Cherokee from her seatmate at school, Polly Keneltz, a "full blood" Cherokee.[78] Hogan Markham "went to school with a boy who lived near us. He was a white boy, he spoke good Cherokee and he taught us a lot of the Cherokee language."[79] In some spaces within the Cherokee Nation, language remained a primary education available to all, including non-Cherokee children, who all learned they had a role to play in sharing that knowledge with others. All of this indicated a propensity on the part of children to recognize, like Granddaughter Water Beetle, that they still had the power to aid other Cherokee people. Polly may have been a student and seatmate to Lucinda, but she was also a teacher. This kind of teaching reached across communities.

By the 1930s, many elite Cherokee women made rhetorical choices to distinguish themselves from "Indians." Just as some women had clarified their social distance from the Pin Indians, Lucinda described "a full blood Cherokee Indian" who "preached in *his* native tongue, with the aid of an interpreter so we could understand him. He was a Baptist preacher, and this meeting was held in a brush arbor."[80] On the one hand, she understood these events to be significant to the history of Cherokee people, but on the other hand, it was no longer *her* native tongue. She viewed herself as distinct from Cherokee language speakers, even though she stated in the same account that she had learned to speak Cherokee from her seatmate at school.

Boarding schools also sent conflicting messages to children about who they should be and how they should identify throughout this period. Some schools, like Dwight Mission and Sequoyah Orphan Training School, promoted clear assimilationist messages. Students at both schools were encouraged to embrace US sports culture, wear uniforms, learn to keep middle-class homes through home economics courses, and conform to rigid time schedules. In a stark shift from the Cherokee-controlled orphanage, and far more representative of what students at Carlisle experienced, the Sequoyah Orphan Training School, including under Jack Brown's leadership, required boys to wear military uniforms and complete drills every day. Students attended compulsory Bible class offered by teachers, and the YWCA and YMCA took turns sending ministers for Sunday evening services.[81] Jack Brown, unlike his Cherokee predecessor Walter Adair Duncan at the Cherokee orphanage, promoted an English-only approach at the school, the one that Luther Standing Bear and many students at Carlisle reviled.[82]

Federal boarding school officials (and educational endeavors more broadly) controlled all those activities related to Indigenous practices and beliefs that they deemed safe while simultaneously suppressing those activities they considered more dangerous. Native children at boarding schools could *play* at being generic Indians. In 1917, twenty-one students posed for a photo "in various tribal dress" at Dwight Mission.[83] Given that most students attending Dwight were Cherokees and none of the attire represented Cherokee dress at any moment in time, what did the children think about being dressed and posed as Indians? None of them look happy. Programs beyond those administered at boarding schools let all children play at being Indian. For many, it became a childhood rite of passage.

Students at Sequoyah were encouraged to join the Boy Scouts and Girl Scouts, which was endorsed and supported by Charles Eastman, a Santee Dakota, but still in its infancy. By 1915, the Boy Scouts underwent a leadership shift that positioned one of the cofounders against the organization when it increasingly focused on militarism and patriotism at the expense of increasing one's knowledge of the natural world, including flora and fauna. Boarding school youth were on the front lines of this infighting. The Scouts, which targeted non-Native youth for membership in the larger United States and encouraged youth to be "Scouts" and "Braves," also heavily influenced boarding schools. Eastman's involvement with the Scouts likely generated pride among Native students. And even though many of the activities focused on the perceived traditional activities of Native Americans, by the 1920s the merger of Christianity, patriotism, and militarism was well underway. A 1920 songbook encouraged youth to "do my duty to God and my Country, and to obey the Scout Law."[84] Cherokee youth involved in Boy Scouts could be "Scouts" or "Braves," but only if they publicly articulated a commitment to Christianity and the United States.[85] At the same time, the YMCA launched its Y-Indian Guides program to promote father and son bonding by spending time in "free spaces to act out their natural wildness." At the very moment when government officials ripped Native children away from their families to place them in boarding schools and erase their identities, white fathers and sons, and mothers and daughters, were encouraged to play Indian to combat the failures of modernity.[86]

In a similar way, the Pocahontas Club's rituals, mottos, membership, and philosophies reflected the conflicts some elite Cherokee people faced in how to articulate who they were to the larger public and to each other with their Nation no longer intact.[87] Even before the Pocahontas Club came into existence in Oklahoma, the Degree of Pocahontas existed as the women's auxiliary to the Improved Order of Red Man, a secret society for white members located only in the Northeast, which had incorporated playing Indian much earlier. The Pocahontas Club adopted the Golden Rule as its motto. Members answered roll call by "giving an Indian name and its meaning," and the male auxiliary members gave themselves titles like "Medicine Man" and "Keeper of the Wampum," titles they would likely have never obtained within Cherokee society because of their linguistic, class, and cultural distance from those traditions and core communities. They made Blackness a butt of their jokes when they awarded a Black baby doll as a "booby prize" for a guessing game. One of the group's debating exercises took up the question, "Shall the Indian remain Indian?"[88] Yet, they also remained deeply committed to Cherokee political history, but with an emphasis on nineteenth-century Cherokee political history and nationhood.

The members' understanding of themselves remained closely tied to institutional schooling. At one meeting, members named the first school they attended and one of their teachers, and if they were a schoolteacher, they shared the name of the first school at which they taught. Members saw themselves as descendants of the Cherokee Nation but not necessarily as the grandchildren of Ageyutsa or Climber of Trees. In a confounded way, these were Cherokee people who traced a matrilineal line of belonging but only to claim citizenship rights to a Nation. They asserted their identity as Cherokee by playing what they and other Americans would label "Indian" so that they could also be American.[89] Members of the Pocahontas Club had whiteness, class, educational privilege, and Christianity on their side as they navigated their lives post-statehood. They grappled with these complicated external messages, but these same messages played out differently for children from different social, economic, and racial stations.

School histories tied many people back to the Cherokee Nation. Cherokee students at the Sequoyah Orphan Training School wrote articles highlighting the history of the school and the Cherokee Nation and created artwork venerating its namesake. Whether students attended public schools or mission schools, the public school reports and the assimilationist policies more broadly sent clear messages to both Cherokee and non-Cherokee people throughout Oklahoma about the value of Cherokee-speaking children who came from poorer "full blood" families.

After the publication of Lewis Meriam's *Problem of Indian Administration* in 1928 and the fallout from the Great Depression and the Dust Bowl, federal policy toward Native people began shifting, but the legacies of the assimilationist messages broadcast to teachers and the public about Native people since the 1890s wore on. New Deal–era programs aimed to aid people in Oklahoma suffering deep poverty. The Indian Pioneer Papers directly benefited Cherokee people who acted as interviewers and interpreters and recorded the lives and histories of wide swaths of Cherokee people, including women like Elinor Boudinot Meigs, Cherokee Freedmen and Freedwomen and their descendants, and monolingual Cherokee speakers, some of whom had little to no schooling but had received educations.

Many Cherokee people living in rural areas had turned toward community-centered education when Cherokee national education ended and Oklahoma had failed to provide adequate educational options for students living in rural areas. In the years ahead, the continuing consolidation of schools coupled with federal legislative changes would force school officials to take stock of the school divides present in many parts of Oklahoma and among many demographics—rural, poor, Cherokee, and Black. The changes that followed in the public schools of Oklahoma in the decades ahead would produce varied educational outcomes for all of Rachel's children and grandchildren.

And yet, through the bilaterally configured home Rachel made with an intergenerational group of Cherokee women, she fostered a classroom space—a center of gravity—for her children and grandchildren. She sent her children to classroom spaces beyond her home, hoping they would spiral back to her when they needed to or when she needed them.

Aincy (Nancy) Joan in Vian. Artwork by Roy Boney Jr.

CHAPTER 6

Oklahoma Schools
Aincy (Nancy) Joan

A little over a hundred years after Ayohka relocated to what would become Sequoyah County, Oklahoma, a place that would be named after her father, Rachel Johnson Quinton returned home from her husband's kin's allotments to settle on her allotment to raise her children and grandchildren. Rachel's allotment, adjacent to six other family members' allotments, sat on Little Vian Creek, which provided a place for the children to swim, handfish, and catch crawdads. River cane grew along its banks. Mountain lions ranged over the area. The land supported wildlife, especially rabbits and squirrels, the latter often supplementing the family's diet in wintertime. Rachel and her husband Sequoyah farmed separately. Rachel grew spinach, carrots, lettuce, tomatoes, green beans and snap peas, nearly all of which were ideal for canning, according to the federally issued 1918 Cherokee language canning brochure.[1] Sequoyah grew watermelons, pole beans, squash, sweet potatoes, and peanuts up on a bluff. The family grew corn and stored it in the corncrib, just as Cherokee people had done for hundreds of years. Their diet contained many of the same foods Ageyutsa and Climber of Trees would have eaten, plus other foods introduced in their granddaughters' lifetimes. Rachel canned throughout the summer, shelving jars two rows deep in a cellar built into a hillside in the 1940s that still exists today, though no one has used it for canning since before Rachel passed away in 1991 when I was a freshman in high school. With a loan from the Bureau of Indian Affairs, the family purchased chickens, a milk cow, a team of horses, and some pigs. They also received commodities from the federal government, which they picked up in a neighboring town on Wednesdays. Sequoyah raised some cotton and supplemented the family's income by picking cotton for others; sometimes his boys joined him.

Rachel eventually took a job at a grocery store in town, where she became the first Cherokee woman in her family to earn wages outside the home. She introduced her children to the English alphabet, reading, and counting before sending them off to school. Her oldest son, Nelson, the only child she had with Kiah Smith, attended local public schools near where they were living, including schools at Wagoner, Greasy, Bunch, and Union and then Dwight Mission; he eventually attended Sequoyah Orphan Training School, the former Cherokee Orphan Asylum now located roughly thirty-five miles from his home, after the federal government assumed its control and renamed it. Rachel's oldest daughter, Marie, who adored Nelson, went to Greasy, Bunch, Fort Sill, Dwight Mission, and Vian but never finished because she "had the responsibility of helping to raise the family of 6 boys + 3 girls." After going to school at Bunch, Fort Sill, and Dwight Mission, Rachel's daughter Cordelia attended and then ran away from Chilocco Indian School, located near the Kansas border, while it was under federal control. When she returned home—traversing over 200 miles to get there—she enrolled at Vian. Rachel's second youngest daughter, Charlotte, attended Fort Sill, Bunch, Vian, and then Dwight Mission. After attending Dwight Mission, she "had a turn," knew the "Bible very much," and considered becoming a "worlds missionary" like Mollie Comingdeer, a bilingual Cherokee speaker who had been educated in Cherokee schools and had taught school in Vian before statehood.[2] By the time Rachel's youngest daughter, Sue, was born, school consolidation and increasing federal dollars for Native students in rural Oklahoma school districts ensured that her youngest children—Frank, Sue, Tommy, and Jay—exclusively attended school at Vian, and eventually her grandchildren would too.

Those who attended Dwight Mission boarding school could make the decision to leave. One of Rachel's sons, Breezy, would walk a few miles home from Dwight Mission while he was boarding there, a straight shot across Cherokee allotments in the early 1940s but a longer distance today because roads bypass private properties that are no longer in Cherokee people's hands. All of Rachel's children who attended boarding schools—schools that had previously been answerable to Five Tribes officials—spoke Cherokee. The oldest children also benefited from the presence of their Cherokee-speaking grandmothers, Aincy Hogtoater and Jennie Johnson, who died within ten years of each other in the 1930s and 1940s.[3]

Rachel's children, whether they traveled 200 miles, walked 5, or rode a bus from school, returned to a home versed in Cherokee educational materials on the lands her kin had lived on since before forced removal. But educational forces mattered. Once buses were introduced in the 1940s to aid national and state consolidation efforts, her youngest children and oldest grandchildren rode the bus together to the Vian Public School. Her children who exclusively attended Oklahoma public schools never achieved fluency in the Cherokee language, mastering instead what linguists call receptive bilingualism, an understanding of the language but an inability to speak it fluently. Over time, this skill waned.[4] The educational experiences of Rachel's children, grandchildren, and extended kin reflected continuities in Cherokee educational practices but also the trends in both Oklahoma and in federal educational policy that affected Cherokee children in rapid succession from the 1930s through the 1950s.

Three of Rachel's younger children—Sue, Frank, and the youngest, Jay—remember Vian Public School as a safe though largely unremarkable place. They also attended public school with their oldest brother Nelson's children with his first wife, Ada Lee (née Duffield). Nelson and Ada Lee married in Okmulgee, Oklahoma, a Muscogee Creek Nation town in 1942.[5] They married there likely to avoid the wrath of Ada Lee's parents, John and Eva Duffield, who objected to her marrying a "full-blood" Indian and who initially disowned her because of the marriage.

Rachel had sustained a Cherokee educational landscape for her children and grandchildren, but other educational worlds competed with hers and for her grandchildren. Her grandchildren Douglas (my father) and Nancy Joan were born while her son Nelson was in the army, stationed in Mississippi. Douglas was born in March 1943 and Nancy Joan barely ten months later, in January 1944. When Nelson and Ada Lee divorced, Ada Lee did what many divorced women did in the 1940s and 1950s: She reconciled with her parents and left her children with them while she sought employment.[6] Cordelia, Rachel's second oldest daughter, brought her children to Rachel while she worked regularly in the 1950s too.

Rachel worked hard to create a Cherokee educational world for her children and grandchildren, including Nancy Joan and Douglas, in the Sycamore community in Vian. Cherokee women, in pocket communities across northeastern Oklahoma, did the same. In many ways Rachel succeeded, especially in the long term. But in the short term, she was competing with forces working against her, both seen and unseen. Nancy Joan, Nelson's one and only daughter, would grow up less than a mile from her Grandma Quinton and her aunts and uncles, an easy walk even by today's standards. Nancy and Douglas attended church with the Quintons on Sundays, where Rachel played the piano. Rachel would give them an orange and a little bit of candy every Christmas. But Nancy and Doug were being raised by their non-Native grandparents, who forbade them from calling Rachel by the title "Grandma" and insisted they refer to her as "Mrs. Quinton," thus denying the children public claims to kinship and sending a painful message privately to the children about the definitions of family and about who they could or could not be. Nancy would also receive messages about the value of girls in both families that didn't provide a gravitational pull toward Sycamore in the same way it would for my dad and for me. Vian came to represent something very different in her childhood, a feeling that left her untethered from her childhood home in the years to come.

Rachel taught her children the history of who they were and the Cherokee origins of the community where they resided, lessons similar to those Ayohka had received generations earlier. She recorded her children's second names. In both a continuity of and a change to the additional names her parents and grandparents possessed, which were rooted in the Cherokee language, Rachel provided nicknames for all of her children. Nelson was Sonny Boy; Marie was Sis; Cordelia had a nickname, Cordy, and a Cherokee name; Charlotte was Shorty. Curtis had a school and a home nickname; the school name stuck—Breezy. Sue Ann became Sue, Tommy became Doogie, Donald Jacob became Jay, and Frank, born French Roe, legally changed his name to Frank as an adult.[7]

Rivers always scared Rachel, and her children and grandchildren knew it. This stood somewhat at odds with the relationship Ageyutsa and Climber of Trees had formed with rivers in the East. Waterways had always been powerful, symbolic spaces for Cherokee people, connecting layers of the other-than-human world together, so that even Ageyutsa and Climber of Trees respected the power of water. Rachel feared that power for an equally educationally salient reason: She had seen Uktena in a river as a child. Her family told her Uktena had followed Cherokee people west during the Long Removal Era. Rachel shared this story with her children and grandchildren, not so they would be frightened of rivers like her but so they would remember that rivers were powerful spaces, capable of good or ill. Nancy never learned this lesson as a child, even though she grew up within walking distance to a classroom where this lesson was taught.

In contrast, Nancy and Doug received lessons at home and at school that stripped their sense of identity and isolated them from their larger Cherokee community. Nancy (the equivalent of Aincy for Cherokee people) Joan was named for one of her paternal great-grandmothers, Aincy Hogtoater, a monolingual Cherokee speaker who remained a presence in her grandchildren's lives, including Nancy's father, Nelson. Nancy's maternal family never used the name Nancy (Aincy), instead referring to her as Joan, the name I have called her my entire life. Douglas Nelson received his middle name from his father, but no one ever called him anything but Doug.

After the Johnson–O'Malley Act passed in 1934, schools began counting Native kids in order to receive federal funds.[8] Many Cherokee kids were identifiable either by phenotype or by a teacher's knowledge of the family. This was true for Sue, Jay, and Frank, but Joan and Doug presented a problem. They were ambiguous; Joan was fairer than Doug, but both had deep hues of butterscotch to bronze skin depending on the sun, and both had deep black hair and dark eyes. They were being raised by non-Native people. Their mother wasn't Cherokee. Were they Cherokee? The teachers didn't know the answer, so they asked the Indian kids to stand up and identify themselves. Joan and her brother both remember standing for these counts and being confused and ashamed by what it all meant. So when they arrived home they asked their non-Native maternal grandmother, "How much Indian are we?" Their grandmother responded, "You're only a little bit Indian." Joan and Doug gleaned that Indianness had something to do with race and kin and being singled out at school, but it was also something to be denied or downplayed in certain settings.

The lessons they learned about Oklahoma history in school did little to help answer these unsettled feelings about their identity. *A Pupil's Study and Workbook in Oklahoma History*, produced throughout the 1930s and possibly into the 1940s, contained coloring sheets of a tepee and a generic Indian man with a bow and arrow. The "Story of Corn" said nothing about Selu or the significance of corn to tribes; the "Story of Cotton" ignored the exploited labor of formerly enslaved Black people or poor Black, Brown or white tenant farmers who still propped up the cotton industry across the country. Instead, corn and cotton production were about environmental resource extraction and the larger economy. The book contained a section on Indian removal and also reinforced "Big Men's History" in a section titled "Some Important Indian Leaders," which included Cherokees John Ross, Sequoyah, and Stand Watie.[9] If Joan and her brother learned from a textbook like this, they may not have fully understood how they connected to those particular people. If they knew the name of the county they lived in—Sequoyah—they may have drawn some vague association between the place and the man.

Joan and Doug grew up one mile apart from their Cherokee kin, attending the same church and the same school as their Aunt Sue and Uncles Frank, Tommy, and Jay. They had names that linked them to their Cherokee kin, but they lacked the everyday nicknames of the very same kin. All of these factors conspired to create confusion for what it meant to be Cherokee for children like them.

Rachel's children were rarely, if ever, confused about who they were as Cherokee people—and less ashamed. And Rachel was never confused about who her kin were. She kept notebooks with details of her children's and grandchildren's lives: birth dates, illnesses, school histories, dispositions, scars, marriages, divorces, addresses. She documented who her relatives were and, to the best of her ability, where they were in relationship to her.

Joan and Doug's classmates/aunts and uncles, and their grandmother, versed in older Cherokee pedagogical practices, attempted to teach them who they were. Frank taught Doug and Joan the more modern Cherokee words for boy and girl, *chuj* and *geyutsa*. Forty years later and without having used them since he was a boy, Doug still remembered those words when I asked him whether he had ever learned the Cherokee language. Doug and Joan's first Cherokee language teacher was another Cherokee child, just like it had been for Lucinda Hickey. Like Granddaughter Water Beetle in Cherokee origin narratives and like Ayohka during the Long Removal Era, Frank, the son of Rachel, great-grandson of Aincy, understood that even as a child he had a role to play in educating his kin.

Joan remembered a different relationship to the language. As many people did in post-Depression Oklahoma, Joan and Doug loaded into the back of a pickup truck at the ages of five and six, respectively, to drive into Cookson Hills to pick strawberries for five cents a quart. Joan remembered the truck being filled with Cherokee-speaking people. One time, she leaned over to Doug and said, "I wonder what those foreigners are talkin.'"[10] For the Cherokee speakers in the back of the truck with receptive bilingualism, what did it do to their hearts to hear that this Cherokee girl had learned they were foreigners in this place and to one another? One mile apart from their Cherokee family, five-year-old Joan had learned that her Cherokee kin and neighbors were foreigners in a land that Cherokee people had occupied since before forced removal. One mile apart, their educational worlds were not the same.

Ironically, these views came from her maternal grandparents, who had only moved to Sequoyah County in the 1930s. Vian cradled the Stokes-Smith stomp grounds, named in part for Joan's great-grandfather Redbird Smith. It was where her Grandma Quinton resided on her family's allotment. It was now a place where the power of old Cherokee educational practices battled against racialized and non-Native educational systems under the mandate of the State of Oklahoma and pursuant to federal policies.

The education Joan and Doug and their school-age counterparts received took place at home, school, and church and while laboring, and it took place within an old Cherokee community by the standards of Indian Territory and Oklahoma history. And yet, the schooling they received took place within an Oklahoma public school when Oklahoma's takeover of Cherokee education remained incomplete. Many tight-knit rural communities were still able to support schools that provided education to only Cherokee children. County schools were becoming the norm, governed by locally elected school boards. Some counties paid to use school buildings in rural communities to provide schooling. Without buses, students living in the most remote places either relied on travel by foot or simply didn't attend.

In contrast to the Long Removal Era, which had created a centrifugal force away from core educational foundations, allotment, statehood, and school takeovers created a centripetal force, which spun those most committed to older educational systems back to community centers. This produced incongruous outcomes for Cherokee children whose grandparents had been the last generation to interface with the world through a Cherokee administrative state.[11] Civic Cherokees, living in more dense towns and cities, relied more heavily on the State of Oklahoma to create spaces for acknowledging who they were as Cherokees. More rural Cherokee people relied on older Cherokee social welfare and educational systems to move forward. Others left the Cherokee Nation and the post-removal Cherokee world entirely, moving to other states for work or joining the military, thus creating challenges for their descendants' ongoing connections to Cherokee communities.[12]

Lewis Meriam's 1928 report, *The Problem of Indian Administration*, known as the Meriam Report, and the 1930 Senate investigations into the conditions among the Five Tribes had accelerated the move to universal public education in some places but with complex and inconsistent results. The Meriam Report condemned the off-reservation boarding school movement and endorsed a "modern" system that "stress[ed] ... upbringing in the natural setting of home and family life."[13] The report did not radically alter the aims of assimilation but instead made calls for increased budgets and expanded educational offerings.

Many Cherokee students were still attending Christian mission schools when this change began, while others attended federal boarding schools and still others multiple public schools, which often disappeared over time through consolidation. States like Oklahoma began to assume more responsibility for educating students of color, linguistic minorities, and rural students only when federal policies intervened in public education. For Cherokee students, this produced uneven educational experiences. Many families turned toward the oldest and most time-tested educational structures they knew, but even in those families, exposure to other educational possibilities remained a reality. The 1930 Senate investigations interviewed Cherokee family member after family member, most of whom preferred all-Native boarding schools.

More than 100 pocket communities of Cherokee people—thirty-five more towns than in 1799, when prospective missionaries rode through the East after the devastating American Revolution—remained committed to older educational practices, including the Cherokee language, gathering for ceremonies, sharing histories, and keeping a subset of children closely exposed to those curricula. Redbird Smith had revitalized activities at the stomp grounds in Sequoyah County prior to statehood, reintroduced lessons related to wampum belts to members of the community, and advocated for mutual aid societies built on the Cherokee ethos of *gadugi*, working together to elevate everyone.[14] While some people left Sequoyah County due to cotton farming failures, many Cherokee families moved to this area after statehood to maintain this education for the generations to come.[15]

In other communities like Bell, near Stilwell, large families maintained older curricula even as some chose not to participate in the ceremonies at the stomp grounds due to their Christianity. Children grew up hauling buckets of water from a fresh spring two miles away. Younger *anigeyutsa* in families with lots of women were less likely to learn to cook since there were so many hands available to help. But if they were asked how to prepare the dishes, they could explain the step-by-step processes from the years they watched at a distance. Some *anigeyutsa* used grease from hogs, as opposed to bears like Ageyutsa and Climber of Trees had, to mix with roses for their hair. The grease could also be mixed with berries to create tinted lip glosses. Rachel's and Joan's generations were the first without bears as a constant neighbor since Cherokee people arrived in Indian Territory. *Anigeyusta* gathered sand rocks from creeks, which they ground to a paste for face powder. They could augment the color by adding red rocks to the paste to create a rouge. Like so many of their predecessors, they lacked access to mirrors. Instead, they relied on one another to prepare each other's faces and often used water as a mirror.

In many communities, Cherokee foodways had changed little. Cherokees raised the same crops as their ancestors: corn, pumpkins, sweet potatoes, and beans. From the cornmeal, they made breads and coffee. As they had in the East, some families kept cellars under their homes to store crops, including cabbage and turnips, for use during the winter. Children went to waterways, not to gather mollusks but to gather crawdads. They foraged for mushrooms. Families raised their own tobacco for medicine, ceremonies, and consumption. Women cooked outside using heavy pots and open hearths, some using the same pots their grandmothers brought west during the Long Removal Era.[16] Rachel's son Frank created an architectural draft, from his memory of childhood, of a log cabin that the family built. His rendering included a large pot and open hearth just beyond the cabin.[17] Although in a different medium, the spatial layout resembles a photograph taken in the 1890s of two Cherokee women working outdoors. Frank omitted the women but added the recently built cellar for storing canned foods. Even in the absence of Rachel, her labor

Although he drafted this image more than a half century later, Frank Quinton's sketch of his Cherokee home (*bottom*) bears remarkable similarities to the photo taken in the 1890s. Even though Frank's mother is absent in his drawing, her labor and home are present. Two Cherokee women working outdoors, ca. 1890, item no. 79, Kathleen Faux Collection, Western History Collections, University of Oklahoma Libraries, Norman. Frank Quinton's sketch in the author's personal collection.

remained. In almost fifty years' time, Frank documented little change to Cherokee homesteads and lifeways.

Many Cherokee children, like their forebears, still slept outside during the warmer months. While Frank slept outside in the summers, down the road his niece Joan shared a bed with her maternal aunt inside her maternal grandparents' house, while Doug slept on a bed with his uncle on a screened porch year-round. In both families, heated bottles or rocks helped keep those sleeping in the coldest spaces a little warmer. Even though outdoor sleeping was a reality for poor rural families more broadly, Doug might have preferred the *osi* (winter home) that Ageyutsa and Climber of Trees had slept in to the harsh wind and snow he faced on the porch of his grandparents' home. In February 1951, when Doug was almost eight, low temperatures hit zero for multiple days and wind gusts were as high as thirty-two miles per hour. He wrote to his mother, "The floor is cold. I am cold."[18] I cried when I read these words more than fifty years later, in letters I found in her house on the night of my grandmother's funeral. I wanted to warm my father through time.

Taking care of each other remained a priority for Cherokee families, even with more limited medicine cabinets. Cherokee families recognized the limitations of medical knowledge, but grandmothers and mothers still prepared medicines to nurse the sick.[19] Some families knew which bushes could be brewed into teas, which could then be steamed inside tents to create aromatic treatments for children afflicted with measles. Cattails could be used to make a treatment for the common cold. Cane pole could treat whooping cough. Tree bark and animal fat could be used to make treatments for tonsillitis. Most people "knew a little medicine" and could call upon the doctors who were still present in each community. Many of those medicine keepers kept special gardens to grow the ingredients they needed. Cherokee people lamented the lack of a more robust medical library among kin and that many children weren't learning medicine from their elders. Generations after Climber of Trees' lesson that the pride of young people had led to a loss of Cherokee literacy, elder Cherokee people regretted that young people were not learning the medical knowledge of their people.[20]

The intergenerational learning necessary for children to identify their teachers and for teachers to identify those committed to the advanced training in medicine suffered under the more dispersed living patterns of Cherokees since before removal and even more so after allotment. White and Cherokee doctors educated in medical schools were also an option for medical care, and children who attended public schools received clear messages about the superiority of state and national medical and public health policies.[21] If one's own children or grandchildren weren't interested in learning, identifying the other kids in the community who were was increasingly difficult. Because many Cherokee people cataloged their archives in their minds and in the Cherokee language, as children ceased to speak Cherokee it became even more inaccessible to the next generations. The lack of accessible medical care provided by local experts, coupled with the distance from medical facilities, led many Cherokee people to request more facilities in the 1930 Senate hearings.[22]

The public health policies that followed the 1918 flu pandemic profoundly altered educational settings and impacted rural communities in very specific ways. As the controlled burns had done for Ageyutsa and Climber of Trees, the policies that trailed the 1918 flu pandemic produced better health outcomes in many Native American communities.[23] In other communities, though, it produced nightmares.[24] However, these public health reforms merged with public school policies from the 1920s and beyond to produce school reports that derided people of color and immigrants as generally dirty, slovenly, and ignorant. In the 1930s, a Cherokee man living near Salina testified that public schools resisted taking Cherokee students because they were dirty and lacked the right clothing.[25]

Throughout the 1930s, *The Health Officer; a Digest of Current Health Information*, which was distributed by the federal government, reported on the public health policies, practices, and curriculums at federal boarding schools.[26] In other reports, Chilocco, which two of Rachel's daughters attended in the 1940s, touted its extensive course offerings for high school students:

> The school proper provides the following project teaching opportunities: garbage, trash and sewer disposal; the sanitation of toilets, showers, and lavatories; . . . the first aid care of accidents in the treatment of simple ailments; sanitation of food supplies; rodent and insect control; swimming pool sanitation; sanitation of kitchen, dining room, and bakery; and sanitation of the laundry work, and the like. There are also the annual physical examination of the student body; the problem of communicable disease; immunization and quarantine; the special problems of tuberculosis, trachoma, and the venereal disease; the question of conservation of sight and hearing; and the matter of nutrition.[27]

Students in the ninth, eleventh, and twelfth grades carried out projects that reinforced this learning, including swabbing their bodies, kitchen areas, and classroom spaces to uncover the bacteria that lived on them and nearby. Girls exposed to this curriculum understood a range of lessons. As with nearly all boarding schools, the curriculum prepared Native girls to perform domestic labor in service to white women.[28] For many of these girls, they returned home conflicted about what they had been taught about the importance of hygiene and its reflection on one's character, contrasting those lessons with the upkeep they saw in the homes maintained by their own mothers.[29] Many of their mothers still lived in homes with dirt floors, flies were a constant companion in rural areas, and there was a fluidity that existed between the indoor and outdoor worlds. They loved their mothers, but this education led some to judge the homes they kept. Because boarding schools were often "self-consciously grand buildings," most students could only hope for and some only desired a far more modest version of the buildings they had boarded in when they returned home.[30] If women who attended boarding schools instilled these same ideas in their daughters, which schools then reinforced, granddaughters often came of age unable to sit, listen, and learn from their grandmothers in the comfortable and familiar spaces and ways that Ageyutsa, Climber of Trees, and Ayohka had. For civic Cherokees who had adopted these attitudes years earlier or who had promoted their distribution, it sharpened the class and racial divides that had continued to grow and deepen in Cherokee communities since the early decades of the nineteenth century. School reports, federal reports, and teachers weaponized children's judgments against their own mothers' homes and unpaid labor, just as they had explicitly weaponized them against their elders.

By the 1940s, two decades of Senate investigations and public health reports in Oklahoma collided with changing federal and state educational policies to produce new experiences of public health education and treatments for Cherokee children that differed from those their ancestors had received. Cherokee people had pleaded for facilities in rural areas in the 1930s. The 1945 Hill–Burton Act directed federal funds to states to build hospitals and clinics that could serve rural populations. Fourteen projects in Oklahoma increased the number of beds available in rural areas by 399.[31] This also increased the numbers of medical providers living in those areas. Most Oklahoma counties employed rural health nurses, and by the early 1950s rural health officials offered physicals to student athletes at their schools.[32] Indian Health Services provided medical care to Cherokee people, but the hospital was located in Tahlequah, a significant distance from many rural Cherokee people. Rural health nurses examined children at school for signs of trachoma. When Rachel's son Frank showed signs of the contagious eye ailment that could lead to blindness, the school notified Rachel and Sequoyah of his condition. On a predetermined day, Sequoyah walked Frank into town. Frank climbed into the back of a pickup truck loaded with other Indian kids, and the driver took them to Tulsa for a two-week residential treatment. When the two weeks were up, he got in the truck and was driven back to Vian.[33] Despite federal efforts to increase access to medical care in rural communities and county efforts to provide medical care to students through schools, rural Cherokee kids often received segregated care and lived significant distances from many specialized facilities.

Segregated medical treatment was only one aspect of segregation in Cherokee communities. Segregated institutions, which had already existed among the Five Tribes, often remained in use or transformed into other institutions serving Black people. For example, the Muscogee Nation approved the operation of Tullahassee Mission in the 1850s for Muscogee Creek kids. During Reconstruction, which lasted much longer in Indian Territory, the Muscogee Nation designated Tullahassee in 1881 as a boarding school for the children of freedmen and freedwomen. In the period that followed, more Black people moved to Tullahassee. In 1916, the first private college for African Americans in Oklahoma opened in the former Tullahassee Mission building.[34] In all five of the Nations, freedmen and their families pulled together funds to support local schools in the period leading up to statehood, relied on missionaries, or advocated for aid from the federal government.[35] Many of these same institutions remained in use after statehood.

Sequoyah County, which had comprised parts of the Illinois and Sequoyah Districts of the Cherokee Nation, inherited educational institutions that had served Cherokee Freedpeople's children and grandchildren. Ella Lowery had served as a teacher at Redland School from the late 1880s through 1903. Because the area had been a bastion of slaveholding and cotton farming, many Black Cherokees lived in the area at the time of allotment. After statehood, some attended ceremonies at the Stokes-Smith stomp grounds, while others attended the Baptist church started by freedpeople Jack Brown and Katie Brown in 1867.[36] Others held events for Decoration and Memorial Days at cemeteries in the area, which brought family members who had moved away back to the area for reunions. By 1923, the Douglass School had opened in Vian to provide education to Black children in the area.[37] Eight years later, the Sequoyah County Colored Teachers Association held its annual meeting at the school for Black children in Sallisaw, about thirteen miles southwest of Vian.[38]

Former Five Tribes Freedmen and Freedwomen advocated for the educational institutions they had helped build and those they had been denied access to before statehood. In 1934, African Indian and African American people celebrated the opening of a mental health facility for Black people in Taft, Oklahoma, a town built on the allotments of Muscogee Freedpeople.[39] Educational centers for African Indian education often provided predominantly Black towns the foundation to continue offering educational opportunities in the state of

Oklahoma. Lenapah, home to a large number of Cherokee Freedpeople at the time of allotment, was the location of one of the thirty-three accredited high schools serving Black students in Oklahoma in 1940. Of the thirty-three accredited high schools in 1940, fourteen, nearly 50 percent of the overall number accredited, were located on lands formerly governed by the Five Tribes.[40]

Like many Southern states, Oklahoma relied heavily on national philanthropic campaigns to educate rural Black students in the South. With the aid of Booker T. Washington, the Jeanes Fund, also known as the Negro Rural School Fund, was established in 1907, the same year as Oklahoma statehood. Oklahoma used the Jeanes Fund to supplement teacher salaries in counties across Oklahoma. During the 1943–44 school year, overlapping with Doug and Joan's birth years, the Jeanes Fund supplemented salaries in fifteen counties across 296 Oklahoma schools. In 1944 and 1948, the Jeanes Fund supplemented teacher salaries in fourteen counties. In 1944, Black students made up 7.5 percent of the total Oklahoma student population. State annual reports largely ignored how many of these students descended from the histories of enslavement among the Five Tribes, though the counties that Jeanes teachers served—Choctaw, Creek, McCurtain, McIntosh, Muskogee, Okfuskee, Okmulgee, Seminole—provided some of that history.[41]

School consolidation and annexation affected many rural Black families as well. Throughout the 1930s, schools serving fewer than eleven Black students were singled out in reports. If schools dipped below eleven students, the county superintendent could consolidate the school, which then required more busing services but fewer teachers—and therefore less employment for Black educators. The best way to ensure access to schools was to live in towns or cities. Consolidation, annexation, and population shifts led the number of counties served to drop to ten and the total number of schools to 142 for the 1949–50 school year.[42]

While segregation taxed some county resources by forcing counties to maintain separate buildings, it also created jobs for large numbers of Black people with advanced schooling. The Oklahoma State Board of Education reported, "Out of 1,645 Negro teachers in the school year 1948–49, 147 held Master's Degrees, 1,356 held Bachelor's Degrees, 99 had from 90 to 120 college hours, and 44 had below 90 hours."[43] By 1952, of the 1,517 teachers, 221 held master's degrees and 1,232 held bachelor's degrees.[44] Most rural Black students were forced to bypass schools closer to their homes in order to attend their segregated schools.

Instruction in segregated Black schools was similar to that in other schools. Schools had gardens to help supply food and provide an opportunity for canning lessons, and students used flashcards to remember material, learned penmanship, and prepared exhibits for the segregated state fair. Like their rural Cherokee and white counterparts, many Black students attended school in church buildings because those were the only suitable structures available.[45]

The schools that Black students attended, like those across the South, often faced challenges similar to those found in rural schools more broadly and in Cherokee schools specifically. Counties directed more funding to white-serving schools. The accreditation process was highly politicized and subjected Black schools to higher scrutiny, which led some school officials to engage in back-door deals to get their schools through the process. Because of the continued reliance on farming, and tenant farming specifically, in rural areas, Black students often stayed out of school for longer periods of time to support their families' incomes. When they returned to school, some Black students needed remediation. Jeanes teachers often provided this remediation and created flexible school calendars to meet these needs.

For those schools whose descendancy traced directly from the Five Tribes, a certain continuity existed. Even though the US Reconstruction efforts in Indian Territory had led to educational access for Five Tribes Freedmen, with the exception of the Chickasaw, when the United States moved forward with Oklahoma statehood it "abandoned [those] gains."[46] In addition to literacy tests that disenfranchised Black voters, new administrative frameworks and bureaucratic designations within the Oklahoma school system slowly eroded some of the paper trails that had connected Black and Native peoples to one another.

Relationships also eroded between many town-dwelling, white-presenting Cherokee kids and their more rural, phenotypically Native, monolingual or bilingual counterparts; school designations and funding contributed to these fissures. Many of the schools serving Cherokee children remained community schools and, in many instances, family schools created by Cherokee citizen benefactors before statehood or immediately following statehood. These deep connections to community and family enabled some schools to alleviate some of the alienation produced by the curriculums of mission schools and federal Indian boarding schools. However, even in the schools filled with Cherokee children, some of which exhibited core community values, the experiences of students varied widely. Children's feelings toward their school, their success, and their levels of alienation from their identity all depended to some degree on the teachers' pedagogical skills and their attitudes toward their students. It also depended on the home lives of the children, even those Cherokee children related to one another, like Joan, Doug, Frank, Sue, Tommy, and Jay.

Where Cherokees still had sizable core schools and communities, Cherokee people continued to police the actions of teachers who attempted to discriminate against Native children who were racial or linguistic minorities. Because of deep intermarriage, many non-Native teachers mistakenly assumed white-presenting Cherokee children were either not Native or had few allegiances to their Indigenous counterparts. Troy Wayne Poteete described how, when he was a child, bilingual students aided monolingual students in Gore schools. He recalled one time when a teacher grew frustrated because she thought a monolingual student was being recalcitrant. The teacher didn't realize the student spoke Creek, but the other students knew.[47] This was not uncommon in areas southwest of Vian and in and around Notchietown, where multilingualism was still the norm and family members might speak Cherokee, Creek, and Natchez, or in places like Rocky Mountain, Creek and Cherokee, where families descended from both Native nations.

Regardless of what they learned at the different kinds of schools they attended, rural living imposed its own curriculum, comparable to that received by other non-Cherokee children residing in other rural communities. For Cherokee girls like Joan in places like the Sycamore neighborhood in Vian, the purposes of labor and the spaces where it occurred paralleled the labor performed by Ageyutsa and Climber of Trees generations earlier. Cherokee girls gathered water. But for girls living farther away from rivers, springs, or creeks, this task became more onerous than it been for Ageyutsa or Climber of Trees. By the 1940s, girls used eight-gallon buckets to tote water from wells, springs, or creeks, as opposed to the pottery, finely woven baskets, or gourds their predecessors had used. Joan could gather water at a well at her grandparents' home. Occasionally, innovative family members, including Clemmie Tucker's brother, created a wired pulley system, which enabled water to be transported more easily to and from a spring.[48] Clemmie's brother had learned and understood gender complementarity and *gadugi*.

Water may be life, but it was also often deemed burdensome women's labor, unworthy of many men. Daily trips to gather water looked quite different for women and children in the middle of the twentieth century. Going to water for Ageyutsa and Climber of Trees had served as a call to restore and cleanse one's mind and body for the sake of the entire community. As Cherokee people began to name days of the week, Monday, *u-na-do-da-quo-nv-hi*, ᎤᏃᏓᏆᏅᎯ, translated to "washday" in English. By the 1930s, many girls had witnessed a change in women's daily lives. Because most rural Cherokee kids had only two sets of clothes, when compulsory schooling took hold and public health prioritized certain types of cleanliness, Cherokee mothers spent every evening of the school week laundering clothes for their children to wear the next day. After spending their days tending to fields and young children and preparing meals, when their school-age children arrived home, another shift of labor began. Those economically able purchased gas-powered Maytag washing machines and placed them on their porches.[49] Leona Denny Hopper's mother was one who had to launder clothes every day after school.[50] Globally, some women still spend a third of their lives laboring to gain access to water for daily existence.[51]

For the women and older girls who went to water to wash laundry every day so that children could escape some judgment passed by non-Cherokees and attend schools no longer controlled by Cherokee people, it may have been hard to recall the ceremonial purposes of going to water; repetitive labor may have dulled their minds. Mothers likely justified and understood that their tasks were for the sake of their children's well-being, but the monotony absent ceremony and community may have bred resentment or disassociation. For some families without a creek or freshwater supply close to home, washing day continued to serve as a community affair. Women from different households gathered to wash, gossip, and commune. Communities of women and older girls shared the tools of washing, leaving large pots behind for those who came after them to use. There may have been women who preferred cooking to laundry, but they mustered their way through the task knowing they would gather with friends at the creek—just as Ageyutsa had preferred feather cape making to pottery making but tolerated it for social reasons. Those families still performing daily going-to-water rituals, or even those who watched their elders do so, reinforced or perhaps echoed older curriculums to children. When women and girls from those families went to water for more repetitive, monotonous tasks like laundry, the refrain of going-to-water ceremonies may have provided a spiritual foundation to push through. For some, it may have served as a reminder of a world out of balance. When asked by senators why rural Cherokee children failed to attend school, families noted the lack of clothes. But what these families and the women who performed this labor may have really lacked was the physical or emotional energy at the end of the day to haul the water necessary to wash and dry their children's clothes for the next day of school.

Many Cherokee families in Sequoyah County continued to raise and harvest cotton, like Sequoyah Quinton, Rachel's husband. Most able-bodied people, regardless of age or race, helped harvest the cotton. Older girls and boys, grown men and women, all wore harvest bags for the task at hand.[52] Oklahoma schools, attuned to this agrarian reality, shut down in September so that families could harvest cotton. They resumed in November. What was seemingly a shared economic reality that shaped the educational calendar of rural children masked deeper economic truths related to race. Whereas most white and some Native students returned to school in November when the split calendar resumed, many Black children continued to labor on behalf of their families until after Christmas, thus losing an additional two months of schooling compared with their peers.[53] Although in many places, schooling helped level the curricular playing field between urban and rural students, that was not true for many Black and Cherokee students in rural Oklahoma.[54]

While nearly all children labored, it was the labor of women that was seemingly never-ending. Girls continued to carry water from wells, creeks, and springs. They served as caregivers and teachers to younger children while playing outside. They learned to sew, sometimes using those skills to make dolls for play. To turn work into play into artistry, Lorene Drywater embraced doll making, gathering discarded sewing needles from trash piles to create a cache of dolls. Ageyutsa might have recognized the need to gather used or discarded materials in order to begin learning the skill of cape making, 400 years earlier. Lorene carried this skill into motherhood, fashioning dolls for her own daughters when the time came; today she is a well-known doll maker in the community and recognized as a Cherokee National Treasure.[55] For most girls, doll making served as a temporary occupation to fill the lulls of childhood. Other girls lugged the lard buckets of school lunches prepared by their mothers across creeks on foot logs. Girls helped their mothers and fathers weed farms, haul wood for home construction, fish, gather eggs, can vegetables, sell surplus eggs in town, cut wood, gather greens in spring and mushrooms in fall, and hunt squirrels and rabbits.

Weekends offered a different pace and purpose of labor but not a reprieve. When Eva Fourkiller's family prepared a hog for butchering, the men were in charge of the boiling water, but it was her grandmother who sharpened the knives and handled the carving. In a moment of what may have been advocacy or the recognition of the inequities of labor in her family, Eva asked her father, "How come Grandma has to do all this work?" Her father, responding in Cherokee, said, "She's the best one; she doesn't make any mistakes." While the answer complimented her grandmother's skills and attested to the willingness of Cherokee men to watch women perform tasks increasingly assigned to men, it didn't speak to why men in the family didn't sharpen skills of their own to reduce what Eva recognized as an unfair burden of labor on her grandmother.[56]

Whereas girls' labor and the skills they gained often crossed gender lines, the line had hardened in reverse. When Leona Hopper asked her brother to help her carry the lunch bucket across the creek to school, he refused. Eva Fourkiller had seven brothers, but when her mother had surplus eggs to sell in town, "the boys wouldn't do it," so she would handle the sales, a task she despised, possibly for the interactions it involved with men in town.[57] Boys regularly avoided girls' labor or were never assigned it at all.

Men told each other jokes to discourage other men from helping women and mastering the gender complementarity they might be learning at home. Avoiding women's labor became a way to police the boundaries of manhood. A former white missionary schoolteacher, immediately after commenting on the adoption of canning equipment and Maytag washers to aid women's labor in Cookson Hills, added a quip he had heard: "There is two things that you don't want to be caught ever doing, one of 'em is splittin' cook wood for your wife, and most of them had wood stoves, and the other was carryin' water. He said, you'll ruin it for all the rest of us."[58] In his retelling, he seamlessly weaved together stories of mechanized progress aimed at assisting women's labor with hardened gender roles that men should never cross. In a nostalgic nod to the Old South and the racialized enslavement of Black people, the *Sequoyah County Times* ran a story when Jean Dunn, "the last negro in town to carry her laundry home on her head," passed away in 1941. On the surface, the paper offered an homage to a woman's legacy, but it was also pining for a bygone legal and educational system where "Old Mammies taught . . . their young charges to walk and even dance with a glass of water on their heads," a system that degraded women's bodies and one that expected Black women to educate the next generation of girls in their own degradation for the amusement of white people.[59] What women like Jean probably yearned for was the ability to celebrate a cultural lesson carried forward in time by her grandmothers. In reality, though, these tasks stole time from these women and their children and prevented some children from attending school altogether.

Even as some men mocked women's water-related labor, there were others who learned that gender complementarity existed. Clemmie Tucker's brother looked for ways to innovate that enabled everyone to gather water more easily—an approach to innovation rooted in community needs as opposed to profit seeking or sexism. He created the water pulley system to aid his mother and sisters gathering water because he saw their need. When Wilma Mankiller, who was born in 1945 and would later become the first female principal chief of the Cherokee Nation, aided with the Bell Water Project that would bring running water to homes in the Bell community in the 1980s, it wasn't just a Cherokee community project rooted in gender complementarity—though it was that too—it was a gender equity project as well. Maybe for some of those women's granddaughters, going to water could be ceremony and prayer once again, restoring some balance to their lives and the world.

Girls rarely faced limitations when it came to labor, and when they did, those limitations were very specific to families. Joan Jumper's family expected her to gather water, greens, and mushrooms. She also spent her days playing in the woods with her brothers once chores were done. Some mothers refused to let their children experiment with cooking for fear that what little food was available might be ruined, a reasonable concern for people with limited resources.[60] Despite her desire, Joan Jumper's mother never allowed her to gig fish with her brothers and father in the evenings. Ella Thirsty, a self-described "tomboy," played marbles with all the boys and "wrastled" with them in the creek. Most girls learned to ride horses, as Cherokee girls had ever since horses had arrived in Cherokee lands.[61] My Aunt Joan trailed her older brother Doug and her Uncle Jack on their hunting excursions for rabbits and squirrels. Delois NoFire hunted rabbits with her father and brother in winter because, as she said, "that was our food supply as well as our entertainment." Wilma Mankiller described her childhood this way: "The natural world was our playground, and we used our imaginations to invent interesting things to do."[62]

Children who grew up during this period often didn't say much during interviews about the interplay of work and leisure for their mothers, but as with hunting, they did point out their fathers' pastimes. George Polecat described weekends filled with the pursuits of men. On Friday evenings marble playing commenced, and it lasted until Sunday. More than likely, women accompanied George's father's friends to the Polecat home and the women socialized while preparing food together for the weekend's antics.[63]

These gatherings must have served as an intellectual and social reprieve for the women after a week's worth of isolating household labor. This increasing daily isolation stood at odds with the collective work performed by generations of Cherokee women in communities together. Often, the best women could hope for was to have their mothers, their husbands' mothers, or perhaps their oldest daughters to labor beside.

Churches, like they did for women in towns, also filled a social void for women. Rural women labored all week; Sunday school and services provided a reprieve from labor and a time to gather with other women in the community. Sunday schools had long provided the only schooling available to many communities, but by the mid-twentieth century, church services catered some activities to children, relieving women of additional care for a few hours. In the decades following allotment, when schools became less hospitable to Cherokee children, churches often provided Cherokee language education, the reverse of the pre-removal era when Cherokee people sought missions for their ability to teach English. In the Springwater community, Polly Tehee's uncle taught the syllabary in Sunday school.[64] For communities with Cherokee speakers, this provided not only a break from labor but also a welcome intellectual community where women could converse with a wider swath of Cherokee speakers, including those with some of the most advanced and oldest Cherokee vocabularies and oration skills.[65] For families with people not being raised as speakers, kids like Joan and Doug could look "forward to their Christmas party at school and another at Sycamore church," one of the few spaces they could interact with their Grandma Quinton.[66] In Joan and Doug's recollections of Christmas at church, it was not the party but the interactions and gifts from their Grandma Quinton they remembered.

Just like generations of Cherokee mothers before them, starting with Selu, Cherokee women continued to produce and share the food that sustained their children and communities. Mothers and grandmothers prepared buckets of biscuits with jelly or egg or ham that nourished children at school until President Truman signed the National School Lunch Act into law in 1946, which made lunches available at schools across the country. Leona Denny Hopper also noted that it was her mother who canned all the food for winter. Cherokee people's diets in the post-statehood period included few white-tailed deer, which had been plentiful after removal but had declined when settlement exploded in the 1890s. Hunting squirrels and rabbits, while largely carried out by men and boys, was also occasionally the work of girls. In Lorene Drywater's family, in winter it was her mother who killed the squirrels, not her father. Even though places like Sequoyah Orphan Training School reinforced the role of men and boys in raising and slaughtering hogs and cattle, when families slaughtered hogs in the summer it was sometimes left to the women to do the butchering.[67] Women in Vian, including Rachel Quinton and Eva Duffield, Joan's Native and non-Native grandmothers, kept kitchen gardens that aided in the preparation of their family meals. What did girls studying their likely educational trajectories think as they considered their future roles as grown women or mothers? Many learned they would engage in repetitive tasks, some of which they enjoyed but many of which were onerous but necessary and largely in service to their children and grandchildren.

Children did witness other possible labor pursuits for women, but rural living often obscured the full range of creative labor performed each day by women and made identifying and mastering those skills more difficult for children. Most Cherokee families had some knowledge of everyday medicines, but fewer practiced medicine. Johnny Sanders knew of two women in his community who were "old lady Indian" doctors. He remembered one who lived in Greasy and traveled by horse to treat patients. Both doctors would often stay with patients for seven days, a sacred number in Cherokee cosmology, to make sure the treatments took. A few women, like men, recorded their medicine in notebooks in syllabary.[68] Girls still learned treatments and medicinal knowledge from mothers and grandmothers and understood that the trees are medicine.[69] For children with a propensity toward healing, one week with a doctor might not be enough time for them to identify as individuals committed to learning and capable of mentorship. As more and more children learned English, it became even harder to access that training; one has "to be in community to use and rely on it."[70] Access to teachers ebbed and flowed with the illness of family members. The lack of compact towns also placed teachers out of reach of prospective students.

Accessing advanced educational training in older Cherokee-centered curriculums and Euro-American systems grew more difficult in the years following statehood. Cherokee people who valued the curriculums associated with ceremonial grounds or Cherokee-language churches often lived the farthest from the towns that were building high schools. Most rural students—whether white, African American, or Cherokee—never advanced past eighth grade. A single teacher often taught all students from age six through their completion of eighth grade. High schools continued to be out of reach for many rural students. Communities with high schools tended to be more urban and serve predominantly white students—both white-presenting Native and non-Native. For students who lived at a distance, continuing in school required boarding with community members who lived near a high school. The seminaries no longer served Cherokee people seeking a post–eighth grade education. Because of a lack of accessibility of high schools and the rarity of high school diplomas, and not just among rural Cherokee communities, the State of Oklahoma continued to employ many teachers with just an eighth-grade certificate through the 1950s.

Because many Cherokee families continued to value education, especially when it was accessible and under the guidance of people known to the community, achieving an eighth-grade certificate remained the norm throughout the period. Throughout Sequoyah County, the lists of teachers within communities included Cherokee descendants. Dwight Mission continued to provide educational access until the competition with public schools forced its closure in 1948.

Education mattered to Cherokee people. Rachel recorded each of her children's graduations from eighth grade. Rachel's friend and kin Leona Denny Hopper, a first language Cherokee speaker like Rachel, taught in a local school with her eighth-grade education. Joan wrote letters to her mother reporting on how she was doing in school at Vian; her brother Doug did, too.

Joan and Doug as young adults. Photo courtesy of the author.

Because of the continued presence of Cherokee teachers and Cherokee families in schools, girls who attended school did see women who performed labor that could be valued or denigrated by members of the community but that, regardless, was compensated. Female teachers, as they had in the Cherokee Nation before statehood, earned income. Joan remembered having a non-Cherokee relative as a teacher in school. Jay recalled having a Cherokee relative as a teacher. Cherokee and white kin of students vied for teaching positions. As a teacher and a community member, Leona encouraged other young Cherokee people to pursue their education because it was something no one could take away from them.[71] Rachel taught briefly in the local schools with her eighth-grade education. When Jay, the only one of her children to attend a four-year university, quit college, Rachel lamented, "We don't know what to do or say to him."[72]

While many men who taught in the public schools used the position as a stepping stone to other white-collar professional endeavors, for many women, teaching served only as a temporary economic safety net for their families, albeit one that could model possibilities for children—their own or someone else's. Many of the town centers previously occupied by Cherokee-centered businesses or white-owned businesses beholden to Cherokee governance gave way to white-owned and -operated businesses beholden to state officials, thereby providing a model of the professions of non-Native people.

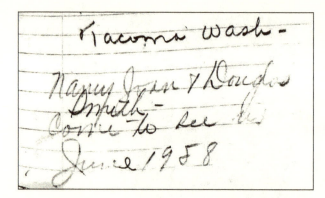

Excerpt from Rachel Quinton's notebook. Image courtesy of the author.

For Ada Lee, Joan and Doug's mother, economic necessity and the lack of employment opportunities had led her to leave them with her parents, the Duffields, who just a few years earlier had disowned her for the relationship that produced them. But that wasn't what had led Joan and Doug to continue to live there or what limited Ada Lee's visits. She and Nelson had remarried other people, and both were on more firm economic footing than they had been when they were married. Yet, the children remained with the Duffields in Vian. Both Joan and Doug remembered sitting on the porch waiting for their mother to arrive for visits, only to be disappointed. Joan would watch her brother disappear from the porch to be alone in his sadness. They don't remember the visits from Nelson and his second wife, Pauline.

Connection matters. Rachel Quinton documented when her children and grandchildren came to visit in her notebooks *and* when they did not. She wrote, "Nancy Joan + Douglas Smith—come to see us June 1958."[73] For Joan, there was a perception that Doug mattered more to Rachel as the oldest son of the oldest son. That is certainly what the *Rollo Code of Morals* worked hard to reinforce at Dwight Mission during the Long Removal Era. I would receive this same message from Ada Lee, now my Grandma Reed, Joan's mother, when every year she sent significantly more money to my brother for his birthday than I received from her for mine. The message I took away was that he was literally worth more. Joan has not felt the same pull to return to Vian as my dad did since they moved away. As hard as Rachel worked to create a Cherokee educational world for her family in Vian, it's a place Joan felt less valued and associated with parental abandonment. And yet, somehow, as Rachel likely intended, it's a place I have come to feel the most at home in the world and that has served as a core part of my Cherokee education.

CHAPTER 7

Global Education

Julie

By the 1970s, Vian and the surrounding area's landscape were markedly changed. From the 1930s through the 1950s, state and federal flood control legislation and the creation of the Grand River Dam Authority created new reservoirs and paths for rivers the community had come to know. The shifts in Oklahoma's land and waterscape were similar to those happening in the Tennessee River Valley to the east, the region from which Cherokee people had been forcibly removed some 130 years earlier. North Carolina Cherokee people, who through the treaties of 1817 and 1819 had broken politically with the Cherokee Nation, maintained a formal community structure and received federal recognition as the Eastern Band of Cherokee Indians in 1889. There, they remained to carve out an enduring core community presence. A different kind of removal commenced in Oklahoma in the mid-1940s, when Nancy Joan was a small child. In 1942, to expand Camp Gruber, the US Army claimed 32,000 acres in Ottawa, Delaware, Craig, and Mayes Counties over the next decade. This forced eighty families to relocate; forty-five of those families lived on allotments held in trust by the federal government.[1] For many families, this was their third forced removal in less than 100 years at the hands of the federal government. When Joan was three, the Army Corps of Engineers completed one of the earliest dams in Oklahoma on the Illinois River. As the dam was built, the nearby Cherokee town of Cookson was relocated wholesale.[2] Closer to Joan's childhood home and Rachel's community, in the late 1960s the federal government used Corps of Engineers land once controlled by the Five Tribes to establish the Sequoyah National Wildlife Refuge. The refuge comprises nearly 21,000 acres that stretches across Sequoyah, Haskell, and McIntosh Counties on the edges of the Kerr Reservoir. The refuge provided lands for cooperative farming and maintained part of the yield to feed the bobcats, deer, and muskrat living on the land.[3]

As the landscape changed, so did important parts of the political structure for Cherokee people and their neighbors. In 1946, a year before dam construction commenced, the federal government agreed to let tribes seek financial redress for lands taken by it through what has come to be known as the Indian Claims

Julie moves into the world. Artwork by Roy Boney Jr.

Commission. Two years later, at the behest of the federal government, Cherokee Chief-for-a-Day J. B. Milam (appointed by Franklin Delano Roosevelt in
1941) called a convention of Cherokee people together, including leaders of the
United Keetoowah Band.[4] The United Keetoowah Band had been attempting
to gain federal recognition since the 1930s. In the intervening years, this group
actively sought federal recognition through the New Deal era's Oklahoma
Indian Welfare Act.[5] At that convention, leaders established an executive committee made up of representatives from each of the Cherokee Nation's nine
previous districts, including an amendment to include two representatives
to serve the interests of those living beyond the boundaries of the Cherokee
Nation, especially those in Tulsa. In the years that followed, Milam and the
appointed executive committee worked to build commercial enterprises, forge
economic partnerships, and garner jobs to increase the economic well-being
of individual Cherokee people. The United Keetoowah Band, which received
federal recognition in 1950 when Joan was six and her brother Doug was seven,
began holding elections among its core communities and identifying federal
funding sources for the most pressing needs.

In 1970, the same year the refuge opened, the federal government finally
passed the Principal Chiefs Act, which enabled the Five Tribes to popularly
select a principal chief for the first time since 1903. The Principal Chiefs Act also
followed on the heels of Nixon's Self-Determination Act; the publication of the
1969 Kennedy Report, a damning report on the lack of educational access and
poor learning outcomes for Indigenous students enrolled in federal boarding
and public schools across the country; and the Red Power movement, collective
actions on the part of mostly young people across the country aimed at ad-
dressing a range of abuses, including local policing in urban areas. Collectively,
these added to a growing recognition of the ways the government was failing
Native people. In response came new federal resources aimed at revitalizing
housing, job training, and education.

As attention to Native peoples and federal allocations for them increased,
new people claiming generationally distant ties or fantastical claims to Native
identity stepped forward as well. Perhaps the best-known fake Indian of the era
was Espera Oscar de Corti, an Italian American also known as Iron Eyes Cody,
or "the Crying Indian" in a federally funded advertisement against pollution.
But many more speculative or outright false claims of Native identity followed
the growing environmental movement's celebration of Indigenous people's
ways and the potential funding for tribal initiatives. Other forms of cultural
appropriation also surged. At the same time the Cherokee Nation was working
to reestablish the political and cultural sovereignty that the federal government,

white settlers, and the State of Oklahoma had tried to dismantle, the YMCA Indian Guides program had grown to 26,000 "tribes" nationwide, with more than 500,000 parent and child participants.[6] As Cherokees in the revitalizing Cherokee Nation and the United Keetoowah Band worked to identify those entitled to resources and those most in need based on connections to Dawes enrollees and living within communities in Oklahoma, they competed with those far from their communities looking to capitalize on distant family lore at best and fraud at worst.

Rachel paid particular attention to the new developments, since during those intervening years she had served as the elected secretary of the United Keetoowah Band.[7] In 1963, while Rachel was secretary, the group amended the 1949 base roll, prepared as part of the federal recognition process, to include many of the children and grandchildren of base roll members. Rachel added her grandchildren Nancy Joan and Douglas Nelson Smith. They had lived apart from Rachel's son Nelson since they were barely toddlers and had moved away from her when their home in Vian burned to the ground. They had both graduated from Norman High School the previous year. And although she had worked hard to document where her children and grandchildren were over the years, she likely did not know where they were when she added them to the roll. In fact, Joan was enrolled in college at the University of Oklahoma, 153 miles away from Vian, and Doug had joined the navy. Because of this, she listed their addresses as Nashville, Tennessee, where Nelson was living with his second wife, Pauline, and their four sons at the time. Although Rachel was unsure where they were in geographic proximity to her, she continued to document who they were in relationship to her and who they were as Cherokee people.

Rachel, who was in her seventies in the 1970s, had given birth to and fostered the leaders and children coming of age in this moment. Some Cherokee girls, like Candessa and Catherine, learned lessons from people like Rachel on porches, in Oklahoma public schools, and in Cherokee people's living rooms in northeast Oklahoma. My schooling, however, took place worlds away from Cherokee communities. I was born in March 1976 at MacDill Air Force Base in Tampa, Florida. I exist in no small part thanks to the legacy of colonial education practices and the history of US empire, with their heavy impacts on Indigenous people worldwide. I join a long line of Cherokee children born from intermarriages. Unlike Catherine and Candessa, who grew up in core Cherokee communities, by the middle of the twenty-first century "hundreds of thousands of youngsters [like me] have received a portion of their elementary or secondary education" in schools set up by the Department of Defense for service members' dependents. Native people serve at rates five times higher than the rest of the population, and my experience as a Cherokee kid attending Department of Defense schools is shared by many other Native students.[8] My schooling simultaneously set me apart from and made me representative of a wide swath of Native and Cherokee youth in the second half of the twentieth century. Collectively, Candessa, Catherine, and I speak to the dynamic ways Cherokee girls' educations have been forged by land, language, and women in the final quarter of the twentieth century.

Girls who grew up in the revitalizing Cherokee Nation received a range of educations from their landscapes of learning. Candessa, who was raised within the boundaries of the Cherokee Nation, spent hours on the front porch of her grandparents' home listening to them tell stories about the five generations of her Cherokee/Creek family who had lived on those lands before her. Her *eduda* (grandfather) waved toward his grandparents' former home, which sat on the same land. She would listen to the cicadas. She believed her grandfather was magical because he could identify their neighbors by the sound of their cars driving by even though he was sitting with his back to the road.[9] Candessa learned that the sensorial educational world mattered; Ageyutsa and Climber of Trees would have shared that understanding.

Catherine, who was born at the W. W. Hastings Hospital in Tahlequah, named for a former Cherokee chief, received a powerful lesson about community as she was growing up in Oklahoma. Beginning in 1969, Congress allocated funds for tribes to employ community health representatives. Early in the program's history, those hired as representatives spent three weeks training for the position, often at locations far from their homes, including Albuquerque, New Mexico, where many Cherokee representatives studied. The position paid $375 a month and mileage. Representatives learned CPR and how to take vital signs from patients, conducted home health checks, served as liaisons between community members and health agencies, and translated for community members.[10] Many bilingual Cherokee women served in these positions, including Rachel Quinton and Catherine's grandmother.

One of Catherine's earliest memories was waking up at 5:00 am to load into her grandmother's van and drive from Warner to Porum to Webber's Falls, old Cherokee communities still filled with Cherokee-speaking people. Catherine's grandmother took people's blood pressure, checked on their prescriptions, and reminded them of appointments. Catherine, at four and five years old, not only was learning the geography of the Cherokee Nation but also visited people's homes and listened to elders speak Cherokee to one another. Attached to her grandmother's hip, as so many Cherokee girls had been over the millennia,

Catherine watched her Cherokee grandmother, fluent in the Cherokee language, tend to the health and well-being of other Cherokee people. As an adult, Rachel's work as a community health representative reinforced the same lesson for her adult children. Watching these women labor as they cared for other Cherokee people was a core part of their children's and grandchildren's education, and now it was being compensated by the federal government.

Catherine attended Warner Public Schools in a formerly Cherokee-controlled community. In third grade, Catherine came home from school and asked her grandmother if she could get a bonnet for Land Run Day, a reenactment held annually around April 22 in Oklahoma public schools to commemorate the opening up of the unassigned lands, lands formerly controlled by Native people, in Indian Territory to white settlement that eventually led to Oklahoma statehood. Catherine's aunt who worked for Warner Public Schools offered to get her the bonnet. Catherine's grandmother, in contrast, looked at Catherine and said, "Just sit there and let them run you over."[11] Just like the full-blood Cherokee woman in Tahlequah at the time of Oklahoma statehood who objected to the politician saying "Our Land and Our Country" by responding "Not our land and *not* our country" two generations earlier, Catherine received a Cherokee-centered education that challenged the schooling she and all other Oklahoma public school students received.[12]

Catherine's education included a world filled with spiritual diversity that highlighted changes that had developed in Cherokee communities over centuries. Every day, her grandmother walked through the house smudging each room with cedar, a powerful medicine for Cherokee people, to rid the house of negativity and offer protection to the people who lived there, including Catherine. Catherine often found medicine bags in her gym bag when she played sports. She learned about the Little People who live near Cherokee people, and although often simply mischievous, they could do real harm if one's actions veered away from the right path.[13] Catherine's family lived near Notchietown, a town associated with Natchez leaders, including Creek Sam, a multilingual speaker, who had advised and mentored Redbird Smith, my great-great-grandfather, before he worked to revitalize the Cherokee grounds at the time of allotment.[14] Catherine grew up attending Cherokee stomp grounds and Muscogee Creek stomp grounds, and she grew up singing Creek hymns. One of Catherine's aunts was heavily involved in the Cherokee Baptist Association, which, when Catherine was young, actively discouraged Cherokee people from attending stomp grounds of any kind. This education left Catherine believing there were medicine wars happening all around her; it left her preferring the safety of her family's land to the larger world around her.

In 1991, when she was just starting high school, Catherine lost her great-grandfather. When she did, she lost a teacher who linked Cherokee educational classrooms across time. He was ninety-nine years old, born in 1892, a full fifteen years before statehood. He preferred to speak in Cherokee and wrote almost exclusively in syllabary. He tied Indian Territory to Oklahoma and the Cherokee language as a viable and sizable curriculum to a time when it was dwindling. He had attended school only until second grade and thereby tethered the darker moment of what it meant for the Cherokee Nation to exercise educational sovereignty to a moment when many Cherokee children were forgotten by schools. He was originally from Porum, a Cherokee community long associated with the Starr family. Sam Starr married Belle Starr, and the two became notorious outlaws in Indian Territory and Oklahoma. Catherine's great-grandfather lost his family lands to the dam projects, one of the many to face multiple removals. Catherine grew up with people who embodied Cherokee educational pasts and presents and paved a way for her future.

Catherine's educational future included a basketball and softball scholarship to Bacone College in Muscogee, Oklahoma. After two months at Bacone, tired of playing sports and unable to keep her scholarship if she didn't, Catherine left school. By the spring of 1995, she had enlisted in the army and was headed to Fort Jackson for basic training. Unlike Cherokee men who joined the military to supplement family incomes, provide a social safety net, do what all men in their Cherokee family had done, or exercise a masculine warrior tradition, Catherine joined because she just needed to get away from Warner. A childhood immersed in Cherokee education followed by her young adulthood acted as a centrifugal force that led her away from the Cherokee Nation. But that force didn't hold.

Unlike Catherine's and Candessa's childhoods, my childhood was marked by far greater mobility and by the sense that there was a Cherokee education that was, at worst, being denied me and, at best, being suppressed. Catherine and I were born the same year, although I was born hundreds of miles from the Cherokee classrooms in the Old Nation, the original homelands of the Southeast, and the new homelands of Oklahoma where my dad and Aunt Joan had been raised. Despite this geographic distance, I do not remember a time I was unaware of being Cherokee through my dad's family. Once old enough, I marked American Indian/Alaska Native on every form I was ever given to fill out in school. My dad's complexion and his eye and hair color were not my own, and his Cherokee-ness was the explanation. When I was very young, race, and to a lesser extent biology, explained what it meant to be Cherokee.

My mother, Martha, born in 1945, was a first-generation college graduate turned public school teacher. Her family, descended from French and German immigrants, had lived in a small farming community called Marilla in western New York, just outside Buffalo. Her paternal grandfather worked as a farmer, as did many of her extended kin. Martha's father, Donald, worked as a carpenter was employed in construction during her childhood. Her mother, Evelyn, didn't work outside the home when Martha was young, but by the time she and her two sisters (Margaret, older, and Marsha, younger) reached school age, Evelyn took a job in the school cafeteria.

My mom attended Iroquois High School—a school name with a degree of specificity about its ties to the region's Indigenous people. As with so many similarly named schools, its mascot until March 2024 was a "chief"—a cartoonish profile of a generic Indian man. But there were also children in the area who identified as Native. One was my mom's fourth-grade classmate; two others she knew were foster children being cared for by a local family, potentially indicative of the removal of children from their families that eventually led to the passage of the Indian Child Welfare Act when I was two years old.[15] Although my mom may have once known their tribal affiliations, she no longer remembers.

Martha loved reading and dreamed of being a teacher from the time she was a child; her dolls transformed into students in her imagined classroom. It was an accessible dream, as teaching had become an acceptable profession for women with college degrees. (She also recalls dreaming of being a scientist, but that one felt out of reach.) After graduating from Iroquois High, she enrolled at SUNY Freedonia. There she remembers meeting other Native people; one of her dormitory hallmates was an Indigenous woman and a bassoonist, deepening her understanding of the diversity of Native peoples. Education and schooling profoundly shaped my mother's life, and in turn it would shape mine.

After an opportunity to study abroad in Belgium in college, beginning her teaching career, and earning a master's degree in education, she applied to be a teacher abroad through the US Department of Defense. She moved to the Philippines to teach, though she did not know about the program's legacy of using white female teachers to advance empire and promote "civilization" of Indigenous people in the United States and around the globe.[16] But after marrying in December 1970, my mom followed my dad when he was assigned to MacDill. There, my brother and I were born. Because of my dad's military service and because of our geographic mobility, I was exposed to schooling informed by a range of educational philosophies and histories.

Each place I lived provided a unique education and contained pieces of a wider history of education. I lived in Germany as a small child, where my parents relied on an array of babysitters, some competent, others far less so, to care for me. Living in Europe was an education unto itself. While there, we visited thirteenth-century castles, toured the tallest church in the world, and traveled by rail and by boats in canals. My brother attended Rhein Mein Elementary, the first official school opened to provide education to service members' children abroad. Rhein Mein began operating schools in the aftermath of World War II, when service members' families made it clear they intended to keep their families together, with or without the support of the military.[17] Since 1976, the year I was born, the school system for children overseas has officially been called Department of Defense Dependents Schools, which now falls under the umbrella of the Department of Defense Education Activity. The schools employ teachers and administrators from across the United States and, internationally, people from the host nation.[18]

For years, I thought of myself as the product of state-run public schools, but that isn't entirely true. When we moved to Fairchild Air Force Base in Spokane, Washington, my mom enrolled me in a Montessori school the year before I started kindergarten. Named for Maria Montessori, an Italian doctor turned educator, the Montessori method turned away from teacher-driven, conscripted, rote memorization and instead embraced "the individual child's independent self-learning, which [Montessori] called 'auto-education.'"[19] Despite efforts by Montessori herself to popularize her methods in the United States in the second decade of the twentieth century, John Dewey's methods won the day in progressive educational institutions. A second generation of Montessori took hold following World War II, including the establishment of the American Montessori Society in 1960.[20] I loved Montessori. To this day, I remember polishing silver, one of the "work" activities we could choose. I loved making the circular motion with the polish and the satisfaction I derived from the before-and-after of my cloth's swirling action. It was my knowledge and positive experiences of Montessori that led me to research and enroll my own daughter in Montessori years later.

I attended kindergarten, first grade, and second grade at Blair Elementary School on Fairchild Air Force Base, a school administered by the Department of Defense and, therefore, federal. In the United States, many bases partner with the local school districts to administer schooling on bases known as Department of Defense Domestic Dependent Elementary and Secondary Schools, DDESS for short; Fairchild, then and now, works with the Medical Lake School District in Spokane.

Even as schooling contributed to my education throughout my childhood, sometimes competing and sometimes complementary classroom spaces offered curriculums on what it supposedly meant to be an Indian. Like the Native children who attended Sequoyah Orphan Training School in the early twentieth

Playing Indian.
Photo courtesy of the
author.

century and thousands of girls across the country, I participated in Brownies
through the Inland Empire Girl Scout Council, Inc. In addition to attending
"Thinking Day," I even got to dress up as an Indian, with face paint, braided hair,
and all, linking me to the legions of kids around the country over the course
of the twentieth century who joined Americanizing projects by transforming
themselves into generic Indians.[21]

My relationship to Scouts, unlike that of the people who ascend through the
ranks, was and is ambivalent at best. In February 1984, our troop took a trip to
the "Indian Museum," as generically named by my troop leader in my Brownie
records.[22] We actually visited the Museum of Native American Cultures, documented on the Massasoit postcard I purchased of the statue located outside
the museum of a Wampanoag leader, long since dead and more than 2,700
miles from his original homelands.[23] A non-Native Girl Scout troop leader
taught us beadwork. When it was time to pick up all the beads off the rug, I
pocketed all of mine. My troop leader confronted me. Rather than admit I was
stealing the beads, which I still hadn't fully committed to, I made the decision
to quit Brownies. From that point forward, I told people I got kicked out of
Girl Scouts. I think, in a way, it felt like I did. I no longer felt like I belonged

because of the shame of what I had thought about doing but also because deep down I also understood that something was wrong with a group that equalized the opportunity to play Indian for all kids and had non-Native people demonstrating Indianness but failed to consider the presence of actual Native kids in their midst, especially blonde-haired, blue-eyed kids that looked like me.

Despite these lessons, when we were in the military, I took diversity for granted. My parents' relationships filled our world with diverse people, people I sometimes interpreted as kin. My parents became godparents to an African American child named Blake, with whose parents and sister we ate dinner regularly, celebrated birthdays, and shared family outings, including a visit to the Grand Coulee Dam. My dad kept Blake and his sister's picture in his wallet for a number of years after he retired. When I moved to Florida just a couple of years later, I articulated the bond I felt to these two children as familial in a school assignment: "My brother and sister live in California and I've been there."[24] My parents also befriended a couple who were the mirror image of them, racially: He was a white man; she was an Alaska Native woman. At least one of the women in my dad's squadron was a lesbian, and another man whom I adored was a Black man named Zack, who was perceived as gay. These were the adults who filled my parents' social world and, therefore, my own. Still, although among enlisted soldiers the military had achieved some semblance of diversity, one needed to look no further than the race of the officers living in the larger houses situated at the corners of each street to reveal the myth of diversity and the failures of equity.[25]

Despite the messages I received at home and in more intimate social settings about diversity, chosen family, friendship, and allyship, the physical design of residential areas made it clear that racial hierarchies existed, that they would be enforced even among relative equals in rank, and that anyone challenging those systems would face consequences.

I learned my first real lessons about the power of racism among those integrated enlisted soldiers. Years later, I identified the homophobia that likely played a role in what I witnessed as well. My dad's squadron would regularly host family events, including picnics, to encourage squadron cohesion. At one of these events, an outdoor picnic at a local park, the kids played in sprinklers, the spouses mingled and kept one eye toward the children, and the men drank beer kept cold in metal drums filled with ice water. At some point, several inebriated men picked up my dad's friend Zack to forcibly submerge him in one of the ice water-filled drums. Zack was fighting to get loose, and he wasn't laughing. I watched as they tried to force him under water. I cried and let loose uncontrollable wails. To this day, I am not sure to what degree what happened next was for me or for Zack, but it stands as one of the bravest things I've ever witnessed.

My dad intervened. He stood up to those three white men. They let Zack go but only after launching a series of the first racial epithets I had ever heard directed toward my Cherokee father. My dad's intervention disrupted those men's violent, racist bullying, but it also called attention to it; for that, they used violent language to exert power and shame him in front of his children, his coworkers, and his spouse.

I have so many interpretations of these events now—now that I know about lynching and homophobia—but what I understood then was that the violence I was witnessing was terribly wrong. After that day, I understood how people used race to intimidate others in a way I never had before, but the educational settings I would later be a part of would work to erase what I learned that day and teach me something very different. I needed a PhD in American history and a much deeper knowledge of African American history to learn to remember what I had fully understood as a child; beyond its institutionalization, the rhetoric of white supremacy gets recycled and repurposed over time to assert power over Black and Brown people.[26]

My dad decided to retire in 1984. This transition would lead to more than just geographic change; it would set me on concurrent educational journeys—one as a Cherokee, one as a student in schools. As I was helping my mom pack for our move back to Florida in anticipation of my dad's retirement, I found my dad's original birth certificate with, as I said to my mom, "the wrong name on it." It revealed that Reed was not my dad's surname at birth; it was Smith. From my mom, I learned that my dad and my Aunt Joan were adopted as teenagers by their stepfather and that my Grandpa Reed was not my biological grandfather. My dad's birth certificate—this was my first primary document.[27] This was an important milestone, but not the only one, in my Cherokee education. When I found it, I learned that dad's birth father was a man named Nelson Smith and it was through him we were Cherokee. This man, absent from my life, represented a mystery, a puzzle that I needed to solve. This mystery became an intellectual and personal project I pursued any time I saw an opportunity to fill in gaps in my understanding.

To answer the first of these questions, I sought out my first teacher—my mom. My father spent a lot of time away on tours of duty for additional pay in places like Diego Garcia and Türkiye, much like Cherokee men had used itinerant labor during the previous two generations and, for hundreds of years before that, had left their homes to hunt. In addition to the core teaching she had provided for my schooling, my mother became my first teacher to discuss

Cherokee history with me; she answered the questions she could. She had met my grandfather's mother, Rachel, and they had exchanged letters for a number of years. In fact, my parents had taken my brother and me to visit her in Oklahoma before we moved to Germany in 1978. I have no memory of that visit, but a single grainy, cropped picture of it still exists—one I would not see until just a few years ago. My dad talked rarely, but affectionately, about his paternal grandmother, Rachel, but his birth father was off-limits.

While driving cross-country on our move from Washington back to Florida in our green Econoline 150 van with my parents, my brother, and our dog when I was nine, I asked my dad when I could meet my *real* grandfather. In his best and angriest Darth Vader voice, my father answered, "You've met your grandfather." My dad sent a clear message to me that biology wasn't everything when it came to fathers, and although I agreed on the surface and loved Grandpa Reed, biology mattered to me.[28] As an adult, I recognize that fathers don't have to occupy the place they do in terms of their societal importance—I need look no further than Cherokee history to see other means of configuring central male figures in one's family—but as a child I didn't think about all of the ways this importance was built into the religious, legal, social, and governmental structures that educated me from birth. And in retrospect, it was a series of women who facilitated my Cherokee education and that led me to Cherokee homelands in the West and East.

From the moment when my dad shut me down, I knew I needed new teachers. We visited Oklahoma fairly regularly when I was young, but as a child I didn't understand that the environment itself was a teacher and a curriculum. We spent most of our time in Norman, two blocks from the University of Oklahoma's campus, where my dad's mother and adopted father lived; we'd also spend time in Eufaula at my grandmother's lake house in the Muscogee (Creek) Nation, a lake that didn't exist when Rachel Johnson was a child and was under construction when Joan and Doug were children. No one told me we were in the Muscogee (Creek) Nation. The highway signs re-marking those older boundary lines wouldn't appear until after my daughter was born. My grandparents kept their pontoon boat at Fountainhead Marina in Checotah, another Muskogee town. I won a kids' fishing contest there. When we returned to their cabin, I watched the men scale the fish we caught and later ate for dinner. I did not want to learn that skill; Ageyutsa, Climber of Trees, and Rachel may have scoffed at my aversion. What I did desire was a better chronology and archive of our family history.

Aunt Joan often came from Colorado to Oklahoma while we visited. Like my mother, she was also a public school teacher. I asked her even more questions. She had written a major paper in college on the Keetoowah society, and through her I learned about the role held in the society by Redbird Smith, her great-grandfather and my great-great-grandfather. She taught me about his significance within Cherokee history. But she knew little about her and my dad's father, Nelson; she barely remembered him. She did know that my dad had visited him in Nashville, before he deployed the first time, but my dad had left that visit believing he had been rejected by his father. Again. This rejection explained my dad's response to my interest. My aunt, partly out of a deep commitment to my dad, shared his view of their father.

I looked to the people and the places I thought could answer questions about Cherokee history. Like most children educated by predominantly white institutions in the United States, I was taught that Indigenous peoples' histories and cultures were interchangeable. On our move back to Florida, we toured what was then Custer Battlefield National Monument, a.k.a. Custer's Last Stand.[29] I am uncertain whether it was my dad's attraction to military history or an affinity with the Lakota and Cheyenne who resisted Custer and his men that took us to Little Bighorn to bear witness to the Battle of Greasy Grass in Montana, probably a reckoning of both. I kept a 1984 brochure produced by the Hardin County Chamber of Commerce. It included a two-sentence history of the Crow Agency, "known as 'Tipi Capitol' of the world," followed by a list of six churches, should one wish to attend Christian services with Crow people. Of course it listed the battlefield as one of its attractions, with the reminder, "Although the Indians won this battle, they lost the war against the white man's efforts to end their independent, nomadic ways."[30] Despite their willingness to market Native American history to generate tourism revenue and do so by filling the pages with images of living Native people, the larger message of the brochure was one of Native defeat, assimilation, and Christianization.

As Catherine learned about a range of spiritual practices that existed in the world in her childhood, the primary teachers in my life filtered their religious beliefs solely through Christianity. The spiritual wars I faced played out in the (non)denominational theologies and social principles of the church of my mother and those of my Grandmother Ada Lee, which came to a head when I was ten. My grandmother, after divorcing Nelson Smith and leaving her two children with her parents to raise, worked a series of jobs to supplement her parents' income and support herself. Later, she moved to Norman and became a real estate agent, one of the first women in Norman to do so. Her career benefited from the surge of home buying and college attendance as a result of the GI Bill after World War II. She married John E. Reed, a postal carrier, in 1948 and with him had her third child.[31] By the time I was a child, she was an established real estate agent, owned a home two blocks from the University of Oklahoma's campus, managed rental properties, drove a series of Cadillacs, always had her hair and makeup done, and was a season ticket holder for the University of Oklahoma's football team.[32]

She also attended a Free Will Baptist church. After my dad retired and my mom no longer took us to services on an air force base, which switched denominations weekly to provide Christian denominational diversity to its service members, we attended a United Methodist church in Riverview, Florida. John Wesley's three principles—"Do no harm. Do good. Stay in love with God"—that I watched my mom model through her service to the church and her work as a public school teacher seemed a mismatch with the preaching I heard when I visited Oklahoma with my dad. Spiritually, I had to discern some kind of truth through the competing messages provided by the women in my life.

During the visit that changed everything, my grandmother's preacher said that if you did not go to church every Sunday, you would never amount to anything and would face damnation. With a few exceptions, my dad attended church only when he visited his mother. When in Florida, he regularly told me if he went to church, the building would fall down on him. I asked my Grandmother Ada what her pastor meant, because in my Methodist church I had never learned that missing church would result in damnation. I also mentioned that my dad, *her son*, didn't attend church. She looked at me and without any hesitation asked, "What *has* he amounted to?" My dad was not a particularly outwardly loving father, he had little patience for girls, his discipline often verged on tyranny, and his temper was explosive, but for a parent to suggest her child was worthless because he didn't attend church taught me more about who she was and how she interpreted the beneficence of her god. It also explained more about my dad's childhood and his parenting style than I had previously understood. My relationship to my grandmother was never the same.

When I was in seventh grade, a flood resulted in my family losing the double-wide mobile home my parents had purchased when we moved back to Florida. During a tropical storm, farmers dammed up the creek we lived on to protect their crops, which forced an overflow of water onto our property. I witnessed millions of fire ants wrap themselves around tree trunks and then cling to each other to survive the flood. I carried my suitcases out over my head with water up to my chest. I still remember the shotgun blasts as our neighbor shot the rattlesnakes that were also seeking safety from the rising waters. In the aftermath, I stayed with friends' families for a couple of months, then in a camper, and then in the flooded-out mobile home for a couple more. My grades dropped, my weight climbed, I had nosebleeds that I had never had before, and my school attendance plummeted. We didn't have flood insurance. Thankfully, with my dad's VA loan we were able to move to a new house right before my thirteenth birthday.

Unlike other Cherokee girls who had come before me, I hadn't learned histories of forced dislocation or the need to respect the power of waterways as places of daily spiritual practice *and* places of danger. I hadn't learned about damning/damming projects that displaced Cherokee people when my dad and aunt were children. I only had the story of Noah and the ark and the message of god's wrath aimed at sinners in the world. This was the message I lived with for many years.

Although I can now critically examine the religious and class biases I had learned by that time and understand the gift of a roof and four walls of any kind, there are some things that your soul carries. My dad associated gathering mustard greens in ditches with the poverty of his childhood. He loved greens of every kind but would never eat mustard greens. For me, I never want to live in another mobile home, as if any house can defend against the power of the land in league with the environment.

By high school, I was beginning to question what it meant to be Cherokee in a world beyond my family. I never fundamentally critiqued my high school's use of an Indian mascot in any real way when I was a teenager. I was class president all four years and won multiple "Brave Spirit" Awards for my leadership and academics. I oozed team spirit. I think in large part a mascot provided some connection to an identity, a history, and a culture I sought desperately to be connected to, much like Indian dress-up had in Brownies. It would take some time and more information for me to change my position.

High school represented a period when I was encouraged to think more deeply in classes and was free to read widely. This led me to Stephen King and Rush Limbaugh, books on serial killers, and works about the Kennedy family, Ross Perot and Bill Clinton. But throughout I lacked a language to help me articulate the questions I was asking about who I was as a Cherokee person in the world. I followed the Oka Crisis, also known as the Kanehsatà:ke Resistance, throughout 1990, an effort by Mohawk people in Quebec to violently resist efforts by the town to develop their sacred lands into a golf course.[33] In my freshman creative writing class in high school, in response to a prompt, I wrote about the mistreatment of Indigenous peoples and listed three distinct tribes, the Mohawk, Cherokees, and Seminoles, as examples. I mentioned that my eighth-grade social studies teacher taught us that no agreements (apparently the word "treaty" was not a part of any earlier lesson I received or not one I remembered) "between Indians and our government have ever been kept."[34]

I didn't stop there. I advocated for the land rights of Indigenous peoples and railed against class privilege and the environmental degradation caused by golf courses.

I wrote a follow-up piece in an editorial style that lamented the unfair treatment of "Mohawk (Iroquois) Indians . . . since at least the 1600s." Echoing my earlier piece, "No Indians have ever been treated fairly. . . . Now the Mohawks must continue the battle with industry, people of power, and the growing disrespect of our earth."[35] Whatever education I was receiving or seeking, fourteen-year-old me failed to articulate assertions of Native nationhood, tribal sovereignty, or the diversity of Mohawk communities. I was growing more attuned to the diversity of Native nations but lacked the vocabulary to use Haudenosaunee, Kahnawá:ke, Kanehsatà:ke, and Ahkwesáhsne. That vocabulary would come years later. I didn't know that for people like Native American and Indigenous studies scholar Leanna Simpson, Oka "was the most profound political education of her life . . . influenc[ing her] professional, artistic, and activist life."[36] Instead, I made a moral argument.

While Catherine was making the decision to leave Bacone and enlist in the army, two events conspired to irrevocably alter my Cherokee education. After high school I attended Salem Women's College, one of the first institutions in the United States to offer education to Cherokee women, although I didn't know this as a college freshman. Principal Chief Wilma Mankiller came to Salem on a speaking tour that accompanied the publication of her book *Mankiller: A Chief and Her People*.[37] She had visited Salem to conduct research in the Moravian archives as she wrote her autobiography, a book that wove together Cherokee history and memoir, a book that I cherish. As a Cherokee student, I was invited to have breakfast with her. In our conversation, I mentioned I was Cherokee. I am sure she initially dismissed me as just another person with a Cherokee princess grandmother in the South, but then I told her who some of my relatives were. She not only knew my Uncle Chad well but also encouraged me to reach out to him and gave me a direct line to do so. She was the first Cherokee woman I had ever witnessed command a public audience in her lecture at Salem. I was inspired. It was the first time I ever thought of history as a subject I existed within. Added to that, she opened a new door to my uncle. I walked through it.

I wrote my Uncle Chad a letter a week before my nineteenth birthday; he wrote back to me two weeks later. He had visited my Aunt Joan after their dad died in order "to understand that part of [his] dad's history." He welcomed a visit with me so that he could tell me about his father and my grandfather, Nelson, and answer questions I had. He also sent me a watch with a Cherokee syllabary face designed by my grandfather and a course book he used to teach Cherokee legal history. "Perhaps," he wrote, "these will help in beginning your Cherokee education."[38] Indeed, they did.

After transferring to the University of South Florida my sophomore year, my education continued to provide me with scholarly opportunities to evaluate the competing and incomplete Christian truths in which I had been immersed. My best friend from elementary school enrolled in the class Literature of the Occult and told me about Lilith, Adam's first wife who chose to leave the Garden of Eden when she learned she would be denied equality. Incredulous that I had never heard this before, I sought out my undergraduate thesis advisor, an ordained Baptist minister with a PhD in Victorian literature, who pulled readings for me.[39] I took a Racism in American Society course and an Introduction to Women's Studies course that undermined so much of what I had been taught as fact and included so much I had never been taught at all. This learning occurred alongside my work as the youth director for my church. I increasingly felt a sense of responsibility to better understand the intellectual origins of what I was imparting to young people. My choice to apply to Southern Methodist University's Perkins School of Theology alongside a number of law schools felt like a response to a very specific moment, but it actually reflected a continuation of a much longer personal, intellectual, and spiritual journey.

Geography and women educators drove my initial decision to apply to Perkins; it was the female professors I encountered and the female thinkers they assigned that continued to transform how I understood the past, present, and future. I applied to Perkins with its proximity to the Cherokee Nation in mind, but it was scholar of the Hebrew Bible Dr. Dana Nolan Fewell's The Book of Genesis exegesis course that once again reminded me how much of the world, past and present, I still needed help to see or consider. Dr. Fewell shared with the class an artist's rendition of the woman at the well, a story found in the gospel of John. The vantage point of the viewer is looking up from the well at the woman, who is quite pregnant, standing next to Jesus. Next to her, barely visible in the scene, are the hands and part of a face of another child, peering into the well at the viewer. That piece of art changed my point of view entirely. Over the next two years, Professors Mary Anne Reed and Pat Davis joined Dr. Fewell in shaping my thinking, as did my classmates who came from a range of spiritual backgrounds and were on equally interesting spiritual journeys. The works of Ada María Isasi-Díaz, Katie Cannon, Emily Townes, and Elizabeth Cady Stanton challenged me to reconsider my theological worldview.

These women invited me to think in ways I had never been asked to before; being in Dallas at Perkins offered me access to a landscape of learning that up until this point had been filtered through my parents and grandparents. A friend from seminary joined me for my first Cherokee National Holidays in 1998, when I was twenty-two. I met more kin, including two of my great-uncles, my grandfather's younger brothers Frank and Jay. We ate lunch together in Tahlequah. One of my uncles told me stories about my dad's childhood. Before he died, my Uncle Frank wrote an autobiography that made sure to mention, "Nelson's two children were always on the bus with us. Doug always come to sit by me."[40] He filled in gaps that my mom, my aunt, and my dad had left blank. He invited me to the family reunion the next day, but I had not made plans to stay longer. I once again had access to new teachers.

I chose to write my major paper in seminary on Cherokee women's spirituality. To accomplish this task, I devoured Theda Perdue's recently published *Cherokee Women* and had the opportunity to interview Wilma Mankiller and her daughters Gina and Felicia Olaya about their spiritual lives. Although I had taken one class and read a book or two that introduced me to surface-level oral history methods and interviewing, my interview says more about my amateur status as an interviewer and my spiritual journey than it does about the rich spiritual lives of Wilma, Felicia, and Gina. The three of them displayed incredible grace, patience, and kindness to me as I fumbled to ask questions and listen intently. From them, I learned there was no single spiritual path or practice required for Cherokee people today, a lesson Catherine learned as a child.

For the next few years, I traveled alone to Oklahoma for the Cherokee National Holidays. My Uncle Chad was elected to the office of principal chief in 1999, and I traveled to Tahlequah for his inauguration at the Cherokee National Holidays that year and attended his first State of the Nation. I faced recurring anxiety that I wasn't Cherokee enough because I had blonde hair and blue eyes and because all these people knew each other. Then I met my dad's other brothers; one of them had fair skin and light hair just like me. All of the externalized racial anxiety I felt as it related to my family washed away. I realized genetics is a crapshoot; I wasn't any less Cherokee than my brother because I had blonde hair and blue eyes like my non-Cherokee mother.

I met my uncles' mother, Pauline, another grandmother. She invited me to the house my Grandpa Nelson Smith had built with his boys' help. I followed her in my rental car down barely paved roads in Oklahoma at what seemed unsafe speeds, dust flying everywhere, to the house they built in Siloam Springs. There, she told me stories about Grandpa Smith and about my dad and my Aunt Joan. She had met them when they were kids. She and Nelson had taken them presents at their other grandparents' house in Vian; neither Joan nor my dad remembered much, if any, of this. Nelson and Pauline had even started to pursue custody of them. What she shared seemed incongruous with the stories of rejection that my dad and aunt lived with and passed on as adults. What she offered was revelatory to me and led me to pen these thoughts:

> I sat very still in his chair.
> I tried to be very quiet.
> I listened.
> I thought maybe I could hear him.
> I didn't.
> I sat on the porch with my other grandmother.
> I looked out over the hillside.
> We watched wild peacocks peck around. We watched squirrels jump
>   between trees. We watched deer stand alert in the distance.
> My other grandma gave me fruit from the trees to take with me.
> Maybe, I did hear my grandfather.[41]

At my uncle's inaugural State of the Nation in 1999 after he was elected chief, I experienced a lot of firsts. I attended the Holiday Powwow and my first stomp dance. I watched a younger cousin scale a tree on the capitol grounds. She paused briefly to let her shoes slip off so she could get a better feel for the tree. She climbed dangerously high. Hundreds of years earlier, Climber of Trees shared this compulsion. I climbed a tree once when I was about my cousin's age when I lived at Fairchild. I was with my brother and his older friends. I was trying to keep up with them. I fell and landed flat on my back. The fall knocked the wind out of me. I mentally called for my mom, but I couldn't get the words out. I truly thought I was dying. Later, I got in trouble for climbing the tree. My cousin's tree climbing was public, whereas my audience and safety net had been a group of older boys who seemed annoyed by my presence. Watching my cousin climb, shoes falling off, but in a public setting, I remembered the freedom of movement from my own childhood, which I perceived as riskier than my cousin's. If she fell, numerous mothers, aunties, uncles, and siblings would be there to provide aid. I sat in awe of her. I longed to reclaim my ability to move and *be* in public settings that seemed cut off to me as a twenty-something young woman.

I didn't dance the first time I attended the stomp grounds. Part of it felt wrong, given the frailty of my beliefs at the time. Another part of me felt like a stranger who had no right to be next to that fire with all those prayers going up with the smoke. Another part of me felt like I had more to learn before I could treat the grounds with the care they deserved. Part of me still feels that way, twenty-five years later. When I did finally dance, I understood something older: that voices and a fire and shell shakers and men, women, and children have been protecting old educational practices so that they could be new to me and to those like me who will come later.

After graduation from seminary in 2000, I returned to Florida. My dad underwent gastric bypass that summer. He experienced complications, lost oxygen to his brain, and was clinically dead briefly. He suffered from septicemia, which the doctors treated in part by keeping him in a medically induced coma for four months. He spent six months in the hospital, most of it in the ICU. When he awoke from the coma, he couldn't speak due to his long-term intubation followed by a tracheotomy.

My relationship with my dad the previous decade-plus had been hard. He had not been kind. He offered little praise and no physical affection and never said, "I love you." He yelled a lot. He held sexist and racist beliefs. He opposed my marriage. Because of that and because I thought the idea of a father *giving a daughter away* reeked of the worst patriarchal practices, I had my dad sit with the other parents at my wedding.

Through the physical act of labor, we had made some headway while I was in seminary. He had driven to Dallas and picked me up for a trip to Oklahoma to join his mother at her cabin to do some construction projects for her. In the period leading up to this trip, I had been working for the Methodist Warehouse, an outreach program in West Dallas that helped recently incarcerated men find jobs and reacclimate to their community. I worked alongside largely African American men, my peers chronologically, doing labor projects in the community. We helped community members avoid citations from the city for things like overgrown yards, cutting and scything our way through them; we dismantled cars up on blocks and hauled them away; and for houses in disrepair, we scraped, painted, and installed windows. I helped build a school and through that process learned to use all sorts of tools, including a nail gun and a nail bar. I earned the nickname Two-Nail Julie. I learned to hammer efficiently. I bought my own nail bar, I loved it so much. Over the course of a week, my dad and I rebuilt the deck at the cabin in Eufaula, but we were also rebuilding something else. And we were beginning to speak the same language. Ageyutsa and Climber of Trees would likely have recognized building and rebuilding as a translatable language.

These skills, a language my dad could have taught me but didn't, were now one of the things that helped draw us back together before his surgery. I also used that time at the cabin to revisit questions with some of my earliest teachers. On a car ride with my dad and my Aunt Joan, I asked them if they had ever learned to speak Cherokee. My dad immediately remembered the abbreviated and more modern words for girl and boy, *geyuj*, and *chuj*, that his Uncle Frank had taught him as a kid. He had not said those words out loud in more than forty years. I also used that week to gently ask my Grandma Reed follow-up questions about our family history. I focused on chronology. I had learned that after the death of my Grandpa Reed, which loosened many family member's tongues, my grandmother had played fast and loose with chronology and with truth when it came to how she represented her early parenting. I now know that my dad and my Aunt Joan had felt abandoned by both parents when they had lived with their grandparents during their formative years.

This knowledge enabled me to be present with my dad in ways I couldn't have imagined just a few years earlier. I visited my dad Monday through Friday at the hospital. I talked to him. I graded papers. I read him the books I was reading. It was the best our relationship had been in a long time, and he was in a coma. At one point, I read him my major paper from seminary about Cherokee women's spirituality, which included the voices of Wilma Mankiller and Gina and Felicia Olaya. When he woke up from the coma and couldn't speak, he was so frustrated. Hospital staff gave him a dry erase board, but between his atrophied muscles, his undiagnosed dyslexia, and his piss-poor handwriting, this was useless. You had to read his lips, and I was the best lip-reader in the family. While reading lips might not have helped Ageyutsa communicate with her family members hundreds of years earlier, it provided another way for my Cherokee father to talk to me. Whether it was the language of work or the months of communication during the coma that readied me for this, we never had a problem communicating ever again.

Whereas for years I had been an ongoing learner, I became like so many women before me, a teacher. For the next few years, I was teaching and learning by day in the public schools and spending my time reading books about Cherokee history on the weekends. During seminary, I bought my first copy of James Mooney's *History, Myths, and Sacred Formulas of the Cherokees*. I had no idea how integral that book would be to me in the decades ahead. While I was teaching, I purchased my first copy of Vine Deloria's *God Is Red*.

In my American government class, we watched a film on the Zapatista movement, an Indigenous leftist movement in some ways defying categorization but at its core focused on Indigenous people's land rights. I used the film to open a discussion of democracy globally. After the film, one of the boys said, "When I have money one day, after I send money to the Mother Country, I'm going to send money to the Zapatistas." At fifteen, he understood the destructive features of colonialism and the radical benevolence it would take to combat it, ideas that I was still learning. Like the lesson reinforced by

Aunt Joan, Uncle Chad, and me, Cherokee National Holiday Powwow, September 2002.
Photo courtesy of the author.

Granddaughter Water Beetle to Grandfather Buzzard, children had lessons I
still needed to learn.

Outside of the teaching and learning I was doing in the public schools,
I fell into a pattern for the Cherokee National Holidays. I'd fly in on Friday
night, wake up early Saturday to run in the Holiday 5K, and attend the parade,
followed by the State of the Nation address on the lawn of the old capitol
building—the same building that Caroline Matilda Fields and her daughter
Elinor would have passed as they headed to the Cherokee Female Seminary.
I'd eat lunch at the Restaurant of the Cherokee if some family came up from
Vian and then browse in the gift shop, Cherokee-controlled spaces unfamiliar
to Ageyutsa, Climber of Trees, and Ayohka. I'd buy books, Dorothy Sullivan
prints, or a Daniel HorseChief print depicting my great-great-grandparents at
the Stokes-Smith stomp grounds. One year my Aunt Joan arrived from Colorado, and we attended the powwow on Saturday night, sitting on a blanket
on the grounds together and visiting with my uncle. I snapped a photo of my
cousin in her tear dress. Otherwise, I'd make my way to Vian late Saturday
afternoon. I'd hug and be hugged. I'd be subjected to NASCAR and teased for
my vegetarianism. I'd hear jokes like, "You know what the Cherokee word for
vegetarian is—bad hunter." I'd laugh a lot. I'd listen a lot. I'd attend stomp. I'd
head back to Tahlequah in the middle of the night. I'd spend Sunday touring
the Heritage Center and buying jewelry from the vendors.

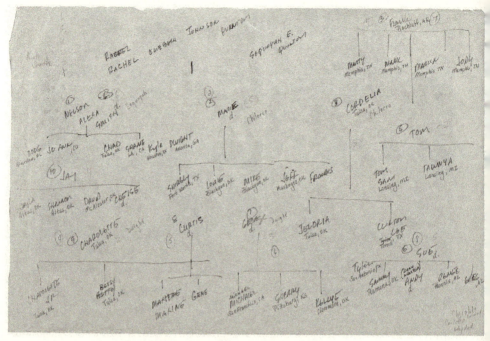

A reconstruction of my family tree. Photo courtesy of the author.

One year, three of my dad's four brothers attended the family reunion in Vian. That year, at the behest of my Uncle Chad, I pulled out construction paper and colored Sharpies and with my uncles, great-uncles, great-aunts, and cousins, I created a color-coded family tree. I rebuilt a family history and mapped Cherokee kinship with my family.

That rebuilding extended beyond construction paper family trees: My dad finally started joining me for the Cherokee National Holidays. The first time he went, we flew to Oklahoma together and rented a car. We attended the powwow; my aunt and uncle were leading grand entry and dragged my dad out there with them. My dad hated having attention drawn to him publicly. I worried about his reaction, but this provided medicine, medicine that healed some part of that little boy who was taught to both stand up and be counted as Cherokee and be ashamed of it at the same time. He was standing up as an Indian man to be counted, but there was no shame in that space.

He attended the family reunion. His uncles told him stories about himself. He remembered another part of who he was. His aunts, who spent a lot of time in the corner speaking Cherokee to one another, derided him for not coming home sooner. He saw one of his brothers for the first time in more than forty years. His brother later said to me with tears in his eyes, "He's just like our dad, the way he turns his wrists and holds his head. It's like watching my dad." It left me asking big questions about nature versus nurture and the power of those earliest years of parenting, the subtle movements that babies, when they are brand-new to this world, study, copy, and remember for later. It left me wondering what travels from one generation to the next through our DNA. He went to the Stokes Ceremonial Grounds with me more than ten years after Nelson had walked on them. Someone who had never met my father said, "That must be Nelson's son; he walks just like him." My dad physically moved through the world just like his dad. My grandfather had been with me all my life.

He started attending the holidays with me more regularly. One year we sat next to Wilma Mankiller and Hastings Shade, the former deputy chief of the Cherokee Nation, and his wife Loretta at the State of the Nation address. The newspaper snapped a photo highlighting the applause of former Chief Mankiller "and others" at the event. My dad and I are the "others." I'm wearing the watch in the photo that my uncle sent to me in college, the year I met Wilma Mankiller and she encouraged me to reach out for home.[42]

My Cherokee education is disjointed and far more incomplete compared with Catherine's and Candessa's, though my porch time has increased over the years. I still have to look at maps to understand where Warner is in relation to Porum and Gore and Webber's Falls and Vian. Catherine knows the geography because it is one of the first lessons she remembers learning as a Cherokee child, just like it was for Ageyutsa. Catherine is Cherokee because her mother, her mother's mother, and all the women before her were Cherokee. I'm Cherokee because in 1825, Cherokee officials changed a law that enabled Cherokee men to produce Cherokee citizens, and the 1976 constitution made room for Cherokee people living beyond the fourteen counties that make up the Cherokee reservation to participate in tribal politics. I am Cherokee because my great-grandmother documented where her children and grandchildren were in relationship to her. I am Cherokee because I found my way home and sought/seek out the teachers I need to continue my education.

The Cherokee language and the language of being Cherokee are intertwined but no longer exactly the same. Despite being raised in a home with Cherokee speakers, Catherine doesn't speak the language. Neither do I, though both of us aspire to keep learning. Candessa, a second language learner and Cherokee language teacher, raised among speakers, will never call herself fluent because, as she has shared, some advanced curriculums come unbroken through our elders before us. As much Cherokee history as the Catherine and I know, there are volumes we can't access because the archives remain linguistically inaccessible.

When someone asks Catherine what Cherokee culture is, she answers, "All I can see is my grandmother"—Ageyutsa, Climber of Trees, Ayohka, Caroline Matilda Fields, and even Rachel would nod in agreement—"[they] know what that is." Catherine's mother didn't raise her, but she always had mothers—Ageyutsa, Climber of Trees, Ayohka, and Rachel would nod in agreement—"[they] know what that is."[43]

The educational classrooms in which my Aunt Joan and I have studied defied the geographic boundaries known to Ageyutsa, Climber of Trees, Ayohka, Caroline Eliza and Caroline Matilda, and even Rachel. And yet, they all knew the worlds they lived in far more intimately than I ever have. I have used schooling, as many disconnected and reconnecting Cherokee people do, to find my way home. But stopping there means my education would be shockingly incomplete. My Cherokee education isn't finished, nor will it ever be.

Conclusion

In April 2023, I visited my Uncle Jay in Vian for the first time since my father passed away in November 2022. As always, a pack of dogs barked and ran alongside my car as I drove down the driveway, though not the same dogs that had greeted me in the late 1990s. Since my uncle wasn't at home when I arrived, I wandered down the dirt road that passed over Little Vian Creek to see my cousin Sherry, sit on her porch, and look out over the family's allotment lands. Later, my uncle hugged me around my neck like always. We looked at pictures and maps. We laughed. We killed flies. We ate dinner on the porch outside my Great-Grandmother Rachel's barely two-bedroom home, the home where my Uncle Jay now lives. After dinner, he handed me one of my great-grandmother's black notebooks with all her children's educational histories. I looked at my uncle and said, "How did she know I would need this?" Part of the reason I'm an agnostic instead of an atheist is because of moments like this—moments that seem too perfect to be random, moments when your ancestors remind you who you are and who you are supposed to be.

My great-grandmother, like generations of Cherokee women before her, was recording and sharing history. She was, as Tiya Miles writes, "allowing us to glimpse what our forebears found worthy of making and keeping, and what, by implication, they held dear."[1] By recording the educational trajectories of her children and writing down their public health histories in a time before rural health offices and schools adequately maintained that information for families, Rachel produced a record of their lives legible to outsiders. She understood what several generations of Cherokee people already knew—institutional affiliations matter—but she was also doing something older: She was locating and mapping her kin in relationship to her. She was telling her children and grandchildren who they were in relationship to her. She no longer had the benefit of a shared community agricultural field like Ageyutsa's and Climber of Trees' teachers had to convey those lessons, nor would she be buried at the edge of her home; instead she used the tools of her moment to record and transmit knowledge that others might need in their moment, no matter how revolutionary, like Ayohka and Sequoyah's syllabary, cocreated in the East and brought to the West, or minor, like my construction paper family tree, created decades later with Rachel's grandsons, my uncles.

When my Aunt Joan was enrolling for citizenship in the Cherokee Nation, it was my Great-Grandmother Rachel who gave my aunt a half sheet of paper with the details of her Cherokee lineage, including roll numbers and blood quantum that my great-grandmother had recorded much earlier, including the handwritten line at the top: "Reed has adopted the Smith boy & girl—Douglas + Joan Smith." On the side of that same sheet of paper, in my aunt's handwriting, it reads, "This was provided for me by Grandma Quinton." My Aunt Joan wrote that before sending it to me when I was in college. My grandmother's black notebook reached across time in a similar way.

That night in April 2023, like so many others in Vian, reminded me of the dialectical quality and incompleteness of my education. I shared allotment maps with my Uncle Jay, who learned something by looking at them, but in considering the maps, he shared far more with me as he talked about where people used to live and what the town of Vian looked like when he was a child. Through this conversation, I learned that my great-grandmother and her husband farmed separate plots of land. He pointed out the locations as it related to the allotment maps.

As I finish this book, I keep asking myself, What is the takeaway? The historian in me knows I should recap my arguments and make some claims about this book's interventions. I'll attempt to do that now. As I did in my first book by examining social welfare policies and the institutions created to deliver those services, I continue to argue that Cherokee people made choices that embedded key pieces of older systems into those they passed forward. In this book, rather than focus on delivery systems, including built institutions, that still privileged non-Native criteria for achieving "civilization" and building a Nation that embedded communitarian ethics within its institutions, I focused on the women and their individual children who were behind the scenes of those efforts, supporting the individuals featured in my first book doing the largely unpaid, silent, "domestic," everyday, multigenerational work of educating the next generation of Cherokee people using the tools handed down by the women before them. And still there is more work to do as it relates to Cherokee Freedpeople's children's experiences of education pre- and post-statehood.

I reject the stories of deficiency or lack still propagated by key historians of American education who describe "American Indian society being forcefully pushed to the margins of the emerging European-based civilization" and rarely, with one exception usually being the Cherokees, having "organized formal institutions to educate the young."[2] While settler colonialism has resulted in many losses, to suggest Indigenous educational systems didn't exist unless they looked like settler systems is simply not true. Instead, this book takes

what others might call "informal" education among one of the supposed exceptions—the Cherokee Nation—to describe and translate formal Indigenous
education to those who use terms like "informal" to excuse themselves from
having to truly contend with Indigenous educational systems in the past or the
present. Yes, the Cherokee Nation adopted schools as a method of education,
but there was and still is an older powerful educational system still functioning
in the lives of Cherokee people.

Similarly, this book supports scholars of Indigenous education focused on
boarding schools for a host of important reasons. Boarding schools produced
generational trauma and did a disservice to Indigenous language use and transmission in this country. This reality is one with which the larger American
public is only now coming to terms. I see portions of this book, like my first
book, contributing to that conversation. But just as in my first book the Cherokee Orphanage stood as an alternative to places like Carlisle Indian Industrial
School, Dwight Mission occupies a more complicated story as it relates to
Indigenous language loss. Boarding schools don't produce singular outcomes;
they produce a diverse set of personal experiences tied to the larger educational
systems to which each child is tethered. Boarding schools produce stories of
loss *and*, to use Gerald Vizenor's term, survivance, but so did public schools.

Long before Secretary of the Interior Deb Haaland unveiled the Federal
Indian Boarding School Initiative in June 2021, the first generation of Indigenous women scholars of boarding schools, including Brenda Child, Tsianina
Lomawaima, Devon Mihesuah, and Amanda Cobb, provided a robust literature
on a variety of institutions. Collectively, these projects, all uncited in the May
2022 *Federal Indian Boarding School Initiative Investigative Report*, worked to
educate scholars of American education and American history and the larger
nation on the effects of what denigrating other cultures' "informal" and sometimes formal educational systems produces.[3] The absence of these women from
that report undergirds how women's work even in "formal," institutional, paid,
and prominent spaces gets overlooked. I refuse to overlook women's roles in
Cherokee educational pasts, presents, or futures. The girls in this book exist
because of the women who came before them. My scholarship exists because
of the women I just named who paved the way for me.

The same week I saw my uncle in Vian and he shared my grandmother's
notebook, I attended Northeastern State University's 50th Annual Symposium
on the American Indian. The theme of the conference was "Envisioning Indigenous Futurity." One of the featured speakers was Laura Harjo, author of *Spiral
to the Stars: Mvskoke Tools of Futurity*. In it, she argues in favor of the core curriculums this book has attempted to document over time: "Everyday community

practices are deep, rich, and meaningful and have sustained Mvskoke people through many moments and in many places."[4] During the panel on ᏛᎣᎣᎦᎢ ᏗᏂᏩᎤᏯ ᎣᎲᏍᏪ (Little Cherokee Seeds), I thought to myself, if someone asked me what I would recommend as a way forward pedagogically for Cherokee education, this would be it. ᏛᎣᎣᎦᎢ ᏗᏂᏩᎤᏯ ᎣᎲᏍᏪ was "born out of a dream of seven Cherokee Nation women. These women, called the ᏭᎵᏋ ᏛᎾᏞ (Second Mothers or Aunts), have come together with the purpose of revitalizing the Cherokee culture and language and specifically creating fluent speakers through cultural and linguistic immersion of Cherokee infants. Our group consists of three fluent Cherokee speakers, four second language learners, four Cherokee language instructors, five mothers, seven aunts, two graduates of the Cherokee Language Master Apprentice Program, and two professors in the field of psychology and family development."[5]

ᏛᎣᎣᎦᎢ ᏗᏂᏩᎤᏯ ᎣᎲᏍᏪ began in 2019 as a weekly Cherokee reading hour for Cherokee women and their babies to facilitate their and their children's language learning. Realizing this was not enough to accomplish their educational goals for their children and for Cherokee society, the women applied for and received a grant from the American Indian Resource Center in Tahlequah, Oklahoma. The women and their babies now meet Monday through Friday, 9:00 a.m. to 3:00 p.m., at Camp Sevenstar, an experiential outdoor center located near Lake Tenkiller. Together the women and their babies sing, farm, prepare traditional meals over an outdoor fire, share meals, perform traditional beadwork and learn how to fire clay beads from elders, attend Cherokee Speakers' Bureau meetings, and harvest pokeweed for salads.

Beyond the intergenerational learning embedded in ᏛᎣᎣᎦᎢ ᏗᏂᏩᎤᏯ ᎣᎲᏍᏪ and the echoes of language learning from centuries ago, while those women sat on the dais during the panel session, babies moved back and forth from one woman to another's arms and a new walker toddled from one seat to another. Those women's partners who sat in the audience occasionally stepped in to offer support. An older child, Amayi, who participated in the reading group and is the child of one of the Cherokee scholars linked to the project worked the room. He appeared onstage at times; he walked among the tables in the audience greeting people he knew; he sat next to the toddler scooting along the edge of the stage. And here we were, as an audience, listening to these women articulate their hopes and dreams for the future of this program and for Cherokee people. One of the women on the stage was my aunt Bobbie, who years before and since has fielded my ignorant questions about language and belonging and community protocols: "We're just teaching like we were taught . . . [during] summers at Grannie's house." We were in an educational space watching a process older than Indian Territory unfolding before our eyes.

Back in 2009, on a summer research trip to Tahlequah with my barely three-year-old in tow, I tried to dream a program like this into being. My daughter was enrolled in a Spanish language immersion home day care, and I desperately wanted her to have something similar to learn Cherokee. I had already purchased some children's books about Cherokee history and culture, but few were written by Cherokee people. We listened to CDs produced by the Cherokee National Youth Choir. I was just beginning to learn the Cherokee language myself and had taken a summer immersion class taught by Bo Taylor at the Museum of the Cherokee People in Cherokee, North Carolina, the previous summer. I scoured the web, searched for programs, and made some phone calls, but nothing like a Cherokee immersion day care or ᎫᎣᏫᏗ ᎠᏂᏣᏫᎩ ᎤᏂᏍᏫ existed.

Since then, Lilith and I have taken Ed Fields's Cherokee language classes offered online through the Cherokee Nation. She has sat at the kitchen table in my great-grandmother's home with my Uncle Frank working on her pronunciation of Cherokee vocabulary, a place I don't remember sitting more than forty-five years ago on my great-grandmother's lap. I am my daughter's teacher in so many ways, but I am also reminded how much she teaches me. She knows more about what it means to be Cherokee at her age than I did. She has taken more language classes, been exposed to more Cherokee speakers, attended more National Holidays, swam in more creeks, lakes, and rivers, hiked on more paths, caught more crawdads, eaten more fry bread, played with more cousins, touched more baby deer, called out to more birds, attended to more elders, and hugged more aunts and uncles in the new and old homelands than I had by eighteen. Education is a constellation of relationships that you orbit again and again. Lilith, now a young woman, like the babies on the stage at the symposium and other children like her, are the past, present, and future of Cherokee education.

Notes

DDC   Doris Duke Collection, Western History Collections, University of Oklahoma Libraries, Norman

IPP   Indian Pioneers Papers, Western History Collections, University of Oklahoma Libraries, Norman

JHPP   John Howard Payne Papers, vol. 1, MS 689, Edward E. Ayer Collection, Newberry Library, Chicago

NARA   National Archives and Records Administration, Washington, DC

RMC   Records of the Moravian among the Cherokees, Moravian Archives, Winston-Salem, NC

Note on the Cherokee Language

1. Most of the Cherokee Nation vocabulary words come from Chris Teuton and Hastings Shades's collection or the Cherokee Nation Language Department's Word List. *Ata* and *awina* come from Duncan and Arch's work. After generating a complete list, I consulted with Eastern Band of Cherokee Indians' citizen, first language Cherokee speaker, and Cherokee language teacher Gilliam Jackson to identify key differences between the Cherokee Nation and EBCI's usage. Gilliam Jackson, conversation with author, December 24, 2024; Christopher B. Teuton and Hastings Shade, *Anitsalagi Elohi Anehi = Cherokee Earth Dwellers: Stories and Teachings of the Natural World* (University of Washington Press, 2023); "Word List," Cherokee Nation Language Department, accessed on December 27, 2024, https://language.cherokee.org/word-list; Barbara R. Duncan and Davey Arch, *The Origin of the Milky Way and Other Living Stories of the Cherokee* (University of North Carolina Press, 2008).

Introduction

1. Carl F. Kaestle, *Pillars of the Republic: Common Schools and American Society, 1780–1860* (Hill and Wang, 1983), 124–28.

2. In 2018, I reread Miles's and Perdue's articles and read Fuentes's brand-new book, which tightened my focus around women for a conference paper I wrote on women's experiences of violence during the Long Removal Era. This turned into an article I have drafted but have yet to publish. In her brief article, Perdue reminds us that we know very little about everyday women's lives during forced removal, and those we do know about often receive "brief mentions" and more than likely "conformed to [the] expectations" of the Civilization Policy. Written thirty-six ago, this remains stubbornly true. Miles's entire body of work has reminded us of the "cost when a society devalues what is precious." Fuentes's book asks us to consider the archival implications of women's cries of pain in the primary record. This exercise opened me to the possibilities of foregrounding girls, thinking about the shreds

of evidence I could work with to examine women's and girls' educational lives over time. Theda Perdue, "Cherokee Women and the Trail of Tears," *Journal of Women's History* 1, no. 1 (1989): 14–30, https://doi.org/10.1353/jowh.2010.0030; Tiya Miles, "'Circular Reasoning': Recentering Cherokee Women in the Antiremoval Campaigns," *American Quarterly* 61, no. 2 (2009): 221–43, https://doi.org/10.1353/aq.0.0078; Marisa J. Fuentes, *Dispossessed Lives: Enslaved Women, Violence, and the Archive* (University of Pennsylvania Press, 2018). The "Long Removal Era" is a concept I have been developing through a series of conference papers since 2015 and that has been used by other scholars since then. The term asks us to think about the multigenerational process of federal and state policy, coercion, settler violence, and eventually removal that divided Cherokee people over time and better captures most Cherokee people's family histories of removal. Rather than focus on the single event of forced removal from 1838 to 1839—also known as the Trail of Tears, an event that deserves the attention it receives for its deadly outcomes as a result of federal policy—"Long Removal Era" enables us to see the generations-long pressures at the hands of a range of actors and the complicated and diverse choices Cherokee people made over time to manage this coercion.

3. Jenny James, "The Sacred Feminine in Cherokee Culture: Healing and Identity," in *Under the Rattlesnake: Cherokee Health and Resiliency*, ed. Lisa Lefler (University of Alabama Press, 2009), 6.

4. Theda Perdue and Michael D. Green, eds., *The Cherokee Removal: A Brief History with Documents* (Bedford Books of St. Martin's Press, 1995).

5. Edmund Schwarze, *History of the Moravian Missions among Southern Indian Tribes of the United States* (Times Publishing Company, 1923), http://hdl.handle.net/2027/nco1.ark: /13960/t6zw1jz2m.

6. Albert L. Wahrhaftig, "Institution Building among Traditional Cherokees," in *Four Centuries of Southern Indians*, ed. Charles Hudson (University of Georgia Press, 1975), 132–47.

7. Kandace D. Hollenbach and Stephen B. Carmody, "The Daily Lives of Early Archaic Foragers in the Mid-South," in *Investigating the Ordinary: Everyday Matters in Southeast Archaeology*, ed. Sarah E. Price and Philip J. Carr (University Press of Florida, 2018), 53–54.

8. Leanne Betasamosake Simpson, "Land as Pedagogy: Nishnaabeg Intelligence and Rebellious Transformation," *Decolonization: Indigeneity, Education & Society* 3 (2014): 1–25.

9. My daughter accompanied me with Jan Simek, Alan Cressler, Stephen Alvarez, and others to Painted Bluff in 2017, when she was eleven years old. Jan F. Simek et al., *The Cosmos Revealed: Precontact Mississippian Rock Art at Painted Bluff, Alabama* (University of Alabama Press, 2021), http://public.eblib.com/choice/PublicFullRecord.aspx?p=28311275.

10. Robert Allen Warrior, *Tribal Secrets: Recovering American Indian Intellectual Traditions* (University of Minnesota Press, 1994).

11. Adrea Lawrence, "Epic Learning in an Indian Pueblo: A Framework for Studying Multigenerational Learning in the History of Education," *History of Education Quarterly* 54, no. 3 (2014): 294–96, https://doi.org/10.1111/hoeq.12068.

12. Juliana Barr, "There's No Such Thing as 'Prehistory': What the Longue Durée of Caddo and Pueblo History Tells Us about Colonial America," *William and Mary Quarterly* 74, no. 2 (2017): 203–40; Robbie Ethridge, "Ancient America: Connecting America's Deep Past to American History and Why It Matters," presidential address at the Meeting of the American Society for Ethnohistory (virtual), November 13, 2021.

13. Cherokee language and grammar structures enable speakers to speak about "past events [as] not separated from the present by the physical distance that is implied in the English-language-based view of time and history." Heidi M. Altman and Thomas N. Belt, "Reading History: Cherokee History through a Cherokee Lens," *Native South* 1, no. 1 (2008): 92, https://doi.org/10.1353/nso.0.0003.

14. Peter N. Stearns, "Challenges in the History of Childhood," *Journal of the History of Childhood and Youth* 1, no. 1 (2008): 35–42, https://doi.org/10.1353/hcy.2008.0000.

15. Tony E. Adams, Stacy Linn Holman Jones, and Carolyn Ellis, *Autoethnography: Understanding Qualitative Research*, Series in Understanding Qualitative Research (Oxford University Press, 2015), 1–2.

16. Bryan McKinley Jones Brayboy, "Toward a Tribal Critical Race Theory in Education," *Urban Review* 37, no. 5 (2005): 425–46, https://doi.org/10.1007/s11256-005-0018-y; Jo-ann Archibald, *Indigenous Storywork: Educating the Heart, Mind, Body, and Spirit* (University of British Columbia Press, 2008); Amanda R. Tachine, "Monsters and Weapons: Navajo Students' Stories on Their Journeys toward College" (PhD diss., University of Arizona, 2015), ProQuest (3704874); Wendy Shelly Greyeyes and Kevin Washburn, *A History of Navajo Nation Education: Disentangling Our Sovereign Body* (University of Arizona Press, 2022); Farina King, *The Earth Memory Compass: Diné Landscapes and Education in the Twentieth Century* (University Press of Kansas, 2018); Meredith L. McCoy and Matthew Villeneuve, "Reconceiving Schooling: Centering Indigenous Experimentation in Indian Education History," *History of Education Quarterly* 60, no. 4 (2020): 487–519, https://doi.org/10.1017/heq .2020.53; Meredith L. McCoy, Leilani Sabzalian, and Tommy Ender, "Alternative Strategies for Family History Projects: Rethinking Practice in Light of Indigenous Perspectives: History Teacher," *History Teacher* 54, no. 3 (2021): 473–508; Corey M. Still and Jami Bartgis, "Using a Community Based Participatory Research Framework to Build Data Leadership, Capacity, and Sovereignty in Indian Country," 50th Annual Symposium on the American Indian: Envisioning Indigenous Futurity, Tahlequah, CN, April 13, 2023; Jeanette Haynes, "An Oral History of the Social Construction of Cherokee Identity" (PhD diss., University of New Mexico, 1997), ProQuest (9727489); Daniel Heath Justice, *Why Indigenous Literatures Matter*, Indigenous Studies Series (Wilfrid Laurier University Press, 2018).

17. Linda Tuhiwai Smith, *Decolonizing Methodologies: Research and Indigenous Peoples* (Bloomsbury Academic and Professional, 2012), 29–30.

18. Embarrassingly late in writing this book, I realized that "Willstown" and "Wattstown" are the same community. Both names are used in primary documents.

19. "Cherokee Heritage, and Natural Resources, Uncovered in Manitou Cave," US Fish and Wildlife Service, December 21, 2022, www.fws.gov/story/2022-12/cherokee-heritage -and-natural-resources-uncovered-manitou-cave.

20. As recently as 2013, a PhD dissertation from an Ivy League institution promoted the idea that Sequoyah did not exist at all and that by extension neither did Ayohka. I have chosen not to list that citation here, but it is a reminder of how fragile the shred of a Cherokee girl's life can be when nonspecialist historians get their hands on it. Samuel L. Knapp, *American Cultural History, 1607–1829: A Facsimile Reproduction of Lectures on American Literature, 1829* (Gainesville, 1961), http://hdl.handle.net/2027/mdp.39015003752253; "Transcripts of John Howard Payne," n.d., vol. 1, JHPP.

21. The Sequoyah Birthplace Museum highlights Ayohka's role at the Cherokee National Council in 1825. Children's books written about Sequoyah often pay particular attention to Ayohka as her father's student, and at least two children's books have focused on her as a central character. This is not surprising given the audience these books are appealing to. "Sequoyah Birthplace Museum," SequoyahMuseum.org, accessed March 10, 2024, https://sequoyahmuseum.org; Randal Rust, "Sequoyah," *Tennessee Encyclopedia* (blog), accessed March 10, 2024, https://tennesseeencyclopedia.net/entries/sequoyah; Catherine Cate Coblentz and Janice Holland, *Ah-Yo-Ka, Daughter of Sequoya* (1950; California State Dept. of Education, 1963); Peter Roop and Connie Roop, *Ahyoka and the Talking Leaves* (Beech Tree, 1994).

22. Thomas Loraine McKenney, *History of the Indian Tribes of North America: With Biographical Sketches and Anecdotes of the Principal Chiefs; Embellished with One Hundred and Twenty Portraits from the Indian Gallery in the Department of War at Washington* (Philadelphia, 1848), http://hdl.handle.net/2027/nyp.33433088721877; "Invention of the Cherokee Alphabet and Creation of a Written Language," *Daily Evening Bulletin* (San Francisco), October 22, 1859, 19th Century US Newspapers, https://link-gale-com.ezaccess.libraries.psu.edu/apps/doc/GT3008897820/NCNP?u=psucic&sid=bookmark-NCNP&xid=7c2dec95.

23. In this early publication about Sequoyah and the syllabary, the discussion of its creation appears in a section titled "Self Taught Men." *American Annals of Education*, vol. 2 (Allen and Ticknor, 1832), 32, http://hdl.handle.net/2027/uiug.30112108067494.

24. Justice, *Why Indigenous Literatures Matter*, 39.

25. Richard White, *Remembering Ahanagran* (Hill and Wang, 1998), 3–4.

26. Cherokee Nation Citizens At-Large website, accessed April 12, 2024, https://cherokeesatlarge.org/communities.

Chapter 1

1. Gary Goodwin records that Kituwha, also spelled Kituwah and Kituhwagi, was also a name used by other Native nations including the Delaware to reference an "important early settlement in the Tuckeskegee River basin." Goodwin notes that rivers provided defense and access to Indigenous exchange routes and economies. Gary C. Goodwin, *Cherokees in Transition: A Study of Changing Culture and Environment prior to 1775* (University of Chicago, 1977), 40n1, 41, http://hdl.handle.net/2027/heb.03785.

2. Milton Gaither, "The History of North American Education, 15,000 BCE to 1491," *History of Education Quarterly* 54, no. 3 (2014): 330, https://doi.org/10.1111/hoeq.12070.

3. One of the key questions in Cherokee archaeology is this: When did the group that archaeologists and Cherokee people call "Cherokee" become recognizably Cherokee? For some Cherokee people, this is insulting and denigrating because they would say Cherokee people have always been in the places they are and have always been Aniyuniwya. Archaeologists would ask, But when did those ancestral peoples refer to themselves as Cherokee? Archaeologists answer this question using a variety of data including, but not limited to, linguistics, pottery, lithics, agricultural patterns, landscape theory and design, ethnography, soil analysis, and climate change. For a summary overview of the deeper history and how the professional approach to the field of archaeology has changed, Vincas Steponaitis describes in his article the longitudinal process in the Southeast from the Paleo-Indian period (? to 8000 BCE) to the Mississippian period (AD 1000 to 1700). He outlines the shift from the prevalence of

small-scale hunter-gatherer societies who hunted megafauna before the Little Ice Age ended to the period of warming following that led to the proliferation of the deciduous forests we still have today that enabled societies to rely on the mast from acorn and chestnut trees and small game to support larger communities and then to the introduction and proliferation of corn that supported larger sedentary societies. Vincas P. Steponaitis, "Prehistoric Archaeology in the Southeastern United States, 1970–1985," *Annual Review of Anthropology* 15 (1986): 363–404. For a discussion of the linguistic origins and (dis)connections among Iroquoian speakers, see Thomas R. Whyte, "Proto-Iroquoian Divergence in the Late Archaic–Early Woodland Period Transition of the Appalachian Highlands," *Southeastern Archaeology* 26, no. 1 (2007): 134–44. Others provide theories of the process of ethnogenesis of Cherokee people and the time frames under which this process took place. To summarize, in different regions, people are becoming Cherokee at different moments in time. Tasha Benyshek, "Archaeological Data Recovery Excavations at the Iotla Site (31ma77) at the Macon County Airport, Macon County, North Carolina," TRC Associates, June 2020; Gerald F. Schroedl, "Cherokee Ethnohistory and Archaeology from 1540 to 1838," in *Indians of the Greater Southeast: Historical Archaeology and Ethnohistory*, ed. Bonnie G. McEwan (University Press of Florida, 2000); Christopher Rodning, "Cherokee Ethnogenesis," in *Archaeological Adaptation: Case Studies of Cultural Transformation from the Southeast and Caribbean*, ed. C. Clifford Boyd (University of Tennessee Press, 2020), 83–134; Gerald F. Schroedl, "Mississippian Towns in the Eastern Tennessee Valley," in *Mississippian Towns and Sacred Spaces: Searching for an Architectural Grammar*, ed. R. Barry Lewis and Charles Stout (University of Alabama Press). And yet, there is a core group of people living in and around Kituwah today, and if they consented and we used DNA, we would likely find they share lineal descendancy to the people who inhabited this region since time immemorial. By the timeline laid out in this chapter, just before the Spanish entradas, Cherokee people in the various ways defined by both archaeologists and Cherokee people today existed.

4. Thomas N. Belt, conversation with author, June 8, 2022.

5. Frans M. Olbrechts, "Cherokee Belief and Practice with Regard to Childbirth," *Anthropos* 26, no. 1–2 (1931): 30; Russell Thornton, "Cherokee Population Losses during the Trail of Tears: A New Perspective and a New Estimate," *Ethnohistory* 31, no. 4 (1984): 291, https://doi.org/10.2307/482714.

6. Lunar cycles mattered and were a way of organizing time and ceremonial schedules. Clara Sue Kidwell, "Native American Systems of Knowledge," in *A Companion to American Indian History*, ed. Philip J. Deloria and Neal Salisbury (John Wiley and Sons, 2002), 87–102; John D. Loftin and Benjamin E. Frey, *People of Kituwah: The Old Ways of the Eastern Cherokees* (University of California Press, 2024), 45, 64.

7. Although this account comes from a later period, archaeologists have documented passenger pigeon bones among other animal remains at sites in the Southeast since the Archaic period, and these types of descriptions continue for another century. It is reasonable to conclude that a child living more than a hundred years earlier would have witnessed similar behaviors of pigeons during her lifetime. Steponaitis, "Prehistoric Archaeology"; John Lawson, *A New Voyage to Carolina* (London, 1709), http://rla.unc.edu/Archives/accounts/Lawson/Lawson.html.

8. Research globally demonstrates that within hunter-gatherer societies, those who gathered produced about 60–90 percent of the caloric energy for their communities. In mast-based

societies that followed the Little Ice Age in the Southeast, gathering likely did the same. The shift to agriculture likely led many women to expand their economic contributions through the continuation of gathering and the addition of farming, both activities that occurred very close to residential sites. Women would have spent significant time laboring together, which I speculate gave them time to discuss a range of issues facing their communities. Herman Pontzer and Brian M. Wood, "Effects of Evolution, Ecology, and Economy on Human Diet: Insights from Hunter-Gatherers and Other Small-Scale Societies," *Annual Review of Nutrition* 41 (October 2021): 363–85, https://doi.org/10.1146/annurev-nutr-111120-105520; Herman Pontzer et al., "Hunter-Gatherer Energetics and Human Obesity," *PLOS ONE* 7, no. 7 (2012): e40503, https://doi.org/10.1371/journal.pone.0040503; Paul E. Minnis, "Introduction," *Ethnobotany: A Reader* (University of Oklahoma Press, 2000), 1–9. In the following piece, the authors examine shared cognates among Iroquoian languages. What stands out to me is the fact that neither the word "corn" (*selu*) or "bean" (*tuya*) shares a cognate with another Iroquoian language. *Selu* stands alone among Iroquoian and Muskogean dialects, which signals that Cherokee peoples developed their own unique linguistic relationship to corn. Michael A. Schillaci et al., "Linguistic Clues to Iroquoian Prehistory," *Journal of Anthropological Research* 73, no. 3 (2017): 448–85, https://doi.org/10.1086/693055. The following pieces lay out the changes in Cherokee peoples' relationship to corn over time, including in Goodwin's piece the six different types of maize that ripened on different timelines. Corn makes its first appearance in what is today western North Carolina around AD 60 and from AD 80–100 in the Tennessee Valley. At old Cherokee towns like Kituwah, corn agriculture did not take hold fully until around AD 900. After AD 1000, it really took off. Goodwin, *Cherokees in Transition*; Kandace D. Hollenbach and Stephen B. Carmody, "The Daily Lives of Early Archaic Foragers in the Mid-South," in *Investigating the Ordinary: Everyday Matters in Southeast Archaeology*, ed. Sarah E. Price and Philip J. Carr (University Press of Florida, 2018); Amber M. VanDerwarker, Jon B. Marcoux, and Kandace D. Hollenbach, "Farming and Foraging at the Crossroads: The Consequences of Cherokee and European Interaction through the Late Eighteenth Century," *American Antiquity* 78, no. 1 (2013): 68–88, https://doi.org/10.7183/0002-7316.78.1.68; Kandace D. Hollenbach, "Plant Use at a Mississippian and Contact-Period Site in the South Carolina Coastal Plain," in *Forging Southeastern Identities: Social Archaeology, Ethnohistory, and Folklore of the Mississippian to Early Historic South*, ed. Gregory A. Waselkov and Marvin T. Smith (University of Alabama Press, 2017).

9. The following authors provide some insights into what archaeologists have defined as the Qualla series of pottery, present at Kituwah, which over time has been divided further into three discrete phases: the Early Qualla phase (ca. AD 1300–1500), the Middle Qualla phase (ca. AD 1500–1650), and the Late Qualla phase (ca. AD 1650–1838). The Qualla series, recently articulated by Jon Bernard Marcoux, "represents a 500-year-long South Appalachian pottery tradition." Brett H. Riggs and M. Scott Shumate, "Archaeological Testing at Kituwah: 2001 Investigations at Sites 31Sw1, 31Sw2, 31Sw287, 31Sw316, 31Sw317, 31Sw318, and 31Sw320," report prepared for the Eastern Band of Cherokee Indians Cultural Resources Program, working paper (North Carolina Office of State Archaeology, July 2003); H. Trawick Ward and R. P. Stephen Davis, *Time before History: The Archaeology of North Carolina* (University of North Carolina Press, 1999); Jon Bernard Marcoux, *Pox, Empire, Shackles, and Hides: The Townsend Site, 1670–1715* (University of Alabama Press, 2010), 70–72. Additionally, contemporary master artists describe a similar path. For example, Harry Oosahwee describes how

he learned to work with clay and that what he has chosen to create includes pipes. "Harry Oosahwee," Osiyo: Voices of the Cherokee People, 2018, https://osiyo.tv/harry-oosahwee.

10. Although none of these studies focuses specifically on Kituwah, the contemporaneous presence of clay pipes at Coweeta, later evidence of clay pipes at Chota and Tanasi, and the continued creation of clay pipes by men through the Long Removal Era suggests that boys would have first witnessed pottery processes with women and over time developed the skill to create clay pipes. Gregory D. Wilson and Christopher B. Rodning, "Boiling, Baking, and Pottery Breaking: A Functional Analysis of Ceramic Vessels from Coweeta Creek," *Southeastern Archaeology* 21, no. 1 (2002): 29–35; Christopher B. Rodning, "Cherokee Towns and Calumet Ceremonialism in Eastern North America," *American Antiquity* 79, no. 3 (2014): 434; Lance Greene, *Their Determination to Remain: A Cherokee Community's Resistance to the Trail of Tears in North Carolina* (University of Alabama Press, 2022), 111; James Frederick Bates, "An Analysis of the Aboriginal Ceramic Artifacts from Chota-Tanasee, an Eighteenth Century Overhill Cherokee Town" (master's thesis, University of Tennessee, 1982), https://trace.tennessee.edu/utk_gradthes/4182; Lawson, *New Voyage to Carolina*; "Harry Oosahwee."

11. This is a creative intervention based on the reality that humor was and is a part of people's lives. As scholars have noted, humor was and is often infused in spiritual activities. The booger dance and the use of booger masks within Cherokee society are examples of Cherokee people using the reimagining of faces to poke fun at others. This imagining is also based on watching my dad interact with my daughter over the course of her lifetime with him. He would sit across a room from her and make a silly face to communicate connection and love and to generate laughter. Marianne Kongerslev, "Enduring Laughter: Introduction to the Special Issue on Native and Indigenous Humor," *Studies in American Humor* 6, no. 2 (2020): 254–64; Michael Tlanusta Garrett et al., "Laughing It Up: Native American Humor as Spiritual Tradition," *Journal of Multicultural Counseling and Development* 33, no. 4 (2005): 194–204, https://doi.org/10.1002/j.2161-1912.2005.tb00016.x; Raymond D. Fogelson, "Person, Self, and Identity: Some Anthropological Retrospects, Circumspects, and Prospects," in *Psychosocial Theories of the Self: Proceedings of a Conference on New Approaches to the Self, Held March 29–April 1, 1979, by the Center for Psychosocial Studies, Chicago, Illinois*, ed. Benjamin Lee (Springer, 1982), 67–109, https://doi.org/10.1007/978-1-4684-4337-0_5; Loftin and Frey, *People of Kituwah*, 69–74; Frank G. Speck, "Concerning Iconology and the Masking Complex in Eastern North America," *University Museum Bulletin* 15, no. 1 (1950), 22–31.

12. Gil, a Cherokee language instructor and first language Eastern Band Cherokee speaker, said at dinner that he would not be able to learn Cherokee as a second language learner today; he was able to speak Cherokee only because he had learned it as a baby from his mother. In a previous conversation with Cherokee Nation first language speaker Tom Belt, he said the following of his language skills: "I speak the way my mom spoke because that's the way it works." Gilliam Jackson, conversation with author, July 2024; Thomas N. Belt, conversation with author, June 9, 2022.

13. Ben Frey, conversation with author, April, 2020.

14. C. Daniel Crews and Richard W. Starbuck, eds., *Records of the Moravians among the Cherokees*, vol. 5, *The Anna Rosina Years*, pt. 3, *Farewell to Sister Gambold, 1817–1821* (Cherokee Heritage Press, 2013), 2185–86.

15. Charles H. Faulkner, "The Winter House: An Early Southeast Tradition," *Midcontinental Journal of Archaeology* 2, no. 2 (1977): 141–59; Charles H. Faulkner, "Origin and Evolution of

the Cherokee Winter House," *Journal of Cherokee Studies* 3, no. 2 (1978): 87–93; Thomas R. Whyte, "[Drawing Depicting Cherokee Winter and Summer Domestic Structures] / [by Thomas R. Whyte]," 1969/1974, Digital Library of Georgia, accessed April 13, 2021, https://dlg.usg.edu/record/dlg_zlna_mm009#item.

16. Recognizing we can never achieve exact numbers, Goodwin estimates that Middletown settlements, where Kituwah is located, averaged about 250–300 people in clusters of concentrated towns. Goodwin, *Cherokees in Transition*, 46–47.

17. For discussion of when Cherokee people became recognizably Cherokee, see note 3 of the introduction. Christopher B. Rodning, "Reconstructing the Coalescence of Cherokee Communities in Southern Appalachia," in *The Transformation of the Southeastern Indians, 1540–1760*, ed. Robbie Ethridge and Charles Hudson (University Press of Mississippi, 2002), 171; Alan Kilpatrick, *The Night Has a Naked Soul: Witchcraft and Sorcery among the Western Cherokee* (Syracuse University Press, 1997), xviii.

18. Although schematic diagrams of Kituwah don't exist, archaeologist Brett Riggs in a professional conversation suggested superimposing a map of Coweeta Creek onto Kituwah to get a sense of how Cherokees structured their space. The larger point about the similar Cherokee town structure is discussed in Brett H. Riggs and Thomas N. Belt, "Cherokee Housing in the North Carolina Mountains," in *Native American Log Cabins in the Southeast*, ed. Gregory A. Waselkov (University of Tennessee Press, 2019), 111–41.

19. Rodning, "Cherokee Ethnogenesis," 90–92.

20. Schroedl, "Mississippian Towns in the Eastern Tennessee Valley."

21. Hollenbach, "Plant Use at a Mississippian and Contact-Period Site."

22. James Mooney, *Myths of the Cherokee* (Government Printing Office 1902), 244–45, https://catalog.hathitrust.org/Record/010939061.

23. Scarry and Scarry note that during the late pre-European contact periods as agricultural endeavors intensified at major population centers, women's femur and humerus strength increased and "stress-related robusticity in shoulders and upper arms [was] consistent with the movements involved in hoeing and pounding corn with large mortars and pestles." Clark Spencer Larsen and Christopher Ruff note that these transitions led to specific stresses on women's bodies, including more osteoarthritis in bones associated with activities related to agriculture. Although the authors highlight that these changes occurred in an earlier period, the continuing proliferation of corn across the Southeast suggests these physical realties would have continued for women farmers. C. Margaret Scarry and John F. Scarry, "Native American 'Garden Agriculture' in Southeastern North America," *World Archaeology* 37, no. 2 (2005): 259–74; Clark Spencer Larsen and Christopher Ruff, "'An External Agency of Considerable Importance': The Stresses of Agriculture in the Foraging-to-Farming Transition in Eastern North America," in *Human Bioarchaeology of the Transition to Agriculture*, ed. Ron Pinhasi and Jay T. Stock (John Wiley and Sons, 2011), 293–315, https://doi.org/10.1002/9780470670170.ch12.

24. Late eighteenth-century accounts, oral narratives, and archaeology support the need for winter hunting largely on the part of groups of men. Gerald F. Schroedl and James F. Bates, *Overhill Cherokee Archaeology at Chota-Tanasee* (University of Tennessee, Dept. of Anthropology, 1986), 470–73; Benjamin Hawkins, *The Collected Works of Benjamin Hawkins, 1796–1810*, ed. Howard Thomas Foster (University of Alabama Press, 2003), 20–22, 45–46.

25. Figurines of female figures associated with corn, including the Birger figurine, were common at Cahokia and the surrounding area in the early Mississippian period. Etowah, in what is today the state of Georgia, contained gorgets with female figures. John Howard Payne recorded oral narratives about the role of women and Selu in his accounts. Archaeologist Gerald Schroedl and more recently Jane Eastman and Brett Riggs have noted that town layouts in what are today East Tennessee and Western North Carolina correspond to solstices. "Transcripts of John Howard Payne," n.d., JHPP; Schroedl and Bates, *Overhill Cherokee Archaeology*; Jane M. Eastman and Brett H. Riggs, "The Sky at Watauga," paper presented at Annual Meeting Southeastern Archaeological Conference, Little Rock, AR, November 9, 2022; Susan C. Power, *Early Art of the Southeastern Indians: Feathered Serpents and Winged Beings* (University of Georgia Press, 2004).

26. Olbrechts, "Cherokee Belief and Practice," 20–21.

27. Frank G. Speck, Leonard Broom, and Will West Long, *Cherokee Dance and Drama* (University of Oklahoma Press, 1993), 7–8.

28. Nancy Shoemaker, *A Strange Likeness: Becoming Red and White in Eighteenth-Century North America* (Oxford University Press, 2006), 65–68. For the Cherokee language of birds, I drew from Christopher B. Teuton and Hastings Shade, *Anitsalagi Elohi Anehi = Cherokee Earth Dwellers: Stories and Teachings of the Natural World* (University of Washington Press, 2023), 172–73.

29. Although it is not clear from the documentary record alone when the eagle dance took hold, the record supports an eagle dance connection between Cherokee people and their Iroquoian-speaking cousins. Additionally, it is clear from the documentary record that by the first half of the eighteenth century, traveler accounts recorded ceremonies that treated eagle feathers as an integral part of sacred practice between and among Indigenous communities. Mooney, *Myths of the Cherokee*, 280–84; William N. Fenton, *The Iroquois Eagle Dance: An Offshoot of the Calumet Dance*, Bulletin 156, Smithsonian Institution American Bureau of American Ethnology (Government Printing Office, 1953), 90–96, https://hdl.handle.net /2027/nyp.33433101977472?urlappend=%3Bseq=13; James Adair, *The History of the American Indians* (E. and C. Dilly, 1775), 42, http://archive.org/details/GR_10.

30. Teuton and Shade, *Anitsalagi Elohi Anehi*, 172–73.

31. Grade-based learning unevenly spread across the United States. In urban areas, common schools, grammar schools, and high schools existed by the middle of the nineteenth century, but not until cost-saving consolidation efforts throughout rural areas to eliminate the inefficiencies of one-room schoolhouses in the twentieth century did grade-based learning really take hold in the United States. John L. Rury, *Education and Social Change: Contours in the History of American Schooling*, 5th ed., (Routledge, 2016), 73–75, 126–37.

32. Robbie Etheridge describes the basic layouts of chiefdoms and the "buffer zones" that existed between towns during the period. Robbie Ethridge, "Navigating the Mississippian World: Infrastructure in the Sixteenth Century Native South," in *Forging Southeastern Identities: Social Archaeology, Ethnohistory, and Folklore of the Mississippian to Early Historic South*, ed. Gregory A. Waselkov and Marvin T. Smith (University of Alabama Press, 2017), 63.

33. Rachel J. Collins et al., "American Chestnut: Re-Examining the Historical Attributes of a Lost Tree," *Journal of Forestry*, 2017, https://doi.org/10.5849/JOF-2016-014.

34. Linguists estimate that linguistic split occurred between 3,500 and 4,000 years ago. Brad Montgomery-Anderson, *Cherokee Reference Grammar* (University of Oklahoma Press,

2015); William N. Fenton and John Gulick, eds., *Symposium on Cherokee and Iroquois Culture*, Smithsonian Institution Bureau of American Ethnology, Bulletin 180 (Government Printing Office, 1961), https://catalog.hathitrust.org/Record/002496941; Schillaci et al., "Linguistic Clues to Iroquoian Prehistory," 453–54.

35. Although he was recording oral narratives in a much later period, Swanton did record the significance of chestnuts to Muscogee practices. Earlier traveler accounts, including those by William Bartram, who traveled through Muscogee Creek communities in the late 1700s, noted the presence of mature chestnuts throughout Muscogee Creek country. John Reed Swanton, *Early History of the Creek Indians and Their Neighbors* (Government Printing Office, 1922), 384; Robbie Franklyn Ethridge, *Creek Country: The Creek Indians and Their World* (University of North Carolina Press, 2003), 47–48, 90.

36. Mooney, *Myths of the Cherokee.*

37. Collins et al., "American Chestnut," 68.

38. John R. Finger, *Tennessee Frontiers: Three Regions in Transition* (Indiana University Press, 2001), 13, http://search.ebscohost.com/login.aspx?direct=true&scope=site&db=nlebk&AN=66590. Rodning notes, "Fire is one of the major forces that has shaped ancient and more recent past, including naturally occurring fires as well as fire set by people to alter local forest ecology to enhance the productivity of foraging and farming." Rodning, "Cherokee Ethnogenesis," 92.

39. In at least some coastal communities, Native peoples used fire to burn cane along waterways to "drive game from hiding." Heather A. Lapham, "In Feast and Famine: New Perspectives on Black Bears in the Southern Appalachians and Piedmont, AD 1000–1800," in *Bears: Archaeological and Ethnohistorical Perspectives in Native Eastern North America*, ed. Heather A. Lapham and Gregory A. Waselkov (University of Florida Press, 2020), 160–92.

40. Bennie C. Keel, *Cherokee Archaeology: A Study of the Appalachian Summit* (University of Tennessee Press, 1987); Collins et al., "American Chestnut."

41. David N. Cozzo, "Ethnobotanical Classification System and Medical Ethnobotany of the Eastern Band of the Cherokee Indians" (PhD diss., University of Georgia, 2004), 75–76.

42. De Brahm noted these uses of fire among the Overhill Cherokee towns in the mid-eighteenth century, though fire had been in use much longer throughout the Southeast. John Gerar William De Brahm, *De Brahm's Report of the General Survey in the Southern District of North America*, ed. Louis De Vorsey Jr. (University of South Carolina Press, 1971), 101–3, https://hdl.handle.net/2027/uva.x006146763.

43. Cynthia Fowler and Evelyn Konopik, "The History of Fire in the Southern United States," *Human Ecology Review* 14, no. 2 (2007): 167.

44. Victor E. Shelford, *The Ecology of North America* (University of Illinois Press, 1965).

45. Shelford, *Ecology of North America*, 42; Teuton and Shade, *Anitsalagi Elohi Anehi*, 167–83.

46. Heather A. Lapham, *Hunting for Hides: Deerskins, Status, and Cultural Change in the Protohistoric Appalachians* (University of Alabama Press, 2006), 90–97, 139–40.

47. Lapham, *Hunting for Hides*, 90–97, 139–40.

48. James Adair, *The History of the American Indians*, ed. Kathryn H. Braund (University of Alabama Press, 2005).

49. Lisa Rutherford, "Feather Cape Notes," unpublished manuscript, January 21, 2021.

50. Feather capes were not ubiquitous, so even in earlier moments in time, the idea that Cherokee creators would have built up calluses on their fingers to minimize the discomfort

seems unlikely. Kaitlyn Abbott, "Lisa Rutherford: Always Learning, Always Creating," OsiyoTV, April 2, 2018, https://osiyo.tv/lisa-rutherford-always-learning-always-creating.

51. I reconstructed this feather cape process using a description provided by Lisa Rutherford, a Cherokee Nation National Treasure and artist who has learned to make feather capes as an adult. Certainly, this process may have had variations, but Lisa's descriptions of the embodied parts of the process (sore fingers, tracing netting lines) seem appropriately timeless. Will Chavez, "Rutherford Recreating Cherokee Feathered Capes," *Cherokee Phoenix* (Tahlequah, OK), December 27, 2013, www.cherokeephoenix.org/culture/rutherford-recreating-cherokee-feathered-capes/article_2af45f6e-7916-5aa8-9b61-bc6223e273be.html; Abbott, "Lisa Rutherford."

52. Very few archaeologists work on archaeology of childhood in the Native South. Archaeologists have paid little attention to the roles children performed economically, spiritually, or politically, similar to the way few archaeologists paid attention to gender until feminist archaeologists began to do so. Although Patty Crown was not an archaeologist of the Native South, she did remain attuned to women, children, and learning practices. Anthropologists taking a more global approach reach conclusions similar to Crown's about learning. Among the Hadza, Crittenden observes that parents and adults offer little direct instruction to children; instead, it is older children who model learning for younger children. Lancy points out that learners "took advantage of opportunities to observe and emulate the most competent in order to achieve competence and to be helpful and accepted." Patricia L. Crown, "Life Histories of Pots and Potters: Situating the Individual in Archaeology," *American Antiquity* 72, no. 4 (2007): 677–90, https://doi.org/10.2307/25470440; Patricia L. Crown, "The Archaeology of Crafts Learning: Becoming a Potter in the Puebloan Southwest," *Annual Review of Anthropology* 43, no. 1 (2014): 74–75, https://doi.org/10.1146/annurev-anthro-102313-025910; David F. Lancy, "Ethnographic Perspectives on Culture Acquisition," in *Childhood: Origins, Evolution, and Implications,* ed. Courthey L. Meehan and Alyssa N. Crittenden, School for Advanced Research Seminar Series (University of New Mexico Press, 2016), 173–95; Alyssa N. Crittenden, "Children's Foraging and Play among the Hadza: The Evolutionary Significance of 'Work Play,'" in *Childhood: Origins, Evolution, and Implications,* ed. Courthey L. Meehan and Alyssa N. Crittenden, School for Advanced Research Seminar Series (University of New Mexico Press, 2016), 155–72.

53. Crown, "Archaeology of Crafts Learning."

54. Crown, "Archaeology of Crafts Learning," 76.

55. Although Allen was exploring an Overhill town location and Whyte was examining a Pisgah phase site, both of their works note the ability of communities and households to integrate diverse approaches to material culture at different points and locations in time. Christian Allen, "Coalesced Cherokee Communities in the Eighteenth Century: A Spatial and Elemental Analyses of the Ceramic Assemblage at Mialoquo (40mr3), an Overhill Cherokee Town in Monroe County, Tennessee" (master's thesis, University of Tennessee, 2019), https://trace.tennessee.edu/utk_gradthes/5572; Thomas R. Whyte, "Household Ceramic Diversity in the Late Prehistory of the Appalachian Summit," *Southeastern Archaeology* 36, no. 2 (2017): 160, https://doi.org/10.1080/0734578X.2016.1250199.

56. Crown, "Archaeology of Crafts Learning."

57. This line of thought is inspired by Cherokee Nation National Treasure for pottery Victoria Mitchell describing the feel of the mud as part of her inspiration. I contend that some

tactile experiences inspire some people, regardless of the century. Additionally, why would we assume an absence of personal preferences in earlier moments? Even though a person's range of preferences may have been dictated by the activities required and available in their moment, to deny those preferences seems to defy human experience. "Victoria Mitchell," All Things Cherokee, August 26, 2014, www.allthingscherokee.com/victoria-mitchell.

58. Sarah H. Hill, *Weaving New Worlds: Southeastern Cherokee Women and Their Basketry* (University of North Carolina Press, 1997), xv.

59. Sarah H. Hill, "Weaving History: Cherokee Baskets from the Springplace Mission," *William and Mary Quarterly* 53, no. 1 (1996): 115–36, https://doi.org/10.2307/2946826.

60. Megan M. King, Roger Cain, and Shawna Morton Cain, "An Experimental Ethnoarchaeological Approach to Understanding the Development of Use Wear Associated with the Processing of River Cane for Split-Cane Technology," *Southeastern Archaeology* 38, no. 1 (2019): 38–53, https://doi.org/10.1080/0734578X.2018.1484216. It took contemporary basket maker and Cherokee Nation National Treasure Shawna Morton Cain ten years to perfect her skills at split-making. "Introduction to Splitting River Cane," posted November 9, 2015, by Cain on Cane, YouTube, 6 min., 57 sec., www.youtube.com/watch?v=e_HNKYJknDE; Hill, *Weaving New Worlds*, 41–43.

61. Hill, *Weaving New Worlds*, 42; Kathryn A. Jakes and Annette G. Ericksen, "Prehistoric Use of Sumac and Bedstraw as Dye Plants in Eastern North America," *Southeastern Archaeology* 20, no. 1 (2001): 56–66.

62. Some types of more specialized learning—for example, those requiring strength or dexterity—may have fallen into a more graded type of learning that required direct instruction or may not have followed a linear set of steps to master the skill. Lancy, "Ethnographic Perspectives on Culture Acquisition."

63. Kenneth C. Reid, "Fire and Ice: New Evidence for the Production and Preservation of Late Archaic Fiber-Tempered Pottery in the Middle-Latitude Lowlands," *American Antiquity* 49, no. 1 (1984): 55–76, https://doi.org/10.2307/280512; Wilson and Rodning, "Boiling, Baking, and Pottery Breaking"; James K. Feathers, "Explaining Shell-Tempered Pottery in Prehistoric Eastern North America," *Journal of Archaeological Method and Theory* 13, no. 2 (2006): 89–133, https://doi.org/10.1007/s10816-006-9003-3.

64. "Cherokee Bowmaker Richard Fields," OsiyoTV, accessed May 10, 2023, https://osiyo .tv/cherokee-bowmaker-richard-fields.

65. James Mooney, "The Cherokee River Cult," *Journal of American Folklore* 13, no. 48 (1900): 1, https://doi.org/10.2307/533728.

66. Mooney, "Cherokee River Cult," 2; Teuton and Shade, *Anitsalagi Elohi Anehi*, 198–99.

67. Crittenden breaks Hadza children's play into four categories. One of those, physical-locomotor, includes swimming and water collection as an area of play. Crittenden, "Children's Foraging and Play," 164.

68. While regional material variations continued to exist, shell became the dominant temper for Southeastern potters during the Mississippian period. Steponaitis, "Prehistoric Archaeology"; Feathers, "Explaining Shell-Tempered Pottery."

69. Approximately sixty miles to the east of Kituwah, Biltmore Mound, occupied in an earlier moment, "yielded an exceptionally diverse faunal assemblage that includes seldom-preserved fish scales, eggshell, terrestrial snail shells, ossified tendons of large birds, and costal cartilage of large mammals. The 34,532 specimens examined to date represent a minimum

of 65 species, including those of crayfish, mollusks, fish, amphibians, snakes, turtles, birds, and mammals. . . . Remains of box turtles, turkeys, squirrels, and deer are notably abundant, while those of aquatic species and other birds are sparser. Whitetailed deer remains account for 86 percent of mammalian specimens." Mollusk diversity continued in the region for centuries. Larry R. Kimball, Thomas R. Whyte, and Gary D. Crites, "The Biltmore Mound and Hopewellian Mound Use in the Southern Appalachians," *Southeastern Archaeology* 29, no. 1 (2010), 50–51.

70. Megan King's collaborative lithics research with Shawna and Roger Cain, two Cherokee Nation and United Keetoowah Band members, inspired this train of thought. They used lithics to process river cane. Through conversations with all of them, I learned the Cains gave their favorite tools nicknames based on the best fit and the safety of that particular tool in their hands. It is easy to imagine children engaged in similar kinds of processing activities also determining which tools enabled them to "exert pressure on the tool during use without cutting their skin." This, perhaps, should have been obvious to me as the parent of a Montessori-educated child. My daughter's ability to help my dad with construction projects as a small child increased when we bought her a child-size, but real, tool kit through Montessori Services. King, Cain, and Cain, "Experimental Ethnoarchaeological Approach," 43–44.

71. Gaither summarizes that landscape knowledge is acquired in two ways: observation or scientific experimentation. Gaither, "History of North American Education."

72. Schroedl and Bates, *Overhill Cherokee Archaeology*.

73. Harjo chooses the spiral as a symbol of Mvskoke futurity both because it ties to the movement of a stomp dance but also because "the stomp dance spiral is not disappearing but rather appearing in new emergence geographies." Laura Harjo, *Spiral to the Stars: Mvskoke Tools of Futurity*, Critical Issues in Indigenous Studies (University of Arizona Press, 2019), 292–94.

74. Raymond Fogelson, "The Cherokee Ballgame Cycle: An Ethnographer's View," *Ethnomusicology* 15, no. 3 (1971): 334–35, https://doi.org/10.2307/850633.

75. Duncan in her discussion of Cherokee adornments and clothing points out that spiral and concentric lines are ubiquitous throughout the world but also exist in ancestral and Cherokee-designed pottery and jewelry. Barbara R. Duncan, *Cherokee Clothing in the 1700s: With Information from Previous and Following Centuries* (Museum of the Cherokee Indian Press, 2016), 114.

76. Christopher Bernard Rodning, *Center Places and Cherokee Towns: Archaeological Perspectives on Native American Architecture and Landscape in the Southern Appalachians* (University of Alabama Press, 2015).

77. Charles H. Faulkner, ed., *The Prehistoric Native American Art of Mud Glyph Cave* (University of Tennessee Press, 1986), 56–59.

78. Mooney recorded a series of rabbit trickster stories. Mooney, *Myths of the Cherokee*, 250, 264, 268, 273–74, 286–87, 325–29, 411, 436, 446–47, 450–52, 472–74, 504.

79. Teuton and Shade, *Anitsalagi Elohi Anehi*, 112–13.

80. William Harlen Gilbert Jr., "The Eastern Cherokees," *Anthropological Papers, No. 23*, Smithsonian Institution Bureau of American Ethnology, Bulletin 133 (Government Printing Office, 1943), 204, http://archive.org/details/bulletin1331943smit; Mooney, *Myths of the Cherokee*, 264.

81. Lapham, "In Feast and Famine," 198.

82. Mooney, *Myths of the Cherokee*, 262, 327–29; Teuton and Shade, *Anitsalagi Elohi Anehi*, 88–89.

83. Heidi Altman, Tanya M. Peres, and J. Matthew Compton, "Better Than Butter: Yona Go'i, Bear Grease in Cherokee Culture," in *Bears: Archaeological and Ethnohistorical Perspectives in Native Eastern North America*, ed. Heather A. Lapham and Gregory A. Waselkov (University of Florida Press, 2020), 193–216; Lapham, "In Feast and Famine," 160–92.

84. There is a rich ethnographic and archaeological record of how Indigenous people, living in what is today Western North Carolina, used bears, bear meat, and bear fat over time. In the early twentieth century, Lean Soap Carey described substituting pig fat for the previous uses of bear fat when bear populations disappeared in Oklahoma. Lapham, "In Feast and Famine"; "Carey, Lean Soap," DDC, accessed February 14, 2023, https://digital .libraries.ou.edu/cdm/ref/collection/dorisduke/id/13235; Henry Timberlake, *The Memoirs of Lieut. Henry Timberlake: (Who Accompanied the Three Cherokee Indians to England in the Year 1762); Containing Whatever He Observed Remarkable, or Worthy of Public Notice, during His Travels to and from That Nation* [. . .] (printed for the author, 1765), http://archive.org /details/memoirsoflieutheootimb; Clarence Walworth Alvord and Lee Bidgood, *The First Explorations of the Trans-Allegheny Region by the Virginians, 1650–1674* (Arthur H. Clark, 1912), 213, 233, http://archive.org/details/firstexplorationooalv.

85. Mooney, *Myths of the Cherokee*, 264, 325–28.

86. Given that stories provided guidance through relationality as opposed to coercive discipline, it is easy to imagine a wiser child understanding the lesson of the story. Mooney, *Myths of the Cherokee*, 262, 327–29; Teuton and Shade, *Anitsalagi Elohi Anehi*, 32–33, 88–89.

87. Andrew Curry, "Cherokee Holy of Holies," *Archaeology* 55, no. 5 (2002): 70–75. Many, including Cherokee Nation citizen and Qualla Boundary–residing Cherokee language expert Tom Belt, regard Kituwah as the spiritual heart of the nation. Tom Belt, conversation with author, August 2019.

88. Crown, "Archaeology of Crafts Learning," 73–74.

89. As Basso puts it, "If place-making is a way of constructing the past, a venerable means of *doing* human history, it is also a way of constructing social traditions and, in the process, personal and social identities. We *are*, in a sense, the place-worlds we imagine." Keith H. Basso, *Wisdom Sits in Places: Landscape and Language among the Western Apache* (University of New Mexico Press, 1996), 7; Adrea Lawrence, "Epic Learning in an Indian Pueblo: A Framework for Studying Multigenerational Learning in the History of Education," *History of Education Quarterly* 54, no. 3 (2014): 286–302, https://doi.org/10.1111/hoeq.12068.

Chapter 2

1. Longe specifically listed these names as common girls' names when he lived among the Overhill towns in the eighteenth century. Alexander Longe, "A Small Postscript on the Ways and Manners of the Indians Called Cherokees," ed. David H. Corkran, *Southern Indian Studies* 21 (October 1969): 1–50.

2. Records indicate three distinct dialects; Schroedl lists them as follows: Overhill towns— western or Otali dialect; Middle—Kituhwa dialect; Lower—Lower or Elati dialect. Gerald F. Schroedl, "Cherokee Ethnohistory and Archaeology from 1540 to 1838," in *Indians of the Greater Southeast: Historical Archaeology and Ethnohistory*, ed. Bonnie G. McEwan (University

Press of Florida, 2000), 204; Christopher Rodning, "Cherokee Ethnogenesis," in *Archaeo-logical Adaptation: Case Studies of Cultural Transformation from the Southeast and Caribbean*, ed. C. Clifford Boyd (University of Tennessee Press, 2020), 3.

3. Christopher B. Teuton and Hastings Shade, *Anitsalagi Elohi Anehi = Cherokee Earth Dwellers: Stories and Teachings of the Natural World* (University of Washington Press, 2023), 123; Gerald F. Schroedl and James F. Bates, *Overhill Cherokee Archaeology at Chota-Tanasee* (University of Tennessee, Dept. of Anthropology, 1986).

4. Charles H. Faulkner, "The Winter House: An Early Southeast Tradition," *Midcontinental Journal of Archaeology* 2, no. 2 (1977): 141–59; Brett H. Riggs and Thomas N. Belt, "Cherokee Housing in the North Carolina Mountains," in *Native American Log Cabins in the Southeast*, ed. Gregory A. Waselkov (University of Tennessee Press, 2019), 111–41.

5. For a discussion of Cherokee language as it relates to architecture, see Riggs and Belt, "Cherokee Housing in the North Carolina Mountains," 112–16.

6. Daniel J. Tortora, *Carolina in Crisis: Cherokees, Colonists, and Slaves in the American Southeast, 1756–1763* (University of North Carolina Press, 2015), 130–31.

7. Erin Stevens Nelson, "Intimate Landscapes: The Social Nature of the Spaces Between," *Archaeological Prospection* 21, no. 1 (2014): 55, https://doi.org/10.1002/arp.1472.

8. Theda Perdue, *Cherokee Women: Gender and Culture Change, 1700–1835* (University of Nebraska Press, 1998), 29–34.

9. Perdue, *Cherokee Women*, 44; Sarah M. S. Pearsall, *Polygamy: An Early American History* (Yale University Press, 2019), 232.

10. Although primarily focused on the Townsend site, Marcoux points out close averages at Chota-Tanasi. Jon Bernard Marcoux, *Pox, Empire, Shackles, and Hides: The Townsend Site, 1670–1715* (University of Alabama Press, 2010), 118, 134.

11. Archaeologists identified 117 distinct burials at Chota-Tanasi. Although not all women's burials can be definitively dated to the early eighteenth century, several of them were women of child-rearing age. This information suggests the exact possibility I speculate about above. Of note, one of the burials was a woman with a fetus in utero. Schroedl and Bates, *Overhill Cherokee Archaeology*.

12. Longe, "Small Postscript." Using the chart of burials and defining a woman of birthing age as being between 18 and 45, one can determine that there are twenty-three women buried at Chota, any of whom could have left behind babies/toddlers who required additional nursing from female kin. Schroedl and Bates, *Overhill Cherokee Archaeology*, 182–83.

13. Heather A. Lapham, "In Feast and Famine: New Perspectives on Black Bears in the Southern Appalachians and Piedmont, AD 1000–1800," in *Bears: Archaeological and Ethno-historical Perspectives in Native Eastern North America*, ed. Heather A. Lapham and Gregory A. Waselkov (University of Florida Press, 2020), 160–92.

14. Marcoux, *Pox, Empire, Shackles, and Hides*, 143.

15. Perdue, *Cherokee Women*, 20.

16. James Mooney, *Myths of the Cherokee* (Government Printing Office, 1902), 242–43, https://catalog.hathitrust.org/Record/010939061.

17. Perdue, *Cherokee Women*, 19.

18. Teuton and Shade, *Anitsalagi Elohi Anehi*, 123.

19. Nelson, "Intimate Landscapes," 54. Although examining the power of gossip among Muscogee Creek women, Innes lays out how women used gossip and intimate women's

spaces to engage in political activities. Pamela Innes, "The Interplay of Genres, Gender, and Language Ideology among the Muscogee," *Language in Society* 35, no. 2 (2006): 231–59, https://doi.org/10.1017/S0047404506060106.

20. Duane Champagne, "Institutional and Cultural Order in Early Cherokee Society: A Sociological Interpretation," *Journal of Cherokee Studies* 15 (1990): 14–15; Perdue, *Cherokee Women*, 58, 146; Longe, "Small Postscript," 32.

21. Lynne P. Sullivan and Christopher B. Rodning, "Residential Burial, Gender Roles, and Political Development in Late Prehistoric and Early Cherokee Cultures of the Southern Appalachians," *Archaeological Papers of the American Anthropological Association* 20, no. 1 (2010): 79–97, https://doi.org/10.1111/j.1551-8248.2011.01029.x.

22. Although Perdue lays out evidence for the existence of women's councils, there is little description of the form, procedures, or scheduling of these events. We are left to imagine how and when these agendas came together, which I have done here. Perdue, *Cherokee Women*, 146, 156–57.

23. Tom Hatley, *The Dividing Paths: Cherokees and South Carolinians through the Era of Revolution* (Oxford University Press, 1995), 5.

24. Hatley, *Dividing Paths*, 5–7.

25. Paul Kelton, *Epidemics and Enslavement: Biological Catastrophe in the Native Southeast, 1492–1715* (University of Nebraska Press, 2007), 158.

26. Alexander Longe, who lived among the Cherokees in the first two decades of the eighteenth century, wrote that nearly an entire community had immigrated to Augustoghe, around the same time the great smallpox epidemic swept through the region. Longe, "Small Postscript"; Kelton, *Epidemics and Enslavement*, 151–53.

27. Although slightly later chronologically, in his article Chambers points out how some of the confusion created by movements of people from Great Tellico in the 1750s stemmed from the adjournments of groups of women within individual towns. This pattern of women's deliberations would be repeated through the Long Removal Era. It is likely that women played a similar role in earlier moments over decisions to relocate. Ian Chambers, "The Movement of Great Tellico: The Role of Town and Clan in Cherokee Spatial Understanding," *Native South* 3, no. 1 (2010): 89–102, https://doi.org/10.1353/nso.2010.0003.

28. For descriptions of the Green Corn Ceremony, see John Witthoft, *Green Corn Ceremonialism in the Eastern Woodlands* (University of Michigan Press, 1949); and Raymond Fogelson, "The Cherokee Ballgame Cycle: An Ethnographer's View," *Ethnomusicology* 15, no. 3 (1971): 327–38, https://doi.org/10.2307/850633.

29. Jack Martin, "Modeling Language Contact in the Prehistory of the Southeastern United States," in *Perspectives on the Southeast: Linguistics, Archaeology, and Ethnohistory*, ed. Patricia B. Kwachka (University of Georgia Press, 1994), 14–24.

30. John Norton, *The Journal of Major John Norton, 1816*, Publications of the Champlain Society 46 (Champlain Society, 1970).

31. Marcoux, *Pox, Empire, Shackles, and Hides*, 12, 129.

32. Christopher Rodning, "Reconstructing the Coalescence of Cherokee Communities in Southern Appalachia," in *The Transformation of the Southeastern Indians, 1540–1760*, ed. Robbie Ethridge and Charles Hudson (University Press of Mississippi, 2008, 155–76; David H. Dye, "The Art of War in the Sixteenth-Century Central Mississippi Valley," in *Perspectives on the Southeast: Linguistics, Archaeology, and Ethnohistory*, ed. Patricia B. Kwachka (University of Georgia Press, 1994), 44–60.

33. Kelton, *Epidemics and Enslavement*, 71.

34. Milton Gaither, "The History of North American Education, 15,000 BCE to 1491," *History of Education Quarterly* 54, no. 3 (2014): 326, https://doi.org/10.1111/hoeq.12070.

35. Teuton and Shade, *Anitsalagi Elohi Anehi*, 198–201.

36. Alan Cressler, a hydrologic technician for the United States Geological Survey based out of Norcross, Georgia, pointed me to links that monitor gauge data, only some of which provide consistent water temperature data. Most of these sites have been collecting temperature data for less than two decades. Additionally, the use of modern-day water temperatures are irrelevant to the period under study because of the introduction of reservoirs and dams throughout the region. Alan Cressler, conversation with author, April 27, 2021.

37. My favorite contemporary telling of this narrative history is the Cherokee language animation produced by students at Sequoyah Schools in the Cherokee Nation under the direction of Cherokee Nation citizen Joseph Erb. "The Beginning They Told," posted July 1, 2016, by Cherokee Nation, YouTube, 11 min., 5 sec., www.youtube.com/watch?v=UM_84WlnYOs&t=243s; Mooney, *Myths of the Cherokee*, 239.

38. John Gerar William De Brahm, *De Brahm's Report of the General Survey in the Southern District of North America*, ed. Louis De Vorsey Jr. (University of South Carolina Press, 1971), 138, https://hdl.handle.net/2027/uva.x006146763.

39. Robbie Ethridge, "Navigating the Mississippian World: Infrastructure in the Sixteenth Century Native South," in *Forging Southeastern Identities: Social Archaeology, Ethnohistory, and Folklore of the Mississippian to Early Historic South*, ed. Gregory A. Waselkov and Marvin T. Smith (University of Alabama Press, 2017), 71.

40. Paul Woodburn Parmalee, Arthur E. Bogan, and American Pearl Farms, *The Freshwater Mussels of Tennessee* (University of Tennessee Press, 1998), 34–35.

41. This imagining comes from structure data from the Schrodel and Bates report but also from unpublished images and site renderings of a home, known as Structure 5, that likely burned down during the historic phase at Chota and preserved a 5' × 3' pile of mussel shells with a rock in the center. Any evidence of a river cane mat to work on would probably not have survived the fire and time, but this speculation fits with the larger use by Cherokee people who often sat on woven mats to work. Schroedl and Bates, *Overhill Cherokee Archaeology*; "40MR2 Chota 1970-Structure 5 Planview" (McClung Museum of Natural History and Culture, University of Tennessee, 1970), 239; "40MR2 Structure 5 in Area 5-Site Maps" (McClung Museum of Natural History and Culture, University of Tennessee, n.d.); "Structure 5 Floor-40MR2-0101" (McClung Museum of Natural History and Culture, University of Tennessee, n.d.).

42. *A New Map of the Cherokee Nation with the Names of the Towns & Rivers. They Are Situated on No. Lat. from 34 to 36: North Carolina Maps*, North Carolina Maps, accessed February 25, 2021, https://dc.lib.unc.edu/cdm/ref/collection/ncmaps/id/357; *A Draught of the Cherokee Country . . .*, image, Library of Congress, accessed June 23, 2021, www.loc.gov/resource/g3300m.gar00003/?sp=73.

43. Hiram C. Wilburn, "Judaculla Rock," *Southern Indian Studies*, no. 4 (October 1952): 19–21.

44. Marcoux, *Pox, Empire, Shackles, and Hides*, 13.

45. Marcoux, *Pox, Empire, Shackles, and Hides*, 13.

46. Heather A. Lapham, *Hunting for Hides: Deerskins, Status, and Cultural Change in the Protohistoric Appalachians* (University of Alabama Press, 2006), 139.

47. Mooney, *Myths of the Cherokee*, 251.

48. Wilma A. Dunaway, "The Southern Fur Trade and the Incorporation of Southern Appalachia into the World-Economy, 1690–1763," *Review (Fernand Braudel Center)* 17, no. 2 (1994): 233.

49. Dunaway, "Southern Fur Trade," 219–20.

50. Mooney, *Myths of the Cherokee*, 251; Mary Rothrock, "Carolina Traders Among the Overhill Cherokees, 1690–1760," *East Tennessee Historical Society Publications*, no. 1 (1929).

51. "Journal of Colonel George Chicken's Mission from Charleston, S.C. to the Cherokees, 1726," in *Travels in the American Colonies*, ed. Newton Dennison Mereness under the auspices of the National Society of the Colonial Dames of America (1916; repr., Antiquarian Press, 1961), 130–32, https://catalog.hathitrust.org/Record/003242649.

52. As late as 1799, when Moravians Steiner and de Schweinitz traveled through the region without an interpreter, they used sign language to communicate. Edmund Schwarze, *History of the Moravian Missions among Southern Indian Tribes of the United States* (Times Publishing Company, 1923), http://hdl.handle.net/2027/nc01.ark:/13960/t6zw1jz2m.

53. Eleazer Wiggan, one of the earliest traders to the Cherokee people, gained proficiency in the Cherokee language and served as an interpreter. Schroedl and Bates, *Overhill Cherokee Archaeology*, 6–8; Mary U. Rothrock, "Carolina Traders among the Overhill Cherokees, 1690–1760," *East Tennessee Historical Society Publications*, no. 1 (1929): 7–8; Henry Thompson Malone, "A Social History of the Eastern Cherokee Indians from the Revolution to Removal." (PhD diss., Emory University, 1952), ProQuest (5805164).

54. De Brahm, *Report of the General Survey*.

55. I chose to omit the word "shaman" in favor of the more modern and more culturally appropriate term "medicine keeper." David H. Corkran, *The Cherokee Frontier: Conflict and Survival, 1740–62* (University of Oklahoma Press, 1962), 12, https://hdl.handle.net/2027/uc1.32106015374587.

56. Raymond D. Fogelson, "On the 'Petticoat Government' of the Eighteenth-Century Cherokee," in *Personality and the Cultural Construction of Society*, ed. David K. Jordan and Marc J. Swartz (University of Alabama Press, 2010), 177–78.

57. Nancy Shoemaker, *A Strange Likeness: Becoming Red and White in Eighteenth-Century North America* (Oxford University Press, 2006), 64.

58. Shoemaker, *Strange Likeness*, 64–66.

59. Longe, "Small Postscript," 30. In his work, Fischer notes a similar approach to literacy used by Mixtec and Aztec (AD 1100 until first century of Spanish colonization) to create inscriptions, "primarily in painted books of cloth, bark paper or animal hide," which differed from the pre–AD 900 Zapotec, Epi-Olmec, and Mayan who carved on stone monuments. Steven R. Fischer, *A History of Writing* (Reaktion Books, 2004), 217, https://hdl.handle.net/2027/uc1.32106016933001.

60. Teuton and Shade, *Anitsalagi Elohi Anehi*, 209.

61. Kathryn E. Braund, *Deerskins and Duffels: Creek Indian Trade with Anglo-America, 1685–1815* (University of Nebraska Press, 1996), 104–5.

62. John Phillip Reid, *A Better Kind of Hatchet: Law, Trade, and Diplomacy in the Cherokee Nation during the Early Years of European Contact* (Pennsylvania State University Press, 1976), 49, http://catdir.loc.gov/catdir/enhancements/fy1309/75015544-b.html.

63. Kelton, *Epidemics and Enslavement*, 131–33.

64. Raymond D. Fogelson, "Who Were the Aní-Kutání? An Excursion into Cherokee Historical Thought," *Ethnohistory* 31, no. 4 (1984): 255–63, https://doi.org/10.2307/482712.

65. Hatley, *Dividing Paths*, 13.

66. Alejandra Dubcovsky, "One Hundred Sixty-One Knots, Two Plates, and One Emperor: Creek Information Networks in the Era of the Yamasee War," *Ethnohistory* 59, no. 3 (2012): 489–513, https://doi.org/10.1215/00141801-1587442; Alejandra Dubcovsky, *Informed Power: Communication in the Early American South* (Harvard University Press, 2016); William L. Ramsey, *The Yamasee War: A Study of Culture, Economy, and Conflict in the Colonial South* (University of Nebraska Press, 2010), 34–38.

67. Kelton, *Epidemics and Enslavement*, 131–33.

68. Christina Snyder, *Slavery in Indian Country: The Changing Face of Captivity in Early America* (Harvard University Press, 2012); Kelton, *Epidemics and Enslavement*, 120–23; Robbie Franklin Ethridge and Sheri Marie Shuck-Hall, *Mapping the Mississippian Shatter Zone: The Colonial Indian Slave Trade and Regional Instability in the American South* (University of Nebraska Press, 2009), 259–60.

69. Corkran, *Cherokee Frontier*.

70. Although Miles examines a later period, the Indian slave trade produced similar kinds of realities for young women and girls across the Native South. Tiya Miles, "The Narrative of Nancy, a Cherokee Woman," *Frontiers: A Journal of Women Studies* 29, no. 2–3 (2008): 60.

71. Perdue, *Cherokee Women*, 49, 54, 69.

72. Snyder, *Slavery in Indian Country*, 128.

73. Corkran, *Cherokee Frontier*, 299; Theda Perdue, *Slavery and the Evolution of Cherokee Society, 1540–1866* (University of Tennessee Press, 1987).

74. Kristofer Ray, *Cherokee Power: Imperial and Indigenous Geopolitics in the Trans-Appalachian West, 1670–1774*, New Directions in Native American Studies, vol. 22 (University of Oklahoma Press, 2023), 42–45.

75. De Brahm, *Report of the General Survey*.

76. William G. McLoughlin and Walter H. Conser, "'The First Man Was Red': Cherokee Responses to the Debate over Indian Origins, 1760–1860," *American Quarterly* 41, no. 2 (1989): 243, https://doi.org/10.2307/2713024.

77. Shoemaker, *Strange Likeness*, 133–34.

78. Longe, "Small Postscript," 20.

79. Braund, *Deerskins and Duffels*, 49.

80. Mooney, *Myths of the Cherokee*, 297.

81. Christopher B. Teuton, *Cherokee Stories of the Turtle Island Liars' Club: Dakasi Elohi Anigagoga Junilawisdii (Turtle, Earth, the Liars, Meeting Place)* (University of North Carolina Press, 2012), 77.

82. Although census numbers are not perfect or universally available during this period for Chota, in 1721 a census taken by South Carolina officials at Tanasi counted 160 men, 193 women, and 190 children. It is likely the numbers for Tanasi are smaller or potentially overlap. Schroedl and Bates, *Overhill Cherokee Archaeology*.

83. Henry Timberlake, Duane H. King, and Museum of the Cherokee Indian, *The Memoirs of Lieutenant Henry Timberlake: The Story of a Soldier, Adventurer, and Emissary to the Cherokees, 1756–1765* (Museum of the Cherokee Indian, 2007); Duane H. King et al., *Emissaries of Peace: The 1762 Cherokee and British Delegations* (Museum of the Cherokee Indian, 2006).

84. Thomas Loraine McKenney, *History of the Indian Tribes of North America: With Biographical Sketches and Anecdotes of the Principal Chiefs; Embellished with One Hundred and Twenty Portraits from the Indian Gallery in the Department of War at Washington* (Philadelphia, 1848), 45, http://hdl.handle.net/2027/nyp.33433088721877.

85. For a fuller picture of how the second half of the eighteenth century unfolded, I suggest reading Jessica L. Wallace, "More Than 'Strangers to Each Others Persons & Manners': Overhill Cherokees and Fort Loudoun," *Native South* 13, no. 1 (2020): 120–57, https://doi.org/10.1353/nso.2020.0004; Jessica Lynn Wallace, "'Building Forts in Their Hearts': Anglo-Cherokee Relations on the Mid-Eighteenth-Century Southern Frontier" (PhD diss., Ohio State University, 2014), ProQuest (27692295); Jamie Myers Mize, "'To Conclude on a General Union': Masculinity, the Chickamauga, and Pan-Indian Alliances in the Revolutionary Era," *Ethnohistory* 68, no. 3 (2021): 429–48, https://doi.org/10.1215/00141801-8940515; Jamie Myers Mize, "Sons of Selu: Masculinity and Gendered Power in Cherokee Society, 1775–1846" (PhD diss., University of North Carolina at Greensboro, 2017), ProQuest (10602447); Tyler Boulware, "'Our Mad Young Men': Authority and Violence in Cherokee Country," in *Blood in the Hills*, ed. Bruce E. Stewart, A History of Violence in Appalachia (University Press of Kentucky, 2012), 80–98, www.jstor.org/stable/j.ctt2jcv2d.8; Tyler Boulware, "The Effect of the Seven Years' War on the Cherokee Nation," *Early American Studies* 5, no. 2 (2007): 395–426; Tyler Boulware, *Deconstructing the Cherokee Nation: Town, Region, and Nation among Eighteenth-Century Cherokees* (University Press of Florida, 2011); Corkran, *Cherokee Frontier*; Hatley, *Dividing Paths*; Colin G. Calloway, *The American Revolution in Indian Country: Crisis and Diversity in Native American Communities*, Cambridge Studies in North American Indian History (Cambridge University Press, 1995); Perdue, *Cherokee Women*; Kristofer Ray, "Cherokees, Empire, and the Tennessee Corridor in the British Imagination, 1670–1730," in *Before the Volunteer State: New Thoughts on Early Tennessee, 1540–1800* (University of Tennessee Press, 2015); Ray, *Cherokee Power*; and Tortora, *Carolina in Crisis*.

Chapter 3

1. James Mooney, *Myths of the Cherokee* (Government Printing Office, 1902), https://catalog.hathitrust.org/Record/010939061.

2. With the exception of New England, most colonies relied heavily on churches to teach reading and writing. Johann N. Neem, *Democracy's Schools: The Rise of Public Education in America*, How Things Worked (John Hopkins University Press, 2017), 7, http://catalogue.bnf.fr/ark:/12148/cb45550474q; Margaret Szasz, *Indian Education in the American Colonies, 1607–1783*, Indigenous Education (Bison Books, 2007), 26–43, http://catalogue.bnf.fr/ark:/12148/cb41140190p; John L. Rury, *Education and Social Change: Contours in the History of American Schooling*, 5th ed. (Routledge, 2016), 19–34.

3. Edmund Schwarze, *History of the Moravian Missions among Southern Indian Tribes of the United States* (Times Publishing Company, 1923), 31–32, http://hdl.handle.net/2027/nco1.ark:/13960/t6zw1jz2m.

4. Hammerer was an early proponent of gendered vocational labor for Native youth. Samuel Cole Williams, *Early Travels in the Tennessee Country, 1540–1800: With Introductions, Annotations and Index* (Watauga Press, 1928), 256, https://babel.hathitrust.org/cgi/pt?id=inu.3

0000005369362&view=1up&seq=13; Ronald Rayman, "Joseph Lancaster's Monitorial System of Instruction and American Indian Education, 1815–1838," *History of Education Quarterly* 21, no. 4 (1981): 395–409, https://doi.org/10.2307/367922.

5. Schwarze, *History of the Moravian Missions*, 43–44.

6. Clarence Edwin Carter, comp. and ed., *The Territorial Papers of the United States*, vol. 4, *The Territory South of the River Ohio, 1790–1796* (Government Printing Office, 1936), 183, https://hdl.handle.net/2027/mdp.35112104686730?urlappend=%3Bseq=7.

7. Williams, *Early Travels*, 472.

8. Peter Nabokov, *Where the Lightning Strikes: The Lives of American Indian Sacred Places* (Penguin Books, 2007), 62.

9. Jill Lepore, *A Is for American: Letters and Other Characters in the Newly United States*, 1st Vintage Books ed. (Vintage Books, 2003), 5.

10. Randal Rust, "Toqua," *Tennessee Encyclopedia* (blog), accessed June 25, 2021, https://tennesseeencyclopedia.net/entries/toqua; Gerald F. Schroedl, "Louis-Phillipes' Journal and Archaeological Investigations at the Overhill Cherokee Town of Toqua," *Journal of Cherokee Studies* 3 (1978): 206–20; Shannon D. Koerner, Lynne P. Sullivan, and Bobby R. Braly, "A Reassessment of the Chronology of Mound A at Toqua," *Southeastern Archaeology* 30, no. 1 (2011): 134–47.

11. Although it is still unclear the degree to which other town clusters represent urban planning tied to astronomical knowledge, Eastman's and Riggs's work at Watauga suggests that Cherokee communities engaged in these practices elsewhere. Jane M. Eastman and Brett H. Riggs, "The Sky at Watauga," paper presented at Annual Meeting Southeastern Archaeological Conference, Little Rock, AR, November 9, 2022.

12. Albert L. Wahrhaftig, "Institution Building among Oklahoma's Traditional Cherokees," in *Four Centuries of Southern Indians*, ed. Charles Hudson (University of Georgia Press, 2007), 132–47.

13. Thomas Loraine McKenney, *History of the Indian Tribes of North America: With Biographical Sketches and Anecdotes of the Principal Chiefs; Embellished with One Hundred and Twenty Portraits from the Indian Gallery in the Department of War at Washington* (Philadelphia, 1848), http://hdl.handle.net/2027/nyp.33433088721877.

14. Henry Timberlake, *The Memoirs of Lieut. Henry Timberlake: (Who Accompanied the Three Cherokee Indians to England in the Year 1762); Containing Whatever He Observed Remarkable, or Worthy of Public Notice, during His Travels to and from That Nation* [. . .] (printed for the author, 1765), http://archive.org/details/memoirsoflieutheootimb.

15. Gary C. Goodwin, *Cherokees in Transition: A Study of Changing Culture and Environment prior to 1775* (University of Chicago, 1977), 133–36, http://hdl.handle.net/2027/heb.03785; Ethan Moore, "From Sikwa to Swine: The Hog in Cherokee Culture and Society, 1750–1840," *Native South* 4, no. 1 (2011): 105–20, https://doi.org/10.1353/nso.2011.0002.

16. Theda Perdue, *Cherokee Women: Gender and Culture Change, 1700–1835* (University of Nebraska Press, 1998), 53, 116; McKenney, *History of the Indian Tribes of North America*, 40–43.

17. M. Thomas Hatley, "Cherokee Women Farmers Hold Their Ground," in *Powhatan's Mantle: Indians in the Colonial Southeast*, ed. Gregory A. Waselkov and Peter H. Wood (University of Nebraska Press, 2006).

18. "Transcripts of John Howard Payne," n.d., 69, JHPP.

19. McKenney, *History of the Indian Tribes of North America*; Grant Foreman, *Sequoyah* (University of Oklahoma Press, 1938); Stan Hoig, *Sequoyah: The Cherokee Genius* (Oklahoma Historical Society, 1995).

20. McKenney, *History of the Indian Tribes of North America*, 40–43.

21. "Transcripts of John Howard Payne," n.d., 83, JHPP.

22. "Transcripts of John Howard Payne," n.d., 70–73, JHPP.

23. "Transcripts of John Howard Payne," n.d., 78–79, JHPP.

24. Raymond D. Fogelson, "Who Were the Aní-Kutáni? An Excursion into Cherokee Historical Thought," *Ethnohistory* 31, no. 4 (1984): 255–63, https://doi.org/10.2307/482712.

25. Alexander Longe, "A Small Postscript on the Ways and Manners of the Indians Called Cherokees," ed. David H. Corkran, *Southern Indian Studies* 21 (October 1969): 1–50; "Transcripts of John Howard Payne," n.d., 72–74, JHPP.

26. David H. Corkran, *The Cherokee Frontier: Conflict and Survival, 1740–62* (University of Oklahoma Press, 1962), 269, https://hdl.handle.net/2027/uc1.32106015374587; Stan Hoig, *The Cherokees and Their Chiefs: In the Wake of Empire* (University of Arkansas Press, 1998), 53, 80, http://hdl.handle.net/2027/mdp.39015043821282; Carter, *Territorial Papers of the United States*, 4:127.

27. Hoig, *Cherokees and Their Chiefs*.

28. William Gerald McLoughlin, *Cherokees and Missionaries, 1789–1839* (Yale University Press, 1984), 86–88.

29. Williams, *Early Travels*, 246.

30. Williams, *Early Travels*, 445.

31. Schwarze, *History of the Moravian Missions*, 32–33, 43–44.

32. C. Daniel Crews and Richard W. Starbuck, eds., *Records of the Moravians among the Cherokees*, vol. 5, *The Anna Rosina Years*, pt. 3, *Farewell to Sister Gambold, 1817–1821* (Cherokee Heritage Press, 2013), 2089.

33. For a richer picture of Nancy Ward's biography, leadership, and mythology and the degree to which her status has become contested, see Clara Sue Kidwell, "What Would Pocahontas Think Now? Women and Cultural Persistence," *Callaloo* 17, no. 1 (1994): 149–59, https://doi.org/10.2307/2932084; Clara Sue Kidwell, "Indian Women as Cultural Mediators," *Ethnohistory* 39, no. 2 (1992): 97–107, https://doi.org/10.2307/482389; Ben Harris McClary, "Nancy Ward: The Last Beloved Woman of the Cherokees," *Tennessee Historical Quarterly* 21, no. 4 (1962): 352–64; Norma Tucker, "Nancy Ward, Ghighau of the Cherokees," *Georgia Historical Quarterly* 53, no. 2 (1969): 192–200; Tiya Miles, "'Circular Reasoning': Recentering Cherokee Women in the Antiremoval Campaigns," *American Quarterly* 61, no. 2 (2009): 221–43, https://doi.org/10.1353/aq.0.0078; and Michelene E. Pesantubbee, "Nancy Ward: American Patriot or Cherokee Nationalist?," *American Indian Quarterly* 38, no. 2 (2014): 177–206.

34. Christina Snyder, *Great Crossings: Indians, Settlers, and Slaves in the Age of Jackson* (Oxford University Press, 2019), 30.

35. Tiya Miles, *The House on Diamond Hill: A Cherokee Plantation Story* (University of North Carolina Press, 2010), 104–6.

36. William G. McLoughlin and Walter H. Conser, "'The First Man Was Red': Cherokee Responses to the Debate over Indian Origins, 1760–1860," *American Quarterly* 41, no. 2 (1989): 243, https://doi.org/10.2307/2713024.

37. Miles, *House on Diamond Hill*, 85.

38. Miles, *House on Diamond Hill*, 158.

39. Tiya Miles, "The Narrative of Nancy, a Cherokee Woman," *Frontiers: A Journal of Women Studies* 29, no. 2–3 (2008): 59–80.

40. Gary E. Moulton, *John Ross, Cherokee Chief* (University of Georgia Press, 1978), 6.

41. William G. McLoughlin, *Cherokee Renascence in the New Republic*, reprint ed. (Princeton University Press, 1992), 76–77, 112–13.

42. McLoughlin, *Cherokees and Missionaries*, 57.

43. Thurman Wilkins, *Cherokee Tragedy: The Ridge Family and the Decimation of a People* (University of Oklahoma Press, 1989), 39.

44. Rowena McClinton, ed., *The Moravian Springplace Mission to the Cherokees, Volume 1: 1805–1813* (University of Nebraska Press, 2007), 133.

45. McLoughlin, *Cherokees and Missionaries*, 60–63.

46. Missionaries recorded wishing that they lived a greater distance from Vann so that they could not hear the violence in his house. McClinton, *Moravian Springplace Mission*, 65.

47. McLoughlin, *Cherokees and Missionaries*, 156.

48. McLoughlin, *Cherokees and Missionaries*, 60.

49. Catharine Brown may have felt similarly after an attempted rape during the War of 1812. Catharine Brown, *Cherokee Sister: The Collected Writings of Catharine Brown, 1818–1823*, ed. Theresa Strouth Gaul (University of Nebraska Press, 2014), 9–11.

50. McClinton, *Moravian Springplace Mission*, 61.

51. Evan Jones, a Baptist missionary who served the Valley Towns in present-day North Carolina, spent ten years learning the language. His son John, born and raised in the Cherokee Nation, spoke Cherokee and English fluently from the time he was a child. McLoughlin, *Cherokees and Missionaries*, 66–67, 157.

52. McLoughlin, *Cherokees and Missionaries*, 66–67.

53. Williams, *Early Travels*, 478.

54. American Board of Commissioners for Foreign Missions, *The Missionary Herald*, vol. 24 (Crocker and Brewster, Printers, 1828), https://babel.hathitrust.org/cgi/pt?id=hvd.ah6ky4&view=1up&seq=7&skin=2021.

55. Crews and Starbuck, *Records of the Moravians*, 5:2184–85.

56. John Norton, *The Journal of Major John Norton, 1816*, Publications of the Champlain Society 46 (Champlain Society, 1970), 56.

57. Joyce B. Phillips and Paul Gary Phillips, *The Brainerd Journal: A Mission to the Cherokees, 1817–1823*, Indians of the Southeast (University of Nebraska Press, 1998), 54–55.

58. McLoughlin writes about this period, "Fathers replaced uncles as the majority authority figures in the home. Women were restricted to a narrow domestic sphere in their husband's homes. Family farms broke up the communal ethic. . . . A materialistic, acquisitive value system replaced a more easy-going ethic of sharing." I disagree with McLoughlin's dismissal of what was likely harder to see within individual lineages. McLoughlin, *Cherokees and Missionaries*, 127.

59. Even when they had human resources readily available to them, the Moravians squandered opportunities because of their theological standards and distrust of the legitimacy of Cherokee people's conversion experiences. David Taucheechy attended Cornwall, a mission school established by the American Board of Commissioners for Foreign Missions in

Connecticut, which operated from 1817 to 1826. He regularly served as interpreter for the Moravians and tried to join their congregation. The Moravians denied him membership several times; he later joined Brainerd, operated by the American Board of Commissioners for Foreign Missions. He continued to interpret for the Moravians when he was able, but the Moravians' exacting theological standards drove him and his skills elsewhere. Schwarze, *History of the Moravian Missions,* 171.

60. McLoughlin, *Cherokees and Missionaries,* 150–51.

61. Schwarze, *History of the Moravian Missions.*

62. Schwarze, *History of the Moravian Missions,* 174.

63. Perdue, *Cherokee Women,* 27–28.

64. Schwarze, *History of the Moravian Missions,* 171.

65. Jedidiah Morse, *A Report to the Secretary of War of the United States, on Indian Affairs, Comprising a Narrative of a Tour Performed in the Summer of 1820* [. . .] (S. Converse, 1820), 75, 75–77, Library of Congress, accessed June 23, 2021, www.loc.gov/item/02015263.

66. Steven Mintz, *Huck's Raft: A History of American Childhood* (Harvard University Press, 2004), 80.

67. H. Thomas Foster, "Benjamin Hawkins," *Encyclopedia of Alabama,* last updated March 18, 2025, http://encyclopediaofalabama.org/article/h-1058.

68. *Periodical Accounts Relating to the Missions of the Church of the United Brethren Established among the Heathen* (Brethren's Society for the Furtherance of the Gospel, 1818), 336.

69. Laura Harjo, *Spiral to the Stars: Mvskoke Tools of Futurity,* Critical Issues in Indigenous Studies (University of Arizona Press, 2019), 211.

70. Henry Thompson Malone, *Cherokees of the Old South: A People in Transition* (University of Georgia Press, 1956).

71. Malone, *Cherokees of the Old South,* 106–7.

72. Rury, *Education and Social Change,* 58–59.

73. Malone, *Cherokees of the Old South.*

74. Phillips and Phillips, *Brainerd Journal,* 128.

75. Phillips and Phillips, *Brainerd Journal,* 128, 284–85.

76. Phillips and Phillips, *Brainerd Journal,* 128, 284–85.

77. McLoughlin, *Cherokees and Missionaries,* 204, 210.

78. McLoughlin, *Cherokees and Missionaries,* 202–7. In 1801, Cherokee leaders gathered at Oosetenauleh had refused to let Hicks, who was serving as an official interpreter in service to the federal agent, sit in on their meetings because they seemed to "distrust him, as he was in the public service." Benjamin Hawkins, *The Collected Works of Benjamin Hawkins, 1796–1810,* ed. Howard Thomas Foster (University of Alabama Press, 2003), 373–74.

79. Crews and Starbuck, *Records of the Moravians,* 5:2126.

80. *American Annals of Education and Instruction, and Journal of Literary Institutions,* vol. 2 (Allen and Ticknor, 1832), http://hdl.handle.net/2027/uiug.30112108067494.

81. "Transcripts of John Howard Payne," n.d., 75, JHPP.

82. "Transcripts of John Howard Payne," n.d., 77, JHPP.

83. *American Annals of Education and Instruction,* 176.

84. "From Thomas Jefferson to Cherokee Nation, 4 May 1808," Founders Online, National Archives, accessed July 22, 2024, https://founders.archives.gov/documents/Jefferson/99-01-02-7956.

85. Marian H. Blair, "Contemporary Evidence—Salem Boarding School, 1834–1844," *North Carolina Historical Review* 27, no. 2 (1950): 142–61; Anna Smith, "Unlikely Sisters: Cherokee and Moravian Women in the Early Nineteenth Century," in *Pious Pursuits: German Moravians in the Atlantic World*, ed. Michele Gillespie and Robert Beachy (Berghahn Books, 2007), 191–206.

86. Morse, *Report to the Secretary of War*, 74.

87. Phillips and Phillips, *Brainerd Journal*, 81–82.

88. Schwarze, *History of the Moravian Missions*, 173–74.

89. Wilma Dunaway, "Rethinking Cherokee Acculturation: Agrarian Capitalism and Women's Resistance to the Cult of Domesticity, 1800–1838," *American Indian Culture and Research Journal* 21, no. 1 (1997): 180.

90. Dunaway, "Rethinking Cherokee Acculturation."

91. McClinton, *Moravian Springplace Mission*, 82.

92. Phillips and Phillips, *Brainerd Journal*, 94.

93. Phillips and Phillips, *Brainerd Journal*, 81–82.

94. Ridge, called Major Ridge after the War of 1812, sought bicultural education for his son John Ridge so that he could return from Cornwall and "be very useful to his nation." He did exactly that when he returned and later wrote for the bilingual *Cherokee Phoenix*, the national newspaper that began printing in 1828. Morse, *Report to the Secretary of War*, 161–62.

95. William Richardson, "Method in the History of Education," in *The Oxford Handbook of the History of Education*, n.d., 51.

96. *History of American Missions to the Heathen, from Their Commencement to the Present Time* (Worcester, 1840), 253, http://hdl.handle.net/2027/mdp.39015069281387.

97. Samuel Colcord Bartlett and American Board of Commissioners for Foreign Missions, *Historical Sketch of the Missions of the American Board among the North American Indians* ([American Board of Commissioners for Foreign Missions], 1878), 9, https://openlibrary.org/ia/ldpd_11361216_000.

98. Malone, *Cherokees of the Old South*; Phillips and Phillips, *Brainerd Journal*, 16.

99. Phillips and Phillips, *Brainerd Journal*, 338.

100. Perdue, *Cherokee Women*, 182.

101. Phillips and Phillips, *Brainerd Journal*, 352.

102. "Transcripts of John Howard Payne," n.d., 80, JHPP.

103. Carroll suggests adherents of older practices, often referred to by scholars as traditionalists, were going underground to preserve traditional ideas. Although other activities at the time suggest this may not have been the case, the caves suggest people were going underground to meet, communicate, and write. Who all these people were is less clear. Beau Carroll, Cherokee Archaeology Conference paper, October 2015, Cherokee, NC; Beau Duke Carroll et al., "Talking Stones: Cherokee Syllabary in Manitou Cave, Alabama," *Antiquity* 93, no. 368 (2019): 519–36, https://doi.org/10.15184/aqy.2019.15.

104. Theda Perdue, "Traditionalism in the Cherokee Nation: Resistance to the Constitution of 1827," *Georgia Historical Quarterly* 66, no. 2 (1982): 159–70.

105. Jack F. Kilpatrick and Anna G. Kilpatrick, "Letters from an Arkansas Cherokee Chief (1828–29)," *Great Plains Journal* 5, no. 1 (1965): 26–34.

106. Hoig, *Cherokees and Their Chiefs*, 111.

107. *American Annals of Education and Instruction*, 179–80.

108. The Cherokee Nation outlawed blood law in 1808; the Western Cherokees did so in 1824. *Laws of the Cherokee Nation: Adopted by the Council at Various Periods [1808–1835]* (Tahlequah, CN, 1852), 3–4, 172, http://hdl.handle.net/2027/mdp.35112105205258.

109. Kilpatrick and Kilpatrick, "Letters from an Arkansas Cherokee Chief," 32.

110. In my paper at NAISA and in a drafted article, I examine the increase in domestic violence in families during the Long Removal Era. Cherokee political leaders during this time framed the disruptions as disagreements over removal, resulting in families breaking up. This masked the violence playing out in families. Julie Reed, "Nameless 'Indian Women,' Violence, and the Long Removal Era," paper, NAISA Conference, Los Angeles, May 17, 2018; "Memorial and Protest of the Cherokee Nation, Cherokee Mission Miscellaneous Pamphlets & Clippings, Indian Missions," 199.4, microfilm reel 750, Indigenous Peoples of North America, Moravian Archives, Winston-Salem, NC.

111. This image comes from a story that Savannah Hicks shared in more detail with me after she completed the 2015 Remember the Removal Bike Ride. In the video, she says that she can never imagine living anywhere other than in the mountains in the East. In conversation, she shared with me the overwhelming emotion of her last look at those mountains in the homelands before heading west. *Osiyo, Voices of the Cherokee People*, season 1, episode 6, "Remember the Removal Bike Ride," posted July 11, 2015, by OsiyoTV, YouTube, 28 min., 31 sec., www.youtube.com/watch?v=HvYlMmc647M.

Chapter 4

1. R. Alfred Vick, "Cherokee Adaptation to the Landscape of the West and Overcoming the Loss of Culturally Significant Plants," *American Indian Quarterly* 35, no. 3 (2011): 394–417, https://doi.org/10.5250/amerindiquar.35.3.0394. For a more general overview of the environmental changes and continuities confronted in Indian Territory, see Clint Carroll, *Roots of Our Renewal: Ethnobotany and Cherokee Environmental Governance*, First Peoples: New Directions in Indigenous Studies (University of Minnesota Press, 2015), 59–64.

2. Barren Fork Diary, February 1839, M 409-4, RMC.

3. *Message from the President of the United States, in Compliance with a Resolution of the Senate, Communicating a Report of an Expedition Led by Lieutenant Abert, on the Upper Arkansas and through the Country of the Camanche Indians, in the Fall of the Year 1845*, S. Doc. No. 438, 29th Cong., 1st sess. (1846), https://digitalcommons.law.ou.edu/indianserialset/7280.

4. Richard J. Neves et al., "Status of Aquatic Mollusks in the Southeastern United States: A Downward Spiral of Diversity," in *Aquatic Fauna in Peril: The Southeastern Perspective*, ed. George W. Benz and David E. Collins (Southeast Aquatic Research Institute, 1997), www.sherpaguides.com/southeast/aquatic_fauna/chapter_3.

5. Christopher B. Teuton and Hastings Shade, *Anitsalagi Elohi Anehi = Cherokee Earth Dwellers: Stories and Teachings of the Natural World* (University of Washington Press, 2023), 182.

6. Reuben Gold Thwaites, ed., *Early Western Travels, 1748–1846*, vol. 13 (Arthur H. Clark Company, 1905), 174, http://hdl.handle.net/2027/umn.31951002454532m.

7. *Message from the President of the United States*.

8. Charles Robert Goins, Danney Goble, and John W. Morris, *Historical Atlas of Oklahoma* (University of Oklahoma Press, 2006), 17.

9. "Transcripts of John Howard Payne," n.d., 73, JHPP.

10. Nicholas J. Czaplewski and William L. Puckette, "Late Pleistocene Remains of an American Black Bear (*Ursus americanus*) and Two Small Vertebrates from an Oklahoma Ozark Cave," *Proceedings of the Oklahoma Academy of Science* 94 (2014): 1, 12, https://ojs .library.okstate.edu/osu/index.php/OAS/article/view/1728.

11. "Treaty with the Western Cherokee, 1828," Tribal Treaties Database, accessed April 3, 2024, https://treaties.okstate.edu/treaties/treaty-with-the-western-cherokee-1828-0288.

12. After the July 1839 Act of Union following forced removal, officials designated Tahlequah as the new capital. Richard Mize, "Sequoyah County," *Encyclopedia of Oklahoma History and Culture*, Oklahoma Historical Society, accessed April 22, 2020, www.okhistory .org/publications/enc/entry.php?entry=SE022; Cherokee Nation, *The Constitution and Laws of the Cherokee Nation, Passed at Tah-Le-Quah, Cherokee Nation, 1839* (Scholarly Resources, 1975), http://catalog.hathitrust.org/api/volumes/oclc/3104184.html.

13. D. C. Gideon, *Indian Territory, Descriptive, Biographical and Genealogical, Including the Landed Estates, County Seats, Etc., Etc., with a General History of the Territory* (Lewis Publishing Company, 1901), http://hdl.handle.net/2027/wu.89063251656; Gregory A. Waselkov, ed., *Native American Log Cabins in the Southeast* (University of Tennessee Press, 2019); "Dwight Mission," *Encyclopedia of Oklahoma History and Culture*, Oklahoma Historical Society, accessed November 20, 2019, www.okhistory.org/publications/enc/entry.php?entry=DW001; Mabelle True, *"Old Dwight": The Historic Cherokee Mission* (Literature Dept. of the Woman's Board of Home Missions of the Presbyterian Church, 1909).

14. A Cherokee woman recounted the conditions of the streams from her time as a student at Dwight Mission in the 1880s. It is entirely possible the streams were even more plentiful in the 1830s–1840s, when Cherokee people were only beginning to arrive in Indian Territory in large numbers. "Mrs. John H. West Interview," n.d., IPP.

15. Looney Hicks, who was born at Dwight Mission in 1849, described the animals that lived near the school. "Looney Hicks Griffin Interview," IPP.

16. "Fishes of Alabama," *Encyclopedia of Alabama*, accessed April 24, 2020, www .encyclopediaofalabama.org/article/h-1586; H. C. Ward, *Know Your Oklahoma Fishes* (Oklahoma Game and Fish Department, n.d.), accessed April 24, 2020, www.nativefishlab.net /library/textpdf/14870.pdf; Tennessee Wildlife Resources Agency, "The Angler's Guide To Tennessee Fish Including Aquatic Nuisance Species," 2012, 68, www.tn.gov/content/dam /tn/twra/documents/fishing/anglersguide.pdf.

17. Stan Hoig, *Sequoyah: The Cherokee Genius* (Oklahoma Historical Society, 1995), 43, 74–75; Spoliation Claim #225 of Tee-See Guess from the Skin Bayou District, March 9, 1842, Penelope Johnson Allen Cherokee Collection, 1775–1878, Tennessee State Library and Archives, Nashville, https://teva.contentdm.oclc.org/digital/collection/p15138coll52/id /3282/rec/1; *Report of the American Board of Commissioners for Foreign Missions, Read at the Twenty-Fifth Annual Meeting* (Crocker & Brewster, 1834), https://hdl.handle.net/2027/pst .000053166395?urlappend=%3Bseq=7.

18. Goins, Goble, and Morris, *Historical Atlas of Oklahoma*, 26–27.

19. C. C. Trowbridge MS, John Gilmary Shea Papers, box 7, folder 16, Georgetown University Library, accessed May 11, 2020, https://findingaids.library.georgetown.edu/repositories /15/archival_objects/1206792.

20. C. C. Trowbridge MS, John Gilmary Shea Papers, box 7, folder 16.

21. American Board of Commissioners for Foreign Missions, *The Missionary Herald* (Board, January 1830), v, 26.

22. American Board of Commissioners for Foreign Missions, *Missionary Herald*, 10.

23. Jack Baker, *Cherokee Emigration Rolls, 1817–1835* (Baker Publishing, 1977).

24. C. C. Trowbridge MS, John Gilmary Shea Papers, box 7, folder 16.

25. C. C. Trowbridge MS, John Gilmary Shea Papers, box 7, folder 16.

26. During 1818, the missionaries described a series of cases where fathers were objecting to Cherokee women's control of children. Joyce B. Phillips and Paul Gary Phillips, *The Brainerd Journal: A Mission to the Cherokees, 1817–1823*, Indians of the Southeast (University of Nebraska Press, 1998). Martschukat points out that the move toward nuclear families in the larger United States in the early republic was often more rhetoric than reality. He also notes that middle- and upper-class white people favored "republican middle class ideals" and frowned upon men who ruled families through violent authoritarianism. Instead, manuals encouraged fathers to persuade through reason and consistency and withholding rewards but always keeping the rod as a backup plan. Jürgen Martschukat, *American Fatherhood: A History* (New York University Press, 2019).

27. In two different accounts years apart, men from Arkansas reported that Cherokee women wanted to marry only white men. It is not clear in either letter where this information was coming from and seems likely their informants were other men, possibly Cherokee men, but not Cherokee women. This raises real questions about the sexual climate Cherokee women were facing when they arrived in Indian Territory, given the rash of abortions in the 1820s and the legal sanctions for those. Given the very grim statistics on how rape and sexual trafficking impacts Indigenous women and children today, these men's statements, the laws being passed, and the coercive policies of mission schools in this era suggest a continuing highway to the here and now outlined by Deer and Theobald. See "Eyewitness Account of the Trail of Tears, Fayetteville, Arkansas, 1837–40" on the James E. Arsenault & Company website, accessed April 12, 2024, www.jamesarsenault.com/pages/books/8757/stuart-walter -case/a-group-of-eight-letters-by-a-young-clerk-in-fayetteville-describing-the-trail-of-tears -and-the; *Letters of Hiram Abiff Whittington, an Arkansas Pioneer from Massachusetts, 1827–1834* (Pulaski County Historical Society, 1956), 3, www.familysearch.org/search/catalog/120423 ?availability=Family%20History%20Library; Thomas Nuttall, *A Journal of Travels into the Arkansas Territory, during the Year 1819. With Occasional Observations on the Manners of the Aborigines. Illustrated by a Map and Other Engravings* (Thos. H. Palmer, 1821), http://hdl .handle.net/2027/nyp.33433081844205; Thwaites, *Early Western Travels, 1748–1846*; Brianna Theobald, *Reproduction on the Reservation: Pregnancy, Childbirth, and Colonialism in the Long Twentieth Century*, Critical Indigeneities (University of North Carolina Press, 2019); and Sarah Deer, *The Beginning and End of Rape: Confronting Sexual Violence in Native America* (University of Minnesota Press, 2015).

28. Fay A. Yarbrough, "Legislating Women's Sexuality: Cherokee Marriage Laws in the Nineteenth Century," *Journal of Social History* 38, no. 2 (2004): 385–406, https://doi.org /10.1353/jsh.2004.0144; Tiya Miles, *Ties That Bind: The Story of an Afro-Cherokee Family in Slavery and Freedom* (University of California Press, 2006).

29. Daniel Heath Justice, *Why Indigenous Literatures Matter*, Indigenous Studies Series (Wilfrid Laurier University Press, 2018), 11.

30. Julie L. Reed, *Serving the Nation: Cherokee Sovereignty and Social Welfare, 1800–1907* (University of Oklahoma Press, 2016), 48–50.

31. Justice, *Why Indigenous Literatures Matter*, 11.

32. Carolyn Ross Johnston, *Cherokee Women in Crisis: Trail of Tears, Civil War, and Allotment, 1838–1907* (University of Alabama Press, 2003), 111–21.

33. Devon A. Mihesuah, *Cultivating the Rosebuds: The Education of Women at the Cherokee Female Seminary, 1851–1909* (University of Illinois Press, 1993).

34. "Dwight Mission," *Chronicles of Oklahoma* 12, no. 1 (1934): 42.

35. Gerald F. Schroedl and James F. Bates, *Overhill Cherokee Archaeology at Chota-Tanasee* (University of Tennessee, Dept. of Anthropology, 1986); Christopher B. Rodning, "Reconstructing the Coalescence of Cherokee Communities in Southern Appalachia," in *The Transformation of the Southeastern Indians, 1540–1760*, ed. Robbie Ethridge and Charles Hudson (University Press of Mississippi, 2008), 155–76.

36. "Cherokee Syllabic Alphabet," *Arkansas Gazette* (Little Rock), May 23, 1826.

37. Cephas Washburn, *Reminiscences of the Indians* (Presbyterian Committee of Publication, 1869), 36, http://hdl.handle.net/2027/uiug.30112004264823.

38. Washburn, *Reminiscences of the Indians*, 37.

39. Charles A. Anderson, "Journey to Indian Territory, 1833–1835: Letters of Cassandra Sawyer Lockwood," *Journal of the Presbyterian Historical Society (1943–1961)* 23, no. 4 (1945): 195–227.

40. *Report of the American Board of Commissioners for Foreign Missions, Read at the Twenty-Sixth Annual Meeting* (Crocker & Brewster, 1835), https://catalog.hathitrust.org/Record/012293912.

41. Isaac McCoy, *Annual Register of Indian Affairs within the Indian (or Western) Territory* (Shawanoe Baptist Mission House, 1836).

42. McCoy, *Annual Register of Indian Affairs*, no. 1.

43. Spoliation Claims, Skin Bayou District, Penelope Johnson Allen Cherokee Collection, 1775–1878, Tennessee State Library and Archives, Nashville.

44. 409A Diaries, Reports, 1840–61, M 409, RMC.

45. Spoliation claim #260 of Sally Guess from the Skin Bayou District, March 4, 1842, Penelope Johnson Allen Cherokee Collection, 1775–1878, Tennessee State Library and Archives, Nashville, https://teva.contentdm.oclc.org/digital/collection/p15138coll52/id/3092/rec/8; Spoliation claim #225 of Tee-See Guess.

46. *History of American Missions to the Heathen, from Their Commencement to the Present Time* (Worcester, 1840), 253, http://hdl.handle.net/2027/mdp.39015069281387.

47. Washburn, *Reminiscences of the Indians*.

48. Isaac McCoy, *The Annual Register of Indian Affairs within the Indian (or Western) Territory, No. 1* (Shawanoe Baptist Mission House, 1835), www-aihc-amdigital-co-uk.ezaccess.libraries.psu.edu/Documents/Images/Ayer_155_A2_03/4#Sections.

49. Barren Fork Diary, M 409, RMC.

50. Barren Fork Diary, M 409, RMC.

51. Barren Fork Diary, M 409, RMC.

52. 409A Diaries, Reports, 1840–61, M 409, RMC.

53. William G. McLoughlin, *After the Trail of Tears: The Cherokees' Struggle for Sovereignty, 1839–1880* (University of North Carolina Press, 1994), 37–40.

54. *Report of the American Board of Commissioners for Foreign Missions, Presented at the Thirty-First Annual Meeting* (Crocker & Brewster, 1840), https://hdl.handle.net/2027/pst.000053166456?urlappend=%3Bseq=7.

55. January 1–October 10, 1841, M 409-5, RMC.

56. John Norton, "The Journal of Major John Norton, 1816," ed. by Carl F. Klinck and James J. Talman (Champlain Society, 1970), 46, 55, https://archive.org/details /journalofmajorjooooonort.

57. May 27, 1841, RMC.

58. Records of Dwight Mission, Creek Nation, 1822–1862, folder 1, Dwight Mission Church Records Collection Manuscripts, Oklahoma Historical Society Research Center, Oklahoma City.

59. January 1–October 10, 1841, M 409-5, RMC.

60. Karen Sánchez-Eppler, *Dependent States: The Child's Part in Nineteenth-Century American Culture* (University of Chicago Press, 2005), xxiv.

61. As Berry points out, the full series walked students through different phases of learning: *Rollo Learning to Talk*, a picture book; *Rollo Learning to Read*, a combination of reading instruction and stories to read; and the Rollo philosophy series, which built on the morality and citizenship lessons in *Learning to Read* and extended to lessons on intellectual development. Annette Wannamaker and Jennifer Miskec, "Books for Beginners," in *The Routledge Companion to Children's Literature and Culture* (Routledge, 2023); Jani L. Berry, "Discipline and (Dis)Order: Paternal Socialization in Jacob Abbott's Rollo Books," *Children's Literature Association Quarterly* 18, no. 3 (1993): 100–105; Jacob Abbott, *The Rollo Code of Morals, or, The Rules of Duty for Children: Arranged with Questions for the Use of Schools* (Crocker & Brewster, 1841), 73, 76, 90.

62. Stremlau notes that Moravians went door-to-door in the 1840s because their congregants who had lost spouses during removal married using older Cherokee practices, in a sense harassing them to marry in a church as they tried to recover from unimaginable loss. Rose Stremlau, "Historicizing Resilience: Young Cherokees in Post-Removal Indian Territory," Symposium: From Removal to Rebirth: The Cherokee Nation in Indian Territory, Helmerich Center for American Research, Tulsa, OK, April 22, 2016.

63. Records of Dwight Mission, Creek Nation, 1822–1862, folder 1, Dwight Mission Church Records Collection Manuscripts.

64. Dwight Mission School Collection Manuscripts, folder 1, Dwight Mission School, 1842–45, Oklahoma Historical Society Research Center, Oklahoma City.

65. Narcissa Owen, *Memoirs of Narcissa Owen, 1831–1907* (Washington, DC, 1907), http:// hdl.handle.net/2027/uva.x004615992.

66. January 1–October 10, 1841, M 409-5, RMC.

67. 409A Diaries, Reports, 1840–61, M 409, RMC.

68. 409A Diaries, Reports, 1840–61, M 409, RMC.

69. Catharine Brown, *Cherokee Sister: The Collected Writings of Catharine Brown, 1818–1823*, ed. Theresa Strouth Gaul (University of Nebraska Press, 2014).

70. The core families included the Fieldses, Gunters, Barneses, Naves, Bells, Starrs, Harlins, Wilsons, Rileys, and Adairs. Dwight Mission School Collection Manuscripts, folder 1, Dwight Mission School, 1842–45.

71. Abbott, *Rollo Code of Morals*, 68.

72. John Gunter Sr. was an intermarried white man. He and his son Edward, also referred to as Edmond and Ned, who was bilingual, maintained business interests in the East and West throughout the Long Removal Era. Edward's brother Spencer served in Cherokee National

government in the West. Edward maintained businesses in Tahlequah and Alabama even after forced removal. Unlike most Cherokee people, even other slaveholders, the Gunter family seemed immune to the economic violence and dispossession experienced by the vast majority of Cherokee people during this period. Trail of Tears Association, Oklahoma Chapter, *1835 Cherokee Census* (Trail of Tears Association, Oklahoma Chapter, 2002); Carolyn Thomas Foreman, "John Gunter and His Family," *Alabama Historical Quarterly* 9, no. 3 (1947), 412–52, http://archive.org/details/alabama-historical-quarterly-v09n03; Robert A. Myers, "Cherokee Pioneers in Arkansas: The St. Francis Years, 1785–1813," *Arkansas Historical Quarterly* 56, no. 2 (1997): 127–57, https://doi.org/10.2307/40023675.

73. David Lindsay Roberts, *Republic of Numbers: Unexpected Stories of Mathematical Americans through History* (Johns Hopkins University Press, 2019), 43, 44, 47.

74. My thinking here is informed by the work of Stephanie E. Jones-Rogers, *They Were Her Property: White Women as Slave Owners in the American South* (Yale University Press, 2019), https://doi.org/10.2307/j.ctvbnm3fz.1.

75. For a fuller discussion of the denominational positions, see McLoughlin, *After the Trail of Tears*, 136–45.

76. Michael J. Cassity and Danney Goble, *Divided Hearts: The Presbyterian Journey through Oklahoma History* (University of Oklahoma Press, 2009), 72.

77. John B. Jones, *Elementary Arithmetic, in Cherokee and English, Designed for Beginners* (Cherokee National Press, 1870), Yale University Library, https://collections.library.yale.edu/catalog/10927115.

78. Daniel F. Littlefield and Lonnie E. Underhill, "Slave 'Revolt' in the Cherokee Nation, 1842," *American Indian Quarterly* 3, no. 2 (1977): 121–31, https://doi.org/10.2307/1184177; Art T. Burton, "Slave Revolt of 1842," *Encyclopedia of Oklahoma History and Culture*, Oklahoma Historical Society, accessed July 21, 2021, www.okhistory.org/publications/enc/entry.php?entry=SL002.

79. Fay A. Yarbrough, *Race and the Cherokee Nation: Sovereignty in the Nineteenth Century* (University of Pennsylvania Press, 2007).

80. *Laws of the Cherokee Nation: Adopted by the Council at Various Periods* (Scholarly Resources, 1973).

81. Georgia, North Carolina, Louisiana, and Virginia all passed anti-literacy laws between 1830 and 1831, which followed the Cherokee Nation's launch of its printing press in 1828 and coincided with the fight over Indian Removal. Heather Andrea Williams, *Self-Taught: African American Education in Slavery and Freedom* (University of North Carolina Press, 2005), 14–16.

82. "Article 6, Treaty with the Cherokee, 1817," in Charles Kappler, *Indian Affairs: Laws and Treaties* (Government Printing Office, n.d.), 143.

83. In 1825, Cherokee leaders in the West wrote to the federal government that women faced "drudgery" because they lacked a sawmill and gristmill. Letters Received by the Office of Indian Affairs, 1824–81, Cherokee Agency West, reel 77, folder 105, n.d., NARA.

84. Clarence Edwin Carter, comp., *The Territory of Arkansas, 1825–1829*, vol. 20 of *The Territorial Papers of the United States* (Government Printing Office, 1934), 26, 657, https://catalog.hathitrust.org/Record/000495370.

85. Carter, *Territory of Arkansas*.

86. Thwaites spends an inordinate amount of time discussing the class distinctions he saw among the Cherokee people residing in the West. Thwaites, *Early Western Travels, 1748–1846*.

87. Tyler B. Howe, "'Regarding Themselves as Permanently Settled': An Ethnohistory of Cherokee Hyper-Displacement" (PhD diss., University of Tennessee, 2019), 169–75.

88. 409A Diaries, Reports, 1840–61, M 409, RMC.

89. Dwight Mission School Collection Manuscripts, folder 1, Dwight Mission School, 1842–45.

90. For a comprehensive history of the Cherokee Nation's national response to missionaries' efforts and legal challenges to its sovereignty when it came to the criminalization of alcohol, see Izumi Ishii, *Bad Fruits of the Civilized Tree: Alcohol and the Sovereignty of the Cherokee Nation* (University of Nebraska Press, 2008).

91. Dwight Mission School Collection Manuscripts, folder 1, Dwight Mission School, 1842–45.

92. James G. McCullagh, *The Teachers of the Cherokee Nation Public Schools: 1870s–1907* (Cherokee Heritage Press, 2012), 5.

93. McCullagh, *Teachers of the Cherokee Nation*, 8–9.

94. Mihesuah, *Cultivating the Rosebuds*.

95. Mihesuah, *Cultivating the Rosebuds*, 98–108.

96. McLoughlin, *After the Trail of Tears*, 230.

97. "Elinor Boudinot Meigs Interview," n.d., IPP.

98. "Elinor Boudinot Meigs Interview."

99. "Elinor Boudinot Meigs Interview."

100. "Elinor Boudinot Meigs Interview."

101. Dwight Mission School Collection Manuscripts, folder 1, Dwight Mission School, 1842–45.

102. Dwight Mission School Collection Manuscripts, folder 1, Dwight Mission School, 1842–45.

103. Dwight Mission School Collection Manuscripts, folder 1, Dwight Mission School, 1842–45.

Chapter 5

1. For a full picture of the experiences facing the Cherokee Nation and the Fives Tribes, see Angie Debo, *And Still the Waters Run: The Betrayal of the Five Civilized Tribes* (Princeton University Press, 1940); Andrew Denson, *Demanding the Cherokee Nation: Indian Autonomy and American Culture, 1830–1900* (University of Nebraska Press, 2015); Andrew Denson, "A Few Unreasonable Proposals: Some Rejected Ideas from the Cherokee Allotment Negotiations," *Chronicles of Oklahoma* 84, no. 4 (2006): 426–43; Katherine Ellinghaus, *Blood Will Tell: Native Americans and Assimilation Policy*, electronic resource, New Visions in Native American and Indigenous Studies (University of Nebraska Press and American Philosophical Society, 2017); Alexandra Harmon, *Rich Indians: Native People and the Problem of Wealth in American History* (University of North Carolina Press, 2010); H. Craig Miner, *The Corporation and the Indian: Tribal Sovereignty and Industrial Civilization in Indian Territory, 1865–1907* (University of Missouri Press, 1976); Tom Holm, "Indian Lobbyists: Cherokee Opposition to the Allotment of Tribal Lands," *American Indian Quarterly* 5, no. 2 (1979): 115–34, https://doi.org/10.2307/1183752; C. Joseph Genetin-Pilawa, *Crooked Paths to Allotment: The Fight over Federal Indian Policy after the Civil War* (University of North Carolina Press, 2012);

Carolyn Ross Johnston, *Cherokee Women in Crisis: Trail of Tears, Civil War, and Allotment, 1838–1907* (University of Alabama Press, 2003); Grant Foreman, *The Five Civilized Tribes: Cherokee, Chickasaw, Choctaw, Creek, Seminole* (University of Oklahoma Press, 1989); William G. McLoughlin, *Champions of the Cherokees: Evan and John B. Jones* (Princeton University Press, 1990); William G. McLoughlin, *After the Trail of Tears: The Cherokees' Struggle for Sovereignty, 1839–1880* (University of North Carolina Press, 1994); Rose Stremlau, *Sustaining the Cherokee Family: Kinship and the Allotment of an Indigenous Nation* (University of North Carolina Press, 2011); Carolyn Ross Johnston, "'The Panther's Scream Is Often Heard': Cherokee Women in Indian Territory during the Civil War," *Chronicles of Oklahoma* 78, no. 1 (2000): 84–107; Barbara Krauthamer, "Indian Territory and the Treaties of 1866: A Long History of Emancipation," in *The World the Civil War Made*, ed. Gregory P. Downs and Kate Masur (University of North Carolina Press, 2015); Clarissa W. Confer, *The Cherokee Nation in the Civil War* (University of Oklahoma Press, 2012); Annie Heloise Abel, *The American Indian in the Civil War, 1862–1865* (University of Nebraska Press, 1919); and David A. Chang, *The Color of the Land: Race, Nation, and the Politics of Landownership in Oklahoma, 1832–1929* (University of North Carolina Press, 2010).

2. Khaled J. Bloom, "An American Tragedy of the Commons: Land and Labor in the Cherokee Nation, 1870–1900," *Agricultural History* 76, no. 3 (2002): 497–523.

3. "Trout, Henry," DDC, accessed February 14, 2023, https://digital.libraries.ou.edu/cdm /ref/collection/dorisduke/id/7383.

4. "Ketcher, Ellis," IPP, accessed April 19, 2023, https://digital.libraries.ou.edu/cdm/ref /collection/indianpp/id/4788.

5. Donald A. White, "Dust Bowl," *Encyclopedia of Oklahoma History and Culture*, Oklahoma Historical Society, accessed July 29, 2021, www.okhistory.org/publications/enc/entry.php ?entry=DU011.

6. Ryan Hall, "Struggle and Survival in Sallisaw: Revisiting John Steinbeck's Oklahoma," *Agricultural History* 86, no. 3 (2012): 33–56, https://doi.org/10.3098/ah.2012.86.3.33.

7. L. C. Snider, *Petroleum and Natural Gas in Oklahoma* (Harloe-Ratliff Company, 1913), online text, Library of Congress, accessed April 6, 2024, www.loc.gov/item/14000172.

8. Miner, *Corporation and the Indian*; Jeffrey Burton, *Indian Territory and the United States, 1866–1906: Courts, Government, and the Movement for Oklahoma Statehood*, Legal History of North America (University of Oklahoma Press, 1995).

9. Fay A. Yarbrough, "Legislating Women's Sexuality: Cherokee Marriage Laws in the Nineteenth Century," *Journal of Social History* 38, no. 2 (2004): 385–406, https://doi.org/10 .1353/jsh.2004.0144; Theda Perdue, *Cherokee Women: Gender and Culture Change, 1700–1835* (University of Nebraska Press, 1998); Brianna Theobald, *Reproduction on the Reservation: Pregnancy, Childbirth, and Colonialism in the Long Twentieth Century*, Critical Indigeneities (University of North Carolina Press, 2019); Brianna Theobald, "Settler Colonialism, Native American Motherhood, and the Politics of Terminating Pregnancies," in *Transcending Borders: Abortion in the Past and Present*, ed. Shannon Stettner et al. (Springer International Publishing AG, 2017).

10. Mary Frances Berry, *The Politics of Parenthood: Child Care, Women's Rights, and the Myth of the Good Mother* (Viking, 1993), 86; Theobald, "Settler Colonialism."

11. "Johnson, Samuel S. - Fold3 - US, Dawes Packets, 1898–1914," Fold3, accessed April 5, 2024, www.fold3.com/image/63746807/johnson-samuel-s-page-1-us-dawes-packets-1898

-1914; "Hopper, Martin - Fold3 - US, Dawes Packets, 1898–1914," Fold3, accessed April 6, 2024, www.fold3.com/image/61127451/hopper-martin-page-3-us-dawes-packets-1898-1914; "Johnson, Jennie - Fold3 - US, Eastern Cherokee Applications, 1906–1909," Fold3, accessed April 5, 2024, www.fold3.com/image/223233460/johnson-jennie-page-3-us-eastern-cherokee -applications-1906-1909.

12. Samuel S. Johnson, 7540, Applications for Enrollment of the Commission to the Five Civilized Tribes, 1898–1914, M1301, NARA, www.fold3.com:9292/image/63746807?terms= johnson,s,samuel; Sunday Hogtoater, 7539, Applications for Enrollment of the Commission to the Five Civilized Tribes, 1898–1914, M1301, NARA, www.fold3.com:9292/image/63746782 ?terms=cherokee,hogtoater.

13. Jennie Johnson, Eastern Cherokee Applications of the US Court of Claims, 1906–1909, M1104, Records of the US Court of Claims, RG 123, NARA.

14. B. W. Alberty "The Public School," *Cherokee Wigwam* (Westville, Indian Territory), Friday, August 5, 1904, Oklahoma Digital Newspaper Program, The Gateway to Oklahoma History, Oklahoma Historical Society, https://gateway.okhistory.org/ark:/67531/metadc1859105 /m1/1.

15. Clinton McClarty Allen, *The "Sequoyah" Movement* (Harlow Publishing Company, 1925); Mara Darleen Rutten, "The Sequoyah Statehood Movement and the Indian Fight for Sovereignty" (PhD diss., Arizona State University, 2000), ProQuest (9976337); Amos Maxwell, "Sequoyah Constitutional Convention" (master's thesis, Oklahoma Agricultural and Mechanical College, 1950); Stacy L. Leeds, "Defeat or Mixed Blessing—Tribal Sovereignty and the State of Sequoyah Indian Tribes and Statehood: A Symposium in Recognition of Oklahoma's Centennial," *Tulsa Law Review* 43, no. 1 (2007): 5–16; *State of Sequoyah*, image, Library of Congress, accessed July 16, 2020, www.loc.gov/item/2013592417.

16. "New School Regulations," *Tahlequah Arrow* (Indian Territory), May 26, 1906, Oklahoma Digital Newspaper Program, The Gateway to Oklahoma History, Oklahoma Historical Society, https://gateway.okhistory.org/ark:/67531/metadc155887/m1/8.

17. Gustav Straubenmüeller, "Teaching Our Language to Non-English Speaking Pupils," in *Journal of Proceedings and Addresses of the Forty-Fourth Annual Meeting*, by the National Educational Association (National Education Association, 1905), 413–21, https://babel.hathitrust .org/cgi/pt?id=uc1.b3433938&seq=5&q1=%22Teaching+Our+Language.

18. National Education Association, *Journal of Proceedings and Addresses of the Forty-Fourth Annual Meeting* (National Education Association, 1905), 414, https://babel.hathitrust.org /cgi/pt?id=uc1.b3433938&seq=5.

19. National Education Association, *Journal of Proceedings and Addresses*, 414.

20. Straubenmüeller, "Teaching Our Language to Non-English Speaking Pupils," 413.

21. National Education Association, *Journal of Proceedings and Addresses*, 420.

22. Painter points out the ways this language of "new" versus "old" was used in the 1850s to express anxieties about immigration. She also points out the willingness to make concessions for whiteness for former new immigrants who had become the old immigrants by the 1890s. Nell Irvin Painter, *The History of White People* (W. W. Norton, 2011), 201–11.

23. Berry, *Politics of Parenthood*, 87.

24. For more reading on Eaton, see the following: Farina King, "'Loyal Countrywoman': Rachel Caroline Eaton, Alumna, of the Cherokee National Female Seminary," in *This Land Is Herland: Gendered Activism in Oklahoma from the 1870s to the 2010s*, ed. Sarah Eppler Janda and Patricia Loughlin (University of Oklahoma Press, 2021); Oklahoma Historical Society,

Chronicles of Oklahoma 16, no. 4 (December 1938): 393–511; "Many People Are Writing History of Oklahoma," *Cherokee County Democrat* (Tahlequah, OK), April 29, 1915, Oklahoma Digital Newspaper Program, The Gateway to Oklahoma History, Oklahoma Historical Society, https://gateway.okhistory.org/ark:/67531/metadc90328/m1/7; Kirby Brown, "Oppositional Discourse and Revisionist Historiography in Rachel Caroline Eaton's *John Ross and the Cherokee Indians*," in *Stoking the Fire: Nationhood in Cherokee Writing, 1907–1970* (University of Oklahoma Press, 2018).

25. Berry, *Politics of Parenthood*, 88.

26. The article ignored the fact that Cherokee educational funds and Cherokee buildings were still supplementing the budgets of those schools and had paid for the infrastructure providing education to Cherokee kids. From the perspective of the Cherokee Nation, it wasn't its responsibility to educate non-Cherokee citizens; that was the responsibility of the United States or those families. As the writer conceded, the Cherokee Nation extended access to non-Cherokee students if they paid tuition at subscription schools. Part of the attack lodged against the Five Tribes at the time of allotment was the lack of educational opportunity for white settlers' children living within the boundaries of Native nations, some legally, most not. "The Development of the Schools," *The Oklahoman* (Oklahoma City), March 10, 1907.

27. Agnes E. Benedict, *Children at the Crossroads* (The Commonwealth Fund, Division of Publications, 1930), 5–10, https://catalog.hathitrust.org/Record/001281610.

28. "School Land Appraisers Appointed," *State Journal* (Cherokee, OK), September 18, 1908, Oklahoma Digital Newspaper Program, The Gateway to Oklahoma History, Oklahoma Historical Society, https://gateway.okhistory.org/ark:/67531/metadc1977937/m1/6; Charles L. Wilson, "The Mountain Feuds," *Cherokee Messenger* (Cherokee, OK), April 9, 1908, Oklahoma Digital Newspaper Program, The Gateway to Oklahoma History, Oklahoma Historical Society, https://gateway.okhistory.org/ark:/67531/metadc2027714/m1/7.

29. Part of Owen's professional background included serving as a teacher at the Orphan Asylum, where his mother had also been employed, and then as the Cherokee Nation's superintendent of education. William T. Hagan, *Taking Indian Lands: The Cherokee (Jerome) Commission, 1889–1893* (University of Oklahoma Press, 2012); Julie L. Reed, *Serving the Nation: Cherokee Sovereignty and Social Welfare, 1800–1907* (University of Oklahoma Press, 2016); Narcissa Owen and Karen L. Kilcup, *A Cherokee Woman's America: Memoirs of Narcissa Owen, 1831–1907* (University Press of Florida, 2005); Narcissa Owen, *Memoirs of Narcissa Owen, 1831–1907* (Washington, DC, 1907), http://hdl.handle.net/2027/uva.x004615992.

30. Tracy L. Steffes, "Solving the 'Rural School Problem': New State Aid, Standards, and Supervision of Local Schools, 1900–1933," *History of Education Quarterly* 48, no. 2 (2008): 181–220.

31. In McKinney's article, she highlights the proliferation of extension offices in Montana and their educational practices beyond schools. She also points out that part of their popularity was that they connected rural women to each other, thus lessening the isolation faced by many rural women. Amy L. McKinney, "From Canning to Contraceptives: Cooperative Extension Service Home Demonstration Clubs and Rural Montana Women in the Post–World War II Era," *Montana: The Magazine of Western History* 61, no. 3 (2011): 57–96.

32. "Believes in Educating Fullblood Indians," *Cherokee County Democrat*, April 15, 1915, Oklahoma Digital Newspaper Program, The Gateway to Oklahoma History, Oklahoma Historical Society, https://gateway.okhistory.org/ark:/67531/metadc90326/m1/1.

33. "Home Canning Clubs," *Vian (OK) Press*, July 6, 1917.

34. "Indians of North America," n.d., box 10, 1975-006-2-10, Series 2: Cherokee Manuscripts and Documents, Special Collections, McFarlin Library, University of Tulsa, OK.

35. Lomawaima and McCarty point out that many federal boarding schools took a step backward when federal reforms took place. K. Tsianina Lomawaima and T. L. McCarty, *"To Remain an Indian": Lessons in Democracy from a Century of Native American Education* (Teachers College Press, 2006), 68–69. Szasz points out that the vocational education provided at federal boarding schools more broadly often lagged behind non-Indian schools and prepared students for jobs that did not exist in students' communities. Margaret Connell Szasz, *Education and the American Indian: The Road to Self-Determination since 1928*, 3rd ed. (University of Mexico Press, 1999), 15, 34–35.

36. "Names Is Names," *Times-Democrat* (Pawnee, OK) April 6, 1916. Lomawaima and McCarty make the point that Indigenous naming practices are intrinsically bound to Indigenous educational practices. Lomawaima and McCarty, *"To Remain an Indian,"* 32–33.

37. The names listed as aristocracy included Chambers, Wards, McClellans, Eatons, Faulkners, Ruckers, Lutons, Parsleys, Gourds, Hicks, Sanders, Lanes, Fosters, Alltons, Murphys, Wyches, Foremans, Rileys, Rogers, Bards, Dannenburgs, Wolfs, Clarks, Pooles, Hammetts, Hastings, Lerskovs, Whisenhunts, Gulagers, and Rollans. Maude Ward DuPriest, Jennie May Bard, and Anna Foreman Graham, *Cherokee Recollections: The Story of the Indian Women's Pocohontas Club and Its Members in the Cherokee Nation and Oklahoma Beginning in 1899* (Thales Microuniversity Press, 1976), 22.

38. DuPriest, Bard, and Graham, *Cherokee Recollections*.

39. "From Tuesday's *Daily Arrow*," *Cherokee County Democrat*, October 8, 1914, Oklahoma Digital Newspaper Program, The Gateway to Oklahoma History, Oklahoma Historical Society, https://gateway.okhistory.org/ark:/67531/metadc90299/m1/7.

40. King, "'Loyal Countrywoman.'"

41. Wilson, "Mountain Feuds."

42. Luther Jewett Abbott, *History and Civics of Oklahoma* (Ginn and Company, 1910), http://hdl.handle.net/2027/hvd.32044035989789.

43. Charles Henry Roberts, *The Essential Facts of Oklahoma History and Civics* (Benj. H. Sandborn & Co., 1916), http://hdl.handle.net/2027/hvd.32044097049985.

44. "Dwight Mission," *Encyclopedia of Oklahoma History and Culture*, Oklahoma Historical Society, accessed November 20, 2019, www.okhistory.org/publications/enc/entry.php?entry=DW001.

45. "We Are Informed," *Marble City Enterprise* (Indian Territory), January 28, 1904, Newspapers.com, www.newspapers.com/image/611616606/?terms=%22Dwight%20Mission%22&match=1.

46. "Indians of North America," n.d., box 4, 1975-006-2-4, Series 2: Cherokee Manuscripts and Documents, Special Collections, McFarlin Library, University of Tulsa.

47. Szasz makes the point that Native peoples assisted in maintaining the continuation of mission schools but spends more time talking about the efforts of missionaries to extend their institutional lives. This is certainly true, but it is also true that places like Dwight owed their longer institutional existences to the choices of tribal governments to grant permission for their operation, supplementing their funds nationally and sending their children there. Through these actions, many mission schools became neighborhood schools. Szasz, *Education and the American Indian*, 12.

48. McLoughlin, *Champions of the Cherokees*, 128–30.

49. "Markham, Hogan," DDC, accessed April 5, 2023, https://digital.libraries.ou.edu/cdm/ref/collection/dorisduke/id/16576.

50. Markham was born in 1891, eight years before Rachel, and attended school at the Cherokee Male Seminary before students began attending Northeastern State Normal, the previous site of the Cherokee Female Seminary. He left Northeastern to attend Chicago University like Eaton, followed by the University of Oklahoma, where he graduated with a degree in physics in 1913. Markam completed a master's degree at Dartmouth in 1915, where he studied with the physicist Albert A. Michelson, the first American to win a Nobel Prize in Physics. "Markham, Hogan," DDC; Colin G. Calloway, *The Indian History of an American Institution: Native Americans and Dartmouth* (University Press of New England, 2010), https://doi.org/10.1349/ddlp.699.

51. "Responsibility of the Teacher," *Vian Press*, September 23, 1921, 8, Newspapers.com, www.newspapers.com/image/607543462/?terms=Schools&match=1.

52. "Health Tournament to be Held Again in State Schools," *Vian Press*, January 13, 1922, Newspapers.com, www.newspapers.com/image/607531669/?terms=Schools&match=1.

53. "Evils of the Curtis Bill: A Reckless Disregard of Existing Contracts, Etc.," *Indian Chieftain* (Vinita, Indian Territory), July 21, 1898.

54. Szasz, *Education and the American Indian*.

55. US Office of Education, *Public Education in Oklahoma* (Bureau of Education, Washington, DC, 1922), 311, http://hdl.handle.net/2027/loc.ark:/13960/t7pn9qq8v.

56. Mary Jane Appel, *Russell Lee: A Photographer's Life and Legacy* (Liveright Publishing, 2020). The following images are all from the Library of Congress, accessed December 3, 2023: *Bedding of Agricultural Workers' Family near Vian, Sequoyah County, Oklahoma,* www.loc.gov/item/2017740244; *Baby of Migrant Agricultural Day Laborers Asleep on the Ground. There Were No Beds or Cots in This Camp near Spiro, Oklahoma. Sequoyah County,* www.loc.gov/item/2017783706; *Young Son of Agricultural Day Laborer in Bed. Near Vian, Oklahoma, Sequoyah County,* www.loc.gov/item/2017783691; *Main Street during 1936 Drought. Sallisaw, Sequoyah County, Oklahoma,* www.loc.gov/item/2017763094; "[Untitled Photo, Possibly Related to: Kitchen of Agricultural Day Laborer North of Sallisaw, Oklahoma. Sequoyah County]," www.loc.gov/item/2017783774; *Corner of Living Room in Home of Agricultural Day Laborers Living North of Sallisaw, Oklahoma. Sequoyah County,* www.loc.gov/item/2017783773.

57. US Office of Education, *Public Education in Oklahoma*.

58. US Office of Education, *Public Education in Oklahoma*, 313.

59. "Brown, Jack," DDC, accessed February 7, 2023, https://digital.libraries.ou.edu/cdm/ref/collection/dorisduke/id/16594.

60. "Brown, Jack," DDC; *Nuyaka Mission Boarding School*, photograph, 1891, Oklahoma Historical Society Photograph Collection, The Gateway to Oklahoma History, Oklahoma Historical Society, https://gateway.okhistory.org/ark:/67531/metadc231430; Dennis Miles, "'Educate or We Perish': The Armstrong Academy's History as Part of the Choctaw Educational System," *Chronicles of Oklahoma* 89, no. 3 (Fall 2011): 312–37, The Gateway to Oklahoma History, Oklahoma Historical Society, https://gateway.okhistory.org/ark:/67531/metadc2016981.

61. "Sequoyah Orphan Training Institute: 1925–1935, Shawnee: 1910–1923," Fort Worth, TX, n.d., Records of the Bureau of Indian Affairs, RG 75, NARA.

62. Reed, *Serving the Nation*, 260–61.

63. At other federal Indian boarding schools, blood tests were not being used to test for sexually transmitted infections. Medical professionals used physical inspections of children's bodies. Central Classified Files, 1907–39, Phoenix Indian School, Records of the Bureau of Indian Affairs, RG 75, NARA; Phoenix School, Annual Report, Narrative Section, July 21, 1920, Annual Narrative and Statistical Reports from Field Jurisdictions of the Bureau of Indian Affairs, 1907–38, Pawnee, 1935, Pechanga School, 1910–13, Phoenix Sanatorium, 1929, 1931–38, Phoenix School, 1910–27, M-1011, Roll 102, Records of the Bureau of Indian Affairs, RG 75, NARA; "Central Classified Files, 1907–39, Phoenix Indian School," Records of the Bureau of Indian Affairs, RG 75, NARA.

64. US Office of Education, *Public Education in Oklahoma*.

65. *Public Education in Oklahoma. A Report of a Survey of Public Education in the State of Oklahoma, Made at the Request of the Oklahoma State Educational Survey Commission*, (Washington, DC, 1922), 309–10, http://hdl.handle.net/2027/loc.ark:/13960/t7pn9qq8v; US Office of Education, *Public Education in Oklahoma*.

66. "Twelfth Biennial Report of the State Superintendent of Public Instruction Together with the Ninth Report of the State Board of Education," n.d., Vertical Files, Blacks, Oklahoma, Schools, Special Collections, Northeastern State University, Tahlequah, OK.

67. "Sequoyah Orphan Training Institute: 1925–1935, Shawnee: 1910–1923."

68. "Survey of Conditions of the Indians in the United States, Part 14: Oklahoma, Five Civilized Tribes," November 10, 1930, https://congressional-proquest-com.ezaccess.libraries.psu.edu/congressional/docview/t29.d30.hrg-1930-ias-0014?accountid=13158.

69. Jack Frederick Kilpatrick and Anna Gritts Kilpatrick, *Run toward the Nightland: Magic of the Oklahoma Cherokees* (Southern Methodist University Press, 1967).

70. George Vauk Jr., "Condition among the Five Civilized Tribes," *Red Man* 5, no. 4 (1912): 135–47; Dana H. Kelsey, "Condition and Needs of the Five Civilized Tribes of Oklahoma," *Red Man* 6, no. 3 (n.d.): 105–14.

71. Emmet Starr, *History of the Cherokee Indians and Their Legends and Folk Lore* (Warden Company, 1922), 483.

72. Part of my speculation here I credit to Daniel HorseChief's artwork. In it, HorseChief depicts Lucy tending to a younger woman's shell shakers at the stomp grounds. Daniel HorseChief, *Redbird Smith* (n.p., n.d); Starr, *History of the Cherokee Indians*.

73. "Fry, Maggie Culver," DDC, accessed February 17, 2023, https://digital.libraries.ou.edu/cdm/ref/collection/dorisduke/id/16150.

74. "Fry, Maggie Culver," DDC.

75. "Lucinda Hickey," IPP.

76. "Lucinda Hickey," IPP.

77. "Elinor Boudinot Meigs Interview," n.d., IPP.

78. "Lucinda Hickey," IPP.

79. "Markham, Hogan," DDC.

80. "Lucinda Hickey," IPP.

81. "Sequoyah Orphan Training Institute: 1925–1935, Shawnee: 1910–1923."

82. Reed, *Serving the Nation*.

83. Lomawaima and McCarty refer to this as "domesticating difference." By allowing and monitoring Indigenous cultural activities at boarding schools, officials could "symbolically neutralize the Native languages, religions, economies, polities, family structures, emotions,

and lives that seemed to threaten American uniformity and national identity." Lomawaima and McCarty, *"To Remain an Indian,"* 2–3, 58–64.

84. *Boy Scout Song Book* (C. C. Birchard & Company, 1920), https://catalog.hathitrust .org/Record/012104703.

85. Deloria observes that when Charles Eastman donned a headdress in public during this period, he was "imitating non-Indian imitations of Indians." However, in this act he also created a hybrid identity, "distinct in its Indianness but also cross-cultural and assimilatory." Students involved in Scouts at boarding schools may have undergone similar shifts in identity. At the same time, for most non-Native students across the country, Scouts and Y-Indian Guides programs created a generic Indianness equally accessible to everyone. Philip Joseph Deloria, *Playing Indian* (Yale University Press, 1998), 120–25.

86. Jürgen Martschukat, *American Fatherhood: A History* (New York University Press, 2019), 141–63.

87. The Pocahontas Club also created hybrid identities for its members, like Deloria describes, while simultaneously engaging in the American uplift noted by Stremlau. Stremlau, *Sustaining the Cherokee Family.*

88. DuPriest et al., *Cherokee Recollections.*

89. Circe Dawn Sturm, *Blood Politics: Race, Culture, and Identity in the Cherokee Nation of Oklahoma* (University of California Press, 2002), 208–9.

Chapter 6

1. "Indians of North America," n.d., box 10, 1975-006-2-10, Series 2: Cherokee Manuscripts and Documents, Special Collections, McFarlin Library, University of Tulsa, OK.

2. "Indians of North America."

3. Rachel Johnson Quinton, black notebook, n.d., record no. 921, Quinton Family Archive (private collection).

4. Frey proposes that for the Eastern Band, boarding schools alone aren't enough to explain language loss. He ties it to economic verticalization, the moment when Eastern Band people no longer shopped at, worked for, or ate at the restaurants run by Cherokee people. Cited with permission of the author. Benjamin Frey, "Rising Above: Language Revitalization in the Eastern Band of Cherokee Indians," unpublished manuscript, n.d.

5. "Nelson Smith and Ada Lee Duffield Marriage," *Okmulgee (OK) Daily Times,* May 8, 1942.

6. Childcare options existed briefly in urban centers during the war where war industries needed women's labor. However, that was not in Vian, Oklahoma. Mary Frances Berry, *The Politics of Parenthood: Child Care, Women's Rights, and the Myth of the Good Mother* (Viking, 1993), 110.

7. R. Quinton, black notebook.

8. "Report of Indian Students Asked," *McAlester (OK) Democrat,* December 6, 1945; "Funds for Indian Schools Assured," *Muskogee (OK) Daily Phoenix and Times-Democrat,* August 8, 1947.

9. My Great-Aunt Cordelia gave me this textbook. It was the book she used as a child in Oklahoma schools. Imogene Bethel and T. T. Montgomery, *A Pupil's Study and Workbook in Oklahoma History* (The Economy Co., n.d.).

10. Joan Smith Reed Mueller, Vian Childhood, conversation with author, May 8, 2020.

11. Jeanette Haynes, "An Oral History of the Social Construction of Cherokee Identity" (PhD diss., University of New Mexico, 1997), ProQuest (9727489).

12. Daniel Heath Justice and Jean M. O'Brien, *Allotment Stories: Indigenous Land Relations under Settler Siege*, Indigenous Americas (University of Minnesota Press, 2022).

13. Margaret Connell Szasz, *Education and the American Indian: The Road to Self-Determination since 1928*, 3rd ed. (University of Mexico Press, 1999), 346.

14. Albert L. Wahrhaftig, "More Than Mere Work: The Subsistence System of Oklahoma's Cherokee Indians," *Appalachian Journal* 2, no. 4 (1975): 327–31.

15. Albert L. Wahrhaftig, "The Tribal Cherokee Population of Eastern Oklahoma," *Current Anthropology* 9, no. 5 (1968): 510–18.

16. "Carey, Lean Soap," DDC, accessed February 14, 2023, https://digital.libraries.ou.edu/cdm/ref/collection/dorisduke/id/13235; "Back Then . . . Eva Fourkiller Comando," posted April 15, 2016, by Cherokee Nation, YouTube, 9 min., 33 sec., www.youtube.com/watch?v=DI2Qxbr8a5M.

17. In Quinton Family Archive.

18. "Fort Smith, AR Weather History," Weather Underground, accessed April 17, 2023, www.wunderground.com/history/monthly/KFSM/date/1951-2; "JE Duffield to Mr Mrs JE Reed," February 16, 1951, Reed Family Archive (private collection).

19. "Back Then . . . Eva Fourkiller Comando."

20. Alexander Longe, "A Small Postscript on the Ways and Manners of the Indians Called Cherokees," ed. David H. Corkran, *Southern Indian Studies* 21 (October 1969): 1–50.

21. "Carey, Lean Soap," DDC; "Cherokee Nation's Back Then Wanda Girty," posted December 15, 2014, by Cherokee Nation, YouTube, 9 min., 48 sec., www.youtube.com/watch?v=44DS_kVgBaY; "Cherokee Nation's Back Then Johnny Sanders," posted November 3, 2014, by Cherokee Nation, YouTube, 9 min., 56 sec., www.youtube.com/watch?v=qpSuBLXA7Ro.

22. "Survey of Conditions of the Indians in the United States Part 14: Oklahoma, Five Civilized Tribes," November 10, 1930.

23. Clifford E. Trafzer, *Strong Hearts and Healing Hands: Southern California Indians and Field Nurses, 1920–1950* (University of Arizona Press, 2021), x.

24. Preston Scott McBride, "A Lethal Education: Institutionalized Negligence, Epidemiology, and Death in Native American Boarding Schools, 1879–1934" (PhD diss., University of California, Los Angeles, 2020), ProQuest (28031676).

25. "Survey of Conditions of the Indians in the United States Part 14: Oklahoma, Five Civilized Tribes," November 10, 1930, 6273.

26. United States Public Health Service, *The Health Officer; a Digest of Current Health Information* (USPHS, 1939).

27. Willard W. Beatty, "A Practical Boarding School Health Program," in *Indian Education: A Fortnightly Field Letter of the Education Division United States Office of Indian Affairs* (Washington, DC, October 15, 1940), 6, https://books.google.com/books/about/Indian_Education.html?id=3mNGAQAAIAAJ.

28. Whalen and Gilbert make the point that the outing system, which employed Native people most often in service to white families, created a permanent underclass. Kevin Whalen and Matthew Sakiestewa Gilbert, *Native Students at Work: American Indian Labor and Sherman Institute's Outing Program, 1900–1945* (University of Washington Press, 2016); May 1951 edition of *The Indian School Journal* from Chilocco, "Indians of North America," n.d.,

box 10, 1975-006-2-10, Series 2: Cherokee Manuscripts and Documents, Special Collections, McFarlin Library, University of Tulsa.

29. Margaret D. Jacobs, *White Mother to a Dark Race: Settler Colonialism, Maternalism, and the Removal of Indigenous Children in the American West and Australia, 1880–1940* (University of Nebraska Press, 2009), http://hdl.handle.net/2027/heb.08861.

30. K. Tsianina Lomawaima, "'All Our People Are Building Houses': The Civilization of Architecture and Space in Federal Indian Boarding Schools," in *Indian Subjects: Hemispheric Perspectives on the History of Indigenous Education*, ed. Brenda J. Child and Brian Klopotek (School for Advanced Research Press, 2014), 171–72.

31. Paul A. Brinker and Burley Walker, "The Hill-Burton Act: 1948–1954," *Review of Economics and Statistics* 44, no. 2 (1962): 212, https://doi.org/10.2307/1928204.

32. "Athletes Take Physical Exams," *Sequoyah County Times*, October 16, 1953.

33. Frank Quinton, "The Life and Times of Frank Quinton," n.d., Quiton Family Archive (private collection).

34. "Tullahassee," *Encyclopedia of Oklahoma History and Culture*, Oklahoma Historical Society, accessed January 23, 2023, www.okhistory.org/publications/enc/entry.php?entry =TU002.

35. All three of the following touch on the educational experiences and advocacy of freedmen and freedwomen or on the role of mission societies or government officials in their education after the Civil War and statehood. Alaina E. Roberts, *I've Been Here All the While: Black Freedom on Native Land* (University of Pennsylvania Press, 2021), 59–61; Eloise G. Spear, "Choctaw Indian Education with Special Reference to Choctaw County, Oklahoma: An Historical Approach" (PhD diss., University of Oklahoma, 1977), ProQuest (7732883); Kendra Taira Field, *Growing up with the Country: Family, Race, and Nation after the Civil War* (Yale University Press, 2018).

36. *We Are Cherokee: Cherokee Freedmen and the Right to Citizenship* (exhibit), Cherokee National History Museum, Tahlequah, OK, 2023; Ty Wilson and Karen Coody Cooper, *Oklahoma Black Cherokees* (Arcadia Publishing, 2012).

37. "Vian News," *Black Dispatch* (Oklahoma City), December 27, 1923.

38. "Colored Teachers to Meet," *Vian Press*, September 10, 1931.

39. "State Wide Celebration Dedicating State Hospital for Negro Insane at Taft," *Blue Valley Farmer* (Oklahoma City), June 7, 1934.

40. Edison Holmes Anderson, "The Historical Development of Music in the Negro Secondary Schools of Oklahoma and at Langston University" (PhD diss., University of Iowa, 1957), 54, ProQuest (0020916).

41. Oklahoma State Board of Education, *Twenty-Third Biennial Report of the State Department of Education, 1950*, Vertical Files, Blacks, Oklahoma, Schools, Special Collections, Northeastern State University, Tahlequah, OK.

42. Oklahoma State Board of Education, *Twenty-Third Biennial Report*.

43. Oklahoma State Board of Education, *Twenty-Third Biennial Report*.

44. Oklahoma State Board of Education, *Twenty-Third Biennial Report*.

45. Oklahoma State Board of Education, *Twenty-Third Biennial Report*.

46. Roberts, *I've Been Here All the While*, 122–24.

47. Troy Wayne Poteete, Jack Baker, and Tupper Dunbar, discussion at Goingsnake District Heritage Association Meeting, October 19, 2020.

48. "Cherokee Nation's Back Then Clemmie Buckner," posted November 27, 2017, by Cherokee Nation, YouTube, 10 min., 9 sec., www.youtube.com/watch?v=ufZdrPx_blQ.

49. "Reverend Haefker, W. A.," DDC, accessed February 7, 2023, https://digital.libraries.ou.edu/cdm/ref/collection/dorisduke/id/4262.

50. Leona Denny Hopper, interview with the author, June 25, 2022.

51. "UNICEF: Collecting Water Is Often a Colossal Waste of Time for Women and Girls," UNICEF, August 29, 2016, www.unicef.org/press-releases/unicef-collecting-water-often-colossal-waste-time-women-and-girls; Jay P. Graham, Mitsuaki Hirai, and Seung-Sup Kim, "An Analysis of Water Collection Labor among Women and Children in 24 Sub-Saharan African Countries," *PLOS ONE* 11, no. 6 (2016): e0155981, https://doi.org/10.1371/journal.pone.0155981; Vica Marie Jelena Tomberge et al., "The Physical Burden of Water Carrying and Women's Psychosocial Well-Being: Evidence from Rural Nepal," *International Journal of Environmental Research and Public Health* 18, no. 15 (2021), 1–11, https://doi.org/10.3390/ijerph18157908.

52. Sequoyah County History Committee, *The History of Sequoyah County, 1828–1975* (ARC Press of Cane Hill, 1998), 130.

53. Leonard B. Cayton, "A History of Black Public Education in Oklahoma" (PhD diss., University of Oklahoma, 1977), 61.

54. Pamela Riney-Kehrberg, ed., *The Routledge History of Rural America*, The Routledge Histories (Routledge, 2016), 41.

55. "Cherokee Nation's Back Then Lorene Drywater," posted September 5, 2017, by Cherokee Nation, YouTube, 10 min., 5 sec., www.youtube.com/watch?v=wVO1M1qJpBA.

56. "Back Then . . . Eva Fourkiller Comando."

57. Hopper interview; "Back Then . . . Eva Fourkiller Comando."

58. "Reverend Haefker, W. A.," DDC.

59. "Anna 'Jean' Dunn," *Sequoyah County Times*, August 8, 1941.

60. "Cherokee Nation's Back Then Lorene Drywater."

61. "Cherokee Nation's Back Then Ruby Jordan," posted October 6, 2014, by Cherokee Nation, YouTube, 8 min., 15 sec., www.youtube.com/watch?v=6Cv3cfwpM84.

62. Wilma Mankiller et al., *Every Day Is a Good Day: Reflections by Contemporary Indigenous Women*, Memorial ed. (Fulcrum Pub., 2011), 46; "Cherokee Nation's Back Then Delois Nofire," posted September 14, 2016, by Cherokee Nation, YouTube, 9 min., 25 sec., www.youtube.com/watch?v=I8dp-srgR5s.

63. "Cherokee Nation's Back Then George and Francis Polecat," posted August 5, 2014, by Cherokee Nation, YouTube, 10 min., 25 sec., www.youtube.com/watch?v=hTAkVAwEuaI.

64. Poteete, Baker, and Dunbar discussion.

65. This assertion is based on the ongoing meetings of the Choctaw language working group and on conversations with Candessa Tehee. Linguist Aaron Broadwell, a member of the working group, has pointed out that it is not surprising in any culture that most daily conversations occur in a more casual register than in places like churches or at ceremonial grounds where theological and cosmological conversations are happening by design. Similarly, Candessa Tehee noted that many of the teachers whose skills she aspires to achieve are associated with our Cherokee language churches. "PSU/UF Choctaw Language Working Group Meetings," 2020–23, Virtual; Teehee, Candessa. "Cherokee Language." Presented at the Cherokee Scholars Conference Planning, University Park, PA, February 30, 2020.

66. "J. E. Duffield, Vian, OK to Mr Mrs JE Reed, Norman OK," December 9, 1950, Reed Family Archive (Private Collection).

67. Patti Dickinson, *Coach Tommy Thompson and the Boys of Sequoyah* (University of Oklahoma Press, 2009), 76; "Cherokee Nation's Back Then Lorene Drywater," posted September 5, 2017, by Cherokee Nation, YouTube, 10 min., 5 sec., www.youtube.com/watch?v=wVO1M1qJpBA. "Cherokee Nation's Back Then Leona Denny Hooper," posted February 9, 2018, by Cherokee Nation, Youtube, 8 min., 58 sec., www.youtube.com/watch?v=rRcSCfORZpQ.

68. "Indians of North America," n.d., box 7, 1975-006-2-7, Series 2: Cherokee Manuscripts and Documents, Special Collections, McFarlin Library, University of Tulsa.

69. "Back Then . . . Eva Fourkiller Comando"; "Cherokee Nation's Back Then Nadine McLemore Mahaney," posted January 20, 2015, by Cherokee Nation, YouTube, 9 min., 13 sec., www.youtube.com/watch?v=4JAH2LO923E.

70. "Cherokee Nation's Back Then Wanda Girty."

71. Hopper interview.

72. R. Quinton, black notebook.

73. R. Quinton, black notebook.

Chapter 7

1. Howard L. Meredith, *Bartley Milam: Principal Chief of the Cherokee Nation* (Indian University Press, 1985), 70–74.

2. Jonita Mullins, "Three Forks History: Cookson Is Town Moved by Water," *Muskogee Phoenix*, December 26, 2015, www.muskogeephoenix.com/news/three-forks-history-cookson-is-town-moved-by-water/article_234c4ed0-70b8-5600-b252-8f8ed91f0de7.html; "Lakes and Reservoirs," *Encyclopedia of Oklahoma History and Culture*, Oklahoma Historical Society, accessed April 23, 2023, www.okhistory.org/publications/enc/entry?entry=LA010; "Local History Lies below Waters of 'Lake Tenkiller,'" *Tahlequah Daily Press*, December 8, 2014, www.tahlequahdailypress.com/news/local-history-lies-below-waters-of-lake-tenkiller/article_23a75cd2-7efb-11e4-8f93-1b01a163cf00.html.

3. US Fish and Wildlife Service, *Sequoyah National Wildlife Refuge* (brochure), October 1999, http://npshistory.com/brochures/nwr/sequoyah-1999-2.pdf; Wikipedia, "Sequoyah National Wildlife Refuge," Wikipedia, last modified January 7, 2020, 05:19, https://en.wikipedia.org/w/index.php?title=Sequoyah_National_Wildlife_Refuge&oldid=934558715; "Many Uses to Be Made of Refuge Manager Says," *Sequoyah County Times*, August 20, 1970; 2, "National Wildlife Refuge Established in Sallisaw Region 1," *Sequoyah County Times*, June 4, 1970; "Sequoyah National Wildlife Refuge," FWS.gov, accessed April 23, 2023, www.fws.gov/refuge/sequoyah/about-us.

4. FDR reappointed Milam in 1942 and again in 1943 for a four-year term. This significantly lengthened the terms many previous chiefs-for-a-day served. Convention transcript, July 30, 1948, folder 1, box CN-3, RG 2, Cherokee National Archives, Tahlequah, OK.

5. Georgia Leeds, *The United Keetoowah Band of Cherokee Indians in Oklahoma*, American University Studies (Peter Lang, 1996), 15–24.

6. Jürgen Martschukat, *American Fatherhood: A History* (New York University Press, 2019), 152.

7. "UKB Election, 1963," *Stilwell (OK) Democrat-Journal*, May 23, 1963; "UKB Election, 1967," *Stilwell Democrat-Journal*, September 14, 1967.

8. William F. Delaney, "A History of the Department of Defense Dependents Schools, 1965–1980" (PhD diss., Catholic University of America, 1983), 7.

9. Nicole Alia Salis Reyes et al., "(Re)Wiring Settler Colonial Practices in Higher Education: Creating Indigenous Centered Futures through Considerations of Power, the Social, Place, and Space," in *Higher Education: Handbook of Theory and Research: Volume 39*, ed. Laura W. Perna (Springer Nature Switzerland, 2024), 130–32, https://doi.org/10.1007/978 -3-031-38077-8_5.

10. "Help Wanted," *Okmulgee Daily Times*, September 1, 1973; "Mose Weavel," *Sequoyah County Times*, March 24, 1974; "Mrs. Flanagan Instructs First Aid at CNI," *Sequoyah County Times*, March 28, 1974; "Health Program Cuts Mean Less Service at Sallisaw Clinic," *Sequoyah County Times*, February 25, 1982; "Health Clinic Affected by Recent Budget Cuts," *Sequoyah County Times*, February 21, 1982, www.newspapers.com/clip/123464211/health-clinic-affected -by-recent-budget; "Clinic Simplifies Health Care for County Indians," *Sequoyah County Times*, April 11, 1976; Leah Kalm-Freeman, "The Community Health Representative Program: Early Voices and Program History, 1968–1980" (PhD diss., Johns Hopkins University, 2009), ProQuest (3381655).

11. Catherine Foreman Gray, interview with the author, April 12, 2023.

12. "Markham, Hogan," DDC, accessed April 5, 2023, https://digital.libraries.ou.edu/cdm /ref/collection/dorisduke/id/16576.

13. James Mooney, *Myths of the Cherokee* (Government Printing Office, 1902), https:// catalog.hathitrust.org/Record/010939061.

14. Emmanuel Dreschel, "The Natchez Way," *Chronicles of Oklahoma* 65, no. 2 (1987): 174–81.

15. For an explanation of and the history leading up to the passage of the Indian Child Welfare Act, as well as the full act itself, see "About NICWA" and "What Is ICWA," *NICWA* (blog), accessed November 27, 2024, www.nicwa.org/about-icwa and www.nicwa.org/about; Mannes Marc, "Factors and Events Leading to the Passage of the Indian Child Welfare Act," in *A History of Child Welfare*, ed. Eve P. Smith and Lisa A. Merkel-Holguín (Routledge, 2017), 257–75, https://doi.org/10.4324/9781351315920-14; and "25 USC Ch. 21: Indian Child Welfare," USCode.house.gov, accessed November 27, 2024, https://uscode.house.gov/view .xhtml?path=/prelim@title25/chapter21&edition=prelim.

16. My parents met in Manila, Philippines, in 1969 after my dad left the navy and enlisted in the air force. The Department of Defense assigned my mom to teach on the same base where my dad was stationed. I think often of the irony that resulted in their meeting. Stefan Aune, "Indian Fighters in the Philippines: Imperial Culture and Military Violence in the Philippine–American War," *Pacific Historical Review* 90, no. 4 (2021): 419–47, https://doi.org/10.1525/phr.2021.90.4.419; Alyssa A. Hunziker, "Playing Indian, Playing Filipino: Native American and Filipino Interactions at the Carlisle Indian Industrial School," *American Quarterly* 72, no. 2 (2020): 423–48; Sarah Steinbock-Pratt, "'We Were All Robinson Crusoes': American Women Teachers in the Philippines," *Women's Studies* 41, no. 4 (2012): 372–92, https://doi.org/10.1080/00497878.2012.663242; David S. Busch, "The Politics of International Volunteerism: The Peace Corps and Volunteers to America in the 1960s," *Diplomatic History* 42, no. 4 (2018): 669–93, https://doi.org/10.1093/dh/dhx063;

Adrian De Leon, *Bundok: A Hinterland History of Filipino America* (University of North Carolina Press, 2023).

17. The Department of Defense began operating schools in Germany in 1949, four years after Rhein Mein Air Base opened. Rhein Mein Elementary, the first school my brother attended in Germany, traced its origins to the Department of Defense's first organized efforts to provide education to children abroad when families began moving to Germany after World War II with or without the military's approval. Department of Defense schools were a by-product of the war between two "greedy institutions," the military and families. Delaney, "History of Department of Defense Dependents Schools," 1.

18. Lewis A. Coser, *Greedy Institutions: Patterns of Undivided Commitment* (Free Press, 1974); Eiko Strader and Margaret Smith, "Some Parents Survive and Some Don't: The Army and the Family as 'Greedy Institutions,'" *Public Administration Review* 82, no. 3 (2022): 446–58, https://doi.org/10.1111/puar.13467; Mady Wechsler Segal, "The Military and the Family as Greedy Institutions," *Armed Forces & Society* 13, no. 1 (1986): 9–38, Delaney, "History of Department of Defense Dependents Schools," 6.

19. Gerald L. Gutek and Patricia A. Gutek, *Bringing Montessori to America: S. S. McClure, Maria Montessori, and the Campaign to Publicize Montessori Education* (University of Alabama Press, 2016), 44.

20. Nancy McCormick Rambusch, "An American Montessori Elementary Teacher: Indigenous American Montessori Models," ERIC, 1992, https://eric.ed.gov/?id=ED353066.

21. "Inland Empire Girl Scout Council, Inc., Scouts Name Julie Reed, Brownie Patch Record Sheet, Individual Girls Record," n.d., Reed Family Archive (Private Collection).

22. "Inland Empire Girl Scout Council, Inc., Scouts Name Julie Reed, Brownie Patch Record Sheet, Individual Girls Record."

23. Postcard in personal archive, n.d.; Lisa Blee and Jean M. O'Brien, *Monumental Mobility: The Memory Work of Massasoit* (University of North Carolina Press, 2019), 60–65.

24. Third-grade writing assignment, Gibsonton (FL) Elementary, 1984–85, in personal archive.

25. An analysis of the annual data from 1982 to 1985 reveals that, despite a slightly growing military under President Reagan in the early 1980s, the overall number of Native American men in the military decreased. In 1982, enlisted Native American men made up .012 of the totals; in 1983, .011; and in 1984, .010. See charts on Military Personnel by Ethnic Group (Table C-31 and C-20 respectively). My dad's personal interpretation of his final years in the military was that he was being pushed out with the reason being more stringent body weight standards. In 1983, officers were 84.2 percent white men and 82.2 percent white women. Overall, white officers made up 84.3 percent of the total. Policy and Procedures Division, "United States Air Force Summary, 1985, AFD-110404-053," Comptroller of the Air Force, accessed November 18, 2024, https://media.defense.gov/2011/Apr/04/2001329905/-1/-1/0/AFD-110404-053 .pdf; Policy and Procedures Division, "United States Air Force Summary, AFD-110404-051," Comptroller of the Air Force, 1984, https://media.defense.gov/2011/Apr/04/2001329916/ -1/-1/0/AFD-110404-051.pdf.

26. In many ways, I would face a system in which "adult white southerners tried, consciously and unconsciously, to teach both black and white children to 'forget' any possible alternatives to white supremacy at the same time they energetically repressed alternatives that arose in both the public and private spheres." These same spaces had enacted policies that physically

removed Native peoples and had done little to acknowledge their continued presence since. Jennifer Ritterhouse, *Growing Up Jim Crow: How Black and White Southern Children Learned Race* (University of North Carolina Press, 2006), 9.

27. I suspect I join a far greater number of historians than White, Joblanka, and Kuntz, whose questions from childhood drive us to the profession, even though the profession discourages us from admitting this until we reach a certain point in our careers. Richard White, *Remembering Ahanagran* (Hill and Wang, 1998); Ivan Jablonka and Jane Kuntz, *A History of the Grandparents I Never Had* (Stanford University Press, 2016).

28. "Absentee fathers exposed for all to see the fundamentally fragile nature of nuclear families." Martschukat, *American Fatherhood*, 29.

29. It was not renamed Little Bighorn Battlefield National Monument until my freshman year of high school. "Custer Falls Again as Site Is Renamed," *New York Times*, November 27, 1991, www.nytimes.com/1991/11/27/us/custer-falls-again-as-site-is-renamed.html.

30. *Welcome to Big Horn County: "Custer Country"* (brochure) (Hardin Area Chamber of Commerce and Agriculture,1984).

31. "Ada Lee Duffield Marriage to John E. Reed, 1948," *Norman (OK) Transcript*, January 25, 1948.

32. From the *Norman Transcript*: "Open," May 17, 1959; "Air Conditioned," April 3, 1959; "Cecil Woods Agency," March 16, 1959; "Open House," March 5, 1959; "$12,200 Brick Home," 26, 1959; "Cecil Woods Agency," February 24, 1959.

33. Given the ubiquity of the nightly news in homes across the United States (CBS in our house), this is almost certainly how I was following this story. "Canada / Mohawk Indians," Vanderbilt Television News Archive, accessed April 2, 2024, https://tvnews-vanderbilt-edu.ezaccess.libraries.psu.edu/broadcasts/334683; https://tvnews-vanderbilt-edu.ezaccess.libraries.psu.edu/broadcasts/129978; https://tvnews-vanderbilt-edu.ezaccess.libraries.psu.edu/broadcasts/334558; https://tvnews-vanderbilt-edu.ezaccess.libraries.psu.edu/broadcasts/576139.

34. Journal for Ms. Seaman, East Bay High School, Gibsonton, FL, 1990, in personal archive.

35. Journal for Ms. Seaman.

36. Robyn Maynard and Leanne Betasamosake Simpson, "Part III: Summer of Revolt" in *Rehearsals for Living* (Haymarket Books, 2022), ebook.

37. "Ex-Chief of Cherokees Will Speak at Salem," *Winston-Salem Journal*, February 23, 1995.

38. Chad Smith to Julie Reed, personal correspondence, March 28, 1995.

39. Although this is not what my professor shared with me in college, it is a brief overview of the history and lore surrounding Lilith. Wojciech Kosior, "A Tale of Two Sisters: The Image of Eve in Early Rabbinic Literature and Its Influence on the Portrayal of Lilith in the Alphabet of Ben Sira," *Nashim: A Journal of Jewish Women's Studies & Gender Issues*, no. 32 (2018): 112–30, https://doi.org/10.2979/nashim.32.1.10. This moment also overlapped with the short-lived Lilith Fair festival, which highlighted women artists in an effort to draw attention to the sexism in the recording industry. I still have my CD.

40. Frank Quinton, "The Life and Times of Frank Quinton," n.d., private archive.

41. "Spiritual Ebbs and Flows," written for Women's Spiritual Memoirs course, WST 5934, in author personal archive.

42. In author's personal collection.

43. Gray interview.

Conclusion

1. Tiya Miles, *All That She Carried: The Journey of Ashley's Sack, a Black Family Keepsake* (Random House, 2021), 20.

2. John L. Rury, *Education and Social Change: Contours in the History of American Schooling,* 5th ed. (Routledge, 2016), 21–24, 108–12.

3. Amanda J. Cobb, *Listening to Our Grandmothers' Stories: The Bloomfield Academy for Chickasaw Females, 1852–1949* (University of Nebraska Press, 2007); Brenda J. Child, *My Grandfather's Knocking Sticks: Ojibwe Family Life and Labor on the Reservation* (Minnesota Historical Society Press, 2014); Brenda J. Child, *Boarding School Seasons: American Indian Families, 1900–1940* (University of Nebraska Press, 1998); K. Tsianina Lomawaima, *They Called It Prairie Light: The Story of Chilocco Indian School* (University of Nebraska Press, 1994), http://search.ebscohost.com/login.aspx?direct=true&scope=site&db=nlebk&db=nlabk&AN=45247; Bryan Newland, *Federal Indian Boarding School Initiative Investigative Report,* May 2022, www.bia.gov/sites/default/files/dup/inline-files/bsi_investigative_report_may_2022_508.pdf.

4. Laura Harjo, *Spiral to the Stars: Mvskoke Tools of Futurity*, Critical Issues in Indigenous Studies (University of Arizona Press, 2019), 4.

5. "ᏧᎣᏙᎫᎢ ᎠᎮᏳᎳ ᎣᎮᏍᏳ—Little Cherokee Seeds," Facebook, accessed May 22, 2023, www.facebook.com/LittleCherokeeSeeds/about_details.

Index

www.ingramcontent.com/pod-product-compliance
Lightning Source LLC
Chambersburg PA
CBHW030725171225
36910CB00021B/268